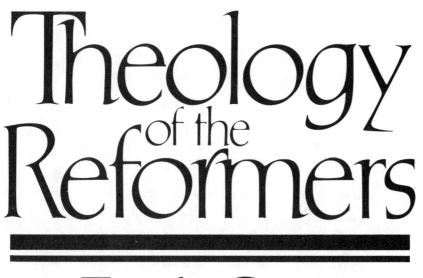

Timothy George

BROADMAN PRESS
Nashville, Tennessee

© Copyright 1988 ● Broadman Press
All rights reserved
4265-73
ISBN: 0-8054-6573-1
Dewey Decimal Classification: 270.6
Subject Headings: REFORMATION//THEOLOGY
Library of Congress Catalog Card Number: 87-27759
Printed in the United States of America

Unless otherwise indicated, Scripture quotations are from the King James Version of the Bible. Scripture quotations marked (RSV) are from the Revised Standard Version of the Bible, copyrighted 1946, 1952, © 1971, 1973.

A section of Chapter 4 appeared as Timothy George, "The Presuppositions of Zwingli's Baptismal Theology," *Prophet, Pastor, Protestant: The Work of Huldrych Zwingli After Five Hundred Years*, E.J. Furcha and H. Wayne Pipkin, eds. (Allison Park, Penn.: Pickwick Publications, 1984), pp. 71-87. Used by permission.

Library of Congress Cataloging in Publication Data

George, Timothy.
  Theology of the reformers.

  Includes index.
  1. Theology, Doctrinal—History—16th century.
2. Reformation.   I. Title.
BT27.G46   1987   230′ .044′09031   87-27759
ISBN 0-8054-6573-1

For
George Huntston Williams,
Hollis Professor of Divinity Emeritus, Harvard University,
master historian, compassionate pilgrim,
citizen of that City which hath foundations,
on the fortieth anniversary of his teaching appointment at
Harvard and the fifty-seventh anniversary of
his ordination to the Christian ministry

Preface

The noted Elizabethan scholar, A. L. Rowse, once complained that "the sixteenth century is full of the useless fooleries of disputes about doctrine."[1] This book is essentially about such disputes, and it assumes that they were neither useless nor foolish insofar as they form a significant chapter in the history of what the church of Jesus Christ "has believed, taught and confessed on the basis of the Word of God."[2] To be sure, most people who live on this side of the Enlightenment in a secular, pluralistic society are acutely indifferent about the niceties of predestinarian theology or the rationale for—or against—the practice of infant baptism. Such issues, and many others discussed in this book, have no measurable influence on the gross national product. At best, they might come in handy in a casual game of theological trivial pursuit. However, for those who stand committedly within the Christian tradition, it is a matter of genuine concern to understand what was so decisively at stake in the great debates of the Reformation.

The Reformation was not merely a tempest in a teacup. Jerome once said that when he read the letters of the apostle Paul, he could hear thunder. That same thunder reverberates through the writings of the reformers as well. Contemporary theologians would do well to listen afresh to the message of these courageous Christians who defied emperors and popes, kings and city councils because their consciences were captive to the Word of God. Their gospel of the free grace of Almighty God, the Lord God Sabaoth, as Luther's great hymn put it, and their emphasis on the centrality and finality of Jesus Christ stand in marked contrast to the attenuated, transcendence-starved theologies which dominate the current scene. It is not the purpose of this study to canonize the reformers. The sixteenth century was an age of violence and coercion, and the mainline reformers

1. A. L. Rowse, *The England of Elizabeth* (London, 1950), p. 387.
2. Jaroslav Pelikan, *The Emergence of the Catholic Tradition* (Chicago: University of Chicago Press, 1971), p. 1.

were not completely innocent of bigotry and intolerance. The Anabaptists, who had warts of their own, offered a counter witness on this score, a witness which still needs to be heard in our own violence-ridden century. Luther's invective against the Jews, Zwingli's complicity in the drowning of Anabaptists, and Calvin's in the burning of Servetus, are all the more tragic because one senses that these, of all people, should have known better. However, what is remarkable about the reformers is that, despite their foibles and sins and blind spots, they were able to grasp with such perspicuity the paradoxical character of the human condition and the great possibility of human redemption through Jesus Christ. This concern undergirded their approach to the church, worship, ministry, spiritual life, and ethics. In each of these arenas we need desperately to hear what they have to say.

Much of this book was assembled during a sabbatical year in Switzerland. Professor H. Wayne Pipkin of the Baptist Theological Seminary in Rüschlikon lent me many books from his valuable collection and made helpful comments on the Zwingli chapter. Professor Fritz Büsser of the Institute für Schweizerische Kirchengeschichte in Zurich and Dres. Pierre Fraenkel and Irena Backus of the Institut de la Réformation in Geneva received me warmly and made available the excellent resources of their respective research facilities. Professor Jan Lochman of the University of Basel was a genial host on my frequent visits to the city where Calvin's *Institutes* were first published in 1536. A section of Chapter 4 appeared earlier as "The Presuppositions of Zwingli's Baptismal Theology" in *Prophet, Pastor, Protestant: The Work of Huldrych Zwingli After Five Hundred Years,* E. J. Furcha and H. Wayne Pipkin, editors. I am grateful for permission to reproduce this material.

Portions of this book were originally presented as lectures to theological students and pastors in a variety of settings. I am indebted to those who heard me and offered valuable suggestions at the Furman Pastors' School, Furman University in Greenville, South Carolina; Union Theological Seminary in Richmond, Virginia; Wake Forest University in Winston-Salem, North Carolina; the Baptist seminaries in Novi Sad, Yugoslavia, and Budapest, Hungary; and the 1986 Amsterdam Colloquium on Anabaptism sponsored jointly by the Doopsgezind Seminarium and the Theologisch Instituut of the University of Amsterdam. My own students at The Southern Baptist Theological Seminary, Louisville, Kentucky, have served as a hospitable nursery in which my ideas could grow and be tested. My colleagues in the departments of church history and theology have been remarkably tolerant of one who has argued, somewhat against the prevailing consensus, that Reformed and Baptist are not mutually exclusive terms. From the beginning of my tenure on the faculty, President Roy L. Honeycutt has been unflagging in his support for me and the discipline to which I am committed. Gaylyn Bishop, Connie Easterling, and Jackie Morcom provided able and cheerful assistance in preparing this manuscript for press. Barbara Bruce, a doctoral candidate in church history, interrupted her translation of Origen's homilies on Joshua to prepare the index for this book.

Like the writings of the four major figures studied in this volume, this book was written amid the struggles and joys of daily family life. I am grateful for the loving support given by my wife, Denise, an accomplished author in her own right and my own special Katie von Bora. It should be recorded that, as this book goes to press, my son, Christian, age six, has mastered the first ten questions of Calvin's Catechism, while my daughter, Alyce, age four, is making good progress on the Apostle's Creed.

Finally, I would like to mention those scholars with whom I have studied Reformation history and theology: Professors William J. Wright, James S. Preus, Arthur C. McGill, Caroline Walker Bynum, Donald R. Kelly, David C. Steinmetz, Ian D. K. Siggins, Heiko A. Oberman, John E. Booty, Peter J. Gomes, and last, but not least, George Huntston Williams. To each of these I owe much more than a prefatory acknowledgment can express. This volume is dedicated to Professor Williams, my mentor and friend, who was a continuing source of encouragement and inspiration during seven years of graduate and postgraduate study at the Harvard Divinity School. One of the premier church historians of the twentieth century, Professor Williams modeled for me the two qualities required of anyone who aspires to the vocation of what Cotton Mather once called "the Lord's remembrancer": a critical reverence for the Christian tradition in all of its varied modalities, and a sense of membership in the church universal, the body of Christ extended throughout time as well as space. This book is dedicated to Professor Williams with affection and esteem, in partial repayment for a debt which can never be cancelled.

TIMOTHY GEORGE
The Southern Baptist
Theological Seminary
Louisville, Kentucky

Epiphany, 1987

Abbreviations

CNTC   *Calvin's New Testament Commentaries,* David W. Torrance and Thomas F. Torrance, eds. 12 vols. Grand Rapids: Eerdmans, 1959-1970.

CO   *Ioannis Calvini opera quae supersunt omnia,* G. Baum, E. Cunitz, and E. Reuss, eds. 59 vols. Brunswick and Berlin: Schwetschke, 1863-1900.

CR   *Corpus Reformatorum.* Halle/Saale, 1835-1860; 1905-

CWE   *Collected Works of Erasmus.* Toronto: University of Toronto Press, 1974-

CWMS   *The Complete Writings of Menno Simons,* John C. Wenger, ed. Scottdale: Herald Press, 1956.

EE   *Opus epistolarum Des. Erasmi Roterodami.* 11 vols. Oxford: Oxford University Press, 1906-1947.

LW   *Luther's Works,* Jaroslav Pelikan and H. T. Lehmann, et al., eds.

MQR   *The Mennonite Quarterly Review.*

OS   *Joannis Calvini Opera Selecta,* P. Barth, W. Niesel, and D. Scheuner, eds. 5 vols. München: Chr. Kaiser, 1926-1962.

PL   *Patrologia Latina,* J. P. Migne, ed. Paris: 1844-1864.

SAW   Spiritual and Anabaptist Writers; George H. Williams and Angel M. Mergal, eds. Philadelphia: Westminster Press, 1957.

WA   *D. Martin Luthers Werke. Kritische Gesamtausgabe.* 58 vols. Weimar: Böhlau, 1833-

WA BR   *Briefwechsel* (Luther's *Letters,* 14 vols. in the Weimar Edition).

WA DB   *Deutsch Bibel* (Luther's *German Bible,* 12 vols. in the Weimar Edition).

WA TR   *Tischreden* (Luther's *Table Talk,* 6 vols. in the Weimar Edition).

Z   *Huldreich Zwinglis Samtliche Werke,* Emil Egli, Georg Finsler, et al., eds. Berlin, Leipzig, Zurich: 1950-

CONTENTS

1

Introduction

In 1518 the Dutch scholar Desiderius Erasmus, having entered upon his fifty-first year and believing his death to be imminent, longed to be rejuvenated for a few years, "for this only reason that I believe I see a golden age dawning in the near future."[1] In retrospect, it seems that Erasmus was unduly pessimistic about his own end—he had nearly twenty years yet to live—and overly optimistic about his times. His heady vision of a "golden age" of peace and learning would soon vanish before renewed war between the pope and the emperor, peasants' uprisings, the assault of the Turks in the East and, above all, a religious crisis of profound impact. This crisis, which we call the Reformation, would shake the foundations of Western Christendom leaving the church permanently divided. Before he died in 1536, Erasmus was referring to his age as "the worst century since Jesus Christ."[2]

This negative assessment, however, must be set alongside other, more positive appraisals. Thus, the Scottish Presbyterian theologian, William Cunningham, opened his massive study of Reformation theology with the bold claim that the Reformation of the sixteenth century "was the greatest event, or series of events, that has occurred since the close of the canon of Scripture."[3] In a similar vein, the philosopher Hegel, a Protestant of a different sort, referred to the Reformation as "the all-illuminating sun,

---

1. The motif of the "golden age" is a recurrent theme in Erasmus's early writings. Compare his exclamation in the *Panegyric* written in 1504 for Archduke Philip of Austria: "O fortunate age of ours, a truly golden age, when . . . the whole crop of virtues from that age of innocence are renewed, restored to life, and bloom again!" CWE 27, p. 48.

2. EE IV, no. 1239.

3. William Cunningham, *The Reformers and the Theology of the Reformation* (Edinburgh: T. and T. Clark, 1866), p. 1.

which follows that day-break at the end of the Middle Ages."[4]

Until quite recently, one's interpretation of the Reformation depended, almost invariably, upon prior confessional or ideological commitments. Roman Catholic partisans, beginning with Johannes Cochlaeus in the sixteenth century and continuing to Heinrich Denifle and Hartmann Grisar in the twentieth, have not been slack in their insistence that the Reformation was—to put it mildly—a mistake. What were its causes? Luther, a mad monk driven by narcissism and sexual compulsion; the German princes, greedy, self-serving autocrats; the Protestant preachers, renegade priests ready to sell their souls to become womanizers. And its consequences? Equally obvious: the rending of the seamless robe of medieval civilization, the splitting apart of faith and reason, nature and grace (so perfectly harmonized by Thomas Aquinas), and the unleashing of the forces of absolutism, nationalism, and secularism.

Protestant polemicists, for their part, responded to the Catholic caricatures in kind. In 1564 the Protestant court chaplain, Jerome Rauscher, published a treatise entitled *One Hundred Select, Great, Shameless, Fat, Well-Swilled, Stinking, Papistical Lies.* The leaders of the Protestant movement, Luther, Zwingli, and Calvin, were depicted as heroes of the faith. Their words and deeds took on cosmic significance in the unfolding of salvation history.[5]

In the tradition of liberal Protestantism, the reformers were frequently extolled not because of, but in spite of, their actual reformatory doctrines. For Hegel, the Reformation, and especially Luther, constituted a crucial moment in the history of thought since it was at this juncture that the concept of human freedom came to the fore. He thus reduced Reformation theology to the dictum: "Man is destined through himself to be free."[6] In this view the Reformation was merely the first phase of the Enlightenment; Luther and Calvin, the precursors of Rousseau and Voltaire!

The German historian, Leopold von Ranke, inaugurated a new era in Reformation historiography when he published his monumental *German*

4. H. Glockner, ed., *Georg Wilhelm Friedrich Hegel, Sämtliche Werke,* (Stuttgart-Bad Constatt, 1956-1965), XI, p. 519. On Hegel as an interpreter of Luther, see Gerhard Ebeling, "Luther and the Beginning of the Modern Age," *Luther and the Dawn of the Modern Era,* Heiko A. Oberman, ed. (Leiden: E. J. Brill, 1974), pp. 11-39.

5. Gordon Rupp, *The Righteousness of God: Luther Studies* (London: Hodder and Stoughton, 1953), p. 20.

6. *Werke,* XI, p. 524.

History in the Age of the Reformation (1839).[7] Although a Lutheran by confession, Ranke sought to rise above denominational prejudice. (He also wrote a history of the popes, in order to prove his evenhandedness!) He stressed the interaction of religion and politics in the period of the Reformation and insisted on extensive and critical use of the primary sources. The proper aim of the historian, as Ranke put it, is to know and reconstruct the actual past *wie es eigentlich gewesen* ("as it actually happened").

Ranke's influence on subsequent Reformation historiography, and indeed on the study of history in general, has been immense. His emphasis on the scrupulous use of sources has raised critical study of the Reformation to a new level. The writings of Luther, Zwingli, and Calvin, as well as those of many Catholic and radical reformers, have since been published in modern critical editions. Much more is known today about the complex of political, social, and cultural factors which characterized the Reformation. At the same time, Ranke's desire for an utterly objective history has not been fulfilled. Nor indeed can it be. History is never the simple recounting of the past as it really was. It is inevitably an interpretation of the past, a retrospective vision of the past, which is limited both by the sources themselves and by the historian who selects and interprets them.

Perspectives in Reformation Studies

Reformation studies today embrace a variety of competing approaches. Before setting forth the aim and perspective of this book, let us look at three general areas of concern in contemporary Reformation scholarship.[8]

The Problem of Periodization

Lord Acton, who was a keen student of the Reformation, once declared that historians should be more concerned with problems than with periods. The attempt to situate the Reformation between the medieval civilization which preceded it on the one hand and modern culture which followed it on the other has proved to be exceedingly awkward. Earlier in this century, Ernst Troeltsch argued that the Reformation, in its seminal tendencies, belonged to the "authoritarian" world view of the Middle Ages. The break-

7. Leopold von Ranke, *Deutsche Geschichte im Zeitalter der Reformation* (Leipzig: Duncter and Humblot, 1873).

8. A helpful introduction to Reformation historiography is Lewis W. Spitz, ed., *The Reformation: Basic Interpretations* (Lexington, Mass.: D. C. Heath, 1962). Cf. also Hans J. Hillerbrand, *Men and Ideas in the Sixteenth Century* (Chicago: Rand McNally, 1969), pp. 1-8.

through to modern times came not in the sixteenth century with the Reformation, but in the eighteenth with the Enlightenment. Troeltsch was rebutted by the famous church historian and Luther scholar, Karl Holl, who claimed that Luther and the Reformers had presaged many positive developments in modern culture, notably in the concepts of personality and community.[9]

Closely related to this debate is the issue of the relationship of the Renaissance to the Reformation. The word *Renaissance,* which was originally only a term in the history of art, has come to represent a period of cultural flourishing—intellectual, literary, artistic—which swept through Italy and then Northern Europe from the fourteenth through the sixteenth centuries. The link between Renaissance and Reformation is often said to be humanism, which refers not to an anthropocentric philosophy of life, but rather to a pattern of education and activism modeled upon a quasi-religious reverence for classical precedence. Humanism deeply affected every branch of the Reformation. Luther developed his insight into Pauline theology while using Erasmus's edition of the Greek New Testament. Zwingli, Calvin, Melanchthon, and Beza, among many others, were steeped in humanistic studies before embracing the Protestant message. Still, we cannot simply equate humanism and the Reformation; for in the wake of the Lutheran schism, humanist was divided from humanist as deeply as Protestant was from Catholic.

Was the Reformation the fulfillment or the antithesis of the Renaissance? Enno van Gelder argued the latter, claiming that the Reformation was basically at odds with positive elements of the Renaissance carried forth by such scholars as Erasmus and Montaigne.[10] On the other hand, William Bouwsma pointed to important affinities between the deep tensions in Renaissance culture and the solutions offered by the Protestant reformers.

9. Cf. Ernst Troeltsch, *Protestantism and Progress: A Historical Study of the Relation of Protestantism to the Modern World* (London: Williams and Norgate, 1912). Holl's seminal essay, "Was verstand Luther unter Religion?" has been translated in *What Did Luther Understand by Religion?* James Luther Adams and Walter Bense, eds. and trans. (Philadelphia: Fortress Press, 1977). See also Holl, *The Cultural Significance of the Reformation* (New York: Meridian, 1959).

10. H. A. Enno van Gelder, *The Two Reformations of the Sixteenth Century* (The Hague: Martinus Nijhoff, 1961). We may compare Gelder's thesis to the starker statement of Friedrich Nietzsche: "If Luther had been burned like Hus, the dawn of the Enlightenment might perhaps have come a little earlier and more brilliantly than we can now imagine." *Nietzsches Werke* (Leipzig, 1899-1904), I, ii, pp. 224-225.

Thus, he described the Reformation as "the theological fulfillment of the Renaissance."[11]

The problem of periodization has defied an easy consensus. It is clear that the Reformation was ambiguously and eclectically related to both medieval and modern impulses. Heiko A. Oberman, whose research on the late medieval context of the Reformation would seem to validate Troeltsch's thesis, has nonetheless found "the birthpangs of the Modern Era" in three characteristics of the later Middle Ages: (1) the discovery of the inductive method in scientific research, (2) a new view of human dignity based on a covenantal understanding of the relationship between God and the human, and (3) the closing of the gap between sacred and secular.[12] Without over-defining our terms, it is best to see the Reformation as an era of transition, characterized by the emergence of a new kind of culture which was struggling to be born even as the old one was still passing away.

Political, Social, and Economic Interpretations

Clearly, the Reformation lends itself to an examination of these factors. In the political sphere, it witnessed the rise of the modern nation-state, the last serious attempt to make the Holy Roman Empire a viable force in European politics, and the beginning of dynastic religious wars. Why the Reformation succeeded in Germany, failed in France, and never took root in Spain can only be understood in the light of the distinct political histories of these states. Economically, the influx of gold from the New World, together with the breakup of feudal land economies, created runaway inflation and economic dislocation. The relationship between the Reformation and the rise of capitalism has been studied extensively and still continues to generate controversy. Likewise, the social forces operative in the Reformation have been investigated in great detail. We now have a much fuller picture of the social realities of the sixteenth century: the resurgence of witchcraft, the impact of printing, the ethos of urban life, changing family structures—all of which impinged directly upon the religious impulses of

11. William J. Bouwsma, "Renaissance and Reformation: An Essay in Their Affinities and Connections," in Oberman, pp. 127-149.

12. H. A. Oberman, "The Shape of Late Medieval Thought: The Birthpangs of the Modern Era," *The Pursuit of Holiness in Late Medieval and Renaissance Religion,* Charles Trinkhaus and H. A. Oberman, eds. (Leiden: E. J. Brill, 1974), pp. 3-25.

the age.[13] Some of the most creative interpretations of the Reformation have been set forth by Marxist historians who, from Friedrich Engels to Gerhard Zschabitz, have interpreted the class struggles of the sixteenth century as a prototype of revolutions in the twentieth.

Ecumenical Historiography

Perhaps no scholar has had more influence on contemporary Roman Catholic interpretations of the Reformation than Joseph Lortz. His two-volume study of *The Reformation in Germany* (1939-1940) broke decisively with earlier Catholic polemics against the Reformation and offered a basically positive, if still critical, appraisal of Luther. An entire "school" of ecumenical Catholic historians has followed in Lortz's footsteps. This tradition of irenic scholarship has received a further impetus since the Second Vatican Council. On the Protestant side, we may mention the new interest in the reformers generated by Emil Brunner, Paul Tillich, and especially Karl Barth. While this emphasis has been decidedly confessional in part (cf. the "Luther renaissance" associated with Karl Holl), it has also contributed to a wider appreciation of the reformers as servants of the entire church.

The Reformation as Religious Initiative

While the foregoing approaches to Reformation history provide valuable insights for understanding such a complex period, we must recognize that the Reformation was essentially a religious event; its deepest concerns, theological. In this study we are not concerned to tell the "whole story" of the Reformation. Our primary focus is neither the political, social, nor the strictly church historical dimensions. Rather we are concerned with the theological self-understanding of four major reformers. Although we shall have occasion for critical assessment, we must not prejudge the validity of the reformers' thought. If F. M. Powicke's dictum, "A vision or an idea is not to be judged by its value for us, but by its value to the man who had it"[14] is not the whole truth, it at least reminds us that we cannot begin to

13. A useful survey of trends in Reformation studies is Steven Ozment, ed., *Reformation Europe: A Guide to Research* (St. Louis: Center for Reformation Research, 1982). A good sampling of recent social history of the Reformation is found in a memorial volume dedicated to Harold J. Grimm: *Pietas et Societas: New Trends in Reformation Social History,* Kyle C. Sessions and Phillip N. Bebb, eds. (Kirksville, Mo.: Sixteenth Century Journal Publishers, 1985).

14. Quoted, G. F. Nuttall, *The Holy Spirit in Puritan Faith and Experience* (Oxford: Blackwell, 1946), p. 168.

evaluate the significance of earlier Christians, especially the reformers, until we have asked ourselves their questions and listened well to their answers.

Such an approach requires an appreciation for what John T. McNeill has called the "religious initiative" in Reformation history.[15] Impressed by the secular context of current events, we are tempted to interpret the past in terms of contemporary standards, rather than those of the age we are studying. It is easy to assume that princes and reformers, like modern statesmen and diplomats, were motivated primarily by secular concerns. Yet the Lutheran, George of Brandenburg, when required by Emperor Charles V to participate in a Corpus Christi procession, replied that he would sooner kneel down and have his head cut off.[16] Likewise, Galaezzo Caracciolo, a relative of the pope who was converted to the reform, preferred a life of exile, including separation from his wife and six children, to the renunciation of his newfound faith.[17] Such examples give poignancy to Luther's lines: "Let goods and kindred go, This mortal life also; The body they may kill: God's truth abideth still, His kingdom is forever." It is well to remember that the age of the Reformation produced more martyrs than all of the persecutions in the early church.

Of course, not everyone in the Reformation was afflicted with martyrdom lust. Montaigne, no doubt, spoke for many when he said: "There is nothing for which I wish to break my neck."[18] Religious toleration was often advocated by those least moved by religious passion, as the case of *les politiques* in France demonstrates. Still, the reformers—Protestant, Catholic, and radical alike—were able to accomplish what they did because they were alive to the deepest struggles and hopes of their age. By tapping this profound reservoir of spiritual yearning, the reformers affected a major change in religious sensibilities. In this sense the Reformation was at once a revival and a revolution.

After an initial chapter, in which a number of the spiritual currents of the Late Middle Ages are described, this book offers a theological profile of four major reformers of the sixteenth century: Martin Luther, Huldrych

15. John T. McNeill, "The Religious Initiative in Reformation History," *The Impact of the Church Upon Its Culture,* Jerald C. Brauer, ed. (Chicago: University of Chicago Press, 1968), pp. 173-205.

16. Roland H. Bainton, *Early and Medieval Christianity* (Boston: Beacon Press, 1962), p. 164.

17. Ibid.

18. Albert Thibaudet, ed., *Essais de Michel de Montaigne,* (Argenteuil, 1933), Bk. II, p. 389.

Zwingli, John Calvin, and Menno Simons. Each of these figures stands at the headwaters of a major confessional tradition in the Reformation. Luther, who is the seminal theological genius of the entire Reformation, left his particular stamp on those Protestants who adhered to the Augsburg Confession. By the end of the sixteenth century the "Lutherans" were the dominant religious party in most of Germany and all of Scandanavia. Zwingli and Calvin, reformers of Zurich and Geneva respectively, are the co-parents of the Reformed tradition which spread far beyond the confines of its native Swiss context to embrace reformatory movements from Scotland and France to Hungary and Poland. Each of these three, Luther, Zwingli, and Calvin, though differing from one another in significant ways, was a *magisterial* reformer, that is, his reform movement was endorsed, indeed established, by magistrates, the ruling civil authorities. Menno Simons is the "odd fellow out" in this foursome. He left his position as priest in the Roman Church to become a leader of the Anabaptists, one of the major groupings of the Radical Reformation. The Mennonites, or Mennists as they were originally called, were very active in the Low Countries. Their influence was felt from England in the west to Russia in the east. By the early seventeenth century they had gained a measure of toleration in some places; in Menno's day they lived under perpetual threat of banishment and death.

Luther and Zwingli were reformers of the first generation; Calvin and Menno, of the second. Zwingli met Luther once; there was no other personal contact among these four reformers. Many other reformers could well have been chosen. Philip Melanchthon, Heinrich Bullinger, and Theodore Beza, the successors respectively of Luther, Zwingli, and Calvin, were all major theologians who transmuted as well as transmitted the traditions they inherited. Among the Anabaptists, Balthasar Hubmaier was more learned and Pilgram Marpeck more incisive than Menno. The Catholic reformers, Ignatius Loyola and Girolamo Seripando; the Anglicans, Thomas Cranmer and Richard Hooker; the Puritans, Thomas Cartwright and William Perkins; the "evangelical rationalists," Michael Servetus and Faustus Socinus; the mediating theologian, Martin Bucer—these and many others could well serve as prisms into the rich diversity of Reformation theology. In this volume, however, we shall attempt an in-depth sounding of several formative figures rather than a broad sampling from a wide range of religious thinkers.

Our interest in the theology of the reformers is neither antiquarian nor obscurantist. Historical theology is the study of what "the church of Jesus

Christ believes, confesses, and teaches on the basis of the Word of God."[19]
The church of Jesus Christ, however, is universal in respect to time as well
as space. The reformers we study are both our fathers in the faith and our
brothers in the community of the faithful. Their struggles and doubts, their
victories and defeats are also ours. Many of the theological issues with
which they wrestled seem far removed from contemporary concerns.

For most modern Christians, the intricacies of predestination, the precise
mode of Christ's presence in the eucharist, the arguments for and against
infant baptism are matters of acute indifference. Concealed in such controverted points, however, are burning questions of life and death, questions
about who God is, how divine revelation is imparted, what constitutes the
true church. The four reformers we focus on in this book faced these and
many other questions with an integrity and lived-out courage which we
cannot only admire but also emulate, even if we cannot agree with all of
their answers. Peter of Blois, a medieval theologian who died nearly three
hundred years before Luther was born, expressed a sense of gratitude for
the Christian writers of antiquity which should also characterize our attitude toward the reformers of the sixteenth century: "We are like dwarfs
standing on the shoulders of giants; thanks to them, we see farther than
they. Busying ourselves with the treatises written by the ancients, we take
their choice thoughts, buried by age and human neglect, and we raise them,
as it were, from death to renewed life."[20]

19. Jaroslav Pelikan, *The Emergence of the Catholic Tradition* (Chicago: University of Chicago Press, 1971), p. 1. Pelikan's definition echoes the opening article
of the Formula of Concord: "We believe, confess, and teach that the only rule and
norm, according to which all dogmas and all doctors ought to be esteemed and
judged, is no other whatever than the prophetic and apostolic writings both of the
Old and of the New Testaments." *Creeds of Christendom,* ed. Philip Schaff (New
York: Harper and Bros., 1877), III, pp. 93-94. For a fuller statement of the perspective on historical theology which informs this study, see Timothy George, "Dogma
Beyond Anathema: Historical Theology in the Service of the Church," *Review and
Expositor* 84 (1987).

20. PL 207, col. 290 AB (Epistola 92): "Nos, quasi nani super gigantum humeros
sumus, quorum beneficio longius, quam ipsi, speculamur, dum antiquorum tractatibus
inhaerentes elegantiores eorum sententias, quas vetustas aboleverat, hominumve
neglectus, quasi jam mortuas in quamdam novitatem essentiae suscitamus."

2

The Thirst for God
Theology and Spiritual Life in the Late Middle Ages

An Age of Anxiety

The Late Middle Ages are frequently described primarily in terms of decline, disintegration, and decay, an interpretation reflected in the title of Johan Huizinga's classic study of this period, *The Waning of the Middle Ages.* An age of adversity and flux, the fourteenth and fifteenth centuries have become a no-man's-land between the medieval synthesis of the thirteenth century, with its Gothic cathedrals and scholastic *summae,* and the great reforming movements of the sixteenth.

In fact, far from being an age of inane decadence, the two centuries prior to the Reformation proved remarkably vital in the face of unprecedented challenge and change. While abuses abounded in the church, so did cries for reform. New forms of lay piety, devotional treatises in the vernacular, renewed interest in relics, pilgrimages, and saints, popular religious movements—the Lollards in England, the Hussites in Bohemia, the Waldensians and Spiritual Franciscans in Italy and France—all testify to a deep-seated, if somewhat frenetic, spirituality. Indeed, we see a steady growth in the power and depth of religious feelings right up to the time of the Reformation.

This is not to deny that late medieval society also faced enormous political, social, economic, as well as religious, upheaval. The sentiment of the poet, Eustache Deschamps, "Now the world is cowardly, decayed, and weak, old, covetous, confused of speech/ I see only female and male fools/ The end approaches, in sooth . . . all goes badly," expressed a common mood of dismay and melancholy.[1] In fact, this sense of malaise, the feeling that the times were out of joint, combined with the rising tide of religious expectations, produced an age of extraordinary anxiety.

Paul Tillich, in his book *The Courage to Be,* outlined the history of

---

1. Quoted in Johan Huizinga, *The Waning of the Middle Ages,* p. 36.

Western civilization in terms of three recurring types of anxiety.[2] The end of classical antiquity was marked by ontic anxiety, an intense preoccupation with fate and death. Toward the end of the Middle Ages, the anxiety of guilt and condemnation predominated. This in turn gave way, at the end of the modern period, to the spiritual anxiety of emptiness and loss of meaning.

While we do not quarrel with Tillich's thesis of a moral crisis on the eve of the Reformation, in fact all three types of anxiety were amply present. Death, guilt, and loss of meaning resound with jarring dissonance in the literature, art, and theology of this period.

These three themes emerge vividly in Luther's struggle to find a gracious God. Struck down by a thunderstorm, and fearing imminent death, Luther vowed to become a monk. Once in the monastery, he was plagued with an overwhelming sense of guilt. Most terrifying of all were the assaults of dread and despair, the *Anfechtungen,* as Luther called them, when he teetered on the brink and nearly collapsed.

While Luther's spiritual struggle was his own, he epitomized the hopes and fears of his age. He was, we might say, just like everybody else, only more so. Furthermore, his doctrine of justification, and his theology of the church which grew out of it, spoke powerfully to the primal apprehensions of his time. In this respect, the theology of the reformers was a specific response to the special anxiety of their age.

A morbid preoccupation with suffering and death pervaded Europe in the late Middle Ages. At the root of this experience were the twin phenomena of famine and plague. So severe was the agrarian crisis in the early fourteenth century that some people resorted to cannibalism: In 1319 it was reported that the corpses of criminals were taken from the gallows and eaten by the poor in Poland and Silesia.[3] Added to this catastrophe was the devastation of the bubonic plague, or Black Death, which reached its peak in England around 1349, and which carried away at least one third of the entire European population. Episodes of the plague recurred down to the

2. Paul Tillich, *The Courage to Be* (New Haven: Yale University Press, 1952), pp. 57-63. Cf. also Tillich's treatment of the Late Middle Ages in his *A History of Christian Thought,* Carl E. Braaten, ed. (New York: Simon and Schuster, 1967), pp. 227-233. Other scholars have also applied the category of anxiety to this period. See especially the insightful article by William J. Bouwsma, "Anxiety and the Formation of Early Modern Culture," *After the Reformation: Essays in Honor of J. H. Hexter,* Barbara C. Malament, ed. (Philadelphia: University of Pennsylvania Press, 1980), pp. 215-246.

3. Robert E. Lerner, *The Age of Adversity: The Fourteenth Century* (Ithaca, N.Y.: Cornell University Press, 1968), pp. 10-11.

sixteenth century when a new plague, syphilis, was brought over from the New World by the sailors of Christopher Columbus.[4] In addition to these "natural" disasters, the invention of the gunpowder cannon elevated warfare to a new savagery.[5]

The vision of death manifested itself in sermons and woodcuts as well as in the painting and sculpture of the times. Tombs were frequently adorned with images of a naked corpse, its mouth agape, its fists clenched, and its bowels devoured by worms. One of the most popular pictorial representations was the Dance of Death. Death, in the form of a skeleton, appeared as a dancing figure leading away his victims. No one could escape his grasp—neither the wealthy merchant, the corpulent monk, nor the poor peasant. An hourglass was usually in a corner of the picture to remind the viewer that life was swiftly passing away.

The certainty of death was a popular theme for preachers as well. A Franciscan friar, Richard of Paris, once preached for ten consecutive days, seven hours a day, on the topic of the Last Four Things: death, judgment, heaven, hell. He delivered his sermons, appropriately enough, in the Cemetery of the Holy Innocents, the most popular burial ground in Paris. Hardly less dramatic was his contemporary, John of Capistrano, who carried a skull into the pulpit and warned his congregation: "Look, and see what remains of all that once pleased you, or that which once led you to sin. The worms have eaten it all."[6]

Theodore Beza, who succeeded John Calvin as the reformer of Geneva, recalled that his conversion to the reformed religion was occasioned by severe illness and the fear of death.

> He approached me through a sickness so severe that I despaired of my life. Seeing His terrible judgment before me, I could not think what to do with my wretched life. Finally, after endless suffering of body and soul, God showed pity upon His miserable lost servant and consoled me so that I could not doubt His mercy. With a thousand tears I renounced my former self,

4. Joseph Lortz, *How the Reformation Came* (New York: Herder and Herder, 1964), p. 6.

5. On the importance of this invention, see J. R. Hale, "Gunpowder and the Renaissance: An Essay in the History of Ideas," *From the Renaissance to the Counter-Reformation: Essays in Honor of Garrett Mattingly,* Charles H. Carter, ed. (New York: Random House, 1965), pp. 13-44; Lynn T. White, Jr., "Tools and Civilization," *Perspectives in Defense Management* 24 (1975-1976), pp. 33-42.

6. Michael Seidlmayer, *Currents of Medieval Thought* (Oxford: Blackwell, 1960), p. 126; cf. also Huizinga, pp. 138-151.

implored His forgiveness, renewed my oath to serve His true church, and in sum gave myself wholly over to Him. So the vision of death threatening my soul awakened in me the desire for a true and everlasting life. So sickness was for me the beginning of true health.[7]

Indeed, death was an ever-present reality for men and women on the eve of the Reformation. The close connection between death and guilt is seen in this statement from Calvin: "Where does death come from but from God's anger against sin? Hence arises that state of servitude through the whole of life, that is the constant anxiety in which unhappy souls are imprisoned."[8] Moral anxiety, which Tillich took to be the dominant motif of the age, arose from the fact that death implied judgment, and judgment brought the sinner face to face with a holy and wrathful God. The dire predicament of this situation is seen in the oft-depicted deathbed scenario where angels and demons alike vie for possession of the dying person's soul.

There were various attempts to assuage the guilt which weighed so heavily on the souls of the people. Most radical of all were the various companies of flagellants, rigorous ascetics who moved from town to town, publicly whipping themselves with leather scourges, in hopes of atoning for their own sins as well as for those of society.[9] Most sinners preferred the more routine channels of forgiveness: the sacraments and the parasacramental aids authorized by the church. Indulgences, pilgrimages, relics, veneration of the saints, the rosary, feast days, adoration of the consecrated Host, recital of many "Our Fathers"—all of these were part of the penitential system whereby one sought to assure a proper standing before God.[10] If the

7. Henri Meylan and Alain Dufour et al., eds., *Correspondence de Théodore de Bèze*, (Geneva: Droz, 1960-   ), III, p. 45 (letter no. 156 to Melchior Wolmar, May 12, 1560), translated in Henry Baird, *Theodore Beza* (New York: G. P. Putnam's Sons, 1899), p. 355.

8. *Comm.* Heb. 2:15: CNTC 2, pp. 485-493.

9. Cf. Norman Cohn, *The Pursuit of the Millennium* (New York: Oxford University Press, 1961), pp. 127-147; Gordon Leff, *Heresy in the Later Middle Ages* (New York: Barnes and Noble, 1967), II, pp. 485-493.

10. Relics were especially in vogue in the fifteenth and early sixteenth centuries. The cathedral at Cologne claimed to house the remains of the three Wise Men. The church at Aachen boasted the outer garments of the virgin Mary, and the bloodied tablecloth on which the severed head of John the Baptist had lain. The castle church in Wittenberg (Luther's church!) contained the valuable collection of Prince Frederick the Wise which included: thirty-five pieces of the true cross, a vial of the virgin Mary's milk, a stick from Moses's burning bush, and 204 parts of the bodies of the Holy Innocents. Cf. John P. Dolan, *History of the Reformation* (New York: Descle

sinner could afford it, he could endow a chantry where masses would be said on his behalf after his death. Emperor Charles V left provision for thirty thousand such masses, whereas Henry VIII of England, who wanted to make doubly sure, required that masses be said for his soul "while the world shall endure."[11]

Nowhere is the burdensome character of late medieval religious life more evident than in the confessional manuals and lay catechisms which came forth in abundance from the newly invented printing presses. Steven Ozment's analysis of these documents shows that the confessional, far from conveying a sense of forgiveness, merely reinforced an already ponderous weight of guilt.[12]

A child was capable of confession as early as age seven, the medieval reckoning of "the age of accountability." He would appear before the priest, recite the Lord's Prayer and Creed, and then respond to the priest's queries. These were designed to show the child the various ways by which he had perhaps transgressed the Ten Commandments. For example, he might be asked:

> Have you believed in magic? Have you loved your father and mother more than God? Have you failed to kneel on both knees or to remove your hat during communion?—These are sins against the first commandment.
>
> Have you cut wood, made bird traps, skipped mass and sermon, or danced on Sundays and holiday?—These are sins against the third commandment.
>
> Have you thrown snowballs or rocks at others? Have you stoned chickens and ducks? Did you kill the emperor with a double-headed ax? [A trick question to see if he was paying attention!]—These are sins against the fifth commandment.[13]

Likewise, for penitent adults the questions were designed to provoke introspection, scrupulosity, and a sense of having fallen short of a complete confession: Have you questioned God's power and goodness when you lost a game? Have you muttered against God because of bad weather, illness, poverty, the death of a child or a friend? Have you dressed proudly, sung and danced lustily, committed adultery, girl-watched, or exchanged adul-

Company, 1965), pp. 204-205.

    11. Seidlmayer, p. 141; "Testamentum Regis Henrici Octavi," Thomas Rymer, *Foedera* (London, 1713), XV, p. 110.

    12. Steven E. Ozment, *The Reformation in the Cities* (New Haven: Yale University Press, 1975), pp. 15-46.

    13. Ibid., quoting from Johannes Geffken, *Bilderkatechismus des funfzehnter Jahrhunderts* (Leipzig: Weigel, 1855).

terous glances in church or while walking on Sunday? Are you a woman who has artificially aborted a child, or killed a newborn and unbaptized infant? Have you miscarried because of overwork, play, or sexual activity? Have you stolen from pilgrims on their way to Rome? Have you thought of committing adultery? Sodomy? Incest?[14]

The pressure to come clean of all sins, including the interior and sometimes unrecognized motives behind them, placed an intolerable burden on the penitent. Once such a confession had been made, one still needed to perform works of satisfaction before absolution could be claimed. Hence the feverish activism of late medieval religion: the building of new churches, the traffic in indulgences, the ceaseless efforts to earn merits.[15]

Beyond all of this, of course, loomed the specter of purgatory and hell whose torments were portrayed in terrifying detail in the art, sculpture, and preaching of the day. Jean Gerson, a leading reformer of the early fifteenth century, described the religious temper of his times as *imaginatio melancholia,* "a melancholy imagination."[16] An example of this imagination is Sir Thomas More's vivid description of the horrors of purgatory. In his *Supplication of Souls* (1529) More placed the following words on the lips of the tormented dead:

> If ye pity the blind, there is none so blind as we, which are here in the dark, saving for sights unpleasant, and loathsome, till some comfort come. If ye pity the lame, there is none so lame as we, that neither can creep one foot out of the fire, nor have one hand at liberty to defend our face from the flame. Finally, if ye pity any man in pain, never knew ye pain comparable to ours; whose fire as far passeth in heat all the fires that ever burned upon earth, as the hottest of all those passeth a feigned fire painted on a wall. If ever ye lay sick, and thought the night long and longed sore for day, while every hour seemed longer than five, bethink you then what a long night we silly souls endure, that lie sleepless, restless, burning and broiling in the fire one long night of many days, of many weeks, and some of many years together . . . . You have your physicians with you, that sometime cure and heal you; no physic will help our pain, nor no plaister cool our heat. Your keepers do you great ease, and put you in good comfort; our keepers are such as God keep you from—cruel, damned sprites, odious, envious and hateful, despite-

14. Ibid.

15. Cf. the following assessment: "These anxious, craning gestures, indicating spiritual destitution and the misery of existence, were of a greater extent and higher intensity than before that time." Bernd Moeller, "Piety in Germany Around 1500," *The Reformation in Medieval Perspective,* Steven E. Ozment, ed. p. 56.

16. Dolan, p. 201.

ous enemies and despiteful tormentors, and their company more horrible and grievous to us than is the pain itself: and the intolerable torment that they do us, wherewith from top to toe they cease not continually to tear us.[17]

If purgatory was that bad, how incomparably worse must hell have been? One illustrated catechism portrayed the inhabitants of hell gnawing at their own vitals and added this commentary: "The pain caused by one spark of hell-fire is greater than that caused by a thousand years of a woman's labor in childbirth."[18] One of the church portals in the cathedral at Mainz depicts the last judgment: Christ the Judge is on top, the redeemed are being by carried by angels into Paradise, while the damned, with grimacing faces, are being led away in chains by demons toward the inferno. This motif, common to all of the major churches of Europe, reflected the medieval ethos of a God of wrath and judgment, before whose anger guilty humans could only quiver.

The themes of death and guilt are related to what was perhaps the overriding anxiety of late medieval society, a crisis of meaning. In every area of life the old static boundaries were being transgressed. The voyages of Columbus, Vespucci, and Magellan shattered the old geography and greatly enlarged the European sphere of influence. The medieval motto for Gibraltar—*ne plus ultra*—became simply *plus ultra*—more beyond. At the same time, the calculations of Copernicus, later confirmed by the observations of Galileo and Kepler, greatly extended the boundaries of the universe by removing earth—and humankind—from the center of created reality.[19] The political boundaries among nations were literally up for grabs, as the Hundred Years War between England and France, and the excursion of Charles VIII into Italy (1494), indicates. At the other end of the social scale, peasants sought to loose themselves from the bonds of feudalism by protest and petition when possible, by bloody revolt when necessary.

All of these conditions posed new and radical questions for late medieval

17. Thomas More, *The Workes of Sir Thomas More . . . wrytten by him in the Englysh tongue* (London: n.p., 1557), pp. 337-338, quoted in A. G. Dickens, *The English Reformation* (New York: Schocken Books, 1964), pp. 5-6.

18. Ozment, *Reformation in the Cities,* p. 28, quoting the *Heidelberger Bildenhandschrift,* Geffken, Appendix 8.

19. This is the basic meaning of the word *eccentric.* On the Nominalist background to the Copernican revolution, see the fascinating article by Heiko A. Oberman, "Reformation and Revolution: Copernicus' Discovery in an Era of Change," in *The Nature of Scientific Discovery,* Owen Gingerich, ed. (Washington, D.C.: Smithsonian Institution Press, 1975), pp. 134-169.

culture. The world view of an ordered universe arranged in a fixed system of celestial hierarchies, perfectly mirrored in an harmonious society on earth, became less and less tenable. Shakespeare, writing in the wake of these developments but still using pre-Copernican imagery, expresses the mood of the age:

> . . . but when the planets
> In evil mixture to disorder wander,
> What plagues and what portents! what mutiny!
> What raging of the sea! shaking of earth!
> Commotion in the winds! frights, changes, horrors,
> Divert and crack, rend and deracinate
> The unity and married calm of states
> Quite from their fixture. Oh, when degree is shak'd,
> Which is the ladder of all high designs,
> The enterprise is sick.[20]

The cosmic disruption, with its counterpart on earth in social and religious unrest, accounts, in part, for the widespread obsession with the strange world of the occult on the eve of the Reformation. In 1484 Pope Innocent VIII issued his bull, *Summis desiderantes,* which authorized two Dominican inquisitors to undertake the systematic extermination of witchcraft. They in turn produced the infamous *Malleus maleficarum,* or Witches' Hammer, an official textbook on witchcraft containing precise instruction for its detection and prosecution. In the witchcraft hysteria which followed, thousands of poor, old, unprotected (because single) women were subjected to unspeakable tortures. In all, some thirty thousand executions for witchcraft had taken place by the end of the sixteenth century.[21] All sorts of calamities were blamed on the witches: hailstorms, drought, the death of farm animals, sexual impotence. Likewise, the connection between witchcraft and heresy was generally accepted. Therefore, it is not surprising that Luther's Catholic detractors circulated the un-

20. This is from Ulysses' speech on "degrees" in Shakespeare, *Troilus and Cressida. The Complete Works of William Shakespeare,* W. G. Clark and W. A. Wright, eds. (New York: Nelson Doubleday, Inc., n.d.), p. 696.

21. This figure comes from Louis of Paramo, a Sicilian inquisitor, who wrote a treatise on the *Origin and Progress of the Inquisition* (1597). Cf. Philip Schaff, *History of the Christian Church* (New York: Charles Scribner's Sons, 1910), VI, p. 529. On the various theories concerning witchcraft see H. C. Erik Midelfort, "Were There Really Witches?" *Transition and Revolution,* Robert M. Kingdon, ed. (Minneapolis: Burgess Publishing Co., 1974), pp. 189-233.

scrupulous rumor that he was born of the illicit union between his mother (a witch!) and a demonic incubus.[22]

We have seen that the Late Middle Ages, far from being a period of decline, was alive with all sorts of spiritual vitalities. It was, as Lucien Febvre described it, an age with "an immense appetite for the divine."[23] The thirst for God was sometimes reflected in bizarre patterns of spirituality: braying at Mass in honor of the donkey on which Mary rode, the name of Jesus tattooed over the heart, veneration of bleeding Hosts. More often it followed the beaten paths of mainline piety. But, in either case, it was for many people a deeply unsatisfying spirituality. The nervous moralism and ceaseless attempts to placate a high and angry God served to intensify the primal anxieties of death, guilt, and loss of meaning. The ultimate achievement of the Reformation was that it was able to redefine these anxieties in terms of new certainties, or, better put, old certainties rediscovered. The spiritual malaise of the late Middle Ages was not the cause of the Reformation, but it was certainly its precondition.

We have said very little about the notorious abuses of the pre-Reformation church: simony, nepotism, the misuse of benefices, clerical concubinage, etc. All of the reformers, Catholic, Protestant, and radical alike, strenuously opposed such practices. However, some among them also realized that something more than a general housecleaning was demanded. It would do no good to sweep out the cobwebs if the foundation itself was rotten. What was needed was a new definition of the church based on a fresh understanding of the gospel.

The Quest for the True Church

Closely related to the anxiety which marked all phases of life in the late Middle Ages was a crisis of confidence in the identity and authority of the church. Unlike the doctrines of the Trinity and Christology, which were subjects of official conciliar definitions in the early church, the doctrine of the church had never received such dogmatic status. Neither Peter Lom-

22. Cf. Ian Siggins, *Luther and His Mother* (Philadelphia: Fortress Press, 1981), pp. 32-44. Belief in witchcraft was, of course, not confined to Catholics. The Puritan theologian, William Perkins, published a *Discourse of the Damned Art of Witchcraft,* and twenty-nine witches were executed in 1544-1545 for causing an epidemic in Calvin's Geneva. Cf. Midelfort, p. 189.

23. Lucien Febvre, "The Origins of the French Reformation: a badly-put question?" *A New Kind of History,* Peter Burke, ed. (New York: Harper and Row, 1973); . . . originally published in *Revue historique* 1929).

bard in his *Book of Sentences* nor Thomas Aquinas in his *Summa Theologica* has a separate *locus* for the church in his systematic theology. However, from the fourteenth century onward, numerous treatises bear the title, *De ecclesia.* This explosion of interest in ecclesiology coincided with extensive institutional changes within the church as well as with the social and political crises we have already touched upon.

The Reformation is often portrayed as having shattered the unity of the medieval church, bequeathing to the modern world the legacy of a divided Christendom. When we look closer at the centuries preceding the Reformation, however, we discover a plurality of ecclesial forms and doctrines. The Protestant reformers, as we shall see, also differed among themselves concerning the nature and function of the church and its ministry. The Reformation of the sixteenth century was thus a continuation of the quest for the true church which had begun long before Luther, Calvin, or the fathers of Trent entered the lists.[24] Let us consider briefly five competing models of the church in the Late Middle Ages.

Curialism

In medieval times the *Curia Romana* referred to the papal court, including all of the officials and functionaries who assisted the pope in the governance of the church. Curialism thus was a theory of church government which invested supreme authority, both temporal and spiritual, in the hands of the papacy.

The Church of Rome, with its dual apostolic affiliation (both Peter and Paul were martyred in Rome), had early on laid claim to a kind of spiritual hegemony. The roots of papal sovereignty, however, go back to the conversion of Constantine, and to the subsequent "Christianization" of the Roman Empire.[25] This event, coupled with the barbarian onslaughts of the fifth century, left the bishop of Rome in a politically strategic position. The

24. On late medieval concepts of the true church, see Gordon Leff, "The Making of the myth of a True Church in the later Middle Ages," *Journal of Medieval and Renaissance Studies* 1 (1971), pp. 1-25; Scott H. Hendrix, "In Quest of the *Vera Ecclesia:* The Crises of Late Medieval Ecclesiology," *Viator* 7 (1976), pp. 347-378.

25. The Constantinian revolution, which the Anabaptists would recognize as the decisive "fall" of the church, was cited as a turning point in the fortunes of the papacy by earlier reformers such as Bernard of Clairvaux. See Bernard, *Sermones in Cantica canticorum* 33.14-16 (PL 183, cols. 958-959). Cf. also Dante's lament: "Ah Constantine, what evil marked the hour—not of your conversion, but of the fee the first rich Father took from you in dower!" *Inferno,* Canto XIX, 109-111: *The Inferno,* John Ciardi, trans. (New York: New American Library, 1954), p. 170.

relationship between the temporal and spiritual realms—often stated in terms of the "two swords" (Luke 22:38)—was given classic formulation by Pope Gelasius I who, in a letter of 494 to Emperor Anastasius, declared:

> Two there are, august emperor, by which this world is chiefly ruled, the sacred authority [*auctoritas*] of the priesthood and the royal power [*potestas*]. Of these the responsibility of the priests is more weighty . . . . And if the hearts of the faithful should be submitted to all priests in general, . . . how much more should assent be given to the bishop of that see which the Most High wishes to be pre-eminent over all priests, and which the devotion of the church has honored ever since.[26]

Although papal power was significantly reduced during feudalism, the Gelasian principle was reasserted with a vengeance in the High Middle Ages. The pronouncements of three popes in particular constitute the high watermark of papal claims to worldly preeminence. Pope Gregory VII, at the height of the Investiture Controversy in 1075, issued his famous *Dictatus Papae,* a list of twenty-seven statements concerning papal power. He claimed, for example, that the pope "is the only one whose feet are to be kissed by all princes," that the pope could depose emperors, convene synods, and absolve subjects of the feudal obligations. Moreover, he insisted that "the Roman Church has never erred, nor ever, by the witness of Scripture, shall err to all eternity."[27] The pope who came closest to putting into effect Gregory's "Dictates" was Innocent III (1198-1216) who presided over a vast world empire. He believed that in the hierarchy of being the pope occupied a middle position between the divine and the human—"lower than God but higher than man." He likened himself to the "greater light" which God had set in the firmament of the universal church, compared to which all other authorities (i.e. the emperor) were but pale reflections.[28] Building on the work of his predecessors, Pope Boniface VIII set forth the most extravagant claims for papal sovereignty in his bull *Unam Sanctam* (1302). Just as there was one ark, guided by one helmsman, so there is "one holy, Catholic, and apostolic church" presided over by one supreme spiritual power, the pope, who can be judged only by God not by man. Hence, he concluded, "We declare, state, define and pronounce that it is altogether

26. Cited in Brian Tierney, *The Crisis of Church and State, 1050-1300* (Englewood Cliffs, N.J.: Prentice Hall, 1964), pp. 13-14.

27. Ibid., pp. 49-50.

28. Ibid., p. 132.

necessary to salvation for every human creature to be subject to the Roman Pontiff."[29]

The pontificate of Boniface marked the end of one phase and the beginning of another in the history of the papacy. His death was followed by the seventy-year exile of the papacy in Avignon, the so-called Babylonian Captivity (1309-1377) and the shocking confusion of the Great Western Schism (1378-1417), when for a while two, and then three, popes claimed simultaneously to be the supreme head of the church. The futility of Boniface's efforts to wield both temporal and spiritual swords was recognized by many of his contemporaries. Thus Dante, who placed Boniface in one of the lowest circles of hell with two other simoniac popes, described the consequences of the curialist position: ". . . since the Church has sought to be two governments at once, she sinks in much, befouling both her power and ministry."[30]

Conciliarism

In the early fifteenth century the demand for *reformatio in capite et in membris*—reformation in head and members—resounded throughout Europe. As one contemporary theologian put it:

> The whole world, the clergy, all Christian people, know that a reform of the Church militant is both necessary and expedient. Heaven and the elements demand it. It is called for by the Sacrifice of the Precious Blood mounting up to heaven. The very stones will soon be constrained to join in the cry.[31]

The specter of the body of Christ divided into three papal obediences, each hurling anathemas and interdicts at the other two, gave urgency to the call for reform. Out of this crisis emerged the conciliar view of the church which affirmed the superiority of ecumenical councils over the pope in the governance and reform of the church.

At the heart of the conciliar theory was the fundamental distinction between the universal church (representatively embodied in a general coun-

29. Ibid., p. 189.

30. *Purgatorio,* Canto XVI, 127-29, John Ciardi, trans., (Franklin Center, Penn.: The Franklin Library, 1983; original ed. 1961), p. 174. A high-curialist view of the church continued to be defended. Cf. the statement of Panormitanus (d. 1453): "Whatever God can do, the Pope can do," quoted in Patrick Granfield, *The Papacy in Transition* (New York: Doubleday, 1980), p. 44.

31. Quoted, L. Pastor, *History of the Popes* (London: Trübner and Co., 1891), I, pp. 202-203.

cil) and the Roman Church (consisting of pope and cardinals).[32] Already
in canon law a loophole to the doctrine that the pope was above human
judgment had been provided in the clause—*nisi deprehendatur a fide devius,*
"unless he deviates from the faith."[33] Such deviation was interpreted to
mean not only manifest heresy but also such acts as threatened the integrity
of the church.

Still the question remained: In the case of multiple schism who was
qualified to hold the popes accountable? William of Ockham had declared
that any Christian, even a woman, could call together a general council in
a time of emergency. After several unsuccessful attempts to settle the crisis
(e.g. by forced resignation and negotiation), the Council of Constance,
summoned by the Emperor Sigismund, convened in 1414. All three existing
popes were deposed. A new pope, Martin V, was elected, and the Great
Western Schism was healed. The papacy had been saved—by the council!

The conciliar theory, as set forth by thinkers such as Pierre d'Ailly
(d. 1420), Jean Gerson (d. 1429), and Dietrich of Niem (d. 1418), did not
seek to abolish the papacy, but to relegate it to its proper role within the
whole church. They did claim that the *plenitudo potestatis,* "fullness of
power" resided only in God, not in any individual man, not even in the
pope. The conciliarists advocated one pope, one undivided church, and a
program of moral reform modeled on the example of the early church. Such
a program, had it been implemented, would have greatly reduced the enormous wealth of the curia by eliminating many sources of its income: exemp-
tions, dispensations, benefices, plenary indulgences, and so on. The failure
of the conciliar movement contributed in part to the success of the Protestant revolt from Rome, as well as the continuing cries for reform from many
who remained faithful to Rome.

Although the Council of Constance passed two decrees, *Sacrosancta*
(1415), affirming conciliar supremacy, and *Frequens* (1417), calling for
future councils to be convened at regular intervals, the later fifteenth century witnessed the revival of the papal monarchy and the demise of the
conciliar movement. The death knell of conciliarism can be heard in the
papal bull, *Execrabilis,* promulgated by Pope Pius II in 1460.

> A horrible abuse, unheard-of in earlier times, has sprung up in our period.
> Some men, imbued with a spirit of rebellion . . . suppose that they can appeal
> from the Pope, Vicar of Jesus Christ . . . to a future council . . . . Desirous,

32. See the magisterial study of Brian Tierney, *Foundations of Conciliar Theory*
(Cambridge: Cambridge University Press, 1955), esp. pp. 1-20, 47-67.
33. Ibid., p. 248.

> therefore, of banishing this deadly poison from the Church of Christ,
> . . . we condemn appeals of this kind, reject them as erroneous and abomina-
> ble, and declare them to be completely null and void.[34]

The decree further warned that anyone attempting to by-pass this injunction would face immediate and irrevocable excommunication. In effect,
Execrabilis nullified both *Sacrocanta* and *Frequens,* bringing to an end the
era of conciliar reform. Henceforth, reform—within the church—could
only be inaugurated by the pope.

Wyclif and Hus

In addition to ending the Great Schism, the Council of Constance also
declared heretical the teachings of the English theologian John Wyclif
(d. 1384) and ordered his bones to be exhumed from the ground and burned.
They then moved to condemn to the stake the leading exponent of Wyclif's
views, the Bohemian reformer, John Hus (d. 1415). Both Wyclif, "The
Morning Star of the Reformation," and Hus are often referred to as forerunners of the Reformation. Indeed, Hus's treatise, *De Ecclesia,* played an
important role in Luther's eventual break with the papacy. At one point,
Luther was forced to confess: "We are all Hussites now."[35] He later realized
that his affinity with Wyclif and Hus was only provisional; neither of them
approached his radical understanding of justification by faith alone.[36]
Nonetheless their own radical ecclesiologies contributed significantly to
Luther's developing doctrine of the church.

Wyclif, whom Gordon Rupp dubbed "the Kierkegaard of the later Middle Ages," leveled a blistering attack against the Christendom of his day.
He denounced priests as "robbers . . . malicious foxes . . . gluttons
. . . devils . . . apes," curates as "spurious offshoots not rooted in the vine
of the Church." The pope was "the head vicar of the fiend," and monaster-

---

34. "Execrabilis," in Gabriel Biel, *Defensorium Obedientiae Apostolicae et Alia
Documenta,* Heiko A. Oberman et al., eds. (Cambridge, Mass.: Harvard University
Press, 1968), pp. 225-226. Cf. also Oberman's discussion of this bull in *Forerunners
of the Reformation,* pp. 212-215.

35. John M. Todd, *Luther: A Life* (New York: Crossroad, 1982), p. 153. On
Luther's relationship to Hus, see Scott H. Hendrix, *Luther and the Papacy: Stages
in a Reformation Conflict* (Philadelphia: Fortress Press, 1981), pp. 85-94; " 'We Are
All Hussites'? Hus and Luther Revisited," *Archiv für Reformationsgeschichte* 65
(1974), pp. 134-161.

36. Thus Luther protested in late 1520: "Non recte faciunt, qui me Hussitam
vocant."

ies, "dens of theives, nests of serpents, houses of living devils."[37]

Wyclif's strident anticlericalism issued from his definition of the church as the predestined body of the elect. Hus later echoed Wyclif's idea: "The unity of the Catholic Church consists in the bond of predestination, since her individual members are united by predestination, and in the goal of blessedness, since all her sons are ultimately united in blessedness."[38] The universal church was not, as the conciliarists had maintained, the congregation of the faithful scattered throughout the earth, but rather the company of the elect extended throughout time. The church on earth, the visible church, could not be identified with the true church since it counted among its members reprobates—the "foreknown" ones (*praesciti*), as Wyclif called them—as well as the redeemed.

Wyclif divided the church into three parts: the Church Triumphant (including the angels) in heaven, the Church Militant on earth, and the Church Dormient in purgatory.[39] As the Church Militant contained both wheat and tares, and as no one could know for sure in this life which of those one was, neither affiliation with the institutional church nor the holding of clerical office guaranteed membership in the invisible church, whose "chief abbot" was Christ. It was thus possible to be *in* the church without being *of* the church. Wyclif applied this concept directly to the papacy: even the popes might be among the reprobates, in which case they were not to be obeyed.[40] Toward the end of his life, Wyclif repudiated the entire papal system and called for its abolition.

If Wyclif's correlation of predestination and ecclesiology proved a solvent to papal supremacy in England, it ignited a national reform movement in Bohemia at the impetus of the martyred Hus. Hus did not merely parrot the doctrine of Wyclif but stood in a tradition of Czech reformers who emphasized preaching, studying the Scriptures, and eliminating clerical

37. E. Gordon Rupp, "Christian Doctrine from 1350 to the Eve of the Reformation," *A History of Christian Doctrine,* Hubert Cunliffe-Jones, ed. (Edinburgh: T. and T. Clark, 1978), p. 292; John Wyclif, *English Works,* F. D. Matthew, ed. (London: Trübner and Co., 1880), pp. 96-104, 477.

38. John Hus, "On the Church," Oberman, *Forerunners,* p. 218.

39. John Wyclif, *De Ecclesia,* Johann Loserth, ed. (London: Trübner and Co., 1886), p. 8: "Sic non dicimus ecclesiam catholicam nisi que in se continet ista tria: partem in celo triumphantem, partem, in purgatorio dormientem et partem in terris militantem."

40. Ibid., p. 32: "Item, iuxta sepe dicta non sic assereret quod sit predestinatus, eo quod non est de substancia fidei catholice quod iste sit predestinatus . . . sed si non sit predestinatus, non est capitaneus in ecclesia sancta Dei."

abuses. He did not teach, as Wyclif was accused of doing, that sacraments administered by a sinful priest had no efficacy. He did insist, however, that wicked priests and popes—presumably among the *praesciti* on the principle of "By their fruits you shall know them"—were not to be obeyed. Concerning the papal office he wrote: "Peter's authority abides in the pope, so long as he does not depart from the law of the Lord Jesus Christ."[41] The principle of moral discrimination served to undercut both papal pretensions and clerical privileges. What Hus called for was not the abolition of the institutional church, nor yet the separation of the godly from the impure (as the later Hussites believed), but the reform of the church based on the example of Christ and apostolic simplicity.

Both Wyclif and Hus were essentially moral reformers who used the concept of predestination to undermine the ecclesiastical claims of a corrupt hierarchy. Their appeal to the invisible church, as well as their evaluation of Scripture as a superior norm for doctrine, provided a critical alternative to both curialism and conciliarism. They bequeathed to the sixteenth-century reformers the unresolved tension between rigid moralism and the true church of the elect.

Spiritual Franciscans

One of the most potent forces of dissent in the late Middle Ages was the radical branch of the Franciscan order, the Spirituals, as they called themselves, as opposed to the compromising Conventuals. The power of their appeal sprang from two sources: Francis's ideal of absolute poverty and the philosophy of history set forth by Joachim of Fiore (d. 1202) which they applied to their own order and to their own times. In combination these elements provided an explosive critique of the contemporary church.

Joachim divided history into three ages associated respectively with the Father, Son, and Holy Spirit. The dawn of the Third Age would be heralded by the coming of a new order of barefooted spiritual men who would oppose the false hierarchy of the church and prepare the way for a millenium of peace which would continue until the last judgment. The Spiritual Franciscans, embittered by their struggles with the papacy, who sided with the Conventuals in the strife over absolute poverty, identified themselves as this new order. They did not hesitate to refer to those popes who opposed them,

41. S. Harrison Thomson, ed., *Magistri Johannis Hus Tractatus de ecclesia* (Boulder, Colo.: University of Colorado Press, 1956), p. 169. On Hus' ecclesiology see Matthew Spinka, *John Hus' Concept of the Church* (Princeton, N.J.: Princeton University Press, 1966); Leff, *Heresy,* II, pp. 655-685.

Boniface VIII and John XXII in particular, as Antichrist. For its part, the church was swift to move against the Spirituals. "Poverty is great," said Pope John, "but integrity is greater, and obedience is the greatest good."[42] In 1318 four Spirituals were tried by the Inquisition and burned at the stake in Marseilles. As a protest movement within the church the Spirituals were effectively crushed. Their influence continued in various sectarian groups in Southern France and Italy.

The story of the Spirituals is laced with irony. Francis who desired to repair the church gave birth to a movement which, by being faithful to his own ideal, seriously disrupted it. In this way, "the figure of Christ as a man became the most potent challenge to the church as divine."[43] Another irony is that Peter John Olivi, an early leader of the Spiritual Franciscans, argued that certain papal decrees which *defended* the Spirituals' doctrine of poverty (notably the bull *Exiit qui seminat,* 1279) were inerrant and infallible! This argument was directed precisely against later *papal* attempts to circumvent the earlier ruling. Thus, as Brian Tierney has shown, the doctrine of papal infallibility, so lethal a weapon in the arsenal of later curialism, was originally an effort to check the excesses of the papal hierarchy.

As Wyclif and Hus opposed the empirical church of their day with the concept of the invisible church of the elect, so the Spiritual Franciscans held out the ideal of the church of the future, the church of the soon-coming Third Age of the Spirit, of which they were forerunners. In the later Middle Ages, the intensity of eschatological expectations and calculations increased. This "pursuit of the millennium" carried into the Reformation, especially among the radical reformers who, in this respect, were heirs to the Joachite-Spiritual Franciscan legacy.

Waldensians

Whereas the Spirituals looked forward to the church of the coming new age, the Waldensians, devoid of apocalyptic fervor, harked back to the *ecclesia primitiva,* modeling their congregations on the simplicity of the early church. The Waldensians traced their origin to a certain Valdès or Waldo (later named "Peter" to show his continuity with the apostle Peter) who forsook his career as a rich merchant for the life of a mendicant

42. Ibid., I, p. 208. On the Joachite influence on the Spirituals, see Marjorie Reeves, *Joachim of Fiore and the Prophetic Future* (New York: Harper and Row, 1976).

43. Leff, "The making of the myth," p. 2.

preacher.[44] The "poor men of Lyons," as his early followers were called, soon gained wide acceptance among the lower classes. The movement quickly spread over most of Europe, from France and Italy to Switzerland, Germany, and even Bohemia where there was a curious blending of Hussite and Waldensian concerns. Because they had stripped themselves of worldly possessions in imitation of Christ Himself, the Waldensians were sometimes referred to as *nudi nudum Christum sequentes,* the naked ones who follow a naked Christ.[45]

The Waldensian view of the church was characterized by a strong perfectionist tendency and an antisacerdotal bias. They believed that the Roman Church had lost all of its spiritual authority when Pope Sylvester I received a gift of property and worldly power from Emperor Constantine in the fourth century.[46] The Waldensian priests, known as *perfecti,* alone could hear confession or grant absolution since they alone were untainted with sin. Thus the Waldensians, much more directly than either Wyclif or Hus, tied the efficacy of the sacraments to the moral quality of the priest. In this sense they represent a revival of the Donatistic principle against which Augustine had argued. Their antisacerdotalism led them to purge their worship of many rituals which were common to the Roman Church. Saints' days, feast days, relics, pilgrimages, indulgences, even belief in purgatory were all swept away as harmful excrescencies of the false church.

The Waldensians were able to survive frequent persecutions because of their separatist model of the church and their practice of clandestine worship. Their obvious affinities with the Protestant movement made them prime candidates for conversion. Indeed, at the Reformation many of the Waldensians merged with the Reformed Church without giving up their

44. On the relation of the Hussite and Waldensian movements, see Amadeo Molvar, "Les vaudois et la réforme tchèque," *Bolletino della Società di Studi Valdesi* 103 (1958), pp. 37-51.

45. On this theme as a characteristic expression of reform groups in the twelfth century, see Giles Constable, "*Nudus Nudum Christum Sequi:* Parallel Formulas in the Twelfth Century," *Continuity and Discontinuity in Church History: Essays Presented to George Huntston Williams on the Occasion of His 65th Birthday,* F. F. Church and Timothy George, eds. (Leiden: E. J. Brill, 1979), pp. 83-91.

46. The fifteenth-century humanist, Lorenzo Valla, proved by linguistic analysis that the "donation of Constantine" was a forgery. Thereafter it was used, in a way very different from that of the Waldensians, as a foil for the argument of papal supremacy.

own identity.[47] They continue to flourish as the Chiesa Evangelica Valdese to this day.

Theologies in Flux

From the foregoing survey of late medieval piety and ecclesiology, it should be clear that the church on the eve of the Reformation was beset by diverse models of spirituality and Christian community. The old idea that the Reformation burst asunder the undisturbed unity of an undivided Christendom must be set aside in the light of what one historian has called the "pregnant plurality" of the fourteenth and fifteenth centuries.[48] Each of the four reformers we shall examine in this book was shaped by the crosscurrents which characterized theological development between the death of Thomas Aquinas (1274) and that of Gabriel Biel (1495). A complete accounting of this controverted period would require a monograph of its own. Here we shall merely introduce several of the major trends with which, in one way or another, Luther, Zwingli, Calvin, and Menno all had to grapple.

Scholasticism

The term *scholasticism* refers to the theology of the schools (*scholae*). In the centuries between the capture of Jerusalem by the Islamic invaders (638) and its recapture by the Christian crusaders (1099), theology was largely the work of monks whose study of the Bible, the Church Fathers, and classical literature was a part of their devotion to the contemplative life. Anselm of Canterbury (1033-1109) has been called "the summit of the early scholastic genius and ripest fruit of the monastic schools."[49] Indeed, Anselm stands at the crossroads of monastic and scholastic cultures. For Anselm theology began with faith and proceeded through understanding toward vision. In theology faith is always in search of understanding: *fides quaerens intellectum.* "I do not seek to understand in order to believe, but I believe

47. For the story of their absorption into Protestantism, see George H. Williams, *The Radical Reformation* (Philadelphia: Westminster Press, 1962), pp. 518-529.

48. Heiko A. Oberman, "Fourteenth Century Religious Thought: A Premature Profile," *Speculum* 53 (1978), p. 80.

49. David Knowles, *The Evolution of Medieval Thought* (New York: Random House, 1962), p. 98. On the monastic origins of scholasticism, see Jean Leclercq, *The Love of Learning and the Desire for God* (New York: Fordham University Press, 1961).

in order to understand."[50] The proper balance between faith and reason on the one hand, and between nature and grace on the other, would be the lingering preoccupation of scholastic theology from the time of Anselm until the Reformation.

The effort to apply the tools of reason to the data of revelation was advanced significantly by Peter Abelard (d. 1142) and his pupil, Peter Lombard (d. 1160), whose *Four Books of Sentences* became the standard textbook for advanced theological study during the next four centuries. This development reached its apex in the thirteenth century with the appearance of the great scholastic *summae* and the efforts of brilliant theologians such as Alexander of Hales, Albertus Magnus, and above all Thomas Aquinas to harmonize the newly rediscovered philosophy of Aristotle with the patristic consensus as it had been filtered through and passed down from Augustine.

By any measure the achievement of Aquinas was remarkable. In the prologue to the *Summa Theologica* he promised "to follow the things which pertain to sacred doctrine with such brevity and clarity as the subject matter allows."[51] The "brevity" which follows extends to 21 volumes, 631 questions, 10,000 objections or replies! The upshot of this vast output was to show that God and all creation was linked together in a great chain of being. God's existence can be proven by natural reason not, as Anselm had supposed, by an analysis of the very concept of God, but rather by observation of God's effects in the visible world. This is the basis of the famous five proofs—from motion, causation, contingency, degree, and design—which constitute Aquinas's cosmological argument for the existence of God. By reason alone one can know *that* God is, but not *what* God is. Most of the *Summa* is concerned with the latter. Here Thomas relied on divine revelation, that is, the Scriptures interpreted through the tradition, to supply the material for his exposition of the Trinity, the incarnation, the sacraments, and so forth. Thomas was convinced, of course, that there was an essential

50. "Neque enim quaero intelligere ut credam, sed credo ut intelligam. Nam et hoc credo: quia 'nisi credidero, non intelligam.' " *Proslogion,* 1. *S. Anselmi Opera Omnia,* F. S. Schmitt, ed. (Edinburgh: Nelson and Sons, 1946), I, p. 100. Significantly, Anselm's famous ontological argument for the existence of God is cast in the form of a prayer.

51. "Haec igitur et alia huiusmodi evitare studentes, tentabimus, cum confidentia divini auxilii, ea quae ad sacram doctrinam pertinet, breviter et dilucide prosequi, secundum quod materia patietur." *Summa Theologiae* (Madrid: Biblioteca de Autores Cristianos, 1961), I, Prologus, p. 3.

harmony between reason and revelation: Both bear witness, each in its proper sphere, to the oneness of God, the unity of all truth, and the fact that grace does not destroy nature, but rather perfects it.

In the seductive hindsight of history, Thomas appears without challenge as the most influential theologian between Augustine and Luther. He became "Saint" Thomas in 1323 when he was canonized by Pope John XXII. At the Council of Trent his *Summa Theologica* was placed on the altar alongside the Bible. In 1879 Pope Leo XIII declared the teaching of Thomas to be the official philosophy of the Roman Catholic Church. Yet the eventual victory of Thomism should not obscure the fact that the late Middle Ages were far from unified in their acceptance of Thomas's theology. In 1277, only three years after Thomas's death, the bishop of Paris, Stephan Tempier, condemned 219 propositions some of which had been held by Thomas. That was primarily an attack on the radical Aristotelianism which had led some thinkers to deny such basics of Christian doctrine as the immortality of the soul and creation *ex nihilo.* While Thomas had tried to harmonize the philosophy of Aristotle with the Christian perspective, many felt that he had not been entirely successful.

In the century following Thomas, the two most important theologians were both Franciscans: Duns Scotus (d. 1308) and William of Ockham (d. 1347). Both of these thinkers were involved in a major transmutation of the scholastic syntheses of the thirteenth century. We can point to three basic shifts which had far-reaching consequences for the development of theology during the period of the Renaissance and Reformation: (1) the shift from *being* to *will* as the primal metaphor for understanding God, (2) the shift from *metaphysics* to *metahistory* as a means of understanding God's relation to the created realm, (3) the shift from *ontological* to *logical* discourse as a method for doing theology.

Thomas had understood God primarily in terms of the effulgence of being. One of his favorite proof texts was Exodus 3:14: "I Am that I Am." However, by stressing so strongly the ontological connection between God and the created order, Thomas came close to limiting God's absolute freedom by entrapping Him in His own system, as it were. Duns Scotus reacted against this tendency by positing the primacy of God's will. Within the being of God, the divine will takes precedence over the divine intellect. An act is virtuous merely because God commands it to be so. If God is not bound by necessity to the great chain of being, He is nonetheless free to bind Himself by His word, His promise. Both Duns Scotus and Ockham made great use of the distinction between God's absolute power (*potentia absoluta*) and God's ordained power (*potentia ordinata*). The former refers to the power by which God, hypothetically, could do anything which does not involve the law of contradiction. God could not make two plus two equal five, but He could (so Duns suggested) have become incarnate in an ass instead of a man. He could have decreed adultery to be a virtue rather than a vice. Within the framework of the absolute freedom of God, it became crucial to stress what in fact God had bound Himself to by His ordained power. By His ordained power, God in fact became incarnate in the man Jesus, not in an ass. By His ordained power, God has decreed that salvation will be dispensed through the sacraments of the church and the earning of merits. God's covenant or pact, that is, God's promise or word, is the basis of the history of salvation. Still, by His absolute power, God might yet suspend the rules. Conceivably, God could save one outside the ordained system of sacraments and merits—*sola fide:* by faith alone.

The third shift from ontological to logical categories was carried through most consistently by William of Ockham. The *via moderna* (modern way) stemmed from his teachings, as opposed to the *via antiqua* (old way) which harked back to the earlier scholastics such as Thomas. Ockham denied the real existence of universal concepts, stressing instead their character as names (*nomina*) or logical constructs. The "nominalism" which developed out of this position focused on individual items of experience, on their concrete meaning and contingent reality rather than their ontological status in the presumed order of being. Such a perspective resulted in a further constriction of the realm of reason. It was no longer possible to argue, as Thomas had, from God's effects in the world back to God's existence as Prime Mover, First Cause, and so forth. This development implied the demise of natural theology as it had been set forth by the scholastic masters. The existence of God and the immortality of the soul were every bit as much articles of faith as the doctrines of the Trinity and incarnation. Steven Ozment has described the impact of these shifts, and Ockham's world view, on the religious life of the Late Middle Ages.

> By dwelling so intently on God's will rather than his being, Ockham created the conditions for a new spiritual anxiety—not the possible nonexistence of God, but the suspicion that he might not keep his word; that he could not be depended upon to do as he had promised; that the power behind all things might ultimately prove to be untrustworthy and unfriendly; that God, in a word, might be a liar. Not God's existence, but his goodness; not the rationality of faith, but the ability to trust God—these became major spiritual problems.[52]

52. Steven Ozment, *The Age of Reform, 1250-1550,* pp. 61-62. For other ac-

Mysticism

At the beginning of the fifteenth century Jean Gerson, chancellor of the University of Paris and one of the leaders of the conciliar movement, distinguished three paths to the knowledge of God. The first path, natural theology, discerned the handiwork of God within creation and sought to understand the Creator by applying the use of human reason to the finite world. The second, dogmatic theology, investigated the sources of God's special revelation in the Scriptures, creeds, and tradition of the church. The third path was mystical theology. By this way the soul was, as it were, "ravished above itself," and received a direct, intuitive, sometimes ecstatic experience of God.[53] From Paul's rapture into the third heaven (2 Cor. 12:1-4) to Francis's reception in his body of the stigmata, the marks of Christ's passion, to Bernard's exposition of the Song of Songs in terms of the soul's intimate union with Christ the Bridegroom, mystical experience had been a mainstay of Christian spirituality. Indeed, it was possible for the same person to be an exponent of all three types of theology. Thomas Aquinas is an example of this. Aquinas's scholastic writings show him a master of both natural and dogmatic theology; and, near the end of his life with his great *Summa Theologica* still unfinished, he was possessed of a profound mystical experience. He was reported to have said, "I have seen that which makes all I have written and thought look small to me."[54]

Scholars have identified at least two major traditions of mystical theology in the Middle Ages. The first is *voluntarist mysticism.* Here the emphasis is on the conformity of the human will to the will of God through the successive stages of purgation, illumination, and contemplation, as Bonaventura outlined it in his classic work, *The Mind's Road to God.*[55] For the most part, this approach to the mystical life posed little challenge to the

counts of this same period, see Gordon Leff, *Medieval Thought* (Chicago: Quadrangle Books, 1958) and *The Dissolution of the Medieval Outlook* (New York: Harper and Row, 1976). Cf. also the helpful survey by David Knowles, "The Middle Ages, 604-1351." *A History of Christian Doctrine,* Hubert Cunliffe-Jones, ed. (Edinburgh: T. and T. Clark, 1978), pp. 246-286.

53. Vide Gerson, *De mystica theologia speculativa,* Cons. 2, quoted in Francis Oakley, *The Western Church in the Later Middle Ages* (Ithaca, N.Y.: Cornell University Press, 1979), pp. 89-90.

54. Quoted in John Ferguson, *An Illustrated Encyclopedia of Mysticism* (London: Thames and Hudson, 1976), p. 196.

55. Bonaventura, *The Mind's Road to God,* George Boas, trans. (Indianapolis: Bobbs-Merrill, 1953).

orthodox structures of church life. Because it was "safe" it had the greater influence in the shaping of popular piety, as the success of Thomas à Kempis's *The Imitation of Christ* demonstrates.

A more virulent strand, *ontological mysticism,* stressed much more starkly the discontinuity between God and the soul. The most sophisticated version of this kind of mystical theology was set forth by Meister Eckhart (d. 1327), a Dominican theologian whose unorthodox ideas were developed in a series of sermons preached to nuns. He proclaimed that deep within each individual there was an "abyss of the soul" (*Seelenabgrund*), a spark of divine life which held the possibility for union with, or absorption into, God. Only by the painful process of detachment from self and all other creatures—Eckhart called this process *Gelassenheit,* "a letting loose of oneself,"—could the moment of ultimate redemption occur, that moment when the Eternal Son would be born within the soul. It seemed to some that Eckhart's doctrine of the birth of the Eternal Son within led him to deny the historicity of Jesus' human birth or at least to downplay its salvific significance. More dangerous still, Eckhart's mystical theology seemed to allow for an "end run" around the established channels of sacramental grace. Put otherwise, ontological mysticism applied the absolute power of God to the individual soul at the expense of God's ordained power as mediated through the priestly ministrations of the church. Churchly authorities were not slow to recognize the potentially explosive character of Eckhart's theology. He was accused of heresy, a charge which he denied saying, "I may err but I may not be a heretic—for the first has to do with the mind and the second with the will!"[56] Nonetheless, Eckhart was condemned, albeit posthumously in 1329, by John XXII, the same pope who six years before had canonized Thomas Aquinas.

Eckhart's ideas did not die with his condemnation. His theology was translated into the popular idiom by his disciples, Johannes Tauler and Heinrich Suso. Some of the late medieval mystics carried their piety to eccentric extremes. Suso was an austere ascetic who cut the name of Jesus into his flesh over his heart. Tauler tended to tone down some of the more questionable aspects of Eckhart's doctrine of the mystical union of the soul with God.

In one form or another the mystical traditions of the late medieval period remained a vital source of spiritual life and theological reflection until, indeed into, the Reformation. The first book which Luther published was

56. Raymond B. Blakney, ed. *Meister Eckhart,* (New York: Harper and Row, 1941), p. xxiii.

an edition of the sermons of Tauler which he called the *Theologia Deutsch* (*German Theology*). As we shall see, mysticism provided Luther with the scaffolding from which he was able to launch his critique of the medieval doctrine of justification, although he was not able to arrive at his own mature formulation of this central tenet until he had abandoned the basic premises of at least ontological mysticism.[57] Zwingli's refined spiritualism, his disdain for materiality in religion, recalls the temperament of the mystics with their stress on the immediacy of grace, on the direct, personal appropriation of Christ by the soul. Calvin, too, perhaps the least mystical of our four reformers, came very near a mystical understanding in his doctrine of the spiritual real presence of Christ in the Eucharist. Calvin could well have prayed the following prayer which actually comes from the *Imitation of Christ:*

> Thou, my Lord God, my Lord Jesus Christ, God and Man, are here wholly present in the Sacrament of the Altar, where the fruit of everlasting health is had plenteously, as oft as Thou art worthily and devoutly received.[58]

Menno specifically disavowed any special mystical revelations. "I am no Enoch," he wrote, "I am no Elijah. I am not one who sees visions . . . or angelic inspirations."[59] Menno was here setting himself over against certain other Anabaptists and spiritualists who used their personal, mystical experiences as a foil for sidestepping strict obedience to the written Word of God. Yet Menno was acquainted with the wider mystical heritage of the Late Middle Ages and drew upon it in his positive construals of the Christian life. None of the reformers took over without qualification the mystical traditions of the Middle Ages, but their own theologies cannot be understood apart from an intense craving for a sense of divine immediacy which called forth and characterized the mystic vision.

Humanism

If mysticism was an "everybody theology" which extended the possibility of intimate union with God to clergy and laity, princes and peasants, women and men alike, then humanism was a movement of reform which originated with, and was dominated by, Europe's intellectual elite. The term *human-*

57. On the much disputed issue of Luther's debt to the mystical tradition, see Heiko A. Oberman, "Simul Gemitus et Raptus: Luther and Mysticism," Ozment, ed. *In Medieval Perspective,* pp. 219-251.

58. Oakley, p. 108.

59. CWMS, p. 310.

ism itself, which is so loosely bandied about in our day, referred in the fifteenth and sixteenth centuries not so much to an all-embracing philosophy of life as to a particular method of learning based upon the recovery and study of the classical sources of both pagan, that is, Roman and Greek, and Christian antiquity. Thus humanism in the period of the Renaissance and Reformation was much closer to what we mean by the *humanities* today. *Ad fontes!* —back to the sources!—was the motto of humanist scholars whose work opened up new vistas in history, literature, and theology.

To some extent humanism was a movement of reaction against the regnant scholasticism of the day. Erasmus, who had studied scholastic theology at the University of Paris, ridiculed the hairsplitting subtleties of contemporary theologians in his *Praise of Folly:*

> Then there are the theologians, a remarkably supercilious and touchy lot
> . . . . They interpret hidden mysteries to suit themselves: how the world was
> created and designed; through what channels the stain of sin filtered down
> to posterity; by what means, in what measure, and how long Christ was
> formed in the Virgin's womb; how, in the Eucharist, accidents can subsist
> without a domicile. But this sort of question has been discussed threadbare.
> There are others more worthy of great and enlightened theologians (as they
> call themselves) which can really rouse them to action if they come their way.
> What was the exact moment of divine generation? Are there several filiations
> in Christ? Is it a possible proposition that God the Father could hate his Son?
> Could God have taken on the form of a woman, a devil, a donkey, a gourd,
> or a flintstone? If so, how could a gourd have preached sermons, performed
> miracles, and been nailed to the cross? And what would Peter have consecrat-
> ed if he had consecrated when the body of Christ still hung on the cross?
> Furthermore, at that same time could Christ have been called a man? Shall
> we be permitted to eat and drink after the resurrection? We're taking due
> precaution against hunger and thirst while there's time. These subtle refine-
> ments of subtleties are made still more subtle by all the different lines of
> scholastic argument, so that you'd extricate yourself faster from a labyrinth
> than from the tortuous obscurities of realists, nominalists, Thomists, Alber-
> tists, Ockhamists, and Scotists—and I've not mentioned all the sects, only the
> main ones.

Erasmus went on to say that the apostles themselves would need the help of another Holy Spirit if they had to debate with "our new breed of theologian."[60]

The problem with scholasticism was not its emphasis upon learning but rather its arid speculations which led to an intellectual labyrinth rather than

60. CWE 27, pp. 126-127.

to the reform of church and society. The *philosophia Christi,* the "philosophy of Christ," as Erasmus called his approach to the Christian life, presupposed reformation by education, education which valued rhetoric over dialectic, the classics over the scholastics, and action in the world over monastic seclusion.

On one level the humanist pruning of classical sources led to a radical critique of ecclesiastical institutions and traditional theology. Lorenzo Valla (d. 1457) proved by linguistic analysis that the so-called *Donation of Constantine,* a document on which much of the papal claim to temporal authority rested, was in fact a forgery from the ninth century. On another score, Valla challenged the traditional translation of the Greek word *metanoia* as "Do penance." He pointed out that the word really meant "repentance"; it referred to a genuine change of mind and heart, not to the ritual performance required by the sacrament of penance. Erasmus incorporated Valla's rendering in his 1516 edition of the Greek New Testament. In turn, Luther found in this fresh reading of the original text a basis for his frontal assault on the practice of indulgences. The first of Luther's *Ninety-five Theses* read: "When our Lord and Master Jesus Christ said, 'Repent' [Matt. 4:17], he willed the entire life of believers to be one of repentance."[61]

Perhaps the most positive contribution of the humanist scholars to the religious renewal of the sixteenth century was the series of critical editions of the Bible and the Church Fathers which were widely disseminated due to the phenomenal success of the printing press. Erasmus' favorite Church Father was Jerome, but by far the most influential patristic source for Reformation theology was Augustine. Indeed, in the centuries just prior to the Reformation there was something of an "Augustinian Renaissance," spawned in part by a renewed interest in the theology of Augustine within the Augustinian Order itself and by the attraction to Augustine of early humanists such as Petrarch, who was drawn especially to the *Confessions.* Whenever he would read it, he said, "it seems to me that I am reading not someone else's history, but the history of my own pilgrimage."[62]

The impact of humanism on the Reformation is still debated by scholars of the period. Without the humanists' early support of Luther, especially

61. LW 31, p. 25.
62. Petrarch quoted in Jaroslav Pelikan, *Reformation of Church and Dogma* (Chicago: University of Chicago Press, 1984), p. 20. On the Augustinian revival within the Augustinian Order, see David C. Steinmetz, "Luther and the Late Medieval Augustinians: Another Look," *Concordia Theological Monthly* 44 (1973), pp. 245-260.

their touting of the *Ninety-five Theses,* it is doubtful whether Luther's attack against Rome would have become the *cause célèbre* which fired the imagination and energies of all Europe. Both Zwingli and Calvin were steeped in the classics, both devotees of the humanist revival of learning, before they became reformers. This perspective continued to inform their biblical studies and their reformatory efforts in Zurich and Geneva. Menno, too, who had less formal training than the others, was nonetheless influenced by the humanist movement and quoted with favor several of the writings of Erasmus. Despite the significance of humanism as a preparation for the Reformation, most of the humanists, Erasmus chief among them, never attained either the sense of the gravity of the human condition or of the triumph of divine grace which marked the theology of the reformers. Humanism, like mysticism, was part of the scaffolding which enabled the reformers to question certain assumptions of the received tradition, but which in itself was not sufficient to provide an enduring response to the haunting questions of the age.

Selected Bibliography

Bentley, Jerry H. *Humanists and Holy Writ.* Princeton: Princeton University Press, 1983. A study of New Testament scholarship in the Renaissance. Excellent chapters on Valla and Erasmus.

Cargill-Thompson, W. D. J. "Seeing the Reformation in Medieval Perspective," *Journal of Ecclesiastical History* 25 (1974), pp. 297-308. A bibliographical survey of recent literature in the field.

Huizinga, Johan. *The Waning of the Middle Ages.* New York: Doubleday, 1949. Originally published in Dutch in 1919, this is an indispensable study of the life, thought, and art of the fourteenth and fifteenth centuries.

Oakley, Francis. *The Western Church in the Later Middle Ages.* Ithaca, N.Y.: Cornell University Press, 1979. Takes into account political, social, intellectual and spiritual forces.

Oberman, Heiko A. *Forerunners of the Reformation.* Philadelphia: Fortress Press, 1966. An anthology of primary sources with helpful introductions.

Ozment, Steven E. *The Age of Reform, 1250-1550.* New Haven: Yale University Press, 1980. A comprehensive overview of the period. Better on the late medieval period than the Reformation.

Ozment, Steven E., ed. *The Reformation in Medieval Perspective.* Chicago: Quadrangle Books, 1971. A valuable collection of essays by eight respected scholars in the field.

Petry, Ray C. *Late Medieval Mysticism*. Philadelphia: Westminster Press, 1957. A
    well-edited anthology of primary sources.
Steinmetz, David C. *Misericordia Dei: The Theology of Johannes von Staupitz in its
    Late Medieval Setting*. Leiden: E. J. Brill, 1968. A superb appraisal of Staupitz
    and the medieval traditions on which he drew.

3

Yearning for Grace
Martin Luther

Luther fought the church not because it demanded too much, but because it demanded too little.   Oswald Spengler[2]

Luther as Theologian

Martin Luther was born on November 10, 1483, in Eisleben, the son of a middle-class silver miner. Destined for the study of law, he turned to the monastery where after many struggles he developed a new understanding of God, faith, and the church. This involved him in conflict with the papacy, followed by his excommunication and the founding of the Lutheran Church, over which he presided until his death in 1546.

Those three sentences summarize the life of Luther. Yet anyone who thinks that such a summary, or even a lengthy biography which explains his lifework in terms of external events, can really account for Luther has hardly penetrated the surface of the subject. Paul Althaus once described Luther as an "ocean."[2] Such an image applies not only to Luther's enormous literary output, over one hundred folio volumes in the great Weimar edition but also to his powerful originality and unnerving profundity. Only two other theologians in the history of the church, Augustine and Aquinas, approach the stature of Luther; only one other corpus of writings, the New Testament documents themselves, have been studied with such close scrutiny as the works of the Wittenberg reformer. It is easy to drown in such an ocean.

Various attempts have been made to interpret Luther in terms of his

1. Oswald Spengler, *The Decline of the West* (New York: Alfred Knopf, 1928), II, p. 296.
2. Paul Althaus, *The Theology of Martin Luther,* Robert C. Schultz, trans., p. vi.

LUTHER

influence on subsequent history.[3] Traditional Catholic historiography portrays a mad monk, a psychotic demoniac pulling down the pillars of Mother Church. To orthodox Protestants Luther was the godly knight, a Moses, a Samson (pulling down the temple of the Philistines!), an Elijah, even the Fifth Evangelist and the Angel of the Lord. To the Pietists he was the warmhearted apostle of conversion. The German nationalists hailed him as a folk hero and "father of his country"; the Nazi theologians made him a proto-Aryan and precursor of the *Führer*. Significantly, Luther texts can be cited in support of each of these caricatures. None of them, however, takes seriously Luther's own self-understanding which is where a proper evaluation of his theology must begin.

Far from attempting to found a new sect, Luther always saw himself as a faithful and obedient servant of the church. Thus his deep chagrin that the first Protestants, in England and France no less than in Germany, were being called "Lutherans":

> The first thing I ask is that people should not make use of my name, and should not call themselves Lutherans but Christians. What is Luther? The teaching is not mine. Nor was I crucified for anyone . . . How did I, poor stinking bag of maggots that I am, come to the point where people call the children of Christ by my evil name?[4]

This disclaimer, written in 1522, was not the protest of a false humility, but rather a genuine effort to deflate an already-burgeoning "personality cult" and to direct attention to the source of the Reformer's thought. "The teaching is not mine." To understand what Luther meant by that statement is to grasp the central thrust of his Reformation theology.

In a sermon of the same year, Luther explained his perception of his own role in the events of the Reformation:

> I simply taught, preached, wrote God's Word; otherwise I did nothing. And then, while I slept, or drank Wittenberg beer with my Philip and my Amsdorf, the Word so greatly weakened the papacy that never a prince or emperor did such damage to it. I did nothing. The Word did it all.[5]

3. The numerous estimations of Luther since the Reformation have been traced by Ernst Walter Zeeden, *The Legacy of Luther* (London: Hollis and Carter, 1954). Cf. also the survey in Bernhard Lohse, *Martin Luther: An Introduction to His Life and Work* (Philadelphia: Fortress Press, 1986), pp. 199-235.

4. WA 8, p. 685.

5. Quoted in Gordon Rupp, *Luther's Progress to the Diet of Worms,* p. 99. *Works of Martin Luther* (Philadelphia: Muhlenberg Press, 1915), II, pp. 399-400.

Such a statement seems fantastic to the modern mind for whom Luther was, if anything, a man of action. Defying the pope, subduing the peasants, intervening in political crises, teaching, preaching, debating, marrying, and giving in marriage: Luther was surely a doer of the Word and not a hearer only. Yet the hearing, the receiving, was primary for Luther. *Fides ex auditu*, "faith out of hearing," "faith by means of listening," is perhaps the best summary of his Reformation discovery.[6]

Luther did not see himself as an agent of ecclesiastical revolution, a sixteenth-century Lenin or Robespierre out to shake the world and overturn kingdoms. That the papacy and empire were shaken, if not overthrown, by the words of a simple German monk was, he thought, merely a providential by-product of his prior vocation. "I have done nothing. I have let the Word act." What Luther did do, what he was called to do, was to listen to the Word. "The nature of the Word is to be heard," he remarked. He also said: "If you were to ask a Christian what his task is and by what he is worthy of the name Christian, there could be no other response than hearing the Word of God, that is faith. Ears are the only organs of the Christian."[7] He listened to the Word because it was his job to do so and because he had come to believe his soul's salvation depended upon it. Luther did not become a reformer because he attacked indulgences. He attacked indulgences because the Word had already taken deep root in his heart.

Luther's life lends itself to dramatic retelling: the crisis in the thunderstorm, the debate with John Eck at Leipzig, the burning of the papal bull, the "Here stand I, God help me" confession at Worms. There is, however, another incident in his career, not as dramatic and seldom retold, which was

6. This is the title of Ernst Bizer's excellent study of Luther's doctrine of justification: *Fides ex Auditu: Eine Untersuchung über die Entwicklung der Gerechtigkeit Gottes durch Martin Luther* (Neukirchen: Moers, 1958).

7. WA 4, p. 9: "Natura verbi est audiri." Cf. the insightful analysis of this text in Gerhard Ebeling, *Luther: An Introduction to His Thought*, pp. 70-75. On "ears as the only organs of the Christian," see WA 57/3, p. 222; LW 29, p. 224: "But the word 'ears' is emphatic and forceful to an extraordinary degree; for in the new law all those countless burdens of the ceremonies, that is, dangers of sins, have been taken away. God no longer requires the feet or the hands or any other member; He requires only the ears. To such an extent has everything been reduced to an easy way of life. For if you ask a Christian what the work is by which he becomes worthy of the name 'Christian,' he will be able to give absolutely no other answer than that it is the hearing of the Word of God, that is, faith. Therefore the ears alone are the organs of a Christian man, for he is justified and declared to be a Christian, not because of the works of any member but because of faith."

of decisive importance for his future work. It took place in September, 1511, just after Luther had come out of one of his spiritual depressions. He and Johann von Staupitz, vicar of the Augustinian order and Luther's mentor and confessor, were sitting under a pear tree in the garden, when the older man declared that young Luther should prepare himself for the profession of preaching and become a Doctor of Theology. Luther, quite amazed at the suggestion, replied: "Your Honor, Mr. Staupitz, you will deprive me of my life." To which Staupitz answered, half in jest: "Quite all right. God has plenty of work for clever men to do in heaven."[8] In fact, Luther had already taken the three degrees prerequisite for the doctorate: *Baccalaureus Biblius,* which entitled him to give introductory lectures on the Bible; *Formatus,* which signified a working knowledge of scholastic terminology, and *Sententiarius,* which authorized him to lecture on the first two books of Peter Lombard's *Sentences,* the standard medieval compendium of doctrine. He now proceeded to complete the requirements for his doctorate in theology. On October 18, 1512, the degree was solemly conferred. Luther received on that occasion a woolen beret, silver ring, and two Bibles, one closed, the other opened. He had been appointed for life *lectura in Biblia* at the University of Wittenberg, succeeding Staupitz himself.[9]

In the winter of 1512, the Reverend Doctor Martin Luther began preparation for his lectures on the Psalms (1513-1515), which were followed in turn by Romans (1515-1516), Galatians (1516-1517), Hebrews (1517), and again Psalms (1518-1519). He later remarked: "In the course of this teaching, the papacy slipped away from me."[10] Also, during these years, Luther moved from an unknown monk in a backwater university to the center stage of European politics. (A *Who's Who* of German universities, compiled in 1514, does not even list Luther's name!) In the turmoil which followed, he was sustained by a compelling sense of the importance of his calling as a professor of the Holy Scriptures. Like Calvin later who felt that God had "thrust" him "into the game," Luther also appealed to divine initiative. With reference to Staupitz's urging, he said: "I, . . . Dr. Martin, was called and forced to become a doctor, against my will, from pure obedience, and

8. This is Roland Bainton's paraphrase of Staupitz's reply in *Here I Stand: A Life of Martin Luther,* p. 59. Cf. the original text in WA TR 3, pp. 187-188.

9. The details of Luther's promotion to the doctorate are reviewed in E. G. Schwiebert, *Luther and His Times* (St. Louis: Concordia, 1950), pp. 193-196.

10. WA 30/3, p. 386; LW 34, p. 103: "While engaged on this kind of teaching, the papacy crossed my path and wanted to hinder me in it. How it has fared is obvious to all, and it will fare worse still. It shall not hinder me."

had to accept a doctor's teaching post, and promise and vow on my beloved Holy Scriptures to preach and teach them faithfully and sincerely."[11] While Luther later renounced his monastic vows and married a former nun, he clung tenaciously to his teaching office and to his doctoral degree.[12] As a teacher of the church, he devoted himself to listening for the Word of God, to brooding over Scripture. Out of this essentially passive activity Luther was given something extraordinary to say.[13]

How are we to understand Luther as a theologian? The Luther corpus contains many diverse genres of writing: commentaries, catechisms, polemical treatises, disputations, hymns, sermons, personal letters, the *Table Talk*, etc. In none of this, however, is there anything remotely resembling a systematic theology. Even the Augsburg Confession, for which Luther was only partially responsible, provides only specific theological statements, not a complete doctrinal system. Luther's writings are invariably contextual, *ad hoc,* addressed to particular situations with definite ends in mind. This does not mean that Luther's theology was casual, nor that there are no overarching themes and patterns in his thought. However, we must let the themes emerge from Luther's own, primarily pastoral, concerns rather than imposing our structure upon him. To do this it will be helpful to examine Luther's basic approach to theology which we may describe in terms of three persistent characteristics. Luther's theology was at once *biblical, existential,* and *dialectical.*

Luther was a biblical theologian. This may mean simply that Luther was a professor of biblical, primarily Old Testament, exegesis at the University of Wittenberg. More largely, however, it signifies a radical break with the standard curriculum of scholastic theology and a reorientation of theology

11. Ibid.

12. In the early years of the Reformation, Andreas Bodenstein von Karlstadt, Luther's senior colleague at Wittenberg who had presided at the conferral of Luther's doctorate in 1512, renounced his own doctoral degrees (he had three!), divested himself of his academic regalia, resigned his university post, and joined the peasants of Orlamünde as their farmer-pastor. Luther rebuked Karlstadt's new life-style in his treatise "Against the Heavenly Prophets": "What think you now? Is it not a fine new spiritual humility? Wearing a felt hat and a gray garb, not wanting to be called doctor, but Brother Andrew and dear neighbor, as another peasant, . . . as though Christian behavior consisted in such external hocus-pocus." LW 40, p. 117; WA 18, pp. 100-101.

13. WA 40/1, p. 610: "In reality our knowing is passive rather than active; that is, we are known by God rather than that we know Him. We must let God work in us. He gives the Word."

to the biblical text. We are not here speaking of Luther's formal doctrine of Scripture, nor of the Reformation principle of *sola scriptura,* both of which are products of this earlier development. What we have in mind is the campaign Luther waged against the scholastic theology of his day and his plans for a sweeping reform of the university curriculum so that "the study of the Bible and the holy Fathers may at once be restored in all its purity."[14]

Luther was thoroughly trained in the nominalist tradition of the Late Middle Ages. On certain issues, such as the question of universals, Luther remained an exponent of the *via moderna* even after his emergence as a reformer.[15] However, very early in his career, while still a *Sententiarius,* Luther revealed a deep-seated scepticism concerning the value of philosophy for the theological enterprise: "Theology is heaven, yes even the kingdom of heaven; man however is earth and his speculations are smoke."[16] Luther's sense of the unbridgeable gulf between theology and human "speculations" intensified as he plunged deeper into the biblical texts. By 1515 he was referring to the nominalists as "hog-theologians."[17] In September, 1517, some two months before the outbreak of the Indulgence Controversy, Luther compressed his attack against scholastic theology into a blast at "Aristotle":

> It is a wrong thing to say that a man cannot become a theologian without Aristotle. The truth is that a man cannot become a theologian unless he becomes one without Aristotle. In short, compared with the study of theology, the whole of Aristotle is as darkness is to the light.[18]

Luther had nothing against Aristotle as such. What he rejected was the whole effort in scholastic theology to make Aristotelian philosophy the

14. WA BR 1, p. 170, No. 74: ". . . ut rursum Bibliae et S. Patrum purissima studia revocentur." This is in a letter of May 9, 1518, which Luther wrote to his former teacher at Erfurt, Jadotus Trutfetter.

15. See Brian A. Gerrish, *Grace and Reason: A Study in the Theology of Luther,* p. 45.

16. WA 9, p. 65. See the analysis of this text by Heiko A. Oberman, *"Facientibus Quod in se est Deus non Denegat Gratiam:* Robert Holcot O.P. and the Beginnings of Luther's Theology," *The Reformation in Medieval Perspective,* Steven Ozment, ed. (Chicago: Quadrangle Books, 1971), pp. 119-141.

17. Heinrich Boehmer, *Luther in the Light of Recent Research* (New York: The Christian Herald, 1916), p. 87.

18. James Atkinson, ed., *Luther: Early Theological Works,* (Philadelphia: Westminster Press, 1962), pp. 269-270.

presupposition of Christian doctrine, to interpret biblical revelation in terms of pagan "sophistry," to reduce the great themes of Scripture, grace, faith, justification, to scholastic jargon. In the spirit of Tertullian, Luther asked what Jerusalem had to do with Athens, the Church with the Academy, faith with reason.

Luther's epithets of reason were so severe—the Devil's Whore, beast, enemy of God, Frau Hulda—that his critics have frequently labeled him an irrationalist. Brian Gerrish has shown that Luther's use of the term *reason* (*ratio, Vernunft*) was more nuanced. Luther in no way denigrated reason in its own sphere of competence, that is, in its ability to judge and discern matters of human society and government. When reason moved beyond this "mundane" level and began to inquire and argue about divine matters, "that smart woman, Madam Jezebel" fell short, for "all God's works and words are against reason."[19]

For Luther, in the realm of true theology reason functioned only ex post facto, that is, as an ordering principle by which the biblical revelation was clearly set forth. Enlightened reason, reason which was incorporated into faith, could thus "serve faith in thinking about something," for reason informed by the Holy Spirit "takes all its thoughts from the Word."[20] This must be clearly borne in mind when we hear Luther's famous utterance at Worms: "Unless I am convicted by Scripture and plain reason, I cannot and I will not recant." Reason was not an independent source of authority alongside Scripture—his conscience was still "captive to the Word of God" —but merely the necessary inference of Scripture itself.[21] Luther did not disparage human rationality; he even assigned redeemed reason a functionary role in the task of theology. What he did reject as a biblical theologian was the arrogance of reason which in scholastic theology had displaced the primacy of revelation.

When we call Luther an *existential* theologian we mean that for him concern with God was a life-and-death matter, involving not merely one's intellect but one's whole existence. For Luther theology was always intensely personal, experiential, and relational. We can better grasp this concept by a brief word study of three crucial phrases in Luther's vocabulary.

19. Gerrish, pp. 19-20.
20. WA TR 1, p. 439; LW 54, p. 71.
21. Gerrish, pp. 24-25.

Coram Deo

Human existence is lived out *coram Deo,* "before God" or "in the presence of God." Calvin made a similar claim when he insisted that in every dimension of life human beings have "business with God" (*negotium cum Deo*).[22] This has nothing to do with formal belief in God, hence Luther's rejection of the classical arguments for the existence of God. For Luther "God" can never be placed in quotation marks. The great sin of scholastic theology (and also, from Luther's perspective, of neo-Kantian philosophy) was precisely the attempt to make of God an ordering concept, the First Principle, or even Necessary Being. Such a procedure placed God at a distance, made God the object of neutral inquiry, and thus exempted the human from deciding for or against God. But the God and Father of our Lord Jesus Christ is not a God we can discuss, or argue about, a God whose existence can be decided in the cool objectivity of a graduate seminar. The living God of the Bible is the God who meets us in judgment and mercy, the God who damns us and saves us. *Coram Deo* means that while we are always at God's disposal, God is never at ours. "To believe in such a God," Luther said, "is to go down on your knees."[23]

Christus pro Me

The heart of Luther's theology was that in Jesus Christ God has given Himself, utterly and without reserve, for us. However, just as Luther accepted no argument for the existence of God, neither did he propose a consistent "theory" of atonement.[24] It is never enough to know simply that Christ died, or even why He died. Such knowledge is the result of a "merely historical faith" which cannot save. The devils also have their theories of atonement; they believe and tremble! Saving faith must break through to personal appropriation. Only when we realize that Christ was given *pro me, pro nobis* ("for me," "for us") have we discerned the import of Christ's accomplishment.

22. CR 11, p. 100: "I am well aware that it is with God that I have to do [mihi esse negotium cum Deo]." Cf. *Institutes* 1.17.2.

23. "Habere deum est colere deum." The translation is that of J. S. Whale, *The Protestant Tradition* (Cambridge: Cambridge University Press, 1955), p. 17.

24. This is a much debated point. Gustaf Aulén has interpreted Luther as an exponent of the "classic" theory of atonement: *Christus Victor* (New York: Macmillan, 1969). I follow here the thesis of Ian Siggins, *Martin Luther's Doctrine of Christ,* pp. 108-143, who holds that while motifs from all the historic atonement theories are present in Luther, he is wedded to none of them.

Read with great emphasis these words, "me," "for me," and accustom
yourself to accept and to apply to yourself this "me" with certain faith.

The words OUR, US, FOR US, ought to be written in golden letters—the
man who does not believe them is not a Christian.[25]

Luther's strong emphasis on the "for me-ness" of the gospel has led some
critics to characterize his theology as subjectivitistic and anthropocentric.
This is a strange charge since Luther's watchword was the theocentric
formula "Let God Be God" and the burden of his Reformation breakthrough the solemn assertion of God's sovereignty in salvation.[26] The good
news is that in Jesus Christ the sovereign God really is for us, not against
us. Luther's point was that this good news cannot be known *in abstracto*,
but only as one grasped it by faith in the depths of experience.[27]

Anfechtung

This word is often weakly translated "temptation," but really means
dread, despair, a sense of foreboding doom, assault, anxiety. Luther used
this word to describe the acute spiritual conflicts which afflicted his conscience in his tortured quest to find a gracious God. He felt, he said, as if
his soul were stretched out with Christ, so that all his bones could be
numbered, "nor is there any corner not filled with the most bitter bitterness,
horror, fear, dolor, and all these things seem eternal." At the bare rustling
of a dry leaf, the whole universe seemed to collapse upon him. So desperate
was his condition that he wanted to creep into a mouse hole. The "whole
wide world" had become too narrow for him, but there was no exit.[28]

The experience of the *Anfechtungen* was more than a momentary phase
in Luther's spiritual pilgrimage. This recurring principle throughout his
entire life defined his approach to theology. In a famous statement Luther
confessed:

I did not learn my theology all at once, but I had to search deeper for it, where

25. WA 40/1, p. 299; 31/2, p. 432.
26. The phrase "Velle deum esse deum" occurs in the "Disputation against
Scholastic Theology" of 1517. Cf. Atkinson, p. 267. See also the classic study by
Philip S. Watson, *Let God Be God!*
27. Cf. this striking statement by Luther: "I have often said that whoever wants
to be saved should act as though no other human being except him existed on earth
and as though all the comfort and promise of God found here and there in Scripture
concerned him alone and was written only for his sake." WA 16, p. 433.
28. Gordon Rupp, *The Righteousness of God,* pp. 108-110. Cf. WA 1, p. 558;
5, p. 208; 19, p. 209.

my temptations [*Anfechtungen*] took me . . . . Not understanding, reading, or speculation, but living, nay, rather dying and being damned make a theologian.[29]

Thus theology is a life-long process of struggle, conflict, and temptation. While faith brings with it a confident assurance, we must ever be on guard against a carnal *securitas.* Christians must daily expect to be incessantly attacked. "No one may go his way securely and heedlessly as if the devil were far from us."[30] Luther was annoyed at those who turned his emphasis on *sola fide* ("by faith alone") into an easy believe-ism. Temptation and experience, he said, certainly teach us that faith is "really a difficult art":

> For when your eyes rest on death, sin, devil, and world, and your conscience struggles when the battle is joined, I dare say you will break into a cold sweat and say: I had rather walk to St. James in armor [a reference to Santiago de Compostella in Spain where the apostle James who stressed works over faith was reputedly buried] than suffer this anguish.[31]

Genuine faith and true theology is wrought on the anvil of temptation for only *experientia* makes a theologian.[32]

A third mark of Luther's theology was its *dialectical* character.[33] Any reading of Scripture and human experience which offers more than a shallow analysis will be to some extent dialectical since neither life nor the Bible lends itself to easy systemization. Luther, however, more than most theologians, seemed to revel in paradox. He spoke almost invariably in sets of twos: law and gospel, wrath and grace, faith and works, flesh and spirit, with respect to God or the world (*coram Deo/coram mundo*), freedom and bondage, God hidden and God revealed. Even when one side of these pairs is not expressly developed, it is always there by implication. Truth can only be arrived at by way of confrontation with a contrasting truth. For example, we could not understand gospel were it not for law which reveals our inability to live rightly and thus points us to Christ. In this example the law/gospel polarity is understood conjunctively: *Both* law *and* gospel are essential to salvation. At other times, the same terms are used disjunctively:

29. WA TR I, p. 146; WA 5, p. 163.
30. WA 30/1, p. 209.
31. WA 33, p. 283; LW 23, p. 179.
32. Cf. Ebeling, p. 32.
33. On Luther as a "dialectical" theologian, see Ernest B. Koenker, "Man: *Simul Justus et Peccator," Accents in Luther's Theology,* Heino O. Kadai, ed. (St. Louis: Concordia, 1967), pp. 98-123.

Either we cling to the law and are damned *or* we trust the gospel and are saved. This way of thinking heightened the tension in Luther's theology. Almost invariably Luther chose to live with the tension rather than dissolve the paradox. We must see now how this dialectic is developed in his doctrine of justification.

From *Simul* to *Semper*: Justification by Faith Alone

Protestantism was born out of the struggle for the doctrine of justification by faith alone. For Luther this was not simply one doctrine among others, but "the summary of all Christian doctrine," "the article by which the church stands or falls." In the *Smalcald Articles* of 1537 he wrote: "Nothing in this article can be given up or compromised, even in heaven and earth and things temporal should be destroyed."[34] At the same time, he admitted that this doctrine was hard to hold on to and that few people were able to teach it correctly.[35] How did Luther arrive at this doctrine, and why did he consider it so vital?

Fortunately, Luther left us an answer to these questions. Near the end of his life Luther remembered how as a monk the phrase "justice of God" (*iustitia Dei*) in Romans, 1:17 had struck terror in his soul. All of his attempts to satisfy God—his prayers, fastings, vigils, good works—left him with a wholly disquieted conscience. His mood swung from despair over his own failures to a simmering rage at God: "I did not love, indeed I hated, that God who punished sinners; and with a monstrous, silent, if not blasphemous, murmuring I fumed against God." Still, he "knocked persistently upon Paul," meditating day and night in his study in the tower, until

> I began to understand that "the justice of God" meant that justice by which the just man lives through God's gift, namely by faith. This is what it means: the justice of God is revealed by the gospel, a passive justice with which the merciful God justifies us by faith, as it is written: "He who through faith is just shall live." Here I felt that I was altogether born again and had entered paradise itself through open gates.[36]

The context makes it clear that this insight occurred in 1519 when Luther began his second exposition of the Psalms. However, many Reformation scholars, finding an evangelical understanding of the gospel in Luther's earlier writings, have laid this late dating to an old man's faulty memory.

34. WA 25, p. 375; 50, p. 119.
35. WA 1, p. 225.
36. WA 54, pp. 179-187; LW 34, p. 328. This famous passage is from the *Preface* to the 1545 edition of Luther's Latin writings.

The point of controversy is where to draw the line between "the young Luther" and "the mature Luther." Or, put in other words, when did Luther make the internal transition from an Augustinian monk to the Protestant reformer?

By the outbreak of the Indulgence Controversy in late 1517 the seed of Luther's later theology had already taken root. He was sure that forgiveness was the gift of God, not the result of human merit. He had broken with scholastic methodology in favor of biblical theology. Yet it was only in the wake of the great struggle which followed the posting of the *Ninety-five Theses* that the mature shape of Luther's doctrine of justification became evident. Could it be that we should distinguish two separate experiences of Luther: one, an initial evangelical awakening prompted by the counsels of Staupitz, dated in 1513 or 1514; the other, a theological discovery which led to a clear and different understanding of justification, dated around 1518 or 1519?

Staupitz had directed Luther to "the wounds of the most sweet Saviour" as a way out of his despair.[37] Thus his confessor and superior in the Augustinian order truly became his "father in God." "If I didn't praise Staupitz, I should be a damnable, ungrateful, papistical ass . . . for he bore me in Christ. If Staupitz had not helped me out, I should have been swallowed up and left in hell."[38] Staupitz planted the seed or, as Luther put it, "started the doctrine," but much germination and growth was required before the doctrine assumed its definitive form. We can best understand Luther's development by briefly describing the doctrine against which he reacted.

The understanding of justification which dominated both patristic and medieval theology derived in part from the wedding of Christian doctrine and Greek philosophy. Reconciliation was understood as effecting a new ontological relationship between the divine and the human, "a belonging to God in the order of being."[39] The secular Greek concept of divinization was Christianized, and salvation became participation in the effulgence of Being which is God. For example, this imagery underlay Athanasius's famous dictum, "Christ became man so that we might become gods," as well as Augustine's whole theology of justification.

A corollary of salvation as deification is the concept of sin as a breach

37. WA 1, p. 525; LW 48, p. 66: "The commandments of God became sweet when they are read not only in books but also in the wounds of the sweetest Savior."
38. WA 58/1, p. 27.
39. Hans Küng, *Justification: The Doctrine of Karl Barth and a Catholic Response* (New York: Thomas Nelson and Sons, 1964), p. 67.

in the order of being, a debilitating sickness which required healing. Irenaeus noted the healing powers released in the incarnation: The enfleshment of the Logos meant the impingement of a divine, substantive power upon the realm of weak, unredeemed nature.[40] This divine power was conveyed to humans in ever new waves through the medium of the sacraments. Ignatius of Antioch had already spoken of the Eucharist as "the medicine of immortality."[41] For Augustine, too, the infusion of grace through the sacramental-penitential system of the church continued the process of justification begun in baptism. In this life the Christian is always a *viator,* a wayfarer, who stands suspended between God's grace, revealed in Christ and mediated through the sacraments, and God's judgment hanging over one's head like an eschatological Damocles's sword ever calling into question one's present spiritual condition.

In scholastic theology the doctrine of justification was further refined by means of the distinction between "actual grace" and "habitual grace." Actual grace effected the forgiveness of actual sins provided they were made known in confession. But actual grace was not strong enough either to remove the guilt of original sin or to transform the sinner ontologically. This required the infusion of habitual grace which imparted a divine quality to the soul and enabled one to perform righteous acts. Habitual grace was pure grace and not the result of merit. Still, one was declared righteous because he had already been made righteous, to some degree at least, by the infusion of a supernatural quality. The verdict of justification was the physician's pronouncement of recovery, a bill of health attesting the patient's transformed nature.

Yet this was precisely Luther's problem. Since only actual sins enumerated in confession could actually be forgiven, Luther was obsessed with the fear that he might have overlooked some sin. He would confess to Staupitz for hours, walk away, then come rushing back with some little foible he had forgotten to mention. At one point Staupitz, quite exasperated, said: "Look here, Brother Martin. If you're going to confess so much, why don't you

40. For a fuller treatment of Irenaeus's concept of salvation see John Lawson, *The Biblical Theology of St. Irenaeus* (London: Epworth Press, 1948), pp. 153-154, 202, and Richard A. Norris, Jr., *God and World in Early Christian Theology* (New York: Seabury Press, 1965), pp. 71-98.

41. ". . . breaking one bread, which is the medicine of immortality, the antidote that we should not die, but live forever in Jesus Christ." Ephesians 20:2. Kirsopp Lake, ed., *The Apostolic Fathers* (Cambridge, Mass.: Harvard University Press, 1912), I, p. 195.

go do something worth confessing? Kill your mother or father! Commit adultery! Quit coming in here with such flummery and fake sins!" Then Luther was plagued with another doubt: "Have I been truly contrite in my confession, or is my repentance motivated merely by fear?" At this point he was driven to the very abyss of despair so that he wished he "had never been created a human being."[42] That hatred turned from self toward God. As Philip Watson has aptly put it, Luther's basic question was no longer whether he was a sheep or a goat, but whether God was herbivorous or carnivorous, a Deliverer or a Destroyer?[43] As we have seen, Staupitz guided Luther through these severe *Anfechtungen* by pointing him to the wounds of Jesus, to the cross of Christ. But this was only the first step in his developing doctrine of justification. A complex of interwoven ideas and influences continually shaped Luther and his thinking about justification during the next five years (1513-1518). Three of the most formative strands of influence were nominalism, German mysticism, and the writings of Augustine.

Luther had cut his theological teeth on the writings of the nominalist theologian Gabriel Biel, under whose students he had studied at Erfurt. Biel stood in a well-established tradition which included William of Ockham and Duns Scotus. Characteristic of this tradition was the well-known distinction between God's absolute power and His ordained power. By His absolute power God could do anything which does not violate the law of contradiction. He could have, for example, become incarnate in a rat or even a stone; he could have decreed adultery a virtue and marital fidelity a vice. In fact, though, we know (through revelation) that by His ordained power, He chose to become incarnate in a man, Jesus Christ, and to make adultery a mortal sin.

As expressed in the theology of Biel this emphasis on the absolute and ordained power of God did not pose a serious threat to the Augustinian concept of progressive justification. Theoretically, *de potentia absoluta*, justification could be effected without the infusion of grace. But, *de potentia ordinata*, God has chosen to justify us through established channels, so to speak. In an Advent sermon (1460) Biel exhorted his flock concerning justification:

> To resume, Gabriel said to Joseph, "You will call His name Jesus for He will save His people from their sins." In truth He has already saved His people by preparing medicine. He continues to save them daily by driving out dis-

42. WA 18, p. 719; LW 33, p. 191.
43. Watson, p. 84.

ease. He will save them ultimately by giving them perfect health and preserving them from every ill . . . . He prepared the medicine when He instituted the medicinal sacraments to heal the wounds inflicted by our sins.[44]

Apart from the sacramental infusion of grace no one could earn a real merit (*meritum de condigno*). However, by "doing one's very best" (*facere quod in se est:* literally, doing what-in-one-is), it was possible to earn a semimerit (*meritum de congruo*). By His ordained power, God had committed Himself to bestow grace on everyone who does the best one can. Thus it was possible for the sinner to have some claim upon God, even to demand certain things from God, on the basis of one's own natural abilities and good works.

We can see how the nominalist picture of the *viator,* suspended between the inscrutable will of a just God and the necessity of doing one's very best, could precipitate the anguish experienced by the young Luther. However, as late as 1515, Luther was still espousing the necessity of doing one's best as a predisposition to the reception of grace. "Hence, just as the law was a figure and preparation of the people for receiving Christ, so our doing what is in us (*factio quantum in nobis est*) disposes us to grace."[45] Luther held to some form of the *facere quod* doctrine until late 1516 or early 1517. During these years, he abandoned the "rancid rules of the logicians" and the terminology of "those grubs, the philosophers."[46] He came to see that which preceded grace was not a disposition, but indisposition and active rebellion.[47] Luther's break with the nominalist concepts of merit and grace was a fundamental step in his developing doctrine of justification.

Staupitz first introduced Luther to the writings of the Dominican mystic Johann Tauler in 1516. Luther found a kindred spirit in the *Theologia Germanica* which he published twice, once in part (1516) and once completely (1518). From Luther's famous dictum, "Mystical rapture is not the passageway to God,"[48] one might conclude that Luther was only affected

44. Heiko A. Oberman, *Forerunners of the Reformation,* (Philadelphia: Fortress Press, 1966) p. 166.

45. WA 4, p. 262: "Unde sicut lex figura fuit et preparatio populi ad Christum suscipiendum, ita nostra factio quantum in nobis est, disponit nos ad gratiam."

46. WA 47, p. 26; 9, p. 29.

47. "Ex parte autem hominis nihil nisi indispositio, immo rebellio gratiae gratiam praecedit." WA 1, p. 225; LW 31, p. 11. This is one of Luther's theses in his "Disputation Against Scholastic Theology."

48. WA 56, p. 300; LW 25, p. 288. A good summary of recent scholarship on Luther's relationship to mysticism is Bengt Hägglund, *The Background of Luther's*

negatively by mysticism. That such was not the case is confirmed by the lavish praise which Luther showered upon Tauler and the other mystics. The perversity of human egoism and the need to conform to Christ's humiliation and sufferings were themes Luther had already developed but found reiterated in the mystics. Luther also agreed that the proper attitude of man before God was one of utter passivity and complete submission (*Gelassenheit*)) exemplified in the passion of Christ. He had experienced resignation to hell as part of his own "preparation" for grace.

For a while Luther embraced the mystic doctrine of synteresis, the ultimate essence of the soul (*Seelenabgrund*) which was the anthropological basis of mystical union. In a sermon on Saint Stephen's Day (December 26, 1515), Luther described this synteresis as sparks under ashes, seed buried in the earth, matter awaiting a form. Isaiah 1:9, "Had the Lord not left us a seed, we should have been as Sodom," he interpreted tropologically as "unless the synteresis and remnants of nature had been kept, all must have perished."[49] Luther further described the synteresis as the ineradicable spark of conscience within natural man, that which the physician calls the natural powers without which no disease could be healed. It is true that the *Seelenabgrund* did not provide the *viator* with an innate standing before God nor with a natural ability to aid in his own salvation. It did, just the same, give the natural person a leg to stand on in that it provided the basis for mystical union through the "birth of God" in the soul. In such a union the self is submerged into God "like a drop of water in the deep sea. He has become much more one with him than the air is united with the brightness of the sun when it shines in broad daylight."[50] To the extent that this process occurs in the human, one is justified: *homo viator* is transformed into *homo deificatus.*

However, as Luther's awareness of the sinner's utter helplessness to save himself or to sustain any righteous standing before God increased, he came to question the notion of synteresis. Gradually Luther came to view sin as a seething rebellion, not merely a passive weakness or a lack of good. The atrocity of sin was not only that it vitiated one's entire being but that it was an uncontrollable energy which could not be conquered by ordinary means. The plight of the human before God (*coram Deo*) was that one was com-

---

Doctrine of Justification in Late Medieval Theology (Philadelphia: Fortress Press, 1971, pp. 2-16. See also Heiko A. Oberman, *"Simul Gemitus et Raptus:* Luther and Mysticism," in Ozment, pp. 219-251.

49. WA 56, p. 300.
50. Hägglund, p. 13.

pletely naked, divested of all natural resources, including the *Seelenabgrund,* with nothing to fall back on. Alienation from God stemmed from the fall, which Luther described graphically:

> So Adam and Eve were pure and healthy. They had eyes so sharp they could have seen through a wall, and ears so good they could have heard anything two miles away. All the animals were obedient to them: even the sun and moon smiled at them. But then the devil came and said, "You will become just like the gods," and so on. They reasoned, "God is patient. What difference would one apple make?" Snap, snap, and it lay before them. It's hanging us all yet by the neck.[51]

This primal sin consisted basically in unfaith toward God, relying on human reasoning instead of God's Word. Most frightening of all was that we are not aware of the seriousness of our sin: "If anyone would feel the greatness of sin he would not be able to go on living another moment; so great is the power of sin."[52] Though Luther continued to use certain mystical terms in later sermons and commentaries, his rejection of the synteresis doctrine was a decisive step toward his new understanding of justification.

We have rejected the thesis that Luther's doctrine of justification was produced *de novo* as the result of one shattering insight. His doctrine developed over a period of years, being influenced by various strands of late medieval thought and undergoing several fundamental shifts. The most crucial of these shifts involved the redefinition of justification in a non-Augustinian framework. Luther's changing attitudes toward Augustine during these years are a helpful gauge in tracing this development. In a letter of May 18, 1517, to his friend Johannes Lang, Luther wrote: "Our theology and St. Augustine are making good progress, and, thanks be to God, they prevail at our university."[53] Luther later evaluated his definitive position on justification vis à vis Augustine thus: "Augustine got nearer to the meaning of Paul than all the Schoolmen, but he did not reach Paul. In the beginning I devoured Augustine, but when the door into Paul swung open and I knew what justification by faith really was, then it was out with him."[54]

51. WA 36, p. 253.

52. WA 39, p. 210. Cf. also WA 39, p. 84: "Radical sin, deadly and truly mortal, is unknown to men in the whole wide world . . . Not one of all men could think that it was a sin of the world not to believe in Christ Jesus the Crucified."

53. *Luthers Briefwechsel,* Enders, ed. (Frankfurt, 1884), I, p. 100.

54. Quoted in Gordon Rupp, "Patterns of Salvation in the First Age of the Reformation," *Archiv fur Reformationsgeschichte* 57 (1966), pp. 52-66.

Luther's break with Augustine coincided with his new understanding of the "justice of God" in Romans 1:17. In his *Lectures on Romans* (1515) Luther's treatment of this verse is very brief, consisting of the exposition of two phrases: "the justice of God is revealed" (eighteen lines including quotations from Augustine and Aristotle) and "from faith to faith" (twenty-four lines with Augustine quoted again). Moreover, the latter phrase is interpreted in terms of progressive justification, a "growing more and more" toward the achievement of righteousness. The Christian life is thus always a "seeking and striving to be made righteous, even to the hour of death."[55] In October, 1518, Luther again expounded Romans 1:17, but now asserted that faith operates without any predisposition or preparation prior to justification, and we find the striking sentence: Faith alone justifies (*Sola fides justificate*).[56] This is the threshold of Luther's new understanding of justification which was set forth clearly for the first time in two sermons published in the winter of 1518-1519: "Sermon on the Twofold Justice" and "Sermon on the Threefold Justice," and later given classic exposition in the *Larger Commentary on Galatians* (1535). Let us examine this doctrine by considering three of its essential features: (1) imputation, (2) its by-faith-alone character, (3) its impact on the phrase "at the same time a sinner and a righteous one."

Luther abandoned the medical imagery of impartation/infusion in favor of the forensic language of imputation. Earlier he had spoken of the Christian's progress in grace as a gradual healing of the wounds of sin. The "weak in faith" of Romans 14:1 (RSV) were those God had taken under His charge to perfect and cure. Their weakness was not reckoned as sin precisely because their cure had begun. Or again, Christ is the good Samaritan who brings the *viator,* half dead and half alive, to the infirmary (the church) to be nursed back to health.[57] The language of imputation moves from the imagery of medicine to that of the law court. God accepts the righteousness of Christ, which is alien to our nature proper, as our own. Though our sins are not actually removed, they cease to be counted against us. Luther described this transaction as a "sweet exchange" between Christ and the sinner:

Therefore, my dear brother, learn Christ and Him crucified; learn to pray to

55. LW 25, pp. 153, 251-252; WA 56, pp. 173, 264-265.
56. Bizer, pp. 97-105.
57. WA 56, p. 441; LW 25, p. 433. Cf. also WA 56, p. 275; LW 25, p. 263: "Ecclesia stabulum est et infirmaria egrotantium et sanandorum." "The church is the inn and the infirmary for those who are sick and in need of being made well."

Him despairing of yourself, saying, "Thou, Lord Jesus, art my righteousness and I am Thy sin; Thou hast taken on Thyself what Thou wast not, and hast given to me what I am not."[58]

Luther believed that he had recovered the original meaning of the Greek verb used by Paul in Romans. Augustine and the scholastic tradition had interpreted it as "to make righteous," whereas Luther insisted on its legal connotation, "to declare righteous."

True, Luther had spoken of imputation before 1518, even of the imputation of Christ's alien righteousness. However, before, justification was a proleptic judgment based on the eradication of actual sins which had already begun and on the eschatological expectation of the complete removal of all sin. Thus, Luther could write before 1518:

For this is the most sweet mercy of God, that He saves real sinners, not imaginary sinners, that He upholds us in our sins, . . . *until* He makes us perfect and consummates us. For He himself is our sole righteousness *until* we are conformed to His likeness.[59]

Luther's new insight was that the imputation of Christ's alien righteousness was based, not on the gradual curing of sin, but rather on the complete victory of Christ on the cross. The once-for-allness of justification was emphasized: "If you believe, then you have it!" Nor is there any direct correlation between the state of justification and one's outward works, as Luther made clear in his sermon on the Pharisee and the publican (1521): "And the publican fulfills all the commandments of God on the spot. He was then and there made holy by grace alone. Who could have foreseen that, under this dirty fellow?"[60]

Luther insisted that we appropriate God's grace, and hence are declared righteous, *by faith alone.*[61] Faith is here understood as *fiducia,* personal

58. Preserved Smith, ed., *Luther's Correspondence and Other Contemporary Letters* (Philadelphia: The Lutheran Publication Society, 1913), I, p. 34.

59. LW 31, p. 63; WA 1, p. 370: "Haec est dulcissima Dei Patris misericordia, quod non fictos, sed veros peccatores salvat, sustinens nos in peccatis nostris et acceptans opera et vitam nostram omni abiectione digna, donec nos perficiat atque consummet." The LW edition mistranslates "misericordia" as "righteousness."

60. WA 17, p. 404. "Et hic statim implevit praecepta dei, ibi mera gratia per sanctitatem, wher het sich des stuck versehen unter dem unflat?"

61. Luther did not, of course, invent this phrase. The German Bible published at Nürnberg in 1483 translated Galatians 2:16 as "gerechtfertigt . . . nur durch den Glauben." Further, the term *sola fide* was well-established in the Catholic tradition having been used by Origen, Hilary, Chrysostom, Augustine, Bernard, Aquinas, and

trust, reliance, a grasping or taking hold of Christ. In the medieval tradition faith was considered as one of the three theological virtues, along with hope and love. Only after overcoming the view of faith as a virtue formed by love could Luther embrace the full meaning of *fiducia* as relationship with God. "If faith is not without all, even the smallest works, it does not justify; indeed it is not even faith."[62] At the same time, Luther was careful to guard against the temptation to consider faith itself a meritorious work. Properly speaking, faith itself does not justify; it is, so to speak, the receptive organ of justification. It does not cause grace to be, but merely becomes conscious of something already in existence. To have faith is to accept the acceptance which is ours in Jesus Christ. But this is not a self-generated human activity; it is a gift of the Holy Spirit.

The person who has thus received the gift of faith Luther described as "at once righteous and a sinner" (*simul iustus et peccator*). Formerly he had understood this term in the Augustinian sense of "partly" a sinner and "partly" righteous, sinners in empirical reality, but justified in hope of the future consummation."[63] Now, however, while retaining the paradox of simultaneity, he sharpened each of the clashing concepts into a sovereign, total realm. Luther continued to use *simul iustus et peccator* after 1518-1519, but he did so in the sense of *semper* (always) *iustus et peccator*. The believer is not only both righteous and sinful at the same time but is also always or completely both righteous and sinful at the same time. What does this mean?

With respect to our fallen human condition we are, and always will be in this life, sinners. However, for believers life in this world is no longer a period of doubtful candidacy for God's acceptance. In a sense we have already been before God's judgment seat and have been acquitted—on account of Christ. Hence we are also always righteous. Luther expressed the paradox thus:

> We are in truth and totally sinners, with regard to ourselves and our first birth. Contrariwise, in so far as Christ has been given for us, we are holy and just totally. Hence from different aspects we are said to be just and sinners at one and the same time.[64]

others but without Luther's particular nuances. Cf. Küng, pp. 249-250.

62. WA 7, p. 231: "Fides nisi sit sine ullis etiam minimis operibus, non iustificat, imo non est fides."

63. WA 56, p. 269: "Peccatores in re, iusti autem in spe."

64. WA 39, p. 523.

So Luther could say that there is no sin at all, and that all is sin; there is hell, and there is heaven. The importance of Luther's shift from *simul* to *semper* has been noted by Paul Tillich: "If God accepted him who is half-sinner and half-just, his judgment would be conditioned by man's half-goodness. But there is nothing God rejects as strongly as half-goodness, and every human claim based on it."[65]

Luther's doctrine of justification fell like a bombshell on the theological landscape of medieval Catholicism. It shattered the entire theology of merits and indeed the sacramental-penitential basis of the church itself. It is no wonder that the Dominican inquisitor of Cologne, Jacob Hochstraten, regarded it as blasphemy for Luther to describe the union of the soul to Christ as a spiritual marriage based on faith alone. How can Christ be thus joined to a sinner? This is to make the soul "a prostitute and adultress" and Christ Himself "a pimp and a cowardly patron of her disgrace."[66] Hochstraten was rightly shocked at the import of Luther's message. But it is no less shocking than the statement of Paul upon which it was based: "God justifies the *ungodly,*" nor, indeed, Jesus' story of the loving father who welcomes home his wayward son even though he is still splattered with mud from the hogpen. Luther would not be happy with the tampered version of John Newton's hymn. The original suits his theology better:

> Amazing grace, how sweet the sound
> That saved a *wretch* like me.

Did Luther, then, have no place at all for good works? Duke George of Saxony thought not when he remarked, "Luther's doctrine is good for the dying, but it is no good for the living." Erasmus was less kind: "Lutherans seek only two things—wealth and wives . . . to them the gospel means the right to live as they please."[67] By emphasizing so strongly God's initiative in salvation, did Luther open the door to antinomianism, the view that Christians are set free by grace from the need of observing any moral law?

Luther was aware of the charge and vigorously denied that he was guilty

65. Paul Tillich, *Systematic Theology* (Chicago: University of Chicago Press, 1963), III, p. 226.

66. Ozment, p. 150.

67. P.S. Allen and H.M. Allen, eds., *Opus Epistolarum Des. Erasmi Roterodami* (Oxford University Press, 1928), VII, p. 366, letter [no. 1977] of March 20, 1528 to Willibald Pirckheimer: "Ubicunque regnat Luteranismus, ibi litterarum est interitus; et tamen hoc genus hominum maxime litteris alitur. Duo tantum querunt, censum et uxorem; cetera praestat illis Evangelium, hoc est potestatem vivendi ut velint."

of it. While we are in no wise justified by works, works should follow faith as its proper fruit:

> "Yes," you say, "but does not faith justify without the works of the Law?" Yes, this is true. But where is faith? What happens to it? Where does it show itself? For it surely must not be such a sluggish, useless, deaf, or dead thing; it must be a living, productive tree which yields fruit.[68]

The fruit of justification is *faith active in love*. Such love is directed in the first instance not toward God in hope of attaining some merit toward salvation, but toward one's neighbor for "the Christian lives not in himself, but in Christ and in his neighbor." Luther urged Christians to perform good works out of spontaneous love in obedience to God for the sake of others. Put otherwise, justification by faith alone frees me to love my neighbor disinterestedly, for his or her own sake, as my sister or brother, not as the calculated means to my own desired ends. Since we no longer carry the intolerable burden of self-justification, we are free "to be Christ's unto one another," to expend ourselves on behalf of one another, even as Christ also loved us and gave himself for us.[69]

Let God Be God: Predestination

The problem of predestination is posed by the particularity of the Judeo-Christian tradition: the fact that God revealed himself uniquely in one people, Israel, and supremely in one man, Jesus of Nazareth. Jesus as well as Paul spoke of "the elect ones" and "the chosen few." The tension between God's free election and genuine human response is present already in the New Testament documents. However, Augustine, in his classic struggle with Pelagius, first developed a full-blown doctrine of predestination.

For Pelagius salvation was a reward, the result of good works freely performed by human beings. Grace was not something other than, above, and beyond nature; grace was present within nature itself. In other words, grace was simply the natural capacity, which everyone has, to do the right thing, to obey the Commandments, and thus to earn salvation. Augustine, on the other hand, saw a great gulf between nature, in its fallen state, and grace. Keenly aware of the radical impotence of his own will to choose rightly, Augustine viewed salvation as the free and surprising gift of God: "Unto thy grace and mercy do I ascribe, for thy hast dissolved my sins as

---

68. LW 24, pp. 264-265; WA 45, p. 702.
69. LW 31, pp. 371, 368.

it were ice.''[70] If, however, the source of our turning to God lies not in ourselves but solely in God's good pleasure, why is it that some respond to the gospel while others spurn it? This question drove Augustine to Paul's discussion of election in Romans 9—11. Here he found the basis for his own "harsh" doctrine of predestination: Out of the mass of fallen humanity God chooses some for eternal life and passes over others who are thus doomed for destruction, and this decision is made irrespective of human works or merits.

In the thousand years between Augustine and Luther, the main drift of medieval theology was devoted to watering down Augustine's stringent predestinarianism. True, Pelagius had been condemned at the Council of Ephesus (431), and semi-Pelagianism, the view that at least the beginning of faith, one's first turning to God, was the result of free will, was rejected by the Second Council of Orange (529). Nonetheless, most theologians tried to modify Augustine's doctrine by qualifying the basis of predestination. Alexander of Hales appealed to the principle of divine equality: "God relates on an equal basis to all.''[71] Others held that predestination was subordinate to foreknowledge, that is, God elects those whom he knows in advance will earn merits of their own free will. None of these theories of salvation was "purely" Pelagian, for all of them required the assistance of divine grace. Still, the crucial factor remained the human decision to respond to God rather than God's free, unfettered decision to choose whom He wills.

We have seen how Luther's doctrine of justification broke decisively with the Augustinian model of a progressive impartation of grace. We are justified not because God is gradually making us righteous, but because we are declared righteous on the basis of Christ's atoning sacrifice. However, on the prior principle of *sola gratia,* Luther—and Zwingli and Calvin after him—stands foursquare with Augustine against the latter-day "Pelagians" who exalt human free will at the expense of God's free grace. In this respect, the mainline Protestant Reformation can be viewed as an "acute Augustinianization of Christianity.''[72] Some historians have regarded Luther's doc-

70. Augustine, *Confessions,* II, 7: "Gratiae tuae deputo et misericordiae tuae, quod peccata mea tamquam glaciem solvisti."

71. Alexander of Hales, *Summa Theologica* (Quaracchi, 1924) L. 320: "Deus se aequaliter habet ad omnes."

72. I am indebted to Professor George H. Williams for this apt phrase which is based on Harnack's description of gnosticism as an "acute Hellenization of Christianity."

trine of predestination as an aberration from his major themes or, at best, as a "merely auxiliary thought."[73] But Luther saw the matter differently. In responding to Erasmus's attack on this doctrine, Luther praised the humanist for not bothering him with extraneous issues such as the papacy, purgatory, or indulgences. "You alone," he said, "have attacked the real thing, that is, the essential issue. . . . You alone have seen the hinge on which all turns, and aimed for the vital spot."[74]

One of Luther's complaints against the "pig-theologians" was their thesis that the human will of its own volition could actually love God above all things, or, that by doing one's best even apart from grace one could earn a certain standing before God. To this optimistic apprisal of human potential Luther opposed a stark contrast between nature and grace. "*Grace* puts God in the place of everything else it sees, and prefers him to itself, but *nature* puts itself in the place of everything, and even in the place of God, and seeks only its own and not what is God's."[75] By "nature" Luther did not mean simply the created realm, but rather the fallen, created realm, and particularly the fallen human will which is "curved in on itself " *(incurvatus in se),* "enslaved," and tainted with evil in all of its actions.[76] At the Heidelberg Disputation in 1518, Luther defended the thesis: "Free will after the Fall exists only in name, and as long as one 'does what in one lies,' one is committing mortal sin."[77] This formulation was included in the bull *Exsurge Domine* by which Pope Leo X excommunicated Luther in 1520.

Was Luther, then, a thoroughgoing determinist? Erasmus and certain modern scholars have thought so.[78] Luther did come perilously close to necessitarian language. Yet he never denied that free will retains its power in matters which do not concern salvation. Thus Luther said to Erasmus: "You are no doubt right in assigning to man a will of some sort, but to credit

73. Werner Elert, *The Structure of Lutheranism,* Walter A. Hensen, trans. (St. Louis: Concordia Publishing House, 1962) I: 123.

74. WA 18, p. 786. English quotations from *De servo arbitrio* are taken from E. Gordon Rupp and Philip S. Watson, eds., *Luther and Erasmus: Free Will and Salvation* (Philadelphia: Westminster Press, 1969).

75. Rupp and Watson, p. 220.

76. Ibid., p. 252.

77. Atkinson, p. 287.

78. Cf. Linwood Urban, "Was Luther a Thoroughgoing Determinist?" *Journal of Theological Studies* 22 (1971), pp. 113-139. The most helpful discussion of the whole question is Harry J. McSorley, *Luther: Right or Wrong?* Cf. also Robert Shofner, "Luther on 'The Bondage of the Will': An Analytical-Critical Essay," *Scottish Journal of Theology* 26 (1973), pp. 24-39.

him with a will that is free in the things of God is too much."[79] Luther freely granted that even the enslaved will is "not a nothing," that with respect to those things which are "inferior" to it, the will retains its full powers. It is only with respect to that which is "superior" to it that the will is held captive in sins and cannot choose the good according to God.[80] Here we find a parallel to Luther's disdain of reason. In its legitimate sphere reason is the highest gift of God, but the moment it transgresses into theology it becomes the "Devil's Whore." So too with free will. Understood as the God-given capacity to make ordinary decisions, to carry out one's responsibilities in the world, free will remains intact. What it *cannot* do is effect its own salvation. On this score free will is totally vitiated by sin and in bondage to Satan.

Luther described the nature of this bondage in terms of a struggle between God and Satan:

> So the will is like a beast standing between two riders. If God rides, it wills and goes where God wills . . . . If Satan rides, it wills and goes where Satan wills; nor can it choose to run to either of the two riders or to seek him out, but the riders themselves contend for the possession and control of it.[81]

Although some scholars have found a nuance of Manichaean dualism in this metaphor, Luther was merely developing an image originally drawn by Jesus: "Every one who commits sin is a slave of sin" and "You are of your father the devil, and your will is to do your father's desires" (John 8:34, 44,RSV). There is a further point Luther developed with regard to the enslaved will. Although our eternal destiny is, in a sense, determined by God, we are not therefore compelled to sin. We sin spontaneously and voluntarily. We go on willing and desiring to do evil in spite of the fact that in our own strength we can do nothing to alter this condition. Herein is the tragedy of human existence apart from grace: We are so curved in upon ourselves that, thinking ourselves free, we indulge in those very things which only reinforce our bondage.

The purpose of grace is to release us from the illusion of freedom, which is really slavery, and to lead us into the "glorious liberty of the children of God." Only when the will has received grace, or to use his other metaphor, only when Satan has been overcome by a stronger rider, "does the power

79. Rupp and Watson, p. 170.
80. Pauck, *Lectures on Romans,* p. 252.
81. Rupp and Watson, p. 140.

of decision really become free, at all events in respect to salvation."[82] The true intention behind Luther's emphasis on the enslaved will now becomes obvious. God desires that we should be truly free in our love toward Him, yet this is not a possibility until we have been *freed* from our captivity to Satan and self. The answering echo to *The Bondage of the Will* is *The Freedom of the Christian.*

Since apart from grace the human possesses neither sound reason nor a good will, "the only infallible preparation for grace . . . is the eternal election and predestination of God"[83] Luther did not shrink from a doctrine of absolute, double predestination, although he admitted that "this is very strong wine, and solid food for the strong."[84] He even restricted the scope of the atonement to the elect: "Christ did not die for all absolutely."[85] Against the objection that such a view turns God into an arbitrary ogre, Luther answered—with Paul—"God wills it so, and because he wills it so, it is not wicked." The "prudence of the flesh" says that "it is cruel and miserable of God that he seeks his glory in my wretchedness. Listen to the voice of the flesh! 'My, my,' it says! Take away this 'my' and say instead: 'Glory be to thee, O Lord!' and you will be saved."[86] The posture of natural reason is always one of egocentricity. God is just as "unjust," strictly speaking, in justifying the ungodly apart from their merits as He is in rejecting others apart from their demerits. Yet no one complains of the former "injustice" because self-interest is involved![87] In both cases God is unjust by human standards, but just and true by His own. Luther refused to subject God to the bar of human justice, as though the "Majesty that is the creator of all things must bow to one of the dregs of his creation."[88] "Let God be good," cried Erasmus the moralist. "Let God be God," replied Luther the theologian.

Although Luther never softened his doctrine of predestination (as did later Lutherans), he did try to set the mystery in the context of eternity. He never admitted that God's inscrutable judgments were in fact unjust, only

82. Pauck, p. 252.

83. Atkinson, p. 268.

84. Pauck, p. 271.

85. Ibid., p. 252.

86. Ibid., p. 253.

87. Rupp and Watson, p. 259: "When therefore Reason praises God for saving the unworthy, but finds fault with him for damning the undeserving, she stands convicted of not praising God as God, but as serving her own interests."

88. Ibid., p. 258.

that we are unable to grasp how they are just. There are, he suggested, three lights—the light of nature, the light of grace, and the light of glory. By the light of grace we are able to understand many problems which appeared insoluable by the light of nature. Even so, in the light of glory God's righteous judgments—incomprehensible to us now even by the light of grace—will be openly manifested. Luther thus appealed to the eschatological vindication of God's decision in election. The answer to the riddle of predestination lies in God's hiddenness behind and beyond His revelation. Ultimately, when we shall have proceeded through the "lights" of nature and grace into the light of glory, the "hidden God" will be shown to be one with the God who is revealed in Jesus Christ and proclaimed in the gospel. In the meantime, Luther admonished, we can only *believe* this. Predestination like justification is also *sola fide*.[89]

No one knew better than Luther the anguish which doubting one's election could produce in a wavering soul. How should a pastor respond to someone who is plagued with this problem? Luther gave two answers to this question, one for the strong Christian, the other for the weaker or newly converted Christian. The highest rank among the elect belongs to those who "resign themselves to hell if God wills this."[90] Resignation to hell was a popular theme in the mystical tradition and signified complete passivity, an utter letting loose of oneself (*Gelassenheit*) before the abyss of God's being. Luther said that God dispensed this gift to the elect briefly and sparingly, most often at the hour of death.

More commonly, Luther was asked to counsel with ordinary Christians who were tormented by the question of election. Luther's basic advice was, "Thank God for your torments!" It is characteristic of the elect, not of the reprobate, to tremble at the hidden counsel of God. Beyond this, he urged a flat refutation of the devil and a contemplation of Christ. Typical was his response to Barbara Lisskirchen, who was distressed she was not among the elect:

> When such thoughts assail you, you should learn to ask yourself, "If you please, in which Commandment is it written that I should think about and deal with this matter?" When it appears that there is no such Commandment, learn to say "Be gone, wretched devil! You are trying to make me worry about myself. But God declares everywhere that I should let him care for me. . .." The highest of all God's commands is this, that we hold up before our eyes the image of his dear Son, our Lord Jesus Christ. Every day he should be our

89. Ibid., pp. 331-332.
90. Pauck, p. 255.

excellent mirror wherein we behold how much God loves us and how well, in his infinite goodness, he has cared for us in that he gave his dear Son for us. In this way, I say, and in no other, does one learn how to deal properly with the question of predestination. It will be manifest that you believe in Christ. If you believe, then you are called. And if you are called, then you are most certainly predestinated. Do not let this mirror and throne of grace be torn away from before your eyes . . . . Contemplate Christ given for us. Then, God willing, you will feel better.[91]

Luther's doctrine of predestination was not motivated by speculative or metaphysical concerns. It was a window into the gracious will of God who freely bound Himself to humanity in Jesus Christ. Predestination, like the nature of God Himself, could only be approached through the cross, through the "wounds of Jesus" to which Staupitz had directed young Luther in his early struggles.

Christ in the Crib: The Meaning of *Sola Scriptura*

While sitting at table Luther recalled the following incident from his early life:

When I was twenty years old I had not yet seen a Bible. I thought that there were no Gospels and Epistles except those which were written in the Sunday postils. Finally I found a Bible in the library and forthwith I took it with me into the monastery. I began to read, to reread, and to read it over again, to the great astonishment of Dr. Staupitz.[92]

The story of Luther's "discovery of the Bible" was retold with considerable embellishment by Luther's early biographers. For example, one version notes that the Bible was chained so as to prevent its examination. In fact, we know that before the invention of bookcases Bibles and other books were frequently chained to reading desks in order to make them more, not less, accessible. This practice continued in Wittenberg long after the Reformation began. Yet there is a kernel of truth in the anecdote. As a movement the Reformation was about books as well as *the Book*. The invention of the printing press together with Luther's German Bible did in a sense "unchain" the Scriptures by making them available not only to scholars and monks but also to ploughboys in the fields and milkmaids at their pails. We cannot appreciate the role of Scripture in Reformation theology without being aware of the enormous revolution in sensibilities which accompanied

91. T. G. Tappert, ed., *Luther: Letters of Spiritual Counsel* (Philadelphia: Westminster Press, 1955), p. 116.

92. Schweibert, p. 121. Cf. WA TR 3, p. 599.

the widespread distribution of the Bible in Europe. A few generations later Thomas Hobbes expressed his horror at the prospect of an "everyman theology":

> After the Bible was translated . . . every man, nay every boy and wench that could read English thought they spoke with God Almighty, and understood what he said when by a certain number of chapters a day they had read the Scriptures once or twice over.[93]

Luther, too, before he was done with it, had reason to complain of "factious spirits" who shouted "God's Word, God's Word," but who wrongly divided its contents.[94]

We have already noted Luther's vocation as *Doctor in Biblia* and his emphasis on the arousal of faith through hearing the Word. We must now ask what the Bible meant for Luther and how he interpreted it in the light of his new understanding of justification by faith alone.

Luther's decisive break from the Church of Rome came not at the Diet of Worms (1521) when he declared his conscience captive to the Word of God, but two years earlier at the Leipzig Debate (July 1519). His opponent was the infamous and very able John Eck, whose name in German means "corner," hence the saying that at Leipzig Eck boxed Luther into a corner. Luther was the better Bible scholar, but Eck was the better church historian. Eck accused Luther of advocating certain theses of John Hus, which had been condemned one hundred years before at the Council of Constance and for which Hus had been burned at the stake. Although Luther protested that he was not defending Hus, Eck kept pressing him on that point. During the lunch break Luther examined the records of the Council of Constance and discovered, to his great surprise, that Eck was right! He had been advocating the same position as Hus. In the afternoon session Luther astonished the whole assembly by declaring in effect: "Ja, ich bin ein Hussite!" Now Luther was really in a corner, for Eck had forced him to ally himself with a condemned heretic and to repudiate the authority of general councils as well as that of the pope. For Luther the old pillars of authority had been shattered. Thenceforth his whole theology was erected on the foundation of *sola scriptura.* In his treatise on *The Babylonian Captivity of the Church* (1520), Luther stated this principle negatively: "What is assert-

93. Thomas Hobbes, *Works,* William Molesworth, ed. (London: n. p. 1839-1845), VI, p. 190.
94. LW 35, pp. 170-171; WA 16, p. 388.

ed without the Scriptures or proven revelation may be held as an opinion, but need not be believed."[95]

The principle of *sola scriptura* was intended to safeguard the authority of Scripture from that servile dependence upon the church which in fact made Scripture inferior to the church. Scripture is the *norma normans* (the determining norm) not a *norma normata* (determined norm) for all decisions of faith and life. Scripture is "the proper touchstone," the "Lydian stone by which I can tell black from white and evil from good."[96] The church, far from having priority over Scripture, is really the creation of Scripture, born in the womb of Scripture. "For who begets his own parent?" Luther asked. "Who first brings forth his own maker?"[97] Although the church approved the particular books included in the canon (about which Luther had some reservations, as we shall see), it was thereby merely bearing witness to the authenticity of Scripture, just as John the Baptist had pointed to Christ.

By placing the Bible above popes and councils was Luther cutting himself off from the tradition of the church? Not at all. He did reject the two-source theory of tradition, later advanced at the Council of Trent, that is, that alongside the tradition embodied in Scripture, there is *another*, extrabiblical, oral tradition deriving from Jesus' post-Easter instruction to the apostles, and passed down to succeeding generations by the magisterium of the church. At the same time, Luther did not simply throw out the preceding 1,500 years of church history. In his treatise against the Anabaptists (1528), he said:

> We do not act as fanatically as the *Schwärmer*. We do not reject everything that is under the dominion of the Pope. For in that event we should also reject the Christian church. Much Christian good is to be found in the papacy and from there it descended to us.[98]

Sola scriptura was not *nuda scriptura*. It was never simply a question of Scripture *or* tradition, Holy Writ *or* Holy Church. The sufficiency of Scripture functioned in the context where the Bible is regarded as the Book given to the church, the community of faith, which is gathered and guided by the Holy Spirit.

95. LW 36, p. 29; WA 6, p. 509: "Nam quod sine scripturis asseritur aut revelatione probata, opinari licet, credi non est necesse."

96. LW 24, pp. 177, 174; WA 45, p. 622.

97. LW 36, p. 107; WA 6, p. 561.

98. LW 40, p. 231; WA 26, p. 147: "Wir bekennen aber, das unter dem Papstum viel Christliches gutes, ia alles Christlich gut sei, und auch deselbs herkomen sei an uns."

We get a better sense of what Luther meant by this when we look at how he used church tradition. He retained the Apostles' Creed, along with the Nicene and Chalcedonian formulations. Although he personally disliked terms such as *homoousios* and *Trinity,* he defended their use against reformers like Martin Bucer who wanted to resort to strictly biblical language. Not that the creeds were supplements to Scripture or a competing authority alongside Scripture. Rather they protected the true intention of Scripture against heretical deviations. What Luther would not compromise was the touchstone quality of Scripture. All creeds, sayings of the Fathers, conciliar decisions must be judged by—and never sit in judgment upon—the "sure rule of God's word":

> Now if anyone of the saintly fathers can show that his interpretation is based on Scripture, and if Scripture proves that this is the way it should be interpreted, then the interpretation is right. If this is not the case, I must not believe him.[99]

Thus Luther argued for the coinherence of Scripture and tradition, Holy Writ and Holy Church, while never wavering in his commitment to the priority of the former.

Historians have frequently referred to the doctrine of *sola scriptura* as the *formal* principle of the Reformation, as compared to the *material* principle of *sola fide.*[100] This is an unfortunate term for it obscures the primary meaning of the Bible for Luther. Luther did not differ from the medieval tradition in his high regard for the inspiration and validity of the Bible. For him the Bible was "the Holy Spirit book," "the vehicle of the Spirit;" not only its words but even its phrases are inspired; while it was written by men, it is neither of men nor from men, but from God.[101] Luther's corpus is filled with lofty statements such as these. Yet they reveal nothing distinctive about Luther's view of Scripture for the scholastic theologians (especially the nominalists) and, indeed, Luther's contemporary opponents were in

---

99. LW 30, p. 166; WA 14, p. 31. On Luther's defense of the ancient creeds see Elert, pp. 185-236.

100. Cf. J. A. Dorner, *History of Protestant Theology* (New York: AMS Press, 1970; original ed., 1871), I, p. 220.

101. WA 48, p. 43; LW 30, p. 321; LW 35, p. 153. On Luther's doctrine of Scripture see Jaroslav Pelikan, *Luther the Expositor* (St. Louis: Concordia, 1959); Watson, pp. 149-189; A. Skevington Wood, *Captive to the Word* (Grand Rapids: Eerdmans, 1969); Jack Rogers and Donald McKim, *The Authority and Interpretation of the Bible* (New York: Harper and Row, 1979), pp. 73-88.

perfect agreement with him here.[102] For this reason Luther did not elevate Scripture to an article of faith in the Augsburg Confession.

What gave Luther's doctrine its unique reformational character was its radical Christocentric basis. As early as 1515, Luther was stessing the Christ-centeredness of Scripture: "He who would read the Bible must simply take heed that he does not err, for the Scripture may permit itself to be stretched and led, but let no one lead it according to his own inclinations but let him lead it to the source, that is, the cross of Christ. Then he will surely strike the center."[103] The great weakness of allegorical exegesis was precisely that it obscured the Christological witness of the plain, literal sense of Scripture. In reaction, Luther abandoned the traditional fourfold schema of interpretation in favor of what he called the "grammatical-historical sense." This is the correct and proper sense, according to Luther, because it "drives home Christ" (*Christum treibet*). Moreover, the Christocentric sense was plainly stated by Christ himself: Study the Scripture "so that in it you discover Me, Me."[104]

Christ is at once the center of Scripture and the Lord of Scripture. While all of Scripture treats of Christ, not all of Scripture speaks equally plainly about Christ. As a result Luther distinguished the letter and form of Scripture from its content: "In the words of Scripture you will find the swaddling clothes in which Christ lies. Simple and little are the swaddling clothes, but dear is the treasure, Christ, that lies in them."[105]

Luther's disdain for the Epistle of James is well known and further illustrates his fixation on Christ as the true and proper center of Scripture.[106] Luther, reading James through the eyes of Paul, found James's theology of

102. Cf. the following statement by William of Ockham: "Qui dicit aliquam partem novi vel veteris testamenti aliquod falsum asserere aut no esse recipiendum a Catholicis est haereticus et pertinax reputandus," *Dialogue,* 449. Cited in B. A. Gerrish, "Biblical Authority and the Continental Reformation," *Scottish Journal of Theology* 10 (1957), pp. 337-360.

103. Ibid.

104. WA 51, p. 2: "Ich wil euch aber ein wunderliche glos und deutung der heiligen Schrifft geben, die ihr noch nicht wisset, das ihr die Schrifft recht lesen und nicht irren moget, nemlich die: Sehet ihr nur zu, das ihr die augen leutert und recht auff thut und also inn der Schrifft studivet, das ihr Mich, Mich drinnen findet."

105. LW 35, p. 236; WA DB 8, p. 12.

106. LW 35, p. 317, p. 280, p. 398; WA TR 1, p. 194, cited in H. G. Haile, *Luther: An Experiment in Biography,* p. 332. On Luther's critical opinions concerning Scripture, see Reinhold Seeberg, *The History of Doctrines* (Grand Rapids, Mich.: Baker Book House, 1977), II: 299-301.

grace wanting. It was "really an epistle of straw," for it had "nothing of the nature of the gospel about it." "Away with James," he said. "I almost feel like throwing Jimmy into the stove, as the priest in Kalenberg did" (a reference to a local pastor who used the wooden statues of the apostles for firewood on occasion). "It is flatly against St. Paul and all the rest of Scripture in ascribing justification to works."[107] Luther then did not read the Bible univocally. He found, we might say, a canon within the canon by which the whole text of Holy Writ was to be evaluated. Put otherwise, while no one may sit in judgment on the Scripture, Scripture itself is its own critic. "Whatever does not teach Christ is not apostolic, even though St. Peter or St. Paul does the teaching. Again, whatever preaches Christ would be apostolic, even if Judas, Annas, Pilate, and Herod were doing it."[108] By "teaching Christ" Luther meant, of course, much more than merely mentioning Christ or presenting Him as a worth exemplar. James does that! Rather Luther had in mind the clear proclamation of Christ as the Savior of sinners, the gospel, the good news that God has redeemed fallen humanity through the cross of Christ. This is what Paul did so consistently, and therefore Luther found Paul's books, especially Romans, to be "the daily bread of the soul"[109] Even so, Luther did not simply excise James from his Bible. He placed it, along with Hebrews, Jude, and Revelation, (Erasmus, too, had doubts about their canonicity) at the end of his Bible, in a sort of limbo between the apocryphal books, which he rejected outright, and "the true and certain chief books" which proclaimed Christ more clearly."[110]

The upshot of this discussion is obvious: Luther's view of the Bible has much closer bonds with his doctrine of the incarnation than with any theory of inspiration. Holy Scripture is God's Word clad in human words, "inlettered," Luther said, "just as Christ, the eternal Word of God, is incarnate in the garment of his humanity."[111] Christ ever remains the Lord of Scripture, which is a means to faith but not an object of faith. Just as "within

---

107. LW 35, pp. 362, 396; WA DB 7, p. 385; LW 34, p. 317. Cf. Althaus, p. 81, 31n. For a fuller discussion of Luther's views on James, see Timothy George, " 'A Right Strawy Epistle': Reformation Perspectives on James," *Review and Expositor* 83 (1986), pp. 369-382.

108. LW 35, p. 396; WA DB 7, p. 385.

109. LW 35, p. 365; WA DB 7, p. 3.

110. LW 35, p. 394; WA DB 7, p. 345.

111. WA 48, p. 31: "Die heilige Schrifft ist Gottes wort, geschrieben und (das ich so rede) gebuchstabet und in buchstaben gebildet, Gleich wie Christus ist das ewige Gottes wort, in die menscheit verhullet, Und gleich wie Christus in der Welt gehalten und gehandelt ist, so gehets dem schrifftlichen Gottes wort auch."

that simple basket of reeds, patched with clay, pitch, and such thing . . . there lies a beautiful living boy, like Moses, even so, Christ lies in the crib, wrapped in swaddling clothes."[112] In this way the formal principle of the Reformation is determined by the material principle: Justification by faith alone based upon the grace and work of Christ alone is the key to understanding God's revelation in Scripture alone.

When saying that Scripture must "drive home" or "inculcate" (*trieben*) Christ, Luther was not thinking of any formal theory of the Bible at all, not even of a properly Christological one. Rather he had in mind that quality of Scripture in which the living and true God always confronts the reader in judgment and grace. "God's Word is living. That means that it makes alive those who believe it. Therefore we must rightly hasten to it before we perish and die."[113] Luther knew nothing of a purely objective, disinterested, or scholarly knowledge of the Bible. Such a knowledge, even if it were possible, would only be the dead letter which kills. The Spirit makes alive! We must therefore "feel" the words of Scripture "in the heart." Experience is necessary for the understanding of the Word. It is not merely to be repeated or known, but to be lived and felt.[114]

This living character of the Word is seen in the way Luther contemporized the biblical text. Just as God is not merely "there" (*da*) but "there for thee" (*dir da*), so, too, the stories in the Bible are not simply historical acts, back there and then, but living events, here and now. Luther called for imaginative participation in the biblical stories, as we see in his treatment of Gideon: "How difficult it was for [Gideon] to fight the enemy at those odds. If I had been there, I'd have befouled my breeches for fright."[115] The distance between the ancient people of God and the contemporary believer collapses before the timeless Word of God. This is not to lessen the historical reality of the biblical event—remember Luther's insistence on the grammatical-historical sense—but to confront every reader with the existential demand and promise of Scripture which requires a present response.

112. WA 10/1, p. 15.

113. Atkinson, p. 94.

114. B. A. Gerrish develops this point in *The Old Protestantism and the New* (Chicago: University of Chicago Press, 1982), pp. 53-58. Cf. WA TR 1, p. 340: "Non solum scriptura . . . sed etiam experientia . . . Habeo rem et experientiam cum Scriptura."

115. WA TR 1, p. 136: "Wenn ich da wer gewest, het ich fur furcht in die hosen geschissen." LW 54, pp. 46-47. This quotation from the *Table Talk* comes in the context of Luther's rejection of allegorization in favor of a literal historical interpretation of the Bible.

Nowhere was Luther better in pulling off this kind of confrontational exegesis than in his treatment of the Psalms. Here the whole range of human emotions is present and the response of the believer to God's message made explicit. In a sermon on the phrase "I called upon the Lord" (Ps. 118:5), Luther admonished his congregation:

> *Call* is what you have to learn. You heard it. Don't just sit there by yourself or off to one side and hang your head, and shake it and gnaw your knuckles and worry and look for a way out, nothing on your mind except how bad *you* feel, how *you* hurt, what a poor guy you are. Get up, you lazy scamp! Down on your knees! Up with your hands and eyes toward heaven! Use a psalm or the Lord's prayer to cry out your distress to the Lord.[116]

Holy Scripture thus reminds us that all of life is lived in the presence of God. It is the inspired testimony of God's perfect revelation of Himself in Jesus Christ and the Christian's daily handbook in the struggles and triumphs of faith.

"To Me She's Dear, the Worthy Maid": Luther on the Church

The last thing in the world Luther wanted to do was start a new church. He was not an innovator but a reformer. He never considered himself anything other than a true and faithful member of the one, holy, catholic, apostolic church. As a doctor of Holy Scripture and as a pastor of souls, Luther protested the abuse of indulgences (the Ninety-five Theses of 1517) and was catapulted into a major confrontation with the Roman Church of his day. In the course of that struggle, he issued a decisive *no* to the entire papal system. He denounced the pope as Antichrist, referred to the Roman hierarchy as the "whore-church of the devil," and burned the whole corpus of canon law as well as the papal bull which had excommunicated him.[117] These were radical acts. They provoked a schism in Western Christendom which has not yet been healed. Luther, however, was no mere iconoclast. He revolted against the church for the sake of the church, against a corrupt church for the sake of the "true, ancient church, one body and one communion of saints with the holy, universal, Christian church."[118]

Far from being a champion of rugged individualism—every tub sitting on its own bottom—Luther stressed the communal character of Christian-

116. WA 31, p. 1. Cited in Haile, p. 65.
117. LW 41, p. 219; WA 51, p. 523. On the steps which led to this decisive break, see the definitive study by Scott H. Hendrix, *Luther and the Papacy* (Philadelphia: Fortress Press, 1981).
118. LW 41, p. 119; WA 51, p. 487.

ity. "The Christian church is your mother," Luther said, "who gives birth to you and bears you through the Word."[119] He also called the church "my fortress, my castle, my chamber." He said, echoing Cyprian, that outside the church there was no salvation. Luther could be lyrical in praising the church, as in this hymn of 1535 which sounds very much like a secular love song:

> To me she's dear, the worthy maid,
> And I cannot forget her;
> Praise, honor, virtue of her are said;
> Then all I love her better.
> I seek her good, And if I should Right evil fare,
> I do not care, She'll make up for it to me,
> With love and truth that will not tire,
> Which she will ever show me;
> And do all my desire.[120]

But what exactly is the church? Luther once responded impatiently to this question: "Why, a seven-year-old child knows what the church is, namely, holy believers and sheep who hear the voice of their Shepherd."[121] We have in this answer a major thrust of Luther's ecclesiology: the essentially spiritual, noninstitutional character of the church. Luther disliked the German word *Kirche* (which, like *church* in English, or *curia* in Latin, derives from the Greek *kuriakon,* the Lord's house) because it had come to mean the building or the institution. He preferred *Gemeine,* "community" or *Versammlung,* "assembly." For him the true church was the people of God, the fellowship of believers, or, as the Apostles' Creed has it, the communion of saints. From this perspective Luther developed a richly nuanced doctrine of the church. We must examine more closely three facets of this doctrine: (1) the priority of the gospel, (2) Word and sacrament, (3) priesthood of all believers.[122]

119. LW 51, p. 166. Cf. LW 26, p. 441.

120. LW 53, p. 293. This hymn is based on the text in Revelation 12:1-2 which describes a woman suffering in childbirth. Luther interpreted this as the church under assault by Satan. The third stanza of the hymn concludes: "On earth, all mad with murder, The mother now alone is she, But God will watchful guard her, And the right Father be."

121. T. G. Tappert, ed., *The Book of Concord* (Philadelphia: Fortress Press, 1949), p. 315.

122. Among the many studies of Luther's ecclesiology, see esp. the following: Karl Holl, "Die Entstehung von Luthers Kirchenbegriff," *Gesammelte Aufsätze zur*

The Priority of the Gospel

Luther had once been, as he put it, "a most enthusiastic papist" ready to gather wood for the burning of any heretic who slandered the mass, celibacy, or the pope.[123] Luther's disillusionment with the papacy evolved out of his discovery of the gospel based on his study of the Bible. As late as 1521, though he had identified the papacy and its priesthood with "the kingdom of the devil and the rule of Antichrist," he still urged that no one deliberately oppose the pope. The papacy was a plague, a punishment, permitted by God's "angry providence"; it was to be endured with all patience.[124] As he grew older his polemic against Rome became sharper. He referred to Pope Paul III as "His Hellishness." Were not the pope and his associates at least members of the church? Yes, as much as spit, snot, pus, feces, urine, stench, scab, smallpox, ulcers, and syphillis are members of the body. Luther was never one to mince words. But we must remember that he had the same kind of invective cast in his teeth. From at least 1520 on, he persistently refused to identify the true church with the papal hierarchy.

> From this then you can answer the screamers and spitters who have nothing in their grabs but "church!": Tell me, dear pope, what is the church? Answer: the pope and his cardinals. Oh, listen to that, you dunce, where is it written in God's Word that Father Pope and Brother Cardinal are the true church? Was it because that was what the fine parrot bird said to the black jackdaw?[125]

Luther's protest against the Roman Church was not primarily moral, as was that of Erasmus and other reformers, but rather theological. God's grace was *God's* grace. It could not be bought, sold, or parceled out in indulgences. "If the pope had control over the souls in purgatory, why doesn't he open the gate and let them all out?" Luther quipped. The papacy, which was of human not divine origin, had arrogated to itself a prerogative which belonged to God alone. The church had become an end unto itself. The Word had become captive to the whims of mere humans. Against the Roman conception of the church Luther stressed the priority of the gospel.

Kirchengeschichte (Tübingen: J.C.B. Mohr, 1948), I, pp. 288-325; Wilhelm Pauck, *The Heritage of the Reformation* (London: Oxford University Press, 1950), pp. 29-59; Elert, pp. 255-402; Scott H. Hendrix, *Ecclesia in via: Ecclesiological Developments in the Medieval Psalms Exegesis and the Dictata super Psalterium of Martin Luther* (Leiden: E. J. Brill, 1974).
    123. LW 34, p. 328; WA 54, pp. 179-180.
    124. LW 39, pp. 210, 101; WA 7, p. 676; 6, p. 321.
    125. LW 51, p. 311; WA 47, p. 778.

Luther insisted that the gospel was constitutive for the church, not the church for the gospel. "The true treasure of the church is the holy gospel of the glory and the grace of God."[126] Like Augustine, Wyclif, and Hus before him, Luther talked about the invisible church whose membership comprised the whole company of the predestined. The church is extended in time as well as space, not bound to any one city, person, or age. Its foundation is God's gracious election revealed in Jesus Christ and attested by Holy Scripture: "The church does not constitute the Word of God, but is constituted by the Word."[127] Its invisibility derives from the fact that faith itself is invisible, "the evidence of things not seen" (Heb. 11:1). If faith were a measurable quantity, we could identify the church by its outward characteristics. But because faith as the radical gift of God is not definable in external terms, the church too is not a physical assembly, but "an assembly of hearts in one faith."[128]

In addition to "invisible," Luther also spoke of the church as "hidden." This is a more complex concept and carries several connotations. It means first of all that the church, while manifest to God, is hidden from the world. In a daring metaphor Luther said that God does not want the world to know when He sleeps with His bride.[129] To the eyes of faith the church is a "worthy maid," but by the standards of the world she is a poor Cinderella beset by numerous dangerous foes:

> If, then, a person desires to draw the church as he sees her, he will picture her as a deformed and poor girl sitting in an unsafe forest in the midst of hungry lions, bears, wolves, and boars, nay, deadly serpents; in the midst of infuriated men who set sword, fire, and water in motion in order to kill her and wipe her from the face of the earth.[130]

126. WA 1, p. 236: "Verus thesaurus ecclesie est sacrosanctum evangelium glorie et gratie dei." This is the sixty-second of the Ninety-five Theses. LW 31, p. 31.

127. WA 8, p. 491; LW 36, p. 145.

128. LW 39, p. 65; WA 6, p. 293: "Also das der Christenheit wesen, leben und natur sei nit leiplich vorsamlung, sondern ein vorsamlung der hertzen in einem glauben."

129. WA 17/2, p. 501: "Denn Got wil die welt nichtt lassen wissen, wenn er bei seiner braut schlafft."

130. WA 40/3, p. 315: "Itaque si, ut videt eam, ita pingere eam velit, pinget deformem et pauperculam puellam, sedentem in infesto nemore, in medio famelicorum leonum, ursorum, luporum, porcorum, denique serpentum venenatorum; item in medio furiosorum hominum, admoventium ferrum, ignem, aquam ad occidendam eam et tollendam de terra."

As there can be no theology of glory, so neither can there be any ecclesiology of glory. Among the seven "holy possessions" of the church, Luther included the "sacred cross."[131] The church always exists in tension with the demonic powers of this present aeon and, like her Lord, must ever be willing to endure every misfortune and persecution.

The hiddenness of the church also extends to its holiness. Unlike the Anabaptists, Luther never espoused a pure church composed only of discernible saints. In this age the church is a *corpus permixtum* containing at once sinners and saints, hypocrites and devout believers, tares and wheat. The purity of the church is not subject to examination, nor does it depend on the moral qualifications of the members or the ministers. "Our holiness is in heaven, where Christ is; it is not in the world, before the eyes of men, like a commodity on the market."[132]

Luther was sure that the true church had never ceased to exist, even though at times its numbers may have been meager—"only two or three, or children."[133] The continuity of the church he located not in a succession of bishops, but in a succession of true believers (*successio fidelium*) reaching all the way back to Adam: "There is always a holy Christian people on earth in whom Christ lives, works, and rules."[134] Again, the church is subservient to the gospel: God's Word cannot be without God's people, nor his people without His Word. Even in the apostate Church of Rome, Luther conceded, the gospel had not been entirely obliterated. Baptism and the Scriptures at least remained, and this sustained the young children and "some old people, but only a few" who at the end of their lives turned once more to Christ.[135]

Word and Sacrament

It seemed to some that Luther's emphasis on the hidden, invisible character of the church would undermine its tangible, historical reality. However, Luther intended neither to dissolve the church into a fairy castle in the clouds, nor to reduce it to a loose-knit association of like-minded individuals. The gospel remained the sole, infallible mark of the church, but the gospel in a particular sense, as it was manifested in the Word rightly preached and the sacraments rightly administered. Wherever these two

131. LW 41, p. 164; WA 50, p. 642.
132. LW 35, p. 411; WA DB 7, p. 420.
133. LW 41, p. 147; WA 50, p. 627.
134. LW 41, p. 144; WA 50, p. 625.
135. LW 41, p. 210; WA 51, p. 506.

"notes" are evident, the true church exists, even if it is composed only of children in the cradle.

Public preaching of the Word of God is an indispensable means of grace and a sure sign of the true church. Through the words of the preacher, the living voice of the gospel (*viva vox evangelii*) is heard. For Luther the church was not a "pen house" but a "mouth house":

> It is the manner of the New Testament and of the gospel that it must be preached and performed by word of mouth and a living voice. Christ himself has not written anything, nor has he ordered anything to be written, but rather to be preached by word of mouth.[136]

Luther recovered the Pauline doctrine of proclamation: Faith comes by hearing, hearing by the Word of God. But how shall they hear without a preacher? (Rom. 10:17). Luther did not invent preaching, but he did elevate it to a new status in Christian worship. He thought it significant that even the common folk spoke of going to church to *hear* Mass, not to see it. The sermon was the best and most necessary part of the Mass. Luther invested it with an almost sacramental quality and made it the central focus of the liturgy. "To hear mass means nothing else but to hear God's Word and thereby serve God."[137] Protestant worship centered around the pulpit and open Bible with the preacher facing the congregation, not around an altar with the priest performing a semisecret ritual. So important was the preaching office that even those church members under the ban were not be excluded from its benefits: "The Word of God shall remain free, to be heard by everyone."[138]

The one who is entrusted with the spoken Word in the community of faith is beset with many temptations. Many use this sacred trust for self-aggrandizement. Yet "Christ did not establish and institute the ministry of proclamation to provide us with money, property, popularity, honor, or friendship."[139] Some preachers are afraid of speaking harsh words of judgment lest they offend the "big shots" who sit in their congregation. Such preachers are really hirelings who "jabber in the pulpit" but who do not proclaim the truth because they love their belly and this temporal life more than Christ. Perhaps the most searing temptation a preacher faces is that

136. WA 10/1, p. 48. On Luther as a preacher, see Wood, pp. 85-94, and John Doberstein's introduction to vol. 51 of *Luther's Works*.

137. LW 51, p. 262; WA 36, p. 354.

138. LW 39, p. 22; WA 6, p. 75.

139. LW 21, p. 9; WA 32, p. 304.

of vainglory. "May God protect us against the preachers who please all people and enjoy a good testimony from everybody," said Luther.[140] Preachers must beware of flatterers who tickle their vanity, for soon they will be saying to themselves: "This you have done, this is your work, you are the first-rate man, the real master." That isn't even worth throwing to the dogs! Faithful preachers should teach only the Word of God and seek only his honor and praise. "Likewise, the hearers should also say: 'I do not believe in my pastor, but he tells me of another Lord whose name is Christ; him he shows me.' "[141]

Luther's writings are full of advice for aspiring preachers. The three marks of a good preachers are these: He stands up, speaks up, and knows when to shut up![142] Let him speak forth vigorously and clearly, not as though he had a leaf in front of his mouth. The church is a mouth house, not a mealy mouth house! More important, the preacher should have something worth saying. Let the preacher be a *bonus textualis* —a good one with the text—well versed in the Scriptures.[143] Luther excoriated those "lazy, no good" preachers who get all their material from others, from homiletical helps and sermon books, without praying, reading, and searching the Scriptures for themselves.[144] The sermon should not be couched in theological jargon, but in the clear, crisp language of the people. "I do not preach to Drs. Pomeranus, Jonas, and Philipp," said Luther, "but to my little Hans and Elizabeth."[145] Above all, preaching must be true to its proper content, which is Christ. Only in this way can it fulfill its role as the main part of all divine service.

Alongside the Word rightly preached are the sacraments rightly administered. In *The Babylonian Captivity of the Church* (1520), Luther attacked the sacramental system of medieval Catholicism, keeping as authentic only two sacraments: baptism and holy communion. (For a while he retained penance, but later rejected it also because, although instituted by Christ, it lacked the necessary accompanying sign.) These two acts share in common

140. WA 28, p. 530.

141. LW 51, p. 388; WA 51, p. 191.

142. WA 32, p. 302; LW 21, p. 7.

143. WA TR 4, p. 356: "Nam qui est solidus in fundamentis et bonus textualis, ille non facile impingit."

144. WA 53, p. 218.

145. WA TR 3, p. 310: "Ich wil Doctorem Pommeranum, Ionam, Philippum in meiner predigt nicht wissen, den sie wissens vorkin dass den ich. Ich predige ihnen auch nicht, sondern meinem Henslein und Elslein."

the following features: (1) They both proclaim the forgiveness of sins, (2) they are not efficacious in their being celebrated but in their being believed in, and (3) they are extensions or separate instances of the Word of God and so convey to the church the unfailing promises of God. There is thus the "closest possible relation between the preached Word and the Word enacted in the sacraments, that is, the 'visible words of God.' "

Just as the gospel is prior to the church, so the sacraments are consequent to faith. Luther attacked the "mechanical" doctrine of the sacraments, that is, the idea that the sacraments by virtue of their being performed (*ex opere operato*) conveyed grace to everyone not in a state of mortal sin. No, the sacraments are a word of address from God. They must be personally received, believed, and appropriated. Luther held that faith even apart from the sacraments could suffice for salvation: "You can believe even though you are not baptized, for baptism is nothing more than an external sign which reminds us of the divine promise."[146] Luther made this statement in reaction to Roman Catholic sacramentalism. He retained nonetheless a high view of the objective character of the sacraments. Baptism and holy communion are assurances of God's promise and, in this sense, completely independent of the recipient's disposition. Gold jewelry loses none of its purity of metal when worn by a harlot! In the same way, the efficacy of the sacraments does not depend on the worthiness of the presiding minister. The holiness of the sacraments, like that of the church, resides in Christ, not in the administrant, so that "even if Judas, Caiaphas, Pilate, the pope, or the devil himself baptized truly, they would still receive the true, holy baptism."[147]

But why do we need sacraments at all? This question was constantly put to Luther by the radical spiritualists who so stressed the "inner word" that they abandoned all external evidences of God's grace. Luther's best answer to this question comes from his powerful "Sermon on Preparation for Dying" (1519) in which he declared a sacrament to be

> a visible sign of divine intent. We must cling to them with a staunch faith as to the good staff which the patriarch Jacob used when crossing the Jordan [Gen. 32:10], or as to a lantern by which we must be guided, and carefully walk with open eyes the dark path of death, sin, and hell . . . . It points to Christ and his image, enabling you to say when faced by the image of death,

146. WA 10/3, p. 142: "Es kan auch ainer glauben, wenn er gleich nit getaufftt ist, dann der tauff ist nit meer dann ain eüsserlich zaichen." This idea was specifically condemned at the Council of Trent.

147. LW 41, p. 218; WA 51, p. 521.

sin, and hell, "God promised and in his sacraments he gave me a sure sign of his grace . . . . This sign and promise of my salvation will not lie to me or deceive me. It is God who has promised it, and he cannot lie."[148]

To Luther the sacraments were, as Heinrich Bornkamm has put it, "tall guideposts along life's highway," reminders in life and death of God's unfailing promise and sustaining grace.[149]

We shall discuss Luther's eucharistic theology in the context of his debate with Zwingli. We must now look at the salient features of his doctrine of baptism. In his *Small Catechism* Luther asked, "What does Baptism give or profit?" Answer: "It works forgiveness of sins, delivers from death and the devil, and gives eternal salvation to all who believe this."[150] He went on to explain that the water itself does not have this power, but the Word of God which is in and with the water and faith which trusts such word in the water. Baptism is the liturgical enactment of Luther's doctrine of justification by faith alone. Performed in the name of the Triune God, baptism is a divine act. God is the Doer in baptism, the minister merely God's agent. In baptism God announces His gracious acceptance of the sinner, for those who receive baptism in faith are none other than those who have been bathed and cleansed in "the beautiful, rosy-red blood of Christ."[151]

Luther, along with all the mainline reformers, defended infant baptism against the Anabaptists. His arguments were various. While Scripture does not explicitly command infant baptism, neither does it forbid it. How could God have allowed the church to be so long deceived about such a vital matter? Infant baptism is analogous to circumcision in the Old Testament; both are seals of God's promise to His people. The knottiest problem with infant baptism derived from Luther's strict correlation of sacrament and faith. How can unreasoning infants believe? Luther met this objection with his singular concept of infant faith. "To be sure, children are brought to baptism by the faith and work of others; but when they get there and the pastor baptizes them in Christ's stead, it is Christ who blesses them and grants them faith and the kingdom of heaven."[152] Faith, so to speak, is imputed to the infant in baptism even though he is not aware of it. This is all the more a confirmation of God's gratuitous mercy since the infant is

148. LW 42, pp. 108-109; WA 2, p. 693.
149. Heinrich Bornkamm, *Luther's World of Thought,* Martin H. Bertram, trans. (St. Louis: Concordia Publishing House, 1958), p. 97.
150. WA 30/1, p. 285.
151. LW 51, pp. 325-326; WA 49, p. 131.
152. WA 17/2, p. 83.

helpless to effect his own baptism. He can only receive it as a sheer gift, *sola gratia*. Luther rejected the idea, widely believed in the Middle Ages, that unbaptized babies went to limbo, the upper level of hell which, though not a place of severe torment, was their eternal home. Thus in the case of miscarriage, water should not be sprinkled on the abdomen of the mother. Rather the endangered infant should be committed to God in prayer. Luther believed in the salvation of unborn and unbaptized infants, although he was reluctant to preach this publicly lest the common folk grow lax in bringing their children to the baptismal font.[153]

Although baptism is a one-time event, its salvific effect sustains the Christian throughout life. We are both "drowned" and given new life in baptism, and to this condition we must constantly return. The "Christian life is nothing else than a daily baptism, once begun and constantly lived in."[154] There is the closest possible relationship between baptism and repentance. We recall the first of Luther's *Ninety-five Theses,* that the Christian's whole life was one of repentance and turning to God. To repent means to return to the power of our baptism. In this sense Luther declared that "we need continually to be baptized more and more" until in death we actually fulfill the sign of baptism. Luther found great solace in the fact that everyone—pope, bishop, and peasant alike—was both baptized naked and died naked. Luther himself died in the same town where he had been born and baptized. Once when he was plagued with doubts about predestination, Luther exclaimed: "I am a son of God. I have been baptized. Let me alone, devil."[155] In birth and death, and in the dark mystery of life in between, our baptism stands as the pledge of God's great love and grace.

Priesthood of All Believers

Luther's greatest contribution to Protestant ecclesiology was his doctrine of the priesthood of all believers. Yet no element in his teaching is more misunderstood. For some it means simply that there are no priests in the church, the secularization of the clergy. From this premise some groups, notably the Quakers, have argued the abolition of the ministry as a distinct

153. WA 53, pp. 203-207. Cf. Jaroslav Pelikan, "Luther's Defense of Infant Baptism," *Luther for an Ecumenical Age,* Carl S. Meyer, ed. (St. Louis: Concordia, 1967), pp. 200-218. On Luther versus the Anabaptists, see John S. Oyer, *Lutheran Reformers Against Anabaptists* (The Hague: Nijhoff, 1964).

154. WA 30/1, p. 220: "Ein Christlich leben nichts anders ist denn ein tegliche Tauffe, ein mal angefangen und immer darin gegangen."

155. Tappert, *Letters,* p. 134.

order within the church. More commonly people believe that the priesthood
of all believers implies that every Christian is his or her own priest and
hence possesses the "right of private judgment" in matters of faith and
doctrine. Both of these are modern perversions of Luther's original intention. The essence of his doctrine can be put in one sentence: Every Christian
is someone else's priest, and we are all priests to one another.

Luther broke decisively with the traditional division of the church into
two classes, clergy and laity. Every Christian is a priest by virtue of his
baptism. This priesthood derives directly from Christ: "We are priests as
he is Priest, sons as he is Son, kings as he is King."[156] Moreover every
member of the *Gemeine* has an equal share in this priesthood. This means
that the priestly offices are the common property of all Christians, not the
special prerogative of a select caste of holy men. Luther listed seven rights
which belong to the whole church: to preach the Word of God, to baptize,
to celebrate Holy Communion, to bear "the keys," to pray for others, to
sacrifice, to judge doctrine.[157] Luther based his claim that all Christians are
priests in equal degree on two New Testament texts, "You are . . . a royal
priesthood" (1 Pet. 2:9) and "Thou hast made them a kingdom and priests"
(Rev. 1:6).

The priesthood of all believers is a responsibility as well as a privilege,
a service as well as a status. God has made us one body, one "cake" (a
favorite image of Luther). Our unity and equality in Christ is demonstrated
by our mutual love and care for one another. "The fact that we are all priests
and kings means that each of us Christians may go before God and intercede
for the other. If I notice that you have no faith or a weak faith, I can ask
God to give you a strong faith."[158]

All of this means that no one can be a Christian alone. Just as we cannot
give birth to ourselves, or baptize ourselves, so neither can we serve God
alone. Here we touch on Luther's other great definition of the church:
communio sanctorum, a community of saints. But who are the saints? They
are not super-Christians who have been elevated to heavenly glory, on
whose "merits" we can draw for help along life's way. All who believe in
Christ are saints. As Paul Althaus said, "Luther brought down the community of saints out of heaven and down to earth."[159]

Whatever it is that you want to do for the saints, turn your attention away

156. LW 40, p. 20; WA 12, p. 179.
157. LW 40, pp. 21-32; WA 12, p. 180.
158. WA 10/3, pp. 308-309. Cf. the discussion in Althaus, pp. 297-303.
159. Althaus, p. 298.

from the dead toward the living. The living saints are your neighbors, the naked, the hungry, the thirsty, the poor people who have wives and children and suffer shame. Direct your help toward them, begin your work here.[160]

A community of intercessors, a priesthood of fellow helpers, a family of mutual sharers and burden-bearers, this is the *communio sanctorum.*

How did Luther relate the priesthood of all believers to the office of the ministry? While all Christians have an equal share in the treasures of the church, including the sacraments, not everyone can be a preacher, teacher, or counselor. There is one common "estate" (*Stand*) but a variety of offices (*Amte*) and functions.

Luther regarded the ministry of the Word as the highest office in the church. The very title, "servant of the divine Word" (*minister verbi divini*), connotes an essentially functional role. Strictly speaking, Luther taught every Christian is a minister and has the right to preach. This right may be freely exercised if one is in the midst of non-Christians, among the Turks, or stranded on a pagan island. However, in a Christian community one should not "draw attention to himself " by assuming this office on his own. Rather he should "let himself be called and chosen to preach and to teach in the place of and by the command of the others."[161] The call is issued through the congregation and the minister remains accountable to the congregation. Luther went so far as to say: What we give him today we can take away from him tomorrow.[162] The rite of ordination confers no indelible character on the ordained. It is merely the public means by which one is commissioned through prayer, Scripture, and the laying on of hands to serve the congregation. Arguing curiously from natural law, Luther excluded women, children, and incompetent persons from the official ministry of the church, although in times of emergency he would have allowed these to fill this office by virtue of their share in the priesthood of all believers.

The exigencies of the Reformation did not conform to Luther's early congregationalism. If the church were to be reformed, the governing authorities had to play a role. Luther referred to the prince as a *Notbischof,* an emergency bishop. Through the institution of the visitation, the territorial prince assumed a larger role in the affairs of the church. Eventually a network of state churches emerged in Germany. This arrangement was given legal sanction by the Peace of Augsburg (1555) which recognized the

160. WA 10/3, p. 407.

161. LW 39, p. 310; WA 11, p. 412.

162. WA 15, p. 721: "Item debent ministerium suum agere, sed non perpetuo: possumus ei hodie commendare, cras iterum adimere." Cf. Elert, p. 347.

religion of the prince as determinative for that of his subjects. Luther saw the dangers as well as the benefits of the state church system. In the doctrine of the two kingdoms, he sought to make clear the proper roles of church and secular authority.

"The Left Hand of God": Luther on the State

Luther, Zwingli, Calvin, and Cranmer were all *magisterial* reformers. This term, coined by George H. Williams, refers to the fact that all of the mainline reformers carried out their reformatory work in alliance with and undergirded by the coercive power of the magistrate, whether it be prince, town council, or, as in the case of England, the monarch himself. (Henry VIII, a mere layman, claimed to be "Head" of the Church of England.) The radical reformers, with few exceptions, renounced this *modus reformandi* and thus broke more decisively with the traditional concept of Christendom as an all-encompassing, unitary society, defined by the interplay of temporal and spiritual authorities. Menno Simons, for example, represents the Anabaptist rejection of the "official" Reformation. Nonetheless the mainline reformers themselves were not of the same mind concerning the nature, purpose, and limit of civil power. A major difference between the Lutheran and Reformed traditions emerges at this point.

Luther developed his theory of the state in relation to his doctrine of the two kingdoms.

> For God has established two kinds of government among men. The one is spiritual; it has no sword, but it has the word, by means of which men are to become good and righteous, so that with this righteousness they may attain eternal life. He administers this righteousness through the word, which he has committed to the preachers. The other kind is worldly government, which works through the sword so that those who do not want to be good and righteous to eternal life may be forced to become good and righteous in the eyes of the world. He administers this righteousness through the sword.[163]

163. LW 46, p. 99; WA 19, p. 629. Luther's basic writing on the state are *To the Christian Nobility of the German Nation* (1520), *Temporal Authority: To What Extent It Should be Obeyed* (1523), and *Whether Soldiers, Too, Can be Saved* (1526). On the two kingdoms doctrine see Rupp, *Righteousness,* pp. 286-309; Paul Althaus, *The Ethics of Luther* (Philadelphia: Fortress Press, 1972); F. Edward Cranz, *An Essay on the Development of Luther's Thought on Justice, Law, and Society* (Cambridge, Mass.: Harvard University Press, 1959); Marc Lienhard, "La 'doctrine' lutherienne des deux regnes et sa fonction critique," *Istina* 17 (1972), pp. 157-172; John R. Stephenson, "The Two Governments and the Two Kingdoms in Luther's Thought," *Scottish Journal of Theology* 34 (1981), pp. 321-337.

The idea of two correlate powers through which God governs the world goes back to Augustine, who divided the human family into two cities: the City of God, composed of the elect, on pilgrimage toward its heavenly destiny, and the City of Earth, also called the City of the Devil, whose inhabitants exist outside of the sphere of grace. In the present aeon, however, the two cities are intermingled. The course of history is thus determined by their coexistence and opposition.

Luther hammered out his own, doctrine of the two kingdoms in opposition to two counter theories: medieval Catholicism and Anabaptism. Papal supremacy over secular rulers was asserted as early as 494 by Pope Gelasius I in a letter to the Emperor Anastasius: "There are, august emperor, two means by which this world is chiefly ruled, the sacred authority of the priesthood and the royal power. Of these the responsibility of the priests is more weighty . . . "[164] What has been called the "runaway inflation of papal claims" during the millennium which separated Luther from Gelasius I can be traced in the dictates of Gregory VII, Innocent III, and Boniface VIII. In the bull *Unam Sanctam* (1302) Boniface asserted that since both temporal and spiritual authority resided in the church the pope had the right to depose secular rulers when they went counter to his will. Against this tradition Luther proclaimed the independence of the secular realm from clerical control. The distinction between the two is crucial: "The Devil himself never ceases cooking and brewing up the two kingdoms together."[165] A major cause of abuses in the church was that the pope refused to "take his fingers out of the pie" of temporal lordship. The pope should have had no authority over the emperor or other secular rulers. He was not a vicar of Christ glorified, but of Christ crucified; his office was not to rule nations but to preach the gospel.[166]

If the Catholics confused the two realms in the direction of papal theocracy, the Anabaptists too sharply separated the realms in the name of religious separatism. Taking literally Christ's injunction to nonresistance (Matt. 5: 39), the Anabaptists refused to participate in the coercive powers of the state. In confrontation with the pacificist reformers, Luther stressed the

164. Pope Gelasius I in a letter to Emperor Anastasius quoted in Brian Tierney, ed., *The Crisis of Church and State* (Englewood Cliffs, N.J.: Prentice-Hall, 1964), p. 13.

165. WA 51, p. 239; LW 13, p. 194.

166. Martin Luther, *Three Treatises* (Philadelphia: Fortress Press, 1970), pp. 53-56.

divine origin of the state, the limits of its power, and the basis for Christian participation in its coercive activity.

Basing his beliefs on Romans 13 and 1 Peter 2:13-14, Luther held that the state was ordained by God primarily to restrain evildoers, to preserve peace and order in the world. If the whole world were composed of Christians, there would be no need for prince, king, sword, or law. However, since "among thousands there is scarcely a single true Christian," the state is necessary to prevent the world from being reduced to chaos.[167] The temporal rulers were "God's jailers and executioners."[168] From this perspective the doctrine of the two kingdoms represents not so much an ethical dualism, the realm of Satan versus the realm of God, as a twofold means by which God's sovereignty is effected within history. Luther used different metaphors to describe these two modes of God's rule. The kingdom of Christ, the church, is "the right hand of God," the worldly kingdom, the state, is "the left hand of God."[169] Again, the secular ruler is a "mask of God" (*larva Dei*) through which God, in disguise as it were, governs the world. Indeed, Luther said that it was not humans, but God, who hanged, tortured, beheaded, killed, and fought! From these images we gather two important conclusions concerning the state: (1) The origin of the state lies neither in an autonomous will to power nor in the consent of the governed, but in God's ordained will. (2) Church and state, the kingdoms of right and left hands, coexist in a necessary tension. The distinction between them must not be blurred, but neither must it be so sharply drawn that neither reinforces the other.

Christians then are in an ambiguous position: They find themselves citizens of both kingdoms. Luther urged Christians to accept civic responsibility (so long as it did not violate the claims of Christ) for the sake of the neighbor. This mandate extended even to those manifestly violent offices of the sword: "If you see that there is a lack of hangmen, constables, judges, lords, princes, and you find that you are qualified, you should offer your services and seek the position. . . ."[170] In *Whether Soldiers, Too, Can Be Saved* (1526), Luther applied the same injunction to the military vocation. This, however, was not a counsel to servile obedience. If the soldier knew that his lord was wrong in going to war, he could conscientiously abstain from fighting. If, having entered the battle, he discovered the cause to be

167. LW 45, p. 91; WA 11, p. 251.
168. WA 11, p. 267; LW 45, p. 113.
169. WA 1, p. 692; 36, p. 385. Cf. LW 46, p. 96.
170. LW 45, p. 95; WA 11, pp. 254-255.

unjust he should "run from the field . . . and save his soul."[171] Whenever the claims of the two kingdoms clash the Christian must say with Peter: "We must obey God rather than men" (Acts 5:29). At the same time Luther was extremely reluctant to countenance rebellion or active resistance even against tyrants, for these two had been placed in office by God and would be deposed by Him when they had served their purpose.

In later Lutheranism the church tended to become a department of the state; consequently its prophetic voice within society was largely muted. Despite approving of the custodial role of the prince in the establishment of the territorial church, Luther vigorously argued for the independence of the spiritual realm. In a letter of 1543 to the town council of Cruezburg, which had attempted to expel the local pastor, Luther admonished the magistrates:

> You are not lords over the pastoral office and over parsons. You have not instituted the office, but God's Son alone has done so. Nor have you contributed anything to it. You have no more right to it than the devil has a right to the Kingdom of Heaven. Accordingly you should not rule over it, dictate to it, or prevent it from rebuking you. For when pastors rebuke you it is not man's but God's rebuke. And God desires the rebuke to be expressed, not suppressed. Keep to your own office and leave God's rule to him, lest he find it necessary to instruct you.[172]

The kingdom of the left hand was not to meddle with the affairs of the church. Its proper business was to provide justice, order, and tranquillity in society. In the kingdom of the right hand God "rules in person" (i.e. not veiled behind a mask, but through His ministers, Word, and sacraments).

We must not confuse Luther's distinction between the two kingdoms with the modern separation of church and state. For Luther the two realms presupposed and reinforced one another: The pastor urged his flock to obey the temporal authority, while the prince protected the church from the violence of the mob. (Hence Luther's dire words against the "robbing and murdering hordes" of peasants whom he admonished the princes to "stab, smite, slay" upon sight).[173] Although he allowed that a Christian could serve as a magistrate, Luther had no doctrine of a Christian magistracy. The state was ordained by God as a concession to human sin. It was not the agent of God's redemptive purpose for humankind. Luther's apocalyptic eschatology prevented him from harboring much hope for improved worldly

171. WA BR 10, p. 36; LW 46, p. 130. Cf. Stephenson, p. 332.
172. Tappert, *Letters,* p. 343.
173. LW 46, pp. 49-55.

conditions. "For the world is a sick thing . . . like a hospital . . . or it is like a fur pelt or skin, on which neither hide nor hair is any good."[174] At best, the state could only patch up the old order, restrain the spread of anarchy, until God's final judgment was unleashed. Yet this task, the work of God's left hand, was extremely important for it enabled the gospel to do its proper work even in the midst of sinful society.

Last Words and Legacy

In early January 1546, at the age of sixty-two, Luther returned to the town of his birth, Eisleben, to settle a political dispute (really a family quarrel) between the princes of Mansfeld. The journey from Wittenberg to Eisleben was eighty miles. Luther, in extremely poor health, was accompanied by his three sons, Hans, Martin, and Paul, as well as his trusted friend, Justus Jonas. Two days after their departure, while still en route, Luther wrote home to Kate concerning the perils of the journey. Apparently warm weather had thawed the river, preventing travel directly to Eisleben.

> Dear Kate, we arrived in Halle today at eight, but did not continue on to Eisleben because a big Anabaptist [the Saale River] met us with waves and hunks of ice. She flooded the land and threatened to rebaptize us. . . . We take refreshment and comfort in good Torgau beer and Rhenish wine, waiting to see whether the Saale will calm down. . . . The devil resents us, and he is in the water—so better safe than sorry.[175]

174. WA 51, p. 214; LW 13, p. 164. David C. Steinmetz, *Luther in Context,* p. 114, gives the following summary of the goals of Luther's political theory. "Luther's goals, I think, are clear. Luther wanted to establish (1) that Christian ethics, though not all human morality, is grounded in justification by faith alone; (2) that all Christians have a civic and social responsibility to discharge and that some Christians may discharge that duty by assuming public office in the state; (3) that the Sermon on the Mount is not merely a monastic ethic or an ethic for the future Kingdom of God but applies to the life of every Christian, even if its moral demands are not applicable to every decision which Christians must make as public persons; (4) that the state has been established by God to achieve divinely willed ends that the Church cannot and should not attempt to achieve; and (5) that God, who rules the Church through the gospel, rules this disordered world through the instruments available to the state—namely, human reason, wisdom, natural law, and the application of violent coercion."

175. WA BR 11, p. 269; LW 50, pp. 286-287. I have followed the translation in Haile, p. 342.

Finally the river subsided, and the journey continued. On Valentine's Day, February 14, Luther succeeded in effecting a reconciliation between the feuding princes. Three days later the agreement was signed and Luther prepared to return to Kate and Wittenberg. Suddenly he was taken ill and fainted with fatigue. Apparently he knew that the end was near, as people at the gate of death often do. He remarked that little babies die by the thousands, "but when I, Doctor Martinus, die at sixty-three, I don't think there'll be more than sixty or a hundred in the whole world who die with me. . . . Well, all right, we old ones must live so long in order to look the devil in the rear."[176]

After the evening meal, Luther made his way upstairs and lay down to pray. The pain grew worse. Friends rubbed him with hot towels. He experienced a series of attacks, and the doctors were summoned. After a few hours of sleep, Luther awakened in pain about one o'clock in the morning. He repeated in Latin Psalm 31:5: *"In manus tuas commendo spiritum meum, redemisti me, domine Deus veritatis."* "Into thy hand I commit my spirit; thou hast redeemed me, O Lord God of truth." Jonas asked him: "Reverend father, will you die steadfast in Christ, and in the doctrine you have preached?" Luther responded loud enough for everyone in the room to hear, "Ja." By daybreak he was dead.

Luther's body was placed in a tin coffin and returned to Wittenberg where it was laid to rest in the Castle Church on the door of which Luther had posted the *Ninety-five Theses* nearly thirty years before. Melanchthon delivered the funeral oration, placing the fallen reformer in the widest possible context of church history, even salvation history. The Old Testament patriarchs, judges, kings, and prophets had been succeeded by John the Baptist, by Christ Himself, and the apostles. Dr. Martinus was also to be counted in "this beautiful order and succession of supreme individuals on earth."[177] Indeed, Melanchthon claimed, the pure Christian gospel had been most clearly set forth by five men: Isaiah, John the Baptist, Paul, Augustine, and Dr. Luther. Thus began what we might call the Protestant version of the canonization of Luther. Within a few years, a medal was published in Saxony which bore the inscription: *"Mart. Luther. Elias ultimi saeculi."* "Martin Luther: the Elijah of the Last Age."[178] Many people believed that

---

176. Ibid., p. 350; WA 54, pp. 988-989.

177. Haile, p. 355. The details of Luther's death are fully recounted in Schwiebert, pp. 745-752.

178. Rupp, *Righteousness,* p. 14.

Luther was the latter-day forerunner of the Messiah, that Luther's life and career signaled nothing less than the approaching end of the world!

Despite these extremely laudatory claims, which were matched, of course, by equally defamatory attacks from Catholic detractors, nothing summarizes Luther's life and legacy so well as the last words he is known to have written before his death in Eisleben. Walt Whitman once asked, "Why do folks dwell so fondly on the last words of the departing?" He then answered, "Those last words . . . are valuable beyond measure to confirm and endorse the varied train, facts, theories and faith of the whole preceding life."[179] After his death, Luther's friends found the following words scrawled on a piece of paper lying on the desk beside his bed:

> Nobody can understand Vergil in his *Bucolics* and *Georgics* unless he has first been a shepherd or a farmer for five years. Nobody understands Cicero in his letters unless he has been engaged in public affairs of some consequence for twenty years. Let nobody suppose that he has tasted the Holy Scriptures sufficiently unless he has ruled over the churches with the prophets for a hundred years. Therefore there is some thing wonderful, first, about John the Baptist; second, about Christ; third, about the apostles. "Lay not your hand on this divine Aeneid, but bow before it, adore its every trace." We are beggars. That is true.[180]

Half in German, half in Latin: *"Wir sein Pettler, Hoc est Verum."* "We are beggars, that is true."

Luther's whole approach to the Christian life is summed up in these last words. The posture of the human vis à vis God is one of utter receptivity. We have no legs of our own on which to stand. No mystical "ground of the soul" can serve as a basis of our union with the divine. We can earn no merits which will purchase for us a standing before God. We are beggars— needy, vulnerable, totally bereft of resources with which to save ourselves. For Luther the good news of the gospel was that in Jesus Christ God had become a beggar too. God identified with us in our neediness. Like the good

---

179. Walt Whitman, *Leaves of Grass* (Franklin Center, Penn.: The Franklin Library, 1979), p. 521.

180. LW 54, p. 476; WA TR 5, pp. 317-318. On Luther's last words, see Heiko A. Oberman, "Wir sein Pettler. Hoc est Verum. Bund und Gnade in der Theologie des Mittelalters und der Reformation," *Zeitschrift für Kirchengeschichte* 78 (1967), pp. 232-252; Eric W. Gritsch, *Martin—God's Court Jester: Luther in Retrospect,* pp. 71-89; Timothy George, "Luther's Last Words: 'Wir Sein Pettler, Hoc Est Verum,' " *Pulpit Digest* 63 (Sept.-Oct., 1983), pp. 29-34.

Samaritan who exposed himself to the dangers of the road to attend to the dying man in the ditch, God "came where we were."

We have spoken of Luther's *Anfechtungen,* his struggles with the devil, the spiritual onslaughts which pursued him throughout his life. In such moments, Luther found the grace of God most sustaining. "I did not come to my theology of a sudden, but had to brood ever more deeply. My trials brought me to it, for we do not learn anything except by experience."[181] Luther also wrote: "One who has never suffered cannot understand what hope is."[182]

Luther once remarked that his insight into the gracious character of God had come to him while he was *"auff diser cloaca,"* literally, "on the toilet." While some scholars have interpreted this saying in terms of Luther's acute suffering from constipation, we know that the expression *in cloaca* was a common metaphor in medieval spiritual writings. It referred to a state of utter helplessness and dependence upon God. Where else are we more vulnerable, more easily embarrassed, and, in Luther's mind, more open to demonic attacks, than when we are—*in cloaca?* Yet it is precisely in a state of such vulnerability—when we are reduced to humility, when like beggars we can only cast ourselves on the mercy of another—that the yearning for grace is answered in the assurance of God's inescapable nearness. Time and again Luther proved the truth of this statement in his own experience: when, shut up in the Wartburg, the devil was so real that he could hear him flipping chesnuts against the ceiling at night; when he was haunted by the demon of self-doubt and faced with the question, Are you alone wise?; when his body was wracked with illness and pain; when the church was beseiged by war and plague from without, by heresy and schism from within. One of the lowest points of his life was when his beloved daughter Magdalena, barely fourteen years of age, was stricken with the plague. Brokenhearted Luther knelt beside her bed and begged God to release her from the pain. When she had died and the carpenters were nailing down the lid of her coffin, Luther screamed out, "Hammer away! On doomsday she'll rise again."[183]

Luther had really said it all long before, in his explanation of the fourth of the *Ninety-five Theses*: "If a person's whole life is one of repentance and a cross of Christ . . . then it is evident that the cross continues until death

181. WA TR 1, p. 146.
182. WA TR 4, pp. 490-491.
183. WA TR 5, pp. 193-194.

and thereby to entrance into the kingdom."[184] Luther's legacy, unlike that of Francis, does not lie in the saintliness of his life. His warts were many; his vices, sometimes more visible than his virtues. Nor does his legacy depend ultimately upon his vast accomplishments as a reformer and theologian. Luther's true legacy is his spiritual insight into the gracious character of God in Jesus Christ, the God who loves us and sustains us unto death, and again unto life. "What else was Luther," asked Karl Barth, "than a teacher of the Christian church whom one can hardly celebrate in any other way but to listen to him?"[185]

Select Bibliography

In addition to the fifty-four-volume set of *Luther's Works,* four volumes of the Library of Christian Classics series are devoted to Luther's writings. A useful anthology of Luther texts has been edited by John Dillenberger, *Martin Luther: Selections from His Writings* (New York: Doubleday, 1961). Also, the Reformation writings of 1520 have been published as a separate volume: *Martin Luther: Three Treatises* (Philadelphia: Fortress Press, 1960). The following is a select sampling from the vast assortment of secondary literature.

Althaus, Paul. *The Theology of Martin Luther.* Translated by Robert Schultz. Philadelphia: Fortress Press, 1966. A comprehensive overview of Luther's theology arranged in systematic order. A supplementary volume on *The Ethics of Martin Luther* was published by the same press in 1972.

Bainton, Roland H. *Here I Stand: A Life of Martin Luther.* Nashville: Abingdon Press, 1950. The most popular biography of Luther in the twentieth century. Eminently readable and handsomely illustrated with contemporary woodcuts.

Ebeling, Gerhard. *Luther: An Introduction to His Thought.* Philadelphia: Fortress Press, 1970. An insightful survey by a master of Luther studies.

Edwards, Mark U., Jr. *Luther and the False Brethren.* Stanford: University Press, 1975. Well-researched study of Luther's relations with the *Schwärmer.*

Gerrish, Brian A. *Grace and Reason: A Study in the Theology of Luther.* New York: Oxford University Press, 1962. An excellent study on the use and limits of reason in Luther's theology.

Gritsch, Eric W. *Martin—God's Court Jester: Luther in Retrospect.* Philadelphia: Fortress Press, 1983. One of the better reviews of Luther's life and thought which was published during the 500th anniversary year of his birth.

Haile, H. G. *Luther: An Experiment in Biography.* New York: Doubleday, 1980. A

184. LW 31, p. 89; WA 1, p. 534.
185. Karl Barth, "Lutherfeier," *Theologische Existenz heute* 4 (1933), p. 11.

fascinating account of the older Luther. Makes good use of the correspondence and *Table Talk.*

Hendrix, Scott H. *Luther and the Papacy.* Philadelphia: Fortress Press, 1981. Traces the developing rupture between Luther and the Roman Church with meticulous care.

Loeschen, John R. *Wrestling with Luther.* St. Louis: Concordia, 1976. Especially good on the polarities and paradoxes in Luther's thought.

McSorley, Harry J. *Luther: Right or Wrong?* New York: Newman Press, 1969. An ecumenical investigation of the Luther-Erasmus debate on free will.

Preus, James Samuel. *From Shadow to Promise: Old Testament Interpretation from Augustine to the Young Luther.* Cambridge: Harvard University Press, 1969. A study of Luther's early lectures on the Psalms in light of medieval hermeneutics.

Rupp, Gordon. *Luther's Progress to the Diet of Worms.* New York: Harper and Row, 1964. A brief but brilliant narrative of Luther's development to 1521.

Rupp, Gordon. *The Righteousness of God.* London: Hodder and Stoughton, 1953. One of the best books on Luther in the postwar period.

Siggins, Ian D. K. *Martin Luther's Doctrine of Christ.* New Haven: Yale University Press, 1970. A thoroughly documented study of Luther's Christology.

Steinmetz, David C. *Luther in Context.* Bloomington: Indiana University Press, 1986. A collection of essays on Luther's theology, several of which focus on his exegetical work.

Watson, Philip S. *Let God Be God!* Philadelphia: Fortress Press, 1970. Originally published in 1947, this remains a landmark interpretation of Luther's "Copernican Revolution."

Wicks, Jared. *Man Yearning for Grace.* Washington: Corpus Books, 1968. One of the finest fruits of ecumenical Catholic Luther research in the tradition of the "Lortz school."

_____. *Luther and His Spiritual Legacy.* Wilmington: Michael Glazier, 1983.

4

Something Bold for God
Huldrych Zwingli

That religion will conquer which can render clear to popular understanding some eternal greatness incarnate in the passage of temporal fact.

Alfred North Whitehead[1]

The Road to Reformation

During the winter of 1510 Martin Luther made a trip to Rome. He walked through eastern Switzerland, crossing the Alps at the Septimer Pass. Far from being impressed favorably by the rough terrain, he regarded the Swiss Alps as huge warts on the face of the earth, a vestige of the curse left over from the Flood. Before the Flood, he surmised, there were no bulging mountains, only gentle "fields in a lovely plain," a description of the Saxon landscape![2] While Luther was trudging through the Alpine snows, in the neighboring canton of Glarus, Huldrych Zwingli went about his duties as a parish priest. He and Luther would emerge as the two leading protagonists of the early Protestant movement. Potential allies in their struggles against Rome, they clashed over the understanding of the Lord's Supper, leaving the Reformation permanently divided.

Zwingli was born on January 1, 1484, in the Toggenburg village of Wildhaus high in the Alps. His earliest biographer Myconius suggested that growing up in the mountains—so near the heavens—made young Huldrych more attuned to the things of God.[3] His writings are filled with allusions to his early years in the Alps: The mountains proclaim "the invincible

1. Alfred North Whitehead, *Adventure of Ideas* (New York: Mentor Books, 1955), p. 40.

2. LW 1, pp. 98-99; WA 42, p. 75. On Luther's trip to Rome, see Heinrich Boehmer, *Martin Luther: Road to Reformation* (Cleveland: Meridian, 1957), pp. 58-81.

3. Samuel M. Jackson, ed., *The Latin Works of Huldreich Zwingli* (New York: Knickerbocker Press, 1912), I, p. 2. Myconius's life of Zwingli was written in 1532, the year following the Reformer's death.

108

ULRIC ZWINGLE

power of the Godhead" and the "vastness of his grandeur;" even the habits of the Alpine rats exemplify divine providence; the "green pastures" of Psalm 23:2 he translated as "a beautiful Alpine meadow."[4] While the profound differences between Luther and Zwingli cannot be reduced to their respective opinions of the Alps, their characters do reflect a unique historical and political context.

Zwingli's early development was shaped by two factors which continued to influence his thought throughout his career: Swiss patriotism and Erasmian humanism. In one of his earliest writings as a reformer, Zwingli described himself as "a Swiss professing Christ among the Swiss."[5] Although still technically a part of the Holy Roman Empire, the Swiss Confederation had gained a measure of independence by the sixteenth century. Its chief export was soldiers. Swiss mercenaries were famous for their fighting ability and were frequently contracted out to the competing sovereigns of Europe, especially the pope, the emperor, and the king of France. Many of these battles were fought on the plains of northern Italy where even today it is said that mothers sometimes threaten their children with the bogeyman by crying, "The Swiss are coming!"[6]

As chaplain to the troops from Glarus, Zwingli accompanied the soldiers on their campaigns. He learned firsthand the horrors of the mercenary trade. In 1515 he was present at Marignano when the Swiss suffered a crushing defeat at the hands of the French and ten thousand men were reported killed. He later lamented: "If only our sons could grow up and not be killed. Murder, murder! What has happened to the Confederacy, that her sons and daughters should be sold like this! Despair, despair! Wretchedness, wretchedness! Sin, sin! . . . O Lord, grant us peace."[7]

4. Ibid., II, pp. 149-150; Oskar Farner, *Huldrych Zwingli: Seine Jugend, Schulzeit and Studenjahre* (Zurich: Zwingli-Verlag, 1943), p. 99. Farner's four-volume study remains the standard biography, although one must also consult Walther Köhler, *Huldrych Zwingli* (Leipzig: Koehler and Amelang, 1943), and especially G. R. Potter, *Zwingli.* A more popular treatment is Jean Rilliet, *Zwingli: Third Man of the Reformation* (Philadelphia: Westminster Press, 1964). Ulrich Gäbler has provided a helpful introduction to Zwingli research in *Huldrych Zwingli: His Life and Work,* Ruth C. L. Gritsch, trans.

5. Jackson, ed., I, p. 217; Z 1, p. 270: "Principio igitur, quid opus erat me Helvetium et apud Helvetios Christum profitentem huius tumultus insimulare?"

6. Gottfried W. Locher, *Zwingli's Thought: New Perspectives* (Leiden: E. J. Brill, 1981), p. 34.

7. Ibid,; Z 13, p. 816. Heinrich Bullinger gave the following account of Zwingli's battlefield activities, which suggests that he may have actually participated in

In 1522 Zwingli addressed a solemn warning against the mercenary connection to the canton of Schwyz. He pointed out that foreign alliances would turn the cantons against each other and threaten their independence. Further, the fine clothing and rich foods which the foreign money provided were corrupting influences on the Swiss. Switzerland may not produce "cinnamon, malmsey, oranges, silk and such feminine delicacies, but she does produce butter, milk, horses, sheep, cattle, home-spun cloth, wine and corn in abundance."[8]

While Zwingli detested war, he was by no means a thoroughgoing pacifist. He believed that young men should undergo military training in order to protect their own country and "those whom God approves."[9] Zwingli himself died on the battlefield wielding a double-headed axe. Jacques Courvoisier has noted that Zwingli was one of the first advocates of the Swiss policy of armed neutrality which has been maintained until the present time.[10] Zwingli's ideal for Switzerland was that of a reformed Alpine "Israel" whose cantons corresponded to the twelve tribes of the ancient people of God. In the end the Zwinglian Reformation itself further divided the country, resulting in the first Protestant-Catholic war of religion and the death of the Zurich reformer.

Zwingli was both a pastor and a patriot, a theologian and a politician. As the "mercenary of Christ" *(Christus, des reiser ich bin),* he applied the Protestant message directly to the social and political conditions of his day. In contrast to Luther's emphasis on the paradox of the two realms, Zwingli insisted that "the kingdom of Christ is also external."[11] Religious awakening implied political reform: "God's Word will make you pious, God-fearing folks. Thus will you preserve your Fatherland."[12] Zwingli's activism, his

---

the fighting: "In the camp he preached diligently and in the battles he was brave and gave a good account of himself, with counsel, words and deeds. Thus he achieved favor, glory, and a good reputation with his countrymen." J. J. Hottinger and H. H. Vogeli, eds., *Heinrich Bullingers Reformationsgeschichte* (Frauenfeld, 1838-1840), I, p. 8.

8. Z 3, p. 106.

9. "Of the Education of Youth," *Zwingli and Bullinger,* G. W. Bromiley, ed., p. 113.

10. Jacques Courvoisier, *Zwingli: A Reformed Theologian,* p. 15.

11. Z 1, p. 394; 9, p. 454: "Sed nos huc solum properamus, ut probemus Christi regnum etiam esse externum . . . . Vult ergo Christus, etiam in externis modum teneri, eumque imperat; non est igitur eius regnum non etiam externum."

12. Z 3, p. 113: "Denn das wirt üch fromm, gotzvörchtig lüt ziehen. Damit werdend ir üwer vatterland behalten."

willingness to unite the tasks of the church with those of the state, his political savvy and flexibility are distinct marks of the Reformed tradition whose origins can be traced to the cities of Switzerland and southern Germany.

Equally decisive for Zwingli's intellectual development was his thorough training in the humanist disciplines. We have identified humanism as a scholarly movement which aimed to reform society by applying the insights of classical antiquity to contemporary life. *Ad fontes*—to the sources—was the motto of scholars who pored over Greek and Latin texts, published new editions of the old classics, and sought a moral-religious renewal through a well-defined program of education and political action. Chief among the humanists was Desiderius Erasmus who exerted a critical influence on Zwingli from about 1514 to 1519. Already well versed in humanism or, as we would say, the humanities, from his university studies at Vienna and Basel, Zwingli was profoundly impressed by the fusion of scholarship and piety he discovered in Erasmus. In fact, Erasmus's poem, "Jesus's Lament to Mankind," in which Christ declares Himself to be the bearer of salvation, the only comfort and treasure of the soul, led Zwingli to abandon his belief in the intercession of the saints.[13] More important still was the 1516 edition of Erasmus's Greek New Testament. Both at Glarus and Einsiedeln, where he held a preaching post from 1516 to 1518, he immersed himself in the text of Holy Writ. His friend and successor in Zurich, Heinrich Bullinger, reported that Zwingli memorized in Greek all of the Pauline Epistles, having copied them down word for word.[14] This spadework would later bear fruit in Zwingli's powerful expository preaching and biblical exegesis. Despite his later break with Erasmus, Zwingli's mature theology reflects his early exposure to humanism. His stress on the spirituality of God, his distaste for externals in religion, his openness to philosophy and reason, his disdain for the mysterious and sacramental, all bear affinity to the Erasmian world of thought.

13. Z 2, p. 217: "Ich hab vor 8. oder 9. jaren ein trostlich gedicht gelesen des hochgelerten Erasmi von Roterdam, an den heren Jesum geschriben, darinn sich Jesus klagt, das man nit alles guts by im sucht, so er doch ein brunn sye alles guten, ein heilmacher, trost und schatz der seel, mit vil gar schönen worten."

14. Bullinger, I, p. 8. Some scholars have doubted the validity of Bullinger's report, but see Locher, p. 239, who points out that Zwingli was merely carrying out the advice of Erasmus. A manuscript preserved in the city archives at Zurich contains portions of the Greek New Testament copied in Zwingli's hand. Cf. Philip Schaff, *History of the Christian Church* (New York: Charles Scribner's Sons, 1910), VIII, p. 31, 2n.

Zwingli's evolution from humanist to Protestant is a matter of debate among Reformation historians. He himself placed the pivotal transition in 1516 when "led by the Word and Spirit of God I saw the need to set aside all these [human teachings] and to learn the doctrine of God direct from his own Word."[15] Another decisive event was the call to serve as "people's priest" at the famous Great Minster church in Zurich. Over the portal of this church today one reads the following inscription: "The Reformation of Huldrych Zwingli began here on January 1, 1519." On this date the new pastor shocked his congregation by announcing his intention to dispense with the traditional lectionary. Instead of "canned" sermons, Zwingli would preach straight through the Gospel of Matthew, beginning with the genealogy in chapter 1. Matthew was followed by Acts, then the Epistles to Timothy, then Galatians, 1 and 2 Peter, and so on until by 1525 he had worked his way through the New Testament and then turned to the Old.[16] This was certainly an important move, one which prepared the citizens of Zurich for the complete acceptance of the Reformation several years later. Zwingli did not break decisively with the Church of Rome until some time after his move to Zurich. During this time he became aware, along with the rest of Europe, of Luther and the goings-on in Germany. He admired Luther's courageous stand against Eck at Leipzig and referred to Luther as an "Elijah." He urged his congregation to buy and read Luther's books, which poured forth from the printing presses of Zurich and Basel. He later refused to be labeled a "Lutheran," denying all dependence on the Wittenberg reformer: "I did not learn my doctrine from Luther, but from God's Word itself."[17] Most modern scholars agree with Zwingli's claim of independence; Zwingli's Reformation insights often paralleled Luther's, but did not derive from them.[18]

In 1519 a terrible plague swept through Zurich. More than two thousand of its seven thousand inhabitants died. Zwingli's brother perished in the epidemic and Zwingli himself nearly died. Out of this experience he wrote

15. Bromiley, pp. 90-91; Z 1, p. 379: "Do kam ich zum letsten dahin, das ich gedacht—doch mit geschrifft und wort gottes ingfurt—, du must das alles lassen liggen und die meinung gottes luter uss sinem eignen ein valtigen wort lernen."

16. Zwingli never preached on Revelation, whose canonicity he doubted. Cf. Potter, p. 61.

17. Z 2, p. 149. This is from Zwingli's *Auslegung und Grunde der Schlussreden* (1523). This first complete English translation of this treatise is in E. J. Furcha and H. W. Pipkin, eds. and trans., *Huldrych Zwingli: Writings,* I, p. 119.

18. The most thorough investigation of this disputed question is Arthur Rich, *Die Anfänge der Theologie Huldrych Zwinglis* (Zurich: Zwingli-Verlag, 1949.)

a "Plague-Song" which some biographers have cited as evidence of deepened theological insight.

> Help me, O Lord
>   My strength and rock;
> Lo, at the door
>   I hear death's knock.
> Uplift thine arm,
>   Once pierced for me,
> That conquered death,
>   And set me free.

And, on recovering from the sickness:

> My God! My Lord!
>   Healed by Thy hand,
> Upon the earth
>   Once more I stand.
>
> Let sin no more
>   Rule over me;
> My mouth shall sing
>   Alone of thee.[19]

Luther had turned to the monastery after a close brush with death. Zwingli emerged from his dire illness chastened and resolved, newly grasped by his total dependence upon God. His discovery of the Pauline doctrine of justification, which he held in common with Luther, did not come "like a flash of lightning," as one biographer has it.[20] His theology developed slowly out of many hours in the study and pulpit. By the early 1520s, Zwingli could no longer retain his status as a priest in the Roman Church. Two events mark his break with Rome and his public adherence to the Protestant cause. In late 1520 he renounced the papal pension he had been receiving for several years. Two years later, on October 10, 1522, he resigned his office as "people's priest" of Zurich, whereupon the city council promptly hired him as preacher to the entire city. Zwingli was now in a position to press for an official reformation in Zurich.

The princes of northern Germany secured the Lutheran Reformation by identifying it with their dynastic and territorial interests. In southern Germany and Switzerland the Reformation coincided with a rising urban mentality. Bernd Moeller has shown that of the eighty-five free, imperial cities

19. Schaff, VIII, pp. 44-45; cf. also Jackson, ed., I, pp. 56-57; Z 1, pp. 67-69.
20. Farner, p. 38.

within the Holy Roman Empire, more than fifty became Protestant during the sixteenth century.[21] In Strasbourg, Basel, Bern, Lausanne, Geneva, Ulm, as well as Zurich, the Reformation reinforced social and political solidarity, enhanced the sense of civic uniformity, and completed the revolution of the guild-dominated middle classes against both external (bishops) and internal (patricians) opponents. In Zurich the common people were among Zwingli's earliest, most ardent supporters. In 1524 Zwingli observed: "The common man adheres to the gospel although his superiors want nothing of it."[22] The struggle over fasting in Lent, which first put Zwingli at odds with the ecclesiastical authorities, was also in part a question of class conflict. Zwingli saw it as a contest between the "laborers" and the "idlers." The latter could afford to abstain from the prohibited meats since they were able to "fill themselves with still richer foods."[23] The poor workmen, on the other hand, had to have their sausages in order to endure their harsh labors.

Zurich lay within the jurisdiction of the bishop of Constance, who regarded Zwingli's strident preaching with growing alarm. The fear of schism was on his mind when he warned the Zurichers to maintain "the unity of the Church, without which there can be no Gospel; Christ is one, and the Church is one." To this admonition Zwingli replied with his *Apologeticus Archeteles* ("my first and last defense"). At points he sounded almost flippant. Is he accused of not listening to the bishops? "Nothing is easier, since they say nothing." As for the charge of abandoning Holy Mother Church, he called on his opponents themselves "to leave the asses and come over to the oxen, abandon the goats for the sheep."[24] That was too much for Erasmus, who fired off a curt reply to his former disciple advising him not to translate the treatise into German until he had consulted with more "learned friends" (i.e. Erasmus!).[25] By this time, however, the die was cast. Zwingli flung down the gauntlet in his final challenge to the bishop:

21. Bernd Moeller, *Imperial Cities and the Reformation,* Erik Midelfort and Mark U. Edwards, trans. (Philadelphia: Fortress Press, 1972), pp. 41-42. Cf. also Steven E. Ozment, *The Reformation in the Cities* (New Haven: Yale University Press, 1975) and Basil Hall, "The Reformation City," *Bulletin of the John Rylands Library* 54 (1971-1972), pp. 103-148.

22. Z 3, p. 446: "Der gmein mann hangt dem evangelio an, obglych ire obren nit daran wellend."

23. Z 1, p. 106; Jackson, I, pp. 86-87.

24. Jackson, pp. 213, 217, 247.

25. Z 7, p. 582. Erasmus wrote this letter after reading only a few pages of Zwingli's treatise—"in the middle of the night *(ad multam noctem)."*

If you wish to maintain that I have not taught the Gospel doctrine truly, try it not by threats nor flattery, not by snares and secret devices, but by the open warfare of the Holy Writ and by public meeting, following the Scripture as your guide and master, and not human inventions.[26]

On Thursday morning, January 29, 1523, some six hundred people, including the two hundred members of the town council and all of the clergy in the canton, crowded into the Zurich town hall, for what has become known as the First Zurich Disputation. They had been summoned by the council at the request of Zwingli. This special assembly gathered for a "public discussion in the German language."[27] As it turned out, the disputation hardly materialized. No one present dared accuse Zwingli of heresy, and the delegation from the bishop, led by Zwingli's sometime friend John Fabri, refused to debate the *Sixty-seven Articles* Zwingli had drawn up for the occasion. They denied that a local city such as Zurich was an appropriate forum for resolving important theological issues. Such matters were better left to a general council or at least a university where learned doctors could discuss them dispassionately and in good Latin not Swiss German! To this evasive tactic Zwingli responded: "I say that here in this room is without doubt a Christian assembly; there is no reason why we should not discuss these matters, speak and decide the truth."[28] This was a remarkable claim. Zwingli regarded this assembly not merely as a special session of the town council but as an evangelical synod on a par with a general council of the church universal, fully competent to pronounce authoritatively on matters of faith and worship. That the governing authorities of Zurich, which did not even have a university and was not the seat of a bishop, felt at ease in arrogating to themselves this prerogative prompted Fabri to charge that Zwingli and his cohorts were "planning to overturn and upset all things."[29]

In the afternoon session the councilmen delivered their verdict: Master Zwingli could "continue and keep on as before to proclaim the holy Gospel and the correct divine Scriptures with the spirit of God in accordance with

26. Jackson, I, p. 288; Z 1, p. 324: "Quamobrem dico edico vobis, ut si evangelicam doctrinam non recte nos docuisse velitis adserere, id non minus, non blandiciis, non insidiis, non cuniculis, sed sacrarum literarum aperto Marte publicoque congressu, quo scripturarum sequamini ducem ac magistram, non humana commenta."

27. Samuel M. Jackson, ed., *Ulrich Zwingli: Selected Works*, p. 25.

28. Ibid., pp. 54-55.

29. Ibid., p. 26.

his capabilities."[30] The action of the council has been compared to Henry
VIII's later assertion of supreme authority in matters religious. Clearly
Zurich became "the first Protestant state by *magisterial* initiative."[31] Still,
the civic supremacy of the Zwinglian Reformation rested on the prior
principle of *sola scriptura.*

This principle had been formally recognized by the council as early as
1520 when it decreed that all preaching within the canton of Zurich was
to be in agreement with the Bible. The retention of Zwingli as a city
employee after his resignation as "people's priest" in 1522 was another step
in the direction of a "Bibliocracy." Zwingli and his associates came to the
disputation carrying their folio volumes of the Greek New Testament,
Hebrew Old Testament, and the Latin Vulgate. Throughout the debate
Zwingli repeatedly appealed to the Scriptures. He demanded to know chapter and verse on Fabri's doctrine of the intercession of saints. He urged that
every priest buy and read his own copy of the Greek New Testament. If he
were too poor to afford it, asserted Zwingli, some pious citizen would buy
one for him or else lend him the money for the purchase. The citizens of
Zurich felt competent to judge spiritual matters because for four years they
had had the pure gospel preached among them. The bishops and priests, the
"big Jacks" *(grossen Hansen),* as Zwingli called them, try to keep the
Scriptures from the common people by claiming that only they had a right
to expound them, as if other Christians had nothing to do with the Spirit
of God or His Word. Toward the end of the disputation, Zwingli issued a
final challenge to Fabri: "If you can prove one of my articles false by means
of the Gospel, I will give you a rabbit cheese. Now let's hear it. I shall await
it." Fabri, apparently unacquainted with the nuanced distinctions among
fine Swiss cheeses, replied: "A rabbit cheese, what is that? I need no cheese."
Having thus achieved a signal victory over his opponents, Zwingli exclaimed: "God be praised and thanked whose divine word will reign in
heaven and upon earth."[32]

The First Zurich Disputation was a decisive moment in the evolution of

30. Ibid., p. 93.

31. Moeller, p. 54, 1n.

32. Jackson, ed., *Selected Works,* pp. 55, 94, 107-108. Heiko A. Oberman has
attempted to place the First Zurich Disputation in the wider context of the civic
traditions in Zurich. See his *Masters of the Reformation* (Cambridge: Cambridge
University Press, 1981), pp. 187-239. For a contrary view on the significance of the
Disputation, see Bernd Moeller, "Die Ursprünge der reformierten Kirche,"
Theologische Literaturzeitung 100 (1975), pp. 642-653.

the Zwinglian Reformation. Zwingli was publicly vindicated of the charge of heresy, and his *Sixty-seven Articles,* which constitute the first Reformed confession of faith, were accepted in principle as the basis for future reforms. Yet much remained to be done before the church in Zurich could be considered fully reformed. In October 1523 a Second Disputation was held, this one dealing with the question of images and the Mass. At the initiative of Leo Jud, Zwingli's fellow reformer, the baptismal liturgy had already been put into German. Zwingli now attacked the Mass as "a blasphemous undertaking, a very work of Antichrist. Christ our Redeemer gave us this only as a food and a memorial of his suffering and his covenant."[33] At the conclusion of this disputation, Zwingli was moved to say:

> Do not be afraid, my friends! God is on our side and He will protect His own. You have indeed undertaken something big and you will encounter much opposition for the sake of the pure Word of God, which only a few bother to think about. Go forth in God's name![34]

Despite the enthusiastic response to Zwingli's preaching, the city council did not order an immediate reform. The "images and idols" remained in the churches until June, 1524, and the Mass was only abolished during Holy Week, 1525. Two reasons caused this delay. A new party, composed mostly of young, ardent supporters of Zwingli, demanded that the reforms be carried out irrespective of the council's directive. Out of this group the earliest Anabaptists evolved. Zwingli and the town council opposed their call for a reformation "without tarrying for any," fearing that precipitate action might trigger public unrest and that weak consciences might take offense. Also, the council was concerned about Zurich's isolation from the other Swiss cantons, most of which were opposed to the new doctrines of Zwingli. The confederation was dividing along religious lines. Only with caution did Zurich decide for that path which would lead to the battlefield of Kappel.

As the process of reform unfolded, Zwingli came increasingly to see himself as a prophet to his people. Like the prophets of the Old Testament, the "shepherd" or "watchman" (Zwingli's preferred words for pastor) needed to guard zealously the flock against attacks from the Evil One and be ready to die fighting for the cause of Christ. "Fearlessness is your armour! You must watch and be ready for battle; for God sends His proph-

33. Z 2, p. 733.

34. Oskar Farner, *Zwingli the Reformer,* D. G. Sear, trans. (New York: Archon Books, 1952), p. 58.

ets everywhere to warn the sinful world."[35] Zwingli continued to guide the Zurich Reformation until his untimely death in 1531. The founding of a theological school, a tribunal of morals (originally a court to settle matrimonial disputes), the translation of the Bible into the Swiss German dialect, the spread of the Reformation to other cantons, especially Bern and Basel, helped to consolidate Zwingli's reforming efforts. During the last years of his life Zwingli's writings became more explicitly theological as he struggled to define his distinct Reformation stance against Roman Catholic apologists such as Fabri and John Eck, the radical Anabaptists who openly split with him in 1525, and Luther, who increasingly regarded him with suspicion and mistrust.

Zwingli as Theologian

Zwingli's role in the history of Christian thought has never been clearly assessed. Claiming that his contribution to the history of theology "will require no more than a brief report," a recent historian of theology assigns only three pages to the Zurich reformer.[36] The reasons for this neglect are obvious. Zwingli composed all of his Reformation writings hurriedly, within less than a decade. He was overshadowed during his lifetime by the great Luther and succeeded by the more effective Calvin, which prompted one scholar to dub him the "third man" of the Reformation. He never wrote anything comparable to the *Institutes.* Most of his sermons were delivered extemporaneously; only a few were later revised for publication. Likewise, his table talk was lost to posterity for lack of devoted fans who jotted down his every word.

What then is the scope of Zwingli's theology? His humanist background and his bent toward rationalism have led some scholars to see him as the forerunner of modern liberal theology. Paul Tillich related Zwingli's theology to the bourgeois ideal of health: "If you are psychologically healthy, then you can have faith, and vice versa."[37] More recent investigations have stressed the Christological focus and spiritualist tenor of his thought.[38]

35. Ibid., p. 56.
36. Bengt Hägglund, *History of Theology* (St. Louis: Concordia, 1968), p. 255.
37. Paul Tillich, *History of Christian Thought* p. 257.
38. See, for example, Christof Gestrich, *Zwingli als Theologe: Glaube und Geist beim Zürcher Reformator* (Zurich: Zwingli-Verlag, 1967); Gottfried W. Locher, *Die Theologie Huldrych Zwinglis im Lichte seiner Christologie* (Zurich: Zwingli-Verlag, 1952). I am especially indebted to Locher's interpretation of Zwingli. Much of his ground-breaking research is now available in English in a superb collection of essays,

We shall attempt to outline the contour of Zwingli's theology in terms of five basic themes in his thought. While we shall frequently contrast Zwingli's ideas to Luther's, this must not obscure the essential agreement of the two reformers. Luther's slogans of *sola gratia, sola fide,* and *sola scriptura* are echoed no less strongly by Zwingli, although with different emphasis. Their doctrines of predestination, while not identical, stand together with Calvin's over against the more positive assessment of free will in both Counter Reformation and Anabaptist theologies. Zwingli, no less than Luther and Calvin, proclaimed salvation through Christ alone: "Christ is the only way to salvation for all who ever were, are and shall be."[39] Likewise the church is seen as the company of those who truly belong to God by faith: "All who dwell in the head are members and children of God, and that is the church or communion of the saints, the bride of Christ, Ecclesia catholica."[40] Only against this common background of agreement can the distinct patterns of Zwingli's theology be discerned.

Unlike Luther, Zwingli never received a doctorate in theology. During the First Zurich Disputation, Fabri was incensed that "Master" Huldrych dared to pronounce on matters better left to bishops and learned doctors. Nonetheless Zwingli was well versed in the scholastic tradition, especially the *via antiqua* which he had studied at the University of Basel. He later claimed that one of his teachers, Thomas Wyttenbach, had had a decisive influence on his rejection of indulgences.[41] Of the scholastic masters he was most impressed with Thomas Aquinas whose views on election he accepted for a while.[42] Luther, however, was even more thoroughly immersed in

Zwingli's Thought. For an assessment of Zwingli studies see therein: "How the Image of Zwingli Has Changed in Recent Research," pp. 42-71. Among Roman Catholic interpretations the article by J. V. M. Pollet remains unsurpassed: "Zwinglianisme," *Dictionnaire de Théologie catholique,* (Paris, 1951), XV, cols. 3745-3928. Cf. also the articles in E. J. Furcha, ed., *Huldrych Zwingli, 1484-1531: A Legacy of Radical Reform* (Montreal: McGill University Faculty of Religious Studies, 1985).

39. This is the third of the *67 Articles:* "Dannenher der enig weg zur säligkeit Christus ist aller, die ie warend, sind und werdend." Z 1, p. 458.

40. The eighth of the *67 Articles,* Z 1, p. 459: "Uss dem volgt: Zu eim, das alle, so in dem houpt läbend, glider und kinder gottes sind, und das ist die kilch oder gemeinsame der heyligen, ein hussfrouw Christi: Ecclesia catholica." Jackson, ed., *Selected Works,* p. 111.

41. Z 2, p. 146; Furcha and Pipkin, eds., I, p. 117.

42. Jackson, *Latin Works,* II, p. 184: "[Thomas's] opinion pleased me once, when I cultivated scholasticism, but when I abandoned that and adhered to the purity of the divine oracles, it displeased me very greatly." On Zwingli's training

scholastic theology and in a different tradition—the *via moderna*. To some extent their distinct theologies reflect these diverse intellectual backgrounds.

Creator Rather than Creatures.

In July of 1523 Zwingli published an extensive commentary on the *Sixty-seven Articles,* which he had prepared for the First Zurich Disputation six months earlier. Here he recalled the impact of Erasmus's beautiful poem in which Jesus laments that not everything good is sought in Him, even though He is the fount of all goodness. Zwingli confessed: "It is ever thus. *Why, indeed do we seek help with creatures?*"[43]

The fundamental point of departure in Zwingli's theology is the absolute distinction between the Creator and all creatures. The doctrine that God created the universe out of nothing *(ex nihilo)* had been commonplace in Christian theology since the early church. Zwingli, however, felt that this emphasis had been muted and even denied in actual practice. In 1524 he wrote to his fellow Toggenburgers:

> Was it not great blindness that God Almighty, who created us, has so often made known to us that he is our Father, and finally even gave his Son for us; and he himself stands there and calls us poor sinners, saying "Come to me, all who are weary and heavy laden and I will give you rest." And we went and turned to the creature, and thought God to be so rough and cruel that we dare not come to him.[44]

The great sin of humanity, then, was *idolatry,* defined as attributing to a creature that which is God's alone.[45] For Zwingli the Reformation essentially was a movement from idolatry to the service of the one, true God.

The danger of idolatry was a resounding theme in Zwingli's preaching. "I call it the depth of impiety, when we are turned from God to created things, when we accept the human for the divine." Again, "I call my flock absolutely away, as far as I can, from hope in any created being to the one true God and Jesus his only begotten Son."[46]

Two considerations stand behind Zwingli's single-minded exhortation.

in the *via antiqua* see Farner, *Huldrych Zwingli,* pp. 205-234.

43. Furcha and Pipkin, eds., I, p. 171; Z 2, p. 217: "Nun ist es ie also. Warumb suchend wir denn hilff by der creatur?"

44. Z 8, pp. 207-208. Cf. Locher, *Zwingli's Thought,* pp. 106-161.

45. Furcha and Pipkin, eds. I, p. 315; Z 1, p. 464: "Welicher sölchs der creatur zugibt, zücht got sin eer ab unnd gibt sy dem, der mitt gott. Ist ein ware abgöttery."

46. Jackson, ed., *Latin Works,* I, p. 278, 239; Z 1, pp. 286, 317.

First, the *derived character of human existence.* Quite apart from the question of the Fall, human beings subsist, insofar as we are creatures, only at the discretion and by the good will of God. Augustine had said that if God should turn His eyes away from us but for a moment, we would all vanish into nothingness. Zwingli, an avid reader of Augustine, echoes the same thought. How can anyone ascribe anything to oneself, Zwingli asked, when "everything he is, is from God?"[47] Much of Zwingli's writing in this vein can be understood as a commentary on Psalm 100:3: "It is God who has made us, and not we ourselves."

Zwingli was also aware of a further concern: the *undivided loyalty owed to God.* Here, of course, his text was the First Commandment: "I am the Lord thy God. . . . Thou shalt have no other gods before me" (Ex. 20:2-3). To ask "Who is your God?" is to ask "In whom do you put your trust?" "If you put your confidence in one of the saints, you have made him a god, to all intents and purposes; for "God" is the good in which we put our trust so that it may afford us the good which we need."[48] But the one true God will not accept halfhearted trust. We cannot, as it were, hedge our bets by trusting in God and in something else too. It cannot be that a person places his trust in God and says, nonetheless, "I trust in creatures and in saints alike." Zwingli compared this attitude to a child who is asked whom in the family he loves most. He says, "I love my father." But then the mother enters the room and says, "I wish I were the dearest." To which the child replies, "But you are the dearest too." In the end the child will say the same thing even to the maid! God, however, does not tolerate confidence and trust to be placed in anyone other than Himself.[49]

Providence Rather than Chance

Zwingli, like Luther before him, affirmed the sovereignty of God in creation and salvation. Indeed, his doctrines of providence and predestination were, if anything, even more clearly delineated than those of the Wittenberg reformer.

Using the language of scholastic theology, Zwingli referred to God as the first moving cause and the highest good *(summum bonum).* As we have seen, God is the Creator, the source of all that is. However, God's unbounded creativity does not work haphazardly. God is not the life and motion of

47. Furcha and Pipkin, eds., I, p. 148; Z 2, p. 184: "Denn wie kan der mensch im selbs et was zuschryben, so er alles, das er ist, von got ist?"

48. Z 2, p. 219; Furcha and Pipkin, eds., I, p. 172.

49. Furcha and Pipkin, eds., I, pp. 154-155; Z 2, pp. 192-193.

all things in such a way that He "blindly" puts breath or motion into them. God's creative power is purposeful, teleological, that is, directed toward a specific goal. God, then, is not just a vast reservoir of unlimited energy, but the personal center of all reality whose power is not divorced from His wisdom, knowledge, and foresight.

God's providence is concerned not only with the great events of history but also with the minutiae of daily life.

> We cannot but admit that not even the least thing takes place unless it is ordered by God. For who has ever been so concerned and curious as to find out how much hair he has on his head? There is no one. God, however, knows the number. Indeed, nothing is too small in us or in any other creature, not to be ordered by the all-knowing and all-powerful providence of God.[50]

Furthermore, the providence of God governs not only the good and pleasant aspects of life but the darker, troublesome parts as well. "Not even the mosquito has its sharp sting and musical hum without God's wisdom." Zwingli did *not* claim that Christians could understand or rationalize God's providential doings. To ask why God created the flea, gadfly, hornet, or wasp is to display a "vain and useless feminine curiosity."[51] Rather they were to contemplate with reverence what God had disclosed to them, and not impudently desire to touch what He had left hidden.

Zwingli's most detailed statement on providence comes from a sermon preached at the Marburg Colloquy in October 1529 and later reworked into a philosophical treatise, *De Providentia Dei.* Here he brought into closest possible harmony the issues of divine providence and human salvation. Even earlier he had written that "the whole business of predestination, free will, and merit rests upon this matter of providence."[52] He further claimed that providence is, so to speak, the "mother of predestination," since with the elect God turns everything to good, even their evil deeds, but not so with those who are rejected.[53]

Peter Lombard and Thomas Aquinas had also treated predestination in the context of providence, as a part of the general doctrine of God. Zwingli did not depart from the scholastic tradition on this point, as Calvin did

50. Furcha and Pipkin, eds., I, p. 145; Z 2, p. 179.

51. Jackson, ed., *Latin Works,* III, pp. 66-67, Z 3, p. 647.

52. Jackson, ed., *Latin Works,* III, p. 70; Z 3, p. 650: "Nam ex providentiae loco praedestinationis, liberi arbitrii meritque universum negotium pendet."

53. Z 3, p. 842; Jackson, ed., *Latin Works,* III, p. 271. Cf. Locher, *Zwingli's Thought,* p. 125, 16n.

later.[54] Seen from this view, predestination is a special (a very special!) example of divine providence.

Zwingli, like Luther, saw predestination as a bulwark against works righteousness. Since people do not elect God, but God chooses and singles them out, believers cannot claim any of the credit for their own salvation. The epitome of human arrogance is to deny the gratuity of God's grace. Zwingli used a homely example to drive home this point. "See how handsomely we stand here and give out airs like a country bumpkin. He always wanted to be a knight yet never had a horse until in the end he became so miserable and sick that they carted him to a hospital on a manure cart."[55] According to Zwingli, "election" should be attributed only to those whom God has destined for salvation. The reprobate are not "elected" to damnation, although, as a matter of fact, God "rejects, expels and repudiates" them nonetheless. Zwingli did teach a doctrine of double predestination since both "election and rejection are the works of God's free will."[56]

Another aspect of Zwingli's doctrine of election deserves special attention: his postulation of the salvation of the so-called "pious heathen." Zwingli held that even among those who had never heard the gospel, those who lived outside the chronological or geographical bounds of salvation history, there were some chosen by God. They were future neighbors in heaven; not only the Old Testament worthies but "Hercules too and Theseus, Socrates, Aristides, Antigonus, Numa, Camillus, the Catos and Scipios," indeed every pious heart and believing soul from the beginning of the world.[57]

This teaching greatly angered Luther, who saw it as a presumption on the grace of God and a capitulation to the kind of rationalistic humanism

54. Zwingli claims to have been a follower of Thomas Aquinas's doctrine of predestination, which he later abandoned for a more "Augustinian" approach. Whether Zwingli rightly understood Thomas's mature doctrine of election as set forth in the *Summa Theologica* is debatable. See James M. Stayer, "Zwingli and the 'Viri Multi et Excellentes': The Christian Renaissance's Repudiation of *Neoterici* and the Beginnings of Reformed Protestantism," in *Prophet, Pastor, Protestant: The Work of Huldrych Zwingli after Five Hundred Years,* E. J. Furcha and H. W. Pipkin, eds. (Pittsburg: Pickwick Press, 1984), pp. 137-154.

55. Furcha and Pipkin, eds., *Writings,* I, p. 148; Z 2, p. 184.

56. Jackson, ed., *Latin Works,* II, p. 188. John Eck characterized Zwingli as a "blockhead, a dolt, a dunce who denies free will." Ibid., p. 72.

57. Ibid., p. 272: "In short there has not been a good man and will not be a holy heart or faithful soul from the beginning of the world to the end thereof that you will not see in heaven with God."

he had opposed in Erasmus. (Erasmus had once written, "St. Socrates, pray for me.") Zwingli's doctrine also went far beyond Calvin, who felt that one of the likely marks of reprobation was the lack of opportunity to hear the gospel.[58]

For Zwingli, however, the presumed salvation of such "heathen" was not based on the universal revelation of God in nature, much less on their own meritorious deeds. It depended instead on the free decision of God to choose whom He will. It was true that some of those elected outside the visible sphere of Christendom might never come to faith in this life. Yet even that was a negligible consideration since faith follows (rather than precedes) election even as a blossom springs from a bud. "For though those heathen knew not religion in the letter of it and in what pertains to the sacraments, yet as far as the real thing is concerned, I say, they were holier and more religious than all the little Dominicans and Franciscans that ever lived."[59]

Zwingli's extension of the scope of salvation to the elected heathen should not be set over against his basic evangelical commitment. No one preached *solus Christus* more strongly than he, as the second and third of the *Sixty-seven Articles* shows.

> The summary of the gospel is that our Lord Christ, true Son of God, has made known to us the will of his Heavenly Father and has redeemed us from death and reconciled us with God by his guiltlessness.
> Therefore, Christ is the only way to salvation of all who were, are now, or shall be.[60]

In accordance with John 14:6, which he often cited, Zwingli insisted that no one could come to the Father except through Christ who is "the way, the truth, and the life." He refused, however, to limit the scope of Christ's redeeming activity to the circumference of the visible church. This was his own way of saying, "Let God be God."

As a pastor Zwingli recognized the danger inherent in his stern doctrine of providence. Some would be inclined to indulge their desires and exclaim, "If I am elect I shall attain felicity however I live." Such persons, Zwingli

---

58. *Institutes* 3.24.12.

59. Jackson, ed., *Latin Works,* II, p. 201. Cf. the study of Rudolf Pfister, *Die Seligkeit Erwählter Heiden bei Zwingli* (Zurich: Evangelischer Verlag, 1952).

60. Furcha and Pipkin, eds., *Writings,* I, pp. 14, 17; Z 1, p. 458: "Summa des evangelions ist, das unser herr Christus Jhesus, warer gottes sun, uns den willen sines himmilischen vatters kundt gethon unnd mit siner unschuld vom tod erlöst and gott versunt hat . . . . Dannenher der einig weeg zur säligkeit Christus ist aller, die ie warend, sind und werdend."

responded, gave evidence either that they were not elect or that they had not yet acquired faith and the knowledge of God.[61] For the true believer, however, the proper recognition of God's providence was a bulwark against the uncertainties and buffetings of life. Both in our personal lives and also on the great stage of history, we have much assurance in knowing that "however we clamor and whatever we devise, the plans of God remain unchanged."[62]

Holy Scripture Rather than Human Tradition

The Bible stood at the center of the Zwinglian Reformation. This is clearly seen in four pivotal moments in the reformation process.

The first moment was Zwingli's own decisive "conversion" to the Scriptural principle. In a sermon on "The Clarity and Certainty of the Word of God," preached before an assembly of nuns in 1522, Zwingli recalled this important shift in his theological pilgrimage.

> When I was younger, I gave myself overmuch to human teaching, like others of my day, and when about seven or eight years ago I undertook to devote myself entirely to the Scriptures I was always prevented by philosophy and theology. But eventually I came to the point where led by the Word and Spirit of God I saw the need to set aside all these things and to learn the doctrine of God direct from his own Word. Then I began to ask God for light and the Scriptures became far clearer to me.[63]

No doubt this devotion to Scripture was motivated in part by Zwingli's strong affinity for Erasmus. No doubt, too, the "setting aside" of human authorities was a gradual process for Zwingli. In keeping with Erasmus, Zwingli preferred the Church Fathers to the scholastic theologians ("sophists," he called them). Though he remained a keen patristic scholar and was much influenced by the Fathers, especially Augustine, he came to distinguish sharply their authority from that of Holy Scripture. For example, when he was preaching at Einsiedeln, he was still enamoured of Jerome (whose works Erasmus had also edited in 1516), yet even then he remarked to one of his colleagues that there "will be a day when neither Jerome nor any other will mean much among Christians except scripture alone."[64] Later he claimed support for the principle of *sola scriptura* in Augustine himself: "Lo, here you have the Scripture as master and teacher and guide,

61. Jackson, ed., *Latin Works*, II, p. 228.
62. Ibid., p. 231.
63. Bromiley, ed., pp. 90-91.
64. Furcha and Pipkin, eds., *Writings*, I, p. 116; Z 2, p. 145.

not the Fathers, not the misunderstood Church of certain people."[65]

The second moment was Zwingli's radical new pattern of preaching which he began when he entered the pulpit of the Zurich Great Minster on New Year's Day 1519. He abandoned the traditional lectionary in favor of a chapter by chapter exposition of the Scripture. Heinrich Bullinger observed that Zwingli refused "to cut up into little pieces, the Lord's Gospel."[66] Although we cannot now reconstruct the content of those early sermons, Zwingli recalled that he preached "without any human addenda and without any hesistancy or wavering because of counter arguments."[67] He not only was preaching *from* the Bible but also was allowing the Bible to speak directly to him and his congregation. Gradually the great cathedral began to fill with those eager to hear the Word of God. Zwingli confessed surprise at the number who came "hurrying" to his expositions. The proclamation of Holy Scripture was the single most important precipitant of reform in the city of Zurich. Zwingli was confident that within a few years all of Switzerland would embrace the gospel, followed by Germany, France, Italy and Spain. For "the Word of God will easily blow all the dust away." To those who opposed his preaching, Zwingli warned: "Do not put yourself at odds with the Word of God. For truly, it will persist as surely as the Rhine follows its course. One can perhaps dam it up for a while, but it is impossible to stop it."[68]

The third moment was the acceptance of the scriptural principle by the city authorities. Zwingli's bold preaching aroused strong opposition in Zurich, especially from the monastic orders. Still, as early as 1520, the city council issued a mandate allowing freedom to preach the "true divine Scriptures of the Old and New Testaments." This was followed in 1521 by another order requiring that preaching should be "from Holy Scripture, to the exclusion of Scotus and Thomas and suchlike."[69] These civic orders were confirmed at the First Zurich Disputation in January 1523, when the Scriptures were again recognized as the "infallible judges" in the debate between Zwingli and his Roman opponents.

What exactly did Zwingli understand by the "Word of God"? Is the

65. Jackson, ed., *Latin Works,* I, pp. 264-265; Z 1, p. 307.

66. Bullinger, I, p. 12.

67. Furcha and Pipkin, eds., *Writings,* I, p. 116; Z 2, p. 145.

68. Z 3, p. 488: "Tund umb gots willen sinem wort gheinen drang an; dann warlich, warlich es wirt als gewüss sinen gang haben als der Ryn; den mag man ein zyt wol schwellen, aber nit gstellen."

69. Bromiley, ed., pp. 24, 26. Cf. Bullinger, I, pp. 32, 38.

Word of God identical with Holy Scripture? While he certainly maintained that the Word encompassed Scripture, and was uniquely expressed therein, in another sense it was a larger more generic term. For example, God's creative word brought forth the world and everything within it before it was ever committed to writing. Likewise, the powerful word spoken to the virgin Mary generated within her womb the child Jesus. Thus "the whole course of nature must be altered rather than that the Word of God should not remain and be fulfilled."[70] The living Word of God was, of course, Christ Himself. Zwingli also referred to the gospel as the Word of God and defined the gospel as "not only what Matthew, Mark, Luke, and John have written, but all that God has ever revealed to men."[71] Just as God's saving ability was not limited to the historical confines of the visible church, neither was His Word restricted to its written expression. To Zwingli's mind, this in no way diminished the authority of Scripture, but rather undergirded it since it pointed to the ultimate source of the Bible, God Himself.

But how does one come to recognize the Word of God in Holy Scripture? Zwingli answered that there is only one way to receive this insight—from God Himself. The same Spirit who inspired the prophets and apostles to write the Scriptures must be present to confirm and persuade us of its truth. In other words, Scripture is self-authenticating. The Holy Spirit enlightens the text of the Bible in such a way that we know and confess it to be the Word of God. In this sense Zwingli could speak of the "prevenient clarity" *(für Kummende klarheit)* of Holy Scripture. Also for this reason Zwingli could dispense with the official channels of approved interpretation—the pope, the councils, the schoolmen and Fathers. "God's Word can be understood by a man without any human direction."[72]

Zwingli thus brought together two affirmations which would be even more closely conjoined by Calvin: the supremacy of Holy Scripture over human tradition and the inward illumination of the individual believer by the Holy Spirit. Hence, Zwingli could say: "I understand Scripture only in the way that it interprets itself by the Spirit of God. It does not require any human opinion."[73] This does not mean, however, that Zwingli dismissed willy-nilly the decisions of the Fathers or the early councils. Indeed, he accepted without hesitation the first four general councils (Nicea, 321;

70. Bromiley, ed., p. 70.
71. Ibid., p. 86; Z 1, p. 374.
72. Bromiley, ed., pp. 75, 78; Z 1, pp. 362, 365.
73. Z 1, p. 559: "Ich verston die geschrifft nit anders, dann wie sy sich selbst durch den geist gottes usslagt; bdarff keins menschlichen urteils."

Constantinople, 381; Ephesus, 431; Chalcedon, 451) along with the Apostles', Nicene, and Athanasian Creeds. His point—no different from Luther's here—was that all these councils and documents had to be subjected to the testing stone of Scripture. If they displayed Christ, they were genuine, "of the Spirit of God." In this case, however, there was no need to cry "Fathers," "Councils," "customs," and "tradition"; these merely reflected the truth contained in the God-inspired Scriptures and made known by the Holy Spirit.

Finally, there was the furtherance of Bible study in the institution of the "Prophecy." Beginning in July 1525, at seven o'clock in the morning in summer (eight o'clock in winter), on every day except Fridays and Sundays, all of the ministers and theological students in Zurich gathered into the choir of the Great Minster cathedral to engage in an hour of intense exegesis and interpretation of Scripture. Zwingli opened the meeting with prayer:

> Almighty, eternal and merciful God, whose Word is a lamp unto our feet and a light unto our path, open and illuminate our minds, that we may purely and perfectly understand thy Word and that our lives may be conformed to what we have rightly understood, that in nothing we may be displeasing unto thy majesty, through Jesus Christ our Lord. Amen.[74]

The text of the day was then read in Latin, Greek, and Hebrew, followed by appropriate textual or exegetical comments. Zwingli or another of the ministers delivered a sermon on the passage in German. The sermon was heard by many of the laity who stopped by the cathedral on their way to work.

The name *Prophecy* was taken from 1 Corinthians 14, where Paul referred to the gift of prophesying or the telling forth of the Word of God for the edification of the church. The influence of the Zurich Prophecy was enormous. It was a kind of theological seminary where ministers, missionaries, preachers, and teachers received a thorough grounding in the Scriptures. This in turn became a model for Reformed academies and seminaries throughout Europe and was not without influence in the founding of Harvard College in New England in 1636. In addition, numerous biblical commentaries, including several by Zwingli himself, as well as the famous Zurich Bible, emerged from the sessions of the Prophecy.

74. Fritz Schmidt-Clausing, "Das Prophezeigebet," *Zwingliana* 12 (1964), pp. 10-34. Eng. tr. from Locher, *Zwingli's Thought,* p. 28.

True Religion Rather than Ceremonial Piety

During the First Zurich Disputation, an interesting exchange took place between Zwingli and John Fabri, vicar of the bishop of Constance, who spoke for the Roman side.

ZWINGLI: We know from the Old and New Testaments of God that our only comforter, redeemer, savior and mediator with God is Jesus Christ, in whom and through whom alone we can obtain grace, help and salvation, and besides from no other being in heaven or on earth.

FABRI: It seems to me the dear saints and the Virgin Mary are not to be despised, since there are few who have not felt the intercession of the Virgin and the saints. I do not care what everyone says or believes. I have placed a ladder against heaven.[75]

Fabri was referring to the biblical story of Jacob's vision of a ladder from earth to heaven, with angels coming and going back and forth. The same image is found in a popular Sunday School song: "We are climbing Jacob's ladder . . . Ev'ry round goes higher, higher." Fabri's ladder was peopled not only with angels but also with Mary and the saints, not to mention images and relics, rosaries, and vestments. These were the rungs on the ladder to heaven, divinely sanctioned "props" which aided Christians in their journey from this world to the next. Zwingli's emphasis on the immediacy of God's grace, available through Christ alone, and imparted directly by the Holy Spirit, knocked the props out from much of medieval religion. The ladder to heaven was rudely toppled over; now the Christian had direct access by faith alone into the very presence of God Himself (cf. Heb. 4:16).

Zwingli had no intention of denigrating either the saints or Mary, whose perpetual virginity he defended as vigorously as any Roman theologian. His point was rather that people were clinging to these "props" and trusting in them for salvation instead of the one true God. In one place Zwingli invented a speech and placed it on the lips of Mary:

O you ignorant people. Whatever honor I may have is not my own. God in his grace has thus enriched me that I am a maidservant and a mother of all the human race. I am neither a goddess nor the fount of goodness; God alone is that fountain. . . . I am none other than a witness of my son that you may see how certainly salvation rests with him.[76]

Zwingli was much more radical than Luther in trying to prune from

75. Jackson, ed., *Selected Works,* pp. 79-80.
76. Furcha and Pipkin, eds., *Writings,* I, pp. 156-157; Z 2, pp. 195-196.

church life those ceremonial rites and religious accoutrements which were the mainstay of medieval piety. Thoughtless prayers, prescribed fasts, the bleached cowls and carefully shaved heads of the monks, holy days, incense, the burning of candles, the sprinkling of holy water, nun's prayers, priest's chatter, vigils, masses, and matins—this "whole rubbish-heap of ceremonials" amounted to nothing but "tomfoolery." To depend upon them at all for salvation was like "placing iceblocks upon iceblocks."[77]

The Catholic authorities were shocked at the rigor with which Zwingli pursued his reforms. John Eck, writing to the Emperor Charles V in 1530, described the dilapidated state of the Zurich churches: "The altars are destroyed and overthrown, the images of the saints and the paintings are burned or broken up or defaced. . . . They no longer have churches but rather stables."[78] In 1527 the organ at the Great Minster was dismantled and removed, despite the fact that Zwingli was an accomplished musician who had mastered a number of instruments. (In 1874 an organ was restored to this church.) Even today the Great Minster, with its whitewashed walls and bare interior, stands in stark contrast to such lavishly adorned churches as the Cathedral of Notre Dame in Paris.

Why was Zwingli so sternly opposed to images and other forms of ceremonial piety? We can point to at least three reasons. First, the principle of scriptural authority relativized all extrabiblical practices. This is clearly expressed in the second of the Ten Conclusions of Bern (1528): "The Church of Christ makes no laws or commandments apart from the Word of God; hence all human traditions are not binding upon us except so far as they are grounded upon or prescribed in the Word of God."[79] In general, the Lutheran tradition has willingly retained in its worship those practices and customs not directly prohibited by Scripture. The Reformed tradition, following Zwingli, has tended to eliminate what is not expressly commanded in Scripture. In the nineteenth century Alexander Campbell summarized this principle in a succinct formula: Where the Bible speaks, we speak; where the Bible is silent, we are silent.

Secondly, Zwingli's training in the *via antiqua* made him supersensitive to the danger of retaining images in worship. The *via antiqua* posited a real ontological relationship between an image and that which the image portrayed. For Zwingli, images had a real power, albeit a destructive, demonic

77. Furcha and Pipkin, eds., *Writings,* I, pp. 70-71, 73; Z 2, pp. 86, 90.

78. Jackson, ed., *Latin Works,* II, p. 66.

79. John H. Leith, ed., *Creeds of the Churches* (Atlanta: John Knox Press, 1982), pp. 129-130.

kind of power. He observed, for example, that images of holy women were shaped so attractively, so smooth and colorful, that they were able to entice men to lust! In like manner, some of the saints' images were so lavishly decked out that women "are moved to great devotion" by just gazing upon them. Thus they became "idols" which had to be removed from places of public worship, lest they detracted from the worship of the one true God. Luther, who was trained in the *via moderna,* was less sensitive to this issue since as a nominalist he posited only a mental relation, not a real, direct connection, between an image and that which it portrayed.[80]

Finally, Zwingli was against ceremonial piety for he saw it as a substitute for true religion, which he defined as "clinging to God, with an unshaken trust in him as the only good, as the only one who has the knowledge and power to relieve our troubles and to turn away all evils or to turn them to his own glory and the benefit of His people, and with filial dependence upon him as a father—this is piety, is religion."[81] For this reason, Zwingli believed that nothing should be added to what God has revealed in his Word, nor anything taken away which is included therein.

Zwingli did not insist that the entire "hodgepodge of human ordinances" be eliminated immediately or en masse. He was willing to tolerate such things as the sign of the cross in praying or priestly vestments until the Word had time to have its effect. He did insist that the Scriptures be read and preached in German: "He who compromises at this point commits sin, for this is the word of life."[82] Only with time were the images removed from the churches; the Mass was not abolished until 1525. Once, however, the reform had been carried out, there was no going back. It was difficult to "cleanse" the temple of such beloved excrescences, but it was necessary for the pure Word of God to prevail. "If you leave the storks' nests undisturbed," warned Zwingli, "they will surely come back to them."[83]

External Kingdom Rather than Privatized Morality

Luther's Reformation was born out of his torturous quest to find a gracious God, to answer the question: How can I be saved? From the beginning, Zwingli was more concerned with the social and political implications of reform. Zwingli's central question was: How can my people be saved? Luther was fond of quoting Jesus' statement that His kingdom was

80. Furcha and Pipkin, eds., *Writings,* I, p. 172; Z 2, p. 218.
81. Jackson, ed., *Latin Works,* III, p. 1.
82. Ibid., pp. 348-349.
83. Potter, p. 314.

not of this world. For Luther this meant that the kingdom of Christ, as manifested in the visible church, should not be preoccupied with "externals" (i.e. with politics, economics, foreign policy, etc.). This was the proper business of the other realm, of the left hand of God. Zwingli did not distinguish between God's right and left hands. In a letter to Ambrosius Blaurer, the reformer of Constance, he insisted that "the kingdom of Christ is also thoroughly external."[84]

Luther's distinction between the two realms was based upon his sharp contrast between law and gospel. While readily agreeing with Luther that we are justified by faith alone apart from any meritorious acts on our part, Zwingli did not feel the need to separate law and gospel into polar opposites. Everything which God has revealed is either command, prohibition, or promise. All of these modes of revelation, including the commands and prohibitions, edify the believer. When God commands not to covet, or not to commit adultery, these are intended to teach and comfort the believer. By contrast, even the promises of God are sheer folly to the unbeliever. Thus:

> I call everything "gospel" which God opens to human beings and demands of them. For whenever God shows his will to people, it delights those who love God and thus it is to them certain and good news. For this reason I call it "gospel," preferring that term to the term "law"; for it is more fittingly named to suit the understanding of believers and not of unbelievers; and at the same time, we overcome the tension between law and gospel. Besides I know well that Christ is the sum and perfection; he is the certain manifestation of salvation, for he is salvation.[85]

To the Lutherans this blurring of the distinction between law and gospel seemed to open the door to a new legalism, a kind of evangelical works-righteousness grafted onto the pure message of *sola fide*. For Zwingli and those who followed him, it implied an intensely *activistic* concept of the Christian life. "Christ will not let his people be idle," Zwingli wrote to his stepson, Gerold Meyer. "Those who have rightly understood the mystery of the gospel will exert themselves to live rightly."[86] The reformers of

---

84. Hans-Ulrich Delius et al., eds., *Reformatorenbriefe*, (Neukirchen-Vluyn: Neukirchener Verlag, 1973), p. 270: "Christus will also auch für die äusserlichen Dinge massgeblich sein und darüber gebieten. Sein Reich ist also durchaus auch äusserlich." Cf. Z 9, p. 454.

85. Furcha and Pipkin, eds., *Writings*, I, p. 64; Z 2, p. 79.

86. Bromiley, ed., p. 108; Z 2, p. 542: "Quisquis igitur evangelii mysterium capit, recte vivere conatur." On Zwingli's view of the state see Robert C. Walton,

southern Germany and Switzerland—Zwingli in Zurich, Bucer in Strasbourg, Oecolampadius in Basel, and later Calvin in Geneva—were much
occupied in determining the precise interdependence between the church
and the structures of profane society. In Zurich, perhaps more than in any
of the other Reformed cities, church and civic community were one indivis-
ible body, governed by the spiritual and secular officers who both accepted
the principle of Scriptural authority as the basis of their joint governance.
For example, in 1525 the Zurich town council established the so-called
"marriage court" which was presided over by both theologians and city
councillors. This court attempted to impose a strict moral code upon all of
the inhabitants of Zurich, anticipating in some respects the consistory in
Calvin's Geneva. Zwingli saw no problem in this sort of cooperation between church and state. In a famous statement written shortly before his
death he stated, "The Christian man is nothing else but a faithful and good
citizen and the Christian city nothing other than the Christian church."[87]

While Zwingli argued for the compatability of law and gospel as a joint
manifestation of the will of God, he did go to considerable pains to distinguish divine and human justice. This was set forth in the sermon "Divine
and Human Justice and How They Relate to One Another," preached on
Saint John the Baptist Day in 1523. Zwingli maintained that God's "pure,
undefiled, unalloyed" justice was unfolded in the precepts of the Sermon on
the Mount. Christians should forgive as they desire God to forgive. They
should not only not kill but not even become angry, refrain not only from
adultery but also from lust. God demands such purity and innocence. Yet,
since Christians were incapable of living up to such a standard of justice,
God has done it for them through His Son Christ Jesus.

Zwingli said that there remained, however, a standard of human justice,
"poor and feeble," in comparison with God's justice, yet nonetheless instituted by God because of disobedience. At the boundary between divine
and human justice stood the magistrate, appointed by God to maintain
order, repress idolatry, and undergird the preaching of the Word. The

Zwingli's Theocracy (Toronto: University of Toronto Press, 1967), and W. P. Stephens, *The Theology of Huldrych Zwingli*, pp. 282-310. Ozment, p. 216, 71n, has
argued that Luther and Zwingli were basically similar in their view on church and
state.

87. Z 14, p. 424. Cf. the helpful discussion by Robert C. Walton, "Zwingli:
Founding Father of the Reformed Churches," *Leaders of the Reformation*, Richard
L. De Molen, ed. (Selinsgrove, Penn.: Susquehanna University Press, 1984), pp.
69-98.

magistrate, no less than the minister, was the servant of the Lord. They were to work in the closest possible harmony to ensure the furtherance of God's kingdom. For Zwingli not merely the church but the "whole world" had become so corrupt, wicked, and shameless that "it absolutely must be reformed." His reforming work aimed to revamp the corporate structures of society and politics, what he called "the present condition of things," as much as to soothe the personal anxieties of individual consciences.[88]

Although Zwingli had considerable confidence in the ability of magistrates to reform the church, he placed at least two checks against the potential abuse of magisterial authority. One was the possibility of deposing a tyrannous magistrate. Though Zwingli counseled strongly against popular resistance or rebellion (he like Luther was shocked by the seditious behavior of the peasants who took up arms against their lords, though he abhorred Luther's vengeful retort against the peasants), he nonetheless allowed that persistently evil rulers could be ousted by the will of the whole people. In speaking of the atrocities of King Manasseh, he alleged: "If the Jews had not allowed the wantonness of their king to go unpunished, God would not have punished them [with the Babylonian Captivity]."[89]

The magistrate was checked further by the faithful admonitions of the pastor, whom Zwingli preferred to call the shepherd or the watchman or the prophet.

> God has placed among his people officials—the Shepherds—who are to watch at all times. God does not want anyone to have power so unqualified that no one may not point out his misdeeds to him. . . . If the authorities help, then vice can be expelled with the greater peace, but if they do not, then the shepherd has to risk his skin and hope for no other help nor liberation than that from God.[90]

Zwingli knew whereof he spoke. He had been forced to leave his pastorate at Glarus because of his outspoken opposition to the mercenary trade. He "risked his skin" a number of times in Zurich as well; not until 1525 could he count on a solid majority of supporters on the council. In that year, the same year the Prophecy was established, Zwingli's sermons, lectures, and commentaries turned more and more to the Old Testament. Not coincidentally, he assumed the role of prophet in the city of Zurich. "If the shepherd would read the prophets then he would find nothing other than an eternal

88. Jackson, ed., *Latin Works,* III, p. 49.
89. Z 2, p. 344; Furcha and Pipkin, eds., *Writings,* I, p. 279.
90. Furcha and Pipkin, eds., *Writings,* II, p. 102; Z 3, p. 36.

battle with the powerful and the vices of this world."[91] Zwingli's own "prophetic" vocation plunged him directly into the intricate politics of Zurich, the Swiss Confederation, and the empire. In the end that preoccupation, as much as any other, led to his tragic death on the field of battle in 1531.

We can easily read Zwingli as a kind of Protestant Machiavelli, a religious statesman bent upon directing the political destiny of his people. No doubt, there is more than a grain of truth in this caricature. It misses, however, the real motive behind Zwingli's political activity, which revolved around his ideal for the community and especially his concern for its poor and marginal members. Part of the polemic against images focused on the fact that so much Christian love was being lavished on inanimate objects while so many of the true "images of God," that is believers, on earth, languished in need. Zwingli asserted that "for the sake of God's glory one should clothe the living images of God, the poor Christians, and not idols of wood and stone."[92] For many centuries wealthy citizens had endowed Masses for the dead which were supposed to speed up their journey through purgatory. When the Mass was abolished in Zwinglian territories, these endowments were converted into a kind of charitable trust for the poor whose needs, Zwingli believed, were more pressing than those of the already departed. Zwingli was also a keen critic of the economic abuses of emerging capitalism. "If a poor mother in childbed wants to buy some medicine, she may have a hard time of it; for she has to pay the monopolies twice as much as the powder is worth."[93]

Zwingli's involvement in political and economic affairs was directed toward a reformation of the whole community, of the entire life of society. Church and state were related as soul and body, distinct yet necessarily conjoined and interdependent. More than any other reformer, Zwingli reacted against the clerical supremacy of the medieval church. The error of the Roman Antichrist had been to set himself above princes and kings. Zwingli believed that the Bible taught (Ex. 4:16) that priests were to be subordinate to the magistrates. Zwingli's message required a leveling of the sacred and the secular and a vision of reform which embraced both minister and magistrate as coservants of the Word of God. That "the kingdom of Christ is also external" meant that no dimension of human existence could be excluded from the claims and promises of the gospel.

91. Furcha and Pipkin, eds., *Writings,* II, p. 101; Z 3, p. 35.
92. Z 3, p. 130. See Locher, *Zwingli's Thought,* p. 20, 61n.
93. Locher, *Zwingli's Thought,* p. 40.

Baptism as Ecclesial Event

At least as early as the Second Zurich Disputation (October 1523), some of Zwingli's more ardent disciples had become disillusioned with the slow pace of reformation in the city. On that occasion, the council declared the Roman doctrine of the Mass to be false, yet decided to postpone its immediate reform. Zwingli supported this decision, believing that the people of Zurich needed to be more thoroughly prepared for such a sweeping change. The dissenters could not accept such temporizing measures. One of their spokesmen, Conrad Grebel, wrote that at the Second Disputation the leading theologians of Zurich had set the Word of God "on its head, trampled it under foot, and put it into slavery."[94]

Soon the focus of dissent shifted to the other sacrament, which was also unreformed in Zurich, baptism. Grebel, among others, refused to submit his infant son to baptism since he could find no justification for this rite in the New Testament. The decisive break with the official policy of baptism occurred on January 21, 1525, in the home of Felix Mantz, another one of Zwingli's disaffected followers. On that evening, following a time of prayer, George Blaurock, a future Anabaptist evangelist, asked Grebel to baptize him.

> And when he knelt down with that request and desire, Conrad baptized him.
> . . . After that was done the others similarly desired George to baptize them,
> which he also did upon their request. Thus they together gave themselves to
> the name of the Lord in the high fear of God.[95]

Such were the humble, yet blatantly illegal, beginnings of the Anabaptist movement in Zurich. Almost overnight, an Anabaptist conventicle sprang up in the village of Zollikon, just four miles down the lake from Zurich. Other baptismal disturbances in and around Zurich followed: newborn infants withheld from baptism, sermons of the official pastors interrupted by Anabaptist preachers, baptismal fonts overturned and smashed, and separatist congregations of rebaptized believers gathered in defiance of the law. In June 1525 some of the peasants from Zollikon entered the city of Zurich and paraded through its streets crying, "Woe, woe, woe, O Zurich." They pilloried Zwingli as "the old dragon" and, in the spirit of the prophet Jonah, gave the city forty days in which to repent! The council regarded

94. Quoted in Fritz Blanke, *Brothers in Christ* (Scottdale, Penn.: Herald Press, 1961), p. 11.

95. George H. Williams, *Radical Reformation* (Philadelphia: Westminster Press, 1962), p. 122.

such disturbances as a direct threat to its authority. It responded to the crisis by banishing the obstinate offenders and by decreeing death by drowning as the penalty for rebaptism. On January 5, 1527, Felix Mantz became the first Anabaptist to be drowned in Zurich. While Zwingli and the other pastors looked on, Mantz was forcibly lowered beneath the icy waters of the Limmat River. The last words he was heard to utter were: "Into thy hands, O Lord, I commend my spirit."[96]

Zwingli's doctrine of baptism was forged against two fronts: the displacement of infant baptism by the Anabaptists and the sacramental objectivism of both Roman Catholic and Lutheran practice. His early statements on baptism focus almost exclusively on the latter concern. He denied vigorously that baptism had the ability to remove the guilt of original sin. For Zwingli original sin was a defect which, despite its devastating effects on the human race, "is not of itself sinful for him who has it. This defect cannot condemn one—no matter what the theologians say—until he acts out of the defect against the law of God, and one can do that only if he knows the law."[97] Baptism could not be the instrumental cause of regeneration since this had been accomplished once and for all by Christ's atoning death on the cross. What was supposedly effected by the splashing of a little water at thousands of baptismal fonts throughout Christendom had in fact been already achieved by the sacrifice of Christ at Calvary. One could not believe both in Jesus Christ and in holy water.

> So completely did he obtain all things from the Father by his death that whatever we ask in his name is granted. Hence no created thing ought to be worshipped or held in such esteem as if it had any power for the cleansing of our consciences or the salvation of souls. . . . Otherwise, the death of Christ were superfluous.[98]

In medieval theology, infants who died without benefit of baptism were consigned to limbo. There was little suffering in limbo but, unlike purgatory, neither was there any hope of escape. Limbo was, so to speak, an air-conditioned compartment of hell. In Zurich the custom had developed of burying unbaptized infants in a certain middle part of the cemetery, halfway between the profane and the holy ground—a vivid representation of limbo! Zwingli staunchly opposed this practice, urging that all children

96. Ibid., p. 146.
97. Z 4, p. 308. An English translation of "Von der Taufe, von der Wiedertaufe und von der Kindertaufe" is found in Bromiley, ed., pp. 129-175.
98. Jackson, ed., *Latin Works,* II, pp. 27, 30.

who died in infancy be given a full, Christian burial. He believed that the children of Christian parents were saved whether baptized or not, since the covenant of grace extended as much to them as to their parents.

Zwingli's stress on the immediacy of grace, imparted directly by the Spirit, made him wary of the liturgical trappings traditionally associated with the baptismal service. In 1523 Leo Jud, one of Zwingli's co-workers, drew up a vernacular order of baptism to be used in Zurich. It retained, however, many of the ceremonies of the old Latin rite, including a double signing with the cross, blowing under the eyes, placement of salt in the mouth and spittle on the ears and nose, and anointment with oil which had been consecrated by a bishop. By 1525 Zwingli repudiated such practices as a "form of magic," worthless "human additions." "How," he asked, "could water, fire, oil, milk, salt, and such crude things make their way to the mind?" In May 1525 Zwingli set forth his own drastically revised order of baptism in which, as the title read, "all the additions, which have no foundation in the word of God, have been removed."[99]

For Zwingli baptism with the Spirit rather than water baptism was the means by which individuals were drawn into the orbit of divine salvation. The Spirit was not bound to external signs: "God baptizes with his Spirit how, whom, and when he will." This emphasis could well have led to the dissolution of external baptism altogether, as it did in certain radical reformers such as Caspar Schwenckfeld. That it did not is due to Zwingli's strong sense of the corporate nature of the visible church. We will now examine the positive aspects of Zwingli's baptismal theology.

Initiation and Identification

Zwingli defined a sacrament as an initiatory ceremony or pledge by which one was publicly bound to carry out the obligations of a certain office or order. Water baptism for him was essentially a *human* action made in response to God's prior act and word. By initiation he meant not simply a "beginning" but an induction into a new way of life. He drew out of his own experience two metaphors to describe the *consignatio publica* of water baptism. As the erstwhile novice at the Dominican monastery in Bern, he was well acquainted with the monastic rite of initiation. He compared baptism to the putting on of a monk's cowl: It signified a lifelong process of learning the rules and statutes of the order, of conformity to a distinct

99. Ibid., III, p. 181; Z 4, pp. 334-337. Zwingli's baptismal order is given in parallel columns with those of Jud and Luther in Fritz Schmidt-Clausing, *Zwingli als Liturgiker* (Göttingen: Vandenhoeck and Ruprecht, 1952), pp. 143-165.

pattern of behavior. As the veteran field chaplain of Swiss mercenary troops, he likened baptism to the white cross sewed onto the uniform of a confederate. Each year on the first Thursday in April the soldiers, clad in their white-crossed attire, gathered at Näfels to celebrate a military victory of their forebears and to declare their Swiss identity. Just so, baptism marked one off as a member of the *militia Christi,* a soldier of the gospel, fighting under the direction of Christ the Captain.[100]

Neither the cowl nor the white cross imparted any special virtue or character to the one who wore them. They were public badges which identified one with a particular cause. Zwingli believed that baptism was not primarily for the sake of the one who received it; it was rather, a guaranty for those who witnessed it. Its purpose was to inform the whole church rather than one's self of the faith which had been inwardly wrought by the baptism of the Holy Spirit. All the same, baptism with water did pledge the one who received it to a lifelong mortification of the flesh. It was a testimony that one was now numbered among those who repent. It was the believers' "visible *(sichtbarlich)* entry and sealing into Christ."[101] Still, the connection between baptism and repentance is of only marginal significance in Zwingli's baptismal theology. He never developed it as clearly or thoroughly as Luther.

Covenantal Continuity

Zwingli's description of water baptism as a public pledge implied that it was applicable only to adults who could consciously make such a commitment. In fact, this is precisely what he seems to have believed in the early years of his reforming career in Zurich. He later admitted to having been "deceived" in believing that children should not be baptized until they came to the age of discretion. Nor was he the only one to hold such an opinion. In the years before the Anabaptist crisis catapulted the issue onto a wholly different plane, Zwingli shared these doubts with several leading reformers, including Erasmus, Farel, Oecolampadius. Zwingli never went so far as to advocate the abolition of infant baptism as the work of the devil, as did

---

100. Z 4, pp. 218, 231. Significantly, Erasmus too compared baptism to military initiation: "If anyone through baptism becomes a solider of Christ, it is just to fight with good faith under his standards." *Desiderii Erasmi Roterodami opera omnia* (Hildesheim, 1962), V, col. 934.

101. Z 4, p. 244.

certain of his "green," inexperienced disciples.[102]

Beginning in late 1524, Zwingli issued a series of writings in which he disabused himself of his earlier doubts about infant baptism and defended the practice by means of a new argument: convenantal continuity between the people of Israel in the old dispensation and the visible church in the new. We can briefly identify three major strands in Zwingli's argument, each of which, with further elaboration by Bullinger and Calvin, became standard features in the Reformed doctrine of infant baptism.

First, the analogy between circumcision and infant baptism: "baptism is the circumcision of the Christians," *"baptismus sit Christianorum circumcisio."* [103] This comparison was, of course, well worn by patristic and medieval usage; Luther referred to it as well. No one, however, had developed it as thoroughly as Zwingli. The bloody Old Testament rites of circumcision and Passover had been replaced by two "gentler" sacraments, baptism and the Lord's Supper. Baptism is gentler in another respect as well—it extends to female infants not just to boys, although even in the former dispensation the girls received the figure of baptism in passing through the Red Sea. We have seen already that Zwingli related election to infant baptism: Salvation is assured for all children of Christian parents who die in infancy. He went so far as to claim that had Esau died as a baby, he would have been elect! Since Christian children so obviously belong to God, how can they be denied the sign of this belonging? Circumcision was not only a sign of Abraham's faith but also of the whole content of the convenant which God concluded with him and his seed. Water baptism was the external, collective sign of the New Israel, the church.

Secondly, Christian baptism derived not from the baptismal command of Matthew 28, but from the baptism of John the Baptist. Jesus submitted Himself both to circumcision and the baptism of John (though, of course, He needed neither), thereby joining the rites of the two dispensations and signifying that they were of equal value. Medieval Catholicism, Anabaptism, and Luther agreed—though for very different reasons—in drawing a

---

102. Ibid., p. 228. Hubmaier, for example, later reminded Zwingli that "in the year 1523, on the day of Philip and Jacob, I personally conferred with you on Graben Street concerning the scriptural teaching on baptism. Then and there you said I was right to hold that children should not be baptized until they were instructed in the faith." *Balthasar Hubmaier, Schriften,* Gunnar Westin and Torsten Bergsten, eds. *Quellen zur Geschichte der Taufer* (Leipzig: n.p., 1930-   ) IX: 186.

103. Z 8, p. 271. This is from a letter of December, 1524 to Franz Lambert and "the other brothers in Strasbourg."

sharp distinction between the baptisms of Jesus and John. Zwingli, too, had formerly supposed the two baptisms to be quite different. His new insight was based on the conviction that Scripture discloses not two covenants in which God acts differently for salvation, but rather *one covenant in two dispensations.* The baptisms of the church and John were precisely the same because the gospel he preached was the very one Christians proclaimed: "Behold, the Lamb of God, who takes away the sins of the world!" (John 1:29, RSV).

Thirdly, while the New Testament does not command infant baptism *expressis verbis,* it can be inferred from various passages. Zwingli cited the embrace of little children by Christ (Luke 18:15-17), household baptisms in Acts and the Epistles, and the fact that Christ nowhere commanded infants *not* to be baptized as probable indications that the New Testament church practiced infant baptism. At points he appears to be skating on pretty thin exegetical ice, as in his surmise that John baptized infants in the Jordan or his claim that the disciples of John who sought rebaptism (Acts 19) had only received a baptism of "teaching," not of water. Long ago, in his seminal study on Zwingli's doctrine of baptism, Usteri observed that whenever Zwingli had in mind adult baptism he quoted copiously from the New Testament but that the moment he began to defend infant baptism he fell back on the argument from circumcision. He could only secure the objectivity of infant baptism in the context of the unity of the covenant.

Baptism and Faith

We have seen that for Zwingli faith was the gift of the Holy Spirit and had no intrinsic connection with water baptism. Yet in the New Testament water baptism is invariably associated with faith; all doctrines of infant baptism must come to grips with the relation between the two. Luther toyed with the idea that the faith of the sponsors sufficed for the child but abandoned this view of a vicarious faith *(fides vicaria)* for a full-blown doctrine of infant faith. "A child becomes a believer if Christ in baptism speaks to him through the mouth of the one who baptizes, since it is his Word, his commandment, and his word cannot be without fruit."[104] The fact that the intellective processes of the infant were in abeyance was no hindrance to the impartation of faith; if anything, it was easier for an infant to receive faith since whorish reason was not as likely to get in the way!

Zwingli would have none of this idea of an infant faith. "Baptism cannot

104. LW 40, pp. 245-246; WA 26, p. 159.

confirm faith in infants because infants are not able to believe."[105] In Zwingli's baptismal liturgy of 1525, faith is mentioned only once, in the so-called "Flood Prayer" where the minister names the baptizand and prays God to kindle "the light of faith in his heart whereby he may be incorporated into thy Son." When and how the Spirit chose to impart faith to the individual being baptized was impertinent to the rite itself.

Zwingli did, however, place great store in the personal faith of the parents who offered the child for baptism. The whole concept of the covenant as the visible manifestation of God's purpose in history hinged on the fact that these were children of *Christian* parents. Only parents who were conscious participants in the covenant community were to present their infants for baptism: "We do not allow children to be brought to baptism unless their parents have first been taught."[106] The parents made a confession on behalf of their child, by proxy as it were, and the church accepted this confession presuming, in the judgment of charity, that the infant was truly elect. For Zwingli, though, the faith of the parents was secondary to the faith of the whole church. This is why he frowned on private baptisms and insisted that baptism be administered "in the presence of the church" by a duly appointed minister of the Word. "The recipient of baptism testifies that he belongs to the Church of God, which worships its Lord in soundness of faith and purity of life."[107] Infant baptism was, for Zwingli, essentially an ecclesial event. The kind of faith which it presupposed was not the personal, subjective faith of the infants or the parents (*fides qua creditur*), but the whole content of the Christian message (*fides quae creditur*).

Baptism and the Social Order

In *In catabaptistarum strophas elenchus* (1527), Zwingli summed up in one phrase his great fear of the Anabaptist movement: "They overturn everything."[108] By 1524 he had discerned that the real danger from the Anabaptists was not so much heresy as schism and sedition. Infant baptism came to be the fulcrum on which both the unity of the church and the integrity of the civic order turned. In 1526 Zwingli persuaded the Zurich Council to establish a baptismal register in every parish. This device, together with the decision to expel those citizens who refused to submit their infants for baptism, enabled the magistrates to make infant baptism an

---

105. Z 4, p. 228. Cf. also Z 5, p. 649.
106. Z 4, p. 238.
107. Jackson, ed., *Latin Works*, II, p. 48.
108. Z 6, p. 46: "Omnia turbant inque pessimum status commutant."

instrument for political conformity. This policy went hand in glove with Zwingli's program of reform, which presupposed the identity of the visible church with the populace of the Christian city or state: "A Christian city is nothing other than a Christian church." The Christian *civitas* might be a *corpus permixtum* of sheep and goats, God alone knowing for sure who was which, but it could not be a company of baptized and unbaptized lest the civic order itself, and the proclamation of the gospel which depended upon it, be imperiled. It is ironic that water baptism which played at best an adiaphorous role in Zwingli's soteriology became the basis for his defense of the visible church.

The development of Zwingli's baptismal theology followed the course of his work as a reformer. If he seemed to undervalue water baptism as a salvific sign, he rallied to its defense as an indispensable symbol of ecclesial unity. We may applaud the later Reformed tradition for recovering a more incarnational theology of the sacraments, but Zwingli's appeal to the apriority and freedom of divine grace stands as a needed warning against every form of institutional idolatry.

Strife Over the Supper

In a world threatened by nuclear war and global famine, we have difficulty appreciating the intensity with which reformers in the sixteenth century argued over the niceties of eucharistic theology. One of the more moderate participants in those debates, Wolfgang Capito of Strasbourg, wrote to his friend Ambrosius Blaurer in 1525: "Future generations will laugh at the pleasure our age takes in quarrelling when we raise such disturbance about the very signs that should unite us."[109] One of the great tragedies of Reformation history was that so much strife and hurt occurred around the meal

109. Quoted in Potter, p. 287. Potter provides one of the best discussions of the eucharistic controversy from the standpoint of political history. The standard study remains the two-volume work by Walther Köhler, *Zwingli und Luther: Ihr Streit über das Abendmahl nach seinen politischen and religiosen Bezeiehungen* (vol. I: Leipzig: M. Hensius Nachfolger, 1924; vol. II: Gutersloh: C. Bertelsmann Verlag, 1953). Among the plethora of secondary studies, I recommend the following recent works: H. Wayne Pipkin, "The Positive Religious Values of Zwingli's Eucharistic Writings," Furcha, ed., pp. 107-143; Stephens, pp. 218-259; Peter Buhler, "Der Abendmahlsstreit der Reformatoren und seine aktuellen Implikationen," *Theologische Zeitschrift* 35 (1979), pp. 228-241; David C. Steinmetz, "Scripture and the Lord's Supper in Luther's Theology," *Interpretation* 37 (1983), pp. 253-265; Locher, *Zwingli's Thought*, pp. 220-228, 303-339; John Stephenson, "Martin Luther and the Eucharist," *Scottish Journal of Theology* 36 (1983), pp. 447-461.

which Jesus intended as a supper of peace. It is a further irony that Protestants who broke with Rome over the principle of *sola scriptura* could not find in this principle sufficient unity to prevent their separating from one another over the Lord's Supper.

We should not, however, be too hasty in our condemnation of the reformers. For both Luther and Zwingli, the very essence of the gospel was at stake in the debate over the supper. They were not merely arguing over words or being stubborn, though they were guilty of both of these as well. They were each guided to their respective points of view by deeply held convictions concerning the person of Christ, the meaning of Scripture, and the place of the Lord's Supper in the life of the church. We shall examine this controversy in terms of its medieval background, political context, exegetical and Christological dimensions, and finally its liturgical consequences.

The Medieval Background

In the early church the celebration of the Lord's Supper was the central focus of Christian worship. The earliest liturgies portray a service of praise and thanksgiving, celebrated every Sunday by the whole community of faith. This service consisted of Scripture reading, preaching, intercessory prayers, and the sharing of the supper proper—the bringing of the bread, the reception of the elements, and often the exchange of the peace of the Lord. By the time of the Reformation, however, this rite had undergone such a drastic development as to be hardly recognizable as the same event.

In the first place, it had become "clericalized." Rather than an act of worship involving the whole church, the Mass became a special task performed by the ordained clergy. The Eucharist continued to be celebrated each Sunday, but the congregation no longer communicated, except at Easter. Since Mass was the function of the priest rather than the people, Latin instead of the vernacular became the language of the liturgy. On those rare occasions when the people did communicate, they were given only bread, the wine still being reserved for the priests. Even before the Reformation, a major protest against this practice had arisen among the Hussite Utraquists (so called from the Latin *utra,* meaning "both") who insisted that both bread and wine be given to the laity.

Closely related to the clerical domination of the Eucharist was the fact that it had also become commercialized. Many Christians believed that special favors could be secured from God by having a "mass priest" offer the Eucharist on one's behalf. These were called "votive" Masses (from the Latin word for *promised* or *devoted*) and were celebrated by the priest in private. Burnaby Googe, a sixteenth-century English poet, put into verse some of the benefits which were believed to derive from such votive Masses:

Mass doth defend the traveller from danger and disease;
Mass doth preserve the sailing ship amid the raging seas.
Mass giveth store of corn and grain, and helpeth husbandry;
Mass blesseth every such as seeks in wealthy state to be.
Mass gets a man a pleasant wife, and gets the maid her mate;
Mass helps the captain in the field, and furthereth debate . . .[110]

Masses came to be offered at weddings and funerals, for protection against disease or bad weather, and in rural areas, even for the safe delivery of cows, ewes, and mares. In the large churches and cathedrals, numerous altars were erected, often in side chapels endowed by wealthy families, where such Masses could be said many times during the day.

We can easily see how this practice was so readily abused, since the priest expected and sometimes charged a fee for services rendered. Like indulgences, Masses too were sold to people who were willing to pay for the personal benefits they believed would result. In this way the supper of the Lord was transformed into a vulgar monetary exchange while the priest became a kind of spiritual mercenary. To the reformers this practice seemed like another useless effort of trying to buy God's grace. Luther spoke for all of them when he said: "I regard the preaching and selling of the mass as a sacrifice or good work as the greatest of all abominations."[111]

Eucharistic theology had tried to keep pace with eucharistic piety; as a result, the Lord's Supper also became "scholastized." After the Fourth Lateran Council in 1215, medieval Catholic theologians explained the presence of Christ in the Eucharist by reference to the dogma of transubstantiation. Using the categories of Aristotelian philosophy, they taught that at the moment in the Mass when the priest consecrates the bread and wine, a miracle occurs: the *substance* of the elements is suddenly changed (transubstantiated) into the body and blood of Christ, while the *accidents* of the elements remain the same. In other words, when the priest lifted the bread off the altar and said, *"Hoc est corpus meum,"* he was really holding in his hands the very body of Christ, although it still looked and tasted like bread.

This doctrine led to a great concentration on the moment of consecration. Our English expression, *hocus-pocus,* which we use as a kind of byword for

110. Quoted, Theodore G. Tappert, *The Lord's Supper: Past and Present Practices* (Philadelphia: Muhlenberg Press, 1961), p. 41.
111. LW 37, pp. 370-371; WA 26, p. 508.

something magical or incredible, comes from the conflation of the Latin words of institution, *Hoc-est-corpus-meum*. Although most people communicated only annually, the elevation of the Host (from the Latin word *hostia*, "sacrifice") in the Mass became the focus of intense devotion in the later Middle Ages. At the moment of consecration, bells would be rung so people in the congregation could look with wonder and adoration upon the elevated host. The feast of Corpus Christi (The Body of Christ) spread from France throughout Europe. On this occasion, the consecrated Host would be paraded through the streets and public squares in a solemn procession, the people bowing in reverence as the host passed by.

The doctrine of transubstantiation lent credence to the magnificent pageantry of the late medieval Eucharist.

> Played out on the splendid stage of the larger Gothic church, lighted from jewelled windows of stained glass, clothed in the sumptuous late-medieval vestments, with the flames of the candles flickering and the sweet-scented smoke of the incense ascending, [the eucharist] presented a complex of light and colour and movement, which engaged the heart, if not the head, of the medieval Christian.[112]

No wonder that the reformers' efforts to reform the Mass met with such violent reaction.

Both Luther and Zwingli recognized that the Mass was at the nerve center of late medieval piety. They also knew that no genuine reform of the church could be brought about without giving serious attention to its reform. Since we are going to look closely at the differences between Luther and Zwingli on the Eucharist, it will be well at this point to mention what they held in common over against the medieval Mass.

First, they decisively rejected the character of the Mass as a spectator event. They wanted to restore full congregational participation in this central act of worship. Thus, they each urged communion in both kinds (the loaf and the cup) for laity as well as clergy, and both developed a service for the Lord's Supper in their native German tongue. Secondly, they each insisted on the centrality of the Word in the celebration of the supper. By the time of the Reformation, the Scripture readings were often given in Latin, which few could understand, and the sermon was frequently omitted altogether. Luther and Zwingli interpreted the sacraments as (to borrow a phrase from the later Reformed tradition) "visible words" of God, which

112. Jean Daniélou, et al., *Historical Theology* (Middlesex: Penguin Books, 1969), p. 224.

were intended to complement, rather than compete with, the legible, audible Word of Gòd. Thus the Augsburg Confession (1530) defines the true church as that place where "the Word is rightly preached and the sacraments are rightly administered" (article VII). Thirdly, both reformers disavowed the Mass as a sacrifice offered to God on behalf of the people. The Eucharist could not displace the unique, unrepeatable sacrifice of Christ on the cross. And, finally, both rejected the scholastic doctrine of transubstaniation, which they saw as a specious explanation of the Eucharist completely unknown to the early church. Luther complained that "the laity have never understood the hair-splitting philosophy of substance and its accidents; nor, if they were taught it, could they grasp it."[113] Given this wide measure of agreement, it remains to see what the fuss was all about.

The Political Context

As early as 1523, before he had developed mature views on the Eucharist, Zwingli was keenly aware that he and Luther differed on this vital topic. He pointed out that Luther's preferred word for the Eucharist was *testament* while he favored *memorial.* At that time, Zwingli could still refer to Luther as "a good warrior of God, the like of which we have not had on earth in a thousand years."[114] He certainly did not anticipate that the differing nuances of their eucharistic theologies would lead to a permanent split. Nonetheless, the later conflict was presaged to some extent in the two words Zwingli mentioned. For Luther, *testament* referred to the fact that the Lord's Supper was a gift of Christ to the church—"This cup is the new testament in my blood" (Luke 22:20). For Zwingli, *memorial* meant that the supper was a service of commemoration by which the church proclaimed its allegiance to Christ. In other words, Luther emphasized the "This is" in the words of institution, while Zwingli stressed the "Do this."

At first Zwingli saw (or claimed to see) no fundamental difference in these two approaches to the supper. In time, however, he came to believe that the Lutheran teaching that in the Eucharist "we eat the body of Christ under the bread," was fraught with serious, even dangerous, problems. It smacked of the Roman doctrine of transubstantiation and could in no wise be squared with the advanced view which Zwingli had embraced.

Luther had already been challenged on the Eucharist by one of his former associates, Andreas Bodenstein von Karlstadt, who denied the real, objec-

---

113. John Dillenberger, ed., *Martin Luther: Selections from his Writings* (New York: Doubleday, 1961), p. 267.

114. Furcha and Pipkin, eds., *Writings,* I, p. 117; Z 2, p. 147.

tive presence of Christ in the supper in favor of a more spiritualist under-standing. When Luther learned that Zwingli, too, had set forth a revised explanation of the Eucharist, he quickly (and unfairly) lumped Zwingli with Karlstadt and the other "sacramentarians": "I regard them all cut out of the same cloth, whoever they are, who are unwilling to believe that the Lord's body in the Supper is his true, natural body."[115]

Zwingli saw Luther as lapsing back into Romanism; Luther believed Zwingli had gone over to the sectarians. The war was on! Between 1526 and 1529 Luther, Zwingli, and their allies blasted one another in treatise after treatise. At the Frankfurt book fair, in the spring of 1527, Luther's treatise *That the Words of Christ . . . Still Stand Firm Against the Fanatics* and Zwingli's rejoinder, *A Friendly Exegesis . . . Addressed to Martin Luther* (which is really not so friendly) were placed on sale side by side. Zwingli wished Luther had remained silent on the topic, for then "we should not have been forced to swallow your loathsome stuff."[116] Luther declared that Zwingli "is seven times more dangerous than when he was a papist . . . I publicly maintain before God and the whole world that I neither am nor ever will be connected with Zwingli's doctrine."[117]

This dispute might well have gone down as just another theological tempest in an ecclesiastical teapot had it not been for the profound political implications of the controversy. In the years immediately following Lu-ther's condemnation at the Diet of Worms in 1521, Emperor Charles V had been unable to suppress the Protestant "heresy" in his German territories due to the press of external events. The Turks were advancing on Vienna in the east while Francis I of France waged war in the west; even the pope was openly hostile to Charles's imperial designs. By the late 1520's, how-ever, the situation changed drastically in the emperor's favor: The Turks had been checked, Rome had been sacked, the pope captured, and, by 1529, the king of France had come to terms with his Hapsburg rival. Charles promised prompt action against the Protestants: "It is highly pleasing to his Imperial Majesty that a suitable medicine shall be prepared to deal with this dangerous plague."[118]

In this context Landgrave Philip of Hesse attempted to negotiate a mili-tary alliance between his fellow Lutheran princes and the powerful city-states of southern Germany and Switzerland. At the time it was thought

115. WA 54, p. 155.
116. Furcha and Pipkin, eds., *Writings*, II, p. 248; Z 5, p. 578.
117. WA 26, p. 342; LW 37, p. 231.
118. Potter, p. 318.

that even France and Venice might be persuaded to join the alliance because of their opposition to the emperor. If this plan were realized, thought Philip, a "buffer zone" stretching from the Baltic to the Adriatic Seas would protect the Protestant territories from the imminent danger of a counter-reformation. Zwingli saw much merit in this schema. Zurich, although it had won important allies in Basel and Berne, was politically isolated and threatened by the inner cantons of Switzerland which had never accepted the Reformation.

One major obstacle stood in the way of such a pan-Protestant alliance: the eucharistic controversy. Most of the south German cities, especially Strasbourg and Basel, sympathized with Zwingli's views. Luther was against any alliance with the "sacramentarians." Philip of Hesse knew that only a summit meeting between Luther and Zwingli could break through the impasse and establish a theological basis for a political alliance. He proposed a conference at his castle in Marburg for October, 1529. At the urging of his own prince, John of Saxony, Luther reluctantly agreed to attend. He was accompanied by Melanchthon and several other associates. Zwingli, Oecolampadius, and Bucer were the principal leaders of the other delegation. For four days these learned theologians debated in person all of the issues they had already rehashed several times in writing. In the end they agreed to disagree. On fourteen major points of the faith they were united. But concerning the fifteenth, the Lord's Supper, they admitted that "we have not agreed at this moment whether the true body and blood of Christ be corporeally present in the bread and wine."[119] When the two sides departed, Zwingli cried out in tears, "There are no people on earth with whom I would rather be at one than the Wittenbergers." Yet there was to be no confessional alliance and no military alliance either. The failure at Marburg paved the way, at least in part, for the success of the Counter Reformation during the next century and a half.

The Exegetical Crux

On the first day of the Marburg Colloquy Luther had been paired in discussion with Oecolampadius; and Zwingli, with Melanchthon. On the next day, however, the two generals met face to face in an explosive encounter. Luther entered the room earlier and, unbeknownst to anyone else, chalked the words *"Hoc est corpus meum"* onto the table in front of his seat. He then covered the inscription with a satin cloth. In the course of the debate the following exchange occurred:

119. Ibid., p. 330, 2n.

ZWINGLI: It would be a shame to believe in such an important doctrine, teach, and defend it, and yet be unable or unwilling to cite a single Scripture passage to prove it.

LUTHER   (taking the cover from the inscription on the table): This is my body! Here is our Scripture passage. You have not yet taken it from us, as you set out to do; we need no other. My dearest lords, since the words of my Lord Jesus Christ stand there, *Hoc est corpus meum,* I cannot truthfully pass over them, but must confess and believe that the body of Christ is there.

Zwingli, of course, recognized the familiar words of institution, but he placed an entirely different meaning upon them. Influenced by the Dutch humanist Cornelius Hoen, he argued that the *"est"* should be understood as *"significat."* "This [bread] *signifies* my body." The bread signified or represented Christ's body in that it called Christians to remember the event of the cross. Zwingli found support for this figurative interpretation in many other passages of Scripture. For example, when Jesus said, "I am the vine," no one imagined that He became a literal, physical vine! Likewise, when Paul declared (1 Cor. 10:4) that "Christ was that rock," he was not proclaiming a Savior made of stone, but rather that Christ was signified by the rock.

Luther, however, was adamant in holding to the literal meaning of "is." He admitted that the Lord's Supper was a symbol, but it was a symbol which contained that which it symbolized. He gave the following illustration:

I pick up a wooden or silver rose and ask: what is this? You answer: it is a rose. For I did not ask about its meaning, but about its being, so you told me what it was, not what it signified . . . "Is" always has to do with being. There is no other way to take it. But you say: it is not a rose, it is a piece of wood. Well, I answer, all right. But it is still a rose. Even if it is not a natural, organic rose out of my garden, it is still essentially a rose, in its own way. There are lots of roses—silver ones, gold ones, cloth, paper, stone, wooden. Nonetheless, each is in its own way, and essentially, a rose in its being. Not just a mere sign. Why, how could there by any *signifying* unless there were first a *being*? Whatever *is* nothing *signifies* nothing. Whatever signifies first has to be, and to be like that other thing.[120]

Both Luther and Zwingli agreed that the bread in the supper was a sign. For Luther, however, that which the bread signified, namely the body of

120. WA 26, p. 383. Trans. in H. G. Haile, *Luther: An Experiment in Biography* (New York: Doubleday, 1980), pp. 126-127.

Christ, was present "in, with, and under" the sign itself. For Zwingli, though, sign and thing signified were separated by a distance—the width between heaven and earth.

If "This is my body" was Luther's favorite text, Zwingli had one of his own, John 6:63: "It is the spirit that gives life, the flesh is of no avail" This text supported Zwingli's emphasis on the direct, unmediated impartation of salvation by the Holy Spirit, and his disparagement of the "husks of externals." It became the centerpiece of his attack on Luther's doctrine of the corporeal presence of Christ in the Supper. At Marburg Zwingli quoted this verse again and again. In a heated exchange, Zwingli warned Luther that this text would break his neck! Luther replied that necks were not so easily broken in German Hesse as in Switzerland!

"The flesh profits nothing." In this verse, said Zwingli, Christ had cut the knot "with an axe so sharp and solid that no one can have any hope that these two pieces—body and eating—can come together again."[121] This text became the buttress from which Zwingli attacked Luther's literal interpretation of the words of institution. Luther claimed that the body of Christ was not eaten in a gross, material way, but rather in some mysterious way which is beyond human understanding. Yet, Zwingli replied, if the words were taken in their literal sense, the body had to be eaten in the most grossly material way. "For this is the meaning they carry: this bread is that body of mine which is given for you. It was given for us in grossly material form, subject to wounds, blows and death. As such, therefore, it must be the material of the supper."[122] Indeed, to press the literal meaning of the text even farther, it follows that Christ would have again to suffer pain, as His body was broken again—this time by the teeth of communicants. Even more absurdly, Christ's body would have to be swallowed, digested, even eliminated through the bowels! Such thoughts were repulsive to Zwingli. They smacked of cannibalism on the one hand and of the pagan mystery religions on the other.

The main issue for Zwingli, however, was not the irrationality nor exegetical fallacy of Luther's views. It was rather that Luther put "the chief point of salvation in physically eating the body of Christ," for he connected it with the forgiveness of sins.[123] The same motive which had moved Zwingli so strongly to oppose images, the invocation of saints, and baptismal regeneration was present also in the struggle over the supper: the fear of idolatry.

121. Z 5, p. 616.
122. Furcha and Pipkin, eds., *Writings,* II, p. 338; Z 5, p. 704.
123. Z V, p. 572; Furcha and Pipkin, eds., *Writings,* II, p. 244.

Salvation was by Christ alone, through faith alone, not through faith *and* bread. The object of faith was that which is not seen (Heb. 11:1) and which therefore cannot be eaten except, again, in a nonliteral, figurative sense. *"Credere est edere,"* said Zwingli: "To believe is to eat." To eat the body and to drink the blood of Christ in the supper, then, simply meant to have the body and blood of Christ present in the mind.

The Christological Divide

In the meeting at Marburg, the discussion between Luther and Zwingli moved quickly from a skirmish over the proper meaning of specific texts to a debate over the location of Christ's body. At heart the basic theological difference between the two reformers was Christological. Both formally affirmed the definition of the Council of Chalcedon (451) that Christ was "one person in two natures." Luther, however, consistently stressed the unity of the person (like the Monophysites in the early church) while Zwingli emphasized the distinction between the two natures (like the Nestorians). That neither reformer fell off the tightrope of Christological orthodoxy is a measure of their theological acumen. Their failure to reach accord on this point, however, further exacerbated their other eucharistic differences.

When pressed by Zwingli to explain how Christ could be bodily present "in, with, and under" the elements of bread and wine, Luther responded with his doctrine of the ubiquity or omnipresence of Christ's humanity. Put simply, Christ's body was able to be in more than one place at the same time. Luther based this teaching on his particular understanding of what the theologians of the early church had called the "exchange of properties" *(communicatio idomatum).* This was a way of explaining how the incarnate Christ could be at once God and man. The attributes of His divine nature were also characteristic of His human nature, while, in like manner, the peculiar characteristics of His human nature were attributed to His divinity. In this way, one could talk about the Son of God being born or suffering or dying. But Luther did not confine the exchange of properties to Christ's earthly life; he extended them into eternity. The ubiquity of Christ's divine nature was shared with His human nature, so that wherever Christ was spiritually present, He could also be corporally present. Thus in the supper what Christians ate was not bread alone but also the body of Christ.

Zwingli had no trouble affirming that Christ was present in the supper according to His divinity. However, He could be present bodily only according to contemplation and memory. The risen, glorified body of Christ remains in heaven, seated on God's right hand. To Luther's claim that

Christ's body was everywhere present after the resurrection, Zwingli opposed the words of the angel to the woman who came to the tomb on Easter morning: "He is risen. He is not here!" (Matt. 28:6). The ascension of Christ was a literal, historical event. Did not the disciples see Him ascend? Did not Stephen see Him there? Now a body in heaven at God's right hand precluded its corporeal presence on the communion table.

In all of this Zwingli sought to safeguard the integrity of Christ's humanity. In the incarnation, the Second Person of the Godhead assumed human nature. His body was henceforth circumscribed by specific places: a crib, a carpenter shop, dusty roads, a cross. The resurrection and ascension did not rob Christ of this finite human nature. Before Christ ascended to the Father, He said to His disciples: "I am no more in the world" (John 17:11). Zwingli pointed out that this sentence contained the same verb as the famous *"Hoc est corpus meum."* Christ's finite session at the right hand of the Father guaranteed His continual advocacy on behalf of believers and His certain coming again. "When we shall see him return as he departed, we shall know that he is present. Otherwise he sits, according to his human nature, at the right hand of His Father until he will return to judge the quick and the dead."[124]

The Theological Consequences

In *Friendly Exegesis* Zwingli wrote to Luther: "We make our inference thus: you affirm that the flesh is eaten; we deny it. Therefore, one or the other must be wrong."[125] For once Luther agreed with his adversary: "One side must be the devil, and God's enemy. There is no middle ground."[126] Looking from the twentieth century, both of these conclusions appear premature and immature. We must confess that the eucharistic controversy was one of the saddest episodes in church history. Yet we say this penitently not arrogantly, for Luther and Zwingli were both persons of deep conviction and genuine piety. It may justly be said that neither took the pains to understand the deepest motivations of the other. Zwingli could only see Luther leading the church back to "the garlics and onions of Egypt," while Luther belittled his Swiss counterpart (whom he disparagingly called "Zwingel") as an enthusiastic fanatic. Yet both reformers emphasized dimensions of the gospel which are essential to a full understanding of the Christian message. We can summarize our survey of the controversy by

124. Jackson, ed., *Latin Works*, II, p. 51.
125. Furcha and Pipkin, eds., *Writings*, II, p. 282.
126. WA 23, pp. 83-85; LW 37, p. 27.

looking at the underlying convictions which, in the end, they were not able to reconcile.

Incarnation. For Luther the supper was in some ways an extension of the incarnation. He believed that when Christ ascended, He did not cease to be present with believers, bodily as well as spiritually. When at Marburg Oecolampadius urged him not to cling so ardently to the humanity of Christ, but to raise his mind to Christ's divinity, Luther erupted: "I know of no God except the one who became man, and I want none other!" For Luther the Eucharist was the place where Christ was palpably present, not because of the so-called miracle of transubstantiation but because God's Word had promised the body and blood of Christ under the elements of bread and wine. Just as John saw the Holy Spirit when he saw the dove, so believers could see and eat Christ's body in the supper.

Zwingli, too, was vitally concerned with the relation between the incarnation and the Eucharist. For him, however, the supper was not so much an extension of the incarnation as it was a sign which pointed to the historical uniqueness of the incarnation. Thus, Christ's death on the cross and not the supposed munching on Christ's body in the Eucharist was "the only way" *(der eynig Weg)* to salvation. Even in the atonement, for Zwingli, the divinity of Christ and not his humanity was crucial for salvation. In the supper this decisive event is recalled, remembered, and thus realized (i.e. made present, to the faith of believers).

Proper Conduct at the Table. Underlying the different theologies of the Eucharist was a perhaps even more neuralgic concern: the correct mode of reverence at communion. We have seen how that in the late Middle Ages the adoration of the Host became the focus of eucharistic piety, even when the congregation did not communicate. Luther retained a considerable measure of medieval reverence toward the consecrated elements. He held that, at the words of institution, the bread ceased to be mere bread; rather, the consecrated bread "wears" the body of Christ. And if Christ were truly present in the bread, then "why should this food not be handled with the highest reverence and worshipped?"[127] On one occasion when Luther was celebrating Communion, he dropped some consecrated wine onto the floor. He immediately fell on his knees and licked up the wine to avoid stepping on it.[128] Luther ordinarily knelt to receive Communion and considered the adoration of Christ in the supper a proper Christian response. Still, he refused to make such adoration a binding law. He considered it a matter

127. WA 30/1, p. 53; WA TR 5, p. 308.
128. Stephenson, "Luther and the Eucharist," p. 448.

of indifference and personal choice since Christ had given no specific commandment about it.

For Zwingli the worship of Christ in the supper was far from being a question of individual whim—"it is no light matter to teach what is to be worshipped." God alone is to be worshiped, not flesh and blood. Zwingli resisted the kind of special reverence Luther displayed toward the concecrated elements because it seemed to border on idolatrous worship, and also because it seemed to place restrictions on Christ's divinity:

> Do you not shut up God in a place? For if you shut him out or leave him free in one place and not in another, you are evidently limiting his divinity. For you make him free or not in connection with place, and this is nothing less than to tie God to the narrow limits of places. . . . We say Christ is everywhere [by his divine nature] and, therefore, is to be worshipped everywhere.[129]

The Role of Faith. In early writings against the Roman doctrine of the Mass, Luther stressed the priority of faith in the supper: "However true it is that the sacrament is real food, yet it is no help at all to him who does not receive it in his heart by faith." He even quoted Zwingli's favorite text from John 6 and declared that the eating and drinking referred to there is "nothing else but believing on the Lord Jesus Christ."[130] However, as the eucharistic controversy became a major issue, Luther stressed more and more the objectivity of God's gift in the supper. For Luther this meant that all who partake of Communion, regardless of their spiritual condition, receive the true body of Christ with their mouths—"whoever presses this bread with teeth or tongue presses the body of Christ with teeth or tongue."[131] He believed the presence of Christ was not tied to the faith of the recipients, although unbelievers who partook "eat and drink damnation" for themselves (1 Cor. 11:29).

This so-called "eating of the unbelievers" *(manducatio infidelium)* made no sense to Zwingli. For him the supper was essentially a response of thanksgiving and praise for the work of grace which had already been received by faith. And even though the supper could be an occasion for the

129. Furcha and Pipkin, eds., *Writings,* II, p. 305; Z 5, p. 657.

130. WA 15, pp. 341, 343. Zwingli later quoted these very passages back to Luther—to his embarrassment. Karl Barth has rightly observed that Luther himself had said everything necessary against his own position long before Zwingli appeared. See his "Luther's Doctrine of the Eucharist: Its Basis and Purpose," *Theology and Church* (London: SCM, 1962), p. 82, 7n.

131. WA 26, p. 942.

strengthening of faith, it had no effect on those who partook in unbelief. Without faith, the supper was only an empty ritual.

Pastoral Purposes of the Supper. Both Luther and Zwingli were pastors as well as theologians. Each had a distinctive pastoral concern in relating the Eucharist to the life of the church. In 1520 Luther sounded the note which would characterize his whole approach to the sacraments: "There is here not duty *(officium)* but benefit *(beneficium),* not work or service, but only enjoyment and profit."[132] The supper was the place where Christ vouchsafed forgiveness and comfort to His people. It was the place where the Word of God became audible, visible, edible. For this reason those were most prepared to receive the supper who felt acutely their shortcomings and neediness: "This bread is a comfort for the sorrowing, a healing for the sick, life for the dying, food for the hungry, and a rich treasure for all the poor and needy."[133] The supper was one of the means of grace by which Luther warded off the assaults of the devil and assured himself of God's gracious forgiveness in Christ.

When we turn to Zwingli the focus of the supper shifts from the individual and his personal anxieties to the community of faith which is gathered around the table. Toward the end of his life, Zwingli's views on the Eucharist underwent what one scholar has called "a decisive transformation."[134] While not abandoning any of his earlier caveats against the Roman and Lutheran doctrines, he moved toward a more positive appreciation of the real presence of Christ in the supper. He gave a much more full-orbed definition of the Eucharist as commemoration:

> By this commemoration all the benefits which God has displayed in his Son are called to mind. And by the signs themselves, the bread and wine, Christ himself is as it were set before our eyes, so that not merely with the ear, but with eye and palate we see and taste that Christ whom the soul bears within itself and in whom it rejoices.[135]

Such a lofty view of the Eucharist cannot fairly be characterized as "mere memorialism."

Still, despite Zwingli's enhanced view of the Eucharist, the primary pastoral purpose of the supper—as with baptism—remained congregational rather than individual. The sacraments were chiefly those signs by which

132. WA 27, p. 156.
133. WA 10/2, pp. 52, 54.
134. Pipkin, p. 125.
135. Ibid., p. 127. This statement is from Zwingli's posthumously published (1536) *Exposition of the Faith.*

the believer proved to the church that he was a soldier of Christ; their purpose was "to inform the whole church rather than yourself of your faith."[136] The supper was like a confederate's oath of allegiance, renewed periodically in solemn remembrance for a past victory.

> Just as each year, on the Day of Ten Thousand Knights, confederates give praise and thanks to God for the victory which he granted to us at Murten, so in this sacrament we should give praise and thanks to God for saving us by the death of his only son, and for redeeming us from the enemy. This is to proclaim the Lord's death.[137]

In Zurich, Zwingli's reformed liturgy was celebrated for the first time on Maundy Thursday, April 13, 1525. On that evening those who assembled in the Great Minster found, instead of an altar in the chancel, a table in the midst of the congregation. Instead of a priest reciting an arcane liturgy in a language they could not understand, a preacher read and proclaimed the Bible in his native Swiss German dialect. Men and women joined responsively in the recitation of the *Gloria in Excelsis* and the Nicene Creed and prayed in unison the Lord's Prayer. The ministers, dressed in simple dark gowns rather than clerical vestments, distributed the loaf of bread and the jug of wine among the worshipers. When all had partaken, they ended the service by singing Psalm 113: "Praise the Lord, you that are his servants." The church in Zurich celebrated this meal four times a year, "to proclaim the Lord's death [and] to bear witness by this very fact that they are members of one body, [that they] are one bread."[138]

Zwingli's Heart

The cold war between the Protestant and Catholic cantons of Switzerland suddenly became hot in 1531. Zwingli rode to battle as the chaplain of the Zurich troops, fully clad in military armor, wielding a double-edged sword. On October 11, 1531, as darkness fell upon the verdent fields surrounding the monastery at Kappel, Huldrych Zwingli was wounded and killed in battle. When the victorious Catholics discovered that the arch-heretic had fallen in battle, they mixed his ashes with dung to prevent their being collected as relics. All the same, a year later, Oswald Myconius, Zwingli's first biographer, related the following bizarre story:

> The enemy having retired after the third day, friends of Zwingli went to see

136. Z 3, p. 761. Cf. Locher, *Zwingli's Thought,* p. 317, 30n.
137. Locher, *Zwingli's Thought,* p. 216, 326n; Z 3, p. 534.
138. Z 3, p. 807. Cf. Potter, p. 208; Pipkin, p. 122.

if they could perchance find any remains of him, and lo! (strange to say) his heart presented itself from the midst of the ashes whole and uninjured. The good men were astounded, recognising the miracle indeed, but not understanding it. Wherefore, attributing everything to God, they rejoiced because this supernatural fact had made more sure the sincerity of his heart. A man whom I knew very well, in fact very intimately, came to me shortly afterwards asking whether I desired to see a portion of Zwingli's heart which he carried with him in a casket. Because a sort of horror on account of this sudden remark pervaded my whole body I declined. Otherwise, I could have been an eyewitness of this thing also.[139]

So Zwingli's heart, like that of Joan of Arc, was miraculously preserved from destruction! It would have been ironic, to say the least, for Zwingli, that staunchest opponent of relics, to have himself become one!

The story of Zwingli's heart is, of course, a legend in the canon of Protestant hagiography. It demonstrates how powerful was the grip of superstition even on the followers of so radical a reformer as Zwingli. Far more plausible is the account of Zwingli's dying words, spoken as he fell mortally wounded to the ground, and still preserved on a stone monument at Kappel: "You may kill the body but you cannot kill the soul."

In this sense the heart of Zwingli did escape his brutal destruction on the field of battle. His legacy was preserved, especially in Zurich. Heinrich Bullinger and later his son-in-law, Rudolf Gwalter, carried forth the reforming work which Zwingli had begun. He was soon eclipsed by the reformer of French-speaking Switzerland, John Calvin, who in 1531 still adhered to the Church of Rome. But Calvin owed much to the Zurich reformer, more probably than he was willing to admit. Zwingli's influence extended even further through the Swiss (Anabaptist) Brethren, his spiritual if illegitimate offspring, and through the radical Puritans in England, who found his theology congenial to their own attack on the temporizing settlement of Queen Elizabeth I.

Of all the major reformers, Zwingli has been the most misunderstood. His tragic death at age forty-seven could perhaps have been avoided had he been less concerned to defend the gospel by means of political intrigue. His invective against his enemies was sometimes cruel, if not unusual, for the age in which he lived. Writing against his Catholic opponenets in 1523, he said: "God shall punish them like hypocrites and cut them to shreds as one

139. Jackson, ed., *Latin Works,* I, p. 23.

quarters spies."[140] It is little wonder that when precisely this very fate befell Zwingli, his adversaries rejoiced in the just vindication of God against a heretic. Luther, as uncharitable to Zwingli in death as he had been in life, remarked that if God had saved Zwingli, He had done so above and beyond the rule! A sympathetic biographer has observed that Zwingli would have been more favorably remembered had he been willing (like John Hus) to accept martyrdom, which he several times skirted, rather than dying on the field of battle with bloodied hands.

When all of this is said, however, we have yet to describe the heart of Zwingli's religion. Perhaps it is best summed up in one of his last admonitions: "Do something bold for God's sake!"[141] From his first sermons in Zurich to his last stand at Kappel, Zwingli's career was characterized by steadfastness and courage in the face of considerable opposition. As the "mercenary of Christ," he knew that his life belonged not to himself but to his Lord. In 1530 he wrote to the city council of Memmingen: "In the business of the Christian religion and faith, we have long since staked our lives and set our minds on pleasing only our heavenly captain, in whose troop and company we have had ourselves enlisted."[142] Zwingli's bold program of reform included a reordering of the whole community, not just the church. From beginning to end he was single-mindedly concerned to uphold the sovereignty of God and to rout out every practice which encouraged the placing of one's trust in the creature. He took more literally than Luther the *sola* in *sola scriptura,* even if the Anabaptists did him one still better in this regard. He strongly emphasized the role of faith in the Christian life and never allowed the work of the Holy Spirit to be compromised by reliance on external means of grace. One scholar has recently characterized his approach to theology as "spiritual theocentrism."[143] If he had a bent toward the rational, he was not a thoroughgoing rationalist, but a biblical theologian whose humanistic impulses were tempered by his Christocentrism no less than by his views on providence and predestination.

Today the visitor to Zurich is shown a statue of Zwingli which stands by the Wasserkirche on the Limmat River, near the spot where the reformer

140. Furcha and Pipkin, eds. *Writings,* I, pp. 50-51; Z 2, p. 66.
141. Z 10, p. 165: "Tund umb gotzwillen etwas dapfers, ich wil üch by minem leben nit verfeuren noch hälen."
142. Z 11, p. 186. Cf. Locher, *Zwingli's Thought,* p. 83.
143. H. Wayne Pipkin, "In Search of True Religion: The Spirituality of Zwingli as Seen in Key Writings of 1523/24," Furcha and Pipkin, eds. *Prophet, Pastor, Protestant,* p. 129, 36n.

landed when he first came to his preaching post at the Great Minster in 1519. Zwingli stands with the Bible in one hand and the sword in the other. This posture dramatically symbolizes not only the tension in Zwingli's career which led to his tragic death but also his desire to bring every realm of life, church and state, theology and ethics, magistracy and ministry, individual and community, into conformity with the will of God. Then, as now, that was indeed to attempt "something bold for God's sake."

Select Bibliography

The standard critical edition of Zwingli's works (Z: *Hudreich Zwinglis Samtliche Werke)* is found in vols. 88-101 of the *Corpus Reformatorum,* although the earlier edition of Schuler and Schulthess (Zurich, 1828-1842, 8 vols.) must be consulted for some texts. In the early twentieth century a three-volume English translation of *The Latin Works of Huldreich Zwingli* was edited by Samuel Macauley Jackson. They have been reprinted recently by Labyrinth Press. Jackson also edited *Ulrich Zwingli: Selected Works* (Philadelphia: University of Pennsylvania Press, 1910; reprinted, 1972). Several of Zwingli's important writings were translated by G. W. Bromiley in *Zwingli and Bullinger* (Philadelphia: Westminster Press, 1953). G. R. Potter has edited a brief anthology of Zwingli texts in *Huldrych Zwingli* (London: Edward Arnold, 1978). Most recently, E. J. Furcha and H. W. Pipkin have edited two volumes of hitherto untranslated Zwingli texts: *Huldrych Zwingli: Writings* (Allison Park, Pa.: Pickwick Publications, 1984). It is a curious fact that there is now more of Zwingli in print in English than in German. The following are among the more important secondary studies in English.

Courvoisier, Jacques. *Zwingli: A Reformed Theologian.* Richmond: John Knox Press, 1963. A brief but useful survey of Zwingli's theology.

Farner, Oskar. *Zwingli the Reformer.* Translated by D. G. Sear. New York: Archon Books, 1952. A popular distillation of Farner's four-volume biographical study.

Furcha, E. J., ed. *Hydrych Zwingli, 1484-1531: A Legacy of Radical Reform.* Montreal: McGill University Faculty of Religious Studies, 1985. A collection of papers presented at the 1984 International Zwingli Symposium.

Furcha, E. J. and H. Wayne Pipkin, eds. *Prophet, Pastor, Protestant: The Work of Huldrych Zwingli After Five Hundred Years.* Allison Park, Penn.: Pickwick Press, 1984. A collection of eleven essays by European and North American scholars.

Gäbler, Ulrich. *Huldrych Zwingli: His Life and Work.* Translated by Ruth C. L. Gritsch. Philadelphia: Fortress Press, 1986. A helpful introduction to Zwingli studies.

Garside, Charles. *Zwingli and the Arts.* New Haven: Yale University Press, 1966.
An excellent study of Zwingli's aesthetics.

Potter, G. R. *Zwingli.* Cambridge: Cambridge University Press, 1976. The definitive
modern biography of Zwingli.

Stephens, W. P. *The Theology of Huldrych Zwingli.* Oxford: Clarendon Press, 1986.
A comprehensive, thoroughly documented study of Zwingli's theology.

Walton, Robert C. *Zwingli's Theocracy.* Toronto: University of Toronto Press, 1967.
A thorough analysis of Zwingli's political theology in the context of its civic
setting.

5

Glory unto God
John Calvin

Teacher: What is the principal end of human life?
Student: It is to know God.
Teacher: Why do you say that?
Student: Because He has created us and put us on earth to be glorified in us. And it is surely right that we dedicate our lives to His glory, since He is the beginning of it.

The Genevan Catechism, 1541[1]

The Crisis of Reformation Theology

In 1921 Karl Barth moved from a country pastorate in rural Switzerland to become professor of Reformed theology at the University of Göttingen in Germany. One of Barth's first tasks was to prepare lectures on the theology of the Reformers. In June 1922 he wrote of his struggles with Calvin to his friend Eduard Thurneysen:

> Calvin is a cataract, a primeval forest, a demonic power, something directly down from Himalaya, absolutely Chinese, strange, mythological; I lack completely the means, the suction cups, even to assimilate this phenomenon, not to speak of presenting it adequately. What I receive is only a thin little stream and what I can then give out again is only a yet thinner extract of this little stream. I could gladly and profitably set myself down and spend all the rest of my life just with Calvin.[2]

Barth could not let go of Calvin! He wrestled with him day and night. "More than once what I presented at 7 a.m. was not ready until 3-5 a.m." On one occasion he even dismissed class because he was not thoroughly

---

1. Translated in Thomas Torrance, *The School of Faith* (New York: Harper and Bros., 1959), pp. 5-6. Another translation is given in *Calvin: Theological Treatises,* ed. J. K. S. Reid (London, SCM Press, 1954), pp. 88-139.

2. Karl Barth, *Revolutionary Theology in the Making,* James D. Smart, trans. (Richmond: John Knox Press, 1964), p. 101.

prepared. Out of these musings emerged a veritable renaissance in Calvin scholarship (in which Peter Barth, Karl's brother, played an important role) and a new appreciation of Calvin's relevance for our troubled times.

Calvin was a reformer of the second generation. When Calvin was born in Northern France in 1509, Luther was already giving lectures at the University of Erfurt, and Zwingli was hurrying about his pastoral duties in Glarus. In England in the same year King Henry VII lay dying, attended at his deathbed by his eighteen-year-old son, the robust and recently married "Harry" soon to became King Henry VIII. On the papal throne in Rome sat Julius II, known as the "warrior pope" from his habit of leading his own soldiers into battle—which prompted Erasmus to ask if he were not more the successor of Julius Caesar than of Jesus Christ! Soon he would issue a plenary indulgence for the rebuilding of Saint Peter's Cathedral. When Calvin became a Protestant in the early 1530s, he inherited a tradition and a theology already well defined by nearly two decades of controversy.

When Luther's gospel first burst into the public arena (say, with his three treatises of 1520), he was confident that it would win the day. Soon, he believed, the papacy would crumble, the emperor would convene a true reforming council, the Jews and the Turks would be converted, Christ would return, and the devil would be vanquished forever!

By the end of the decade, however, Luther's apocalyptic optimism had turned to near despair. Luther stood excommunicated by the pope and banned by the emperor, who was preparing to wage war against the Protestant princes. The Jews had shown no more interest in Luther's attempts to evangelize them than they had in the countless other efforts through the centuries. The Turks, far from succumbing to the new gospel, were fighting a holy *jihad* against all of Europe. By 1525 they had advanced to the gates of Vienna.

> It was the best of times, it was the worst of times.
> It was the spring of hope; it was the winter of despair.
> We were all going direct to heaven; we were all going direct the other way.[3]

So it must have seemed to many earnest believers who followed the course of events from the Diet of Worms in 1521 ("Here I stand") to the Diet of Speyer (where the term *protestant* was coined) in 1529.

Even more unsettling than external threats was the painful unraveling of

---

3. Charles Dickens, *A Tale of Two Cities* (New York: Merill and Baker, 1962), p. 1.

the Reformation from within. Many who had rallied around Luther in his early struggles now defected from the "Wittenberg pope," as Thomas Müntzer unkindly called him. The humanists had made Luther's name a household word by printing and distributing his *Ninety-five Theses* from one end of Europe to the other. However, most of them, like Erasmus, were not in fundamental agreement with Luther's deepest concerns. They would not follow him into schism. The spiritualists, Anabaptists, and sacramentarians, Luther dubbed *Schwärmer* because they sounded like a confused swarm of bees buzzing around a hive. The Zwinglians' disagreement with the Lutherans over the Eucharist widened rather than lessened after the Colloquy of Marburg. Everyone, of course, appealed to the Bible. Caspar Schwenckfeld, one of the spiritualist reformers, observed that on the basis of the Bible "the papists damn the Lutherans, the Lutherans damn the Zwinglians, the Zwinglians damn the Anabaptists, and the Anabaptists damn all of the others."

At this precise moment, with Zwingli dead and Erasmus dying, with Luther quiescent (if not quiet!), the Roman Church resurgent, the Radical Reformation fragmented and soon to be further discredited by the bloody spectacle of Münster, John Calvin emerged as the leader of a new movement and the reformulator of a new theology.

The noted Luther scholar Karl Holl once referred to Calvin as Luther's greatest disciple. The two reformers never met personally. Yet Luther praised some of Calvin's early writings which had been sent to him. Calvin, in turn, addressed Luther as his "most respected father" and later declared: "We regard him as a remarkable apostle of Christ, through whose work and ministry, most of all, the purity of the gospel has been restored in our time."[4] Unlike Zwingli, Calvin never claimed to be theologically independent of Luther. Still, he was no mere imitator of Luther. Calvin's great achievement was to take the classic insights of the Reformation *(sola gratia, sola fide, sola scriptura)* and give them a clear, systematic exposition, which neither Luther nor Zwingli ever did, and to adapt them to the civic setting of Geneva. From Geneva they took on a life of their own and developed into a new international theology, extending from Poland and Hungary in the East to the Netherlands, Scotland, England (Puritanism), and eventually to New England in the West. For this reason the French historian E. G. Léonard entitled the last chapter of his *History of Protestantism:* "Calvin: The Founder of a Civilization."

4. CO, 6, col. 250. For this citation I follow the translation of B. A. Gerrish, "John Calvin on Luther," *Interpreters of Luther,* Jaroslav Pelikan, ed. (Philadelphia: Fortress Press, 1968), p. 79.

The Man Behind the Myth

Few people in the history of Christianity have been as highly esteemed or as meanly despised as John Calvin. Most Christians, including most Protestants, know only two things about him: He believed in predestination, and he sent Servetus to the stake. From these two facts, both true, emerges the common caricature of Calvin as the grand inquisitor of Protestantism, the cruel tyrant of Geneva, a morose and bitter and utterly inhuman figure.

This distorted image stems in part from Calvin's own times in which he was by no means universally loved. For example, in the year 1551, when the canons of the cathedral of Calvin's hometown of Noyon received word of the reformer's death, they celebrated and gave thanks to God for taking the noted heretic from their midst. Their rejoicing was cut short, however, when they discovered that the rumor of his death was premature. They still had thirteen more years to put up with Calvin! In 1577 Jerome Bolsec, a sometime Protestant who had returned to the Roman Church, published a scurrilous attack on the character of Calvin. Bolsec portrayed Calvin not only as imperious and ill-tempered, which in fact he may have been, but also as a drunkard, an adulterer, and a homosexual, which he certainly was not. In an obvious cheap shot, Bolsec also claimed that Calvin's chronic sickness was the punishment of God; his "being eaten with lice and vermin all over his body" was divine chastisement for his heresy. Modern Calvin-despisers have been no more kind. Nineteenth-century liberalism saw Calvin as "the great black phantom, a glacian person, sombre, unfeeling, hurried . . . nothing in him speaks to the heart."[5] For many contemporary Christians, Calvin is an embarassing skeleton they would prefer to keep safely locked in the historical closets. On occasion, I am told, some of these disenchanted heirs of the Reformation stand before the famous statue of Calvin in Geneva and hurl eggs at the dour likeness looking down at them.

At the other extreme from Calvinphobia stands the equally biased posture of Calvinolatry. In 1556 the Scottish reformer John Knox described Calvin's Geneva as "the most perfect school of Christ that ever was in the earth since the days of the apostles."[6] Others have gone so far as to depict Calvin as not only the greatest teacher of Christian doctrine since Paul but

5. Quoted in Richard Stauffer, *The Humanity of John Calvin*, George A. Shriver, trans. (Nashville: Abingdon Press, 1971), p. 20. On the spurious nature of Bolsec's claims, see Frank Pfeilschifter, *Das Calvinbild bei Bolsec* (Augsburg: F D L Verlag, 1983), pp. 123-177.

6. John T. McNeill, *The History and Character of Calvinism* (New York: Oxford University Press, 1954), p. 178.

also as a near infallible guide in every arena of human endeavor from art and architecture to politics and economics. Without doubt, the most notable attempt to present a "Calvin without warts" is the classic biography by Emile Doumergue which appeared in seven folio volumes around the turn of the century. Doumergue produced what will surely remain the most thorough and detailed study of Calvin's life ever written. But, despite the virtues of this impressive work, it is essentially an exercise in hagiography. Doumergue's Calvin is too good to be true, just as Bolsec's Calvin is too demonic to be human. We do no service to the truth by depicting Calvin as either angelically good or diabolically evil. He was, as Luther declared all Christians to be, at one and the same time both a sinner and a saint.

Unlike Luther, Calvin can be said to have been born into the church. His father, Gérard Cauvin, was the administrative assistant to the bishop of Noyon. His mother Jeanne, the daughter of an innkeeper, was reportedly a very beautiful and pious woman. Jeanne Cauvin died when Jean, her fourth son, was only five or six. Though his father remarried soon thereafter, young Calvin must have felt the loss of his mother very deeply. This no doubt contributed to his sense of personal anxiety and unrest.[7] Nonetheless, Calvin knew something of the warmth of social life from his contacts with the aristocratic Montmor family, with whom he lived for several years. He dedicated his first book to a member of this family, claiming, "I owe you all that I am and have. . . . As a boy I was brought up in your home and was initiated in my studies with you. Hence I owe to your noble family my first training in life and letters."[8] Although Calvin once described himself as "merely a man from among the common people," he moved with ease among the higher echelons of society. He was an aristocrat by heart if not by lineage proper. He never forgot this fact about himself, nor did he let others forget it. Once on the streets of Geneva a grateful but overly enthusiastic refugee addressed him as "Brother Calvin" only to be informed that the correct title was "Monsieur Calvin."

At the age of twelve Calvin received a benefice from the bishop of Noyon, thanks to his father's prudent influence. The holding of a benefice required the entering of minor orders—John became a *clerc* and received the tonsure

7. This argument has been pressed by Suzanne Selinger in her insightful study, *Calvin Against Himself* (Hamden, Conn.: Archon Books, 1984), pp. 85-88. She goes too far, however, in deriving Calvin's alleged bias against sexuality and his presumed coolness toward his wife from this traumatic event.

8. *Calvin's Commentary on Seneca's De Clementia,* eds. Ford L. Battles and André M. Hugo (Leiden: E. J. Brill, 1969), pp. 12-13.

—and the performance of ecclesiastical duties. By the time of the Reformation the system of farming out benefices to relatives and friends was one of the most common abuses in the church. A semiliterate priest would usually be hired to perform the actual duties of the office (which in Calvin's case involved caring for one of the altars in the cathedral) for a paltry sum while the incumbent received the lion's share of the benefice. In fact, the income from this benefice was a kind of scholarship by which young Calvin, already a precocious student, was able to continue his studies.

In August 1523 John Calvin (from the Latinized form of his name: Calvinus) arrived in Paris to begin his formal training at the most famous university in Europe. In the same month, an Augustinian monk named Jean Vallière was burned alive for belonging to "the party of the heretic Luther." He was the first martyr of the reform in France. We do not know what impression this event made on Jean, then only fourteen years of age. Twelve years later he would recoil in horror at the burning to death of his friend Etienne de la Forge, a saintly Protestant with whom he had lived for a while. Indeed, he published the first edition of the *Institutes* partly, as he said, "to vindicate from undeserved insult my brethren whose death was precious in the sight of the Lord."[9] What turned the bright young student from Noyon into the eloquent apologist for the faith? From 1523 until 1541, when he definitively settled in Geneva, many forces were at work in the making of Calvin the reformer. We can survey his life during these turbulent years in terms of his preparation, his conversion, and his vocation.

Calvin's Preparation

Calvin first enrolled in the Collège de la Marche where he perfected his knowledge of Latin grammar and syntax. Here for a while he was taught by Mathurin Cordier, one of the greatest Latin teachers of his day, whose *Grammatica Latina* was still being used as late as the nineteenth century. Years later Calvin remembered this venerable teacher and dedicated to him his commentary on 1 Thessalonians:

> When I was a child and had merely tasted the rudiments of Latin, my father sent me to Paris. There God's goodness gave you to me for a little while as preceptor, to teach me the true way to learn so that I might continue with

9. John Calvin, *Commentary on the Book of Psalms,* James Anderson, trans. (Edinburgh: Calvin Translation Society, 1845), I, p. xlii.

greater profit. . . . I was so helped by you that whatever progress I have since made I gladly ascribe to you.[10]

Cordier was later summoned by Calvin to teach Latin at the academy in Geneva. He remained in this post until he died (in the same year as Calvin) at age eighty-five.

Calvin soon advanced to the Collège de Montaigu, a famous school known for its stern discipline and its bad food. Erasmus, who studied here a few years before Calvin, later complained of the spoiled eggs he was forced to eat in the refectory. Calvin's lifelong problems with indigestion and insomnia probably derived from the rigid fare and his penchant for burning the midnight oil at Montaigu. Later legend has it that during these years his fellow students awarded Calvin the nickname of "the accusative case." While this is not true, Beza, in his adoring biography, acknowledged that the young scholar was indeed "a strict censor of every thing vicious in his companions."[11] While his classmates were cavorting in the streets or running off to wild parties, Calvin was busied with the niceties of nominalist logic or the *quaestiones* of scholastic theology.

As a compulsive student Calvin did extremely well in his studies, but he also acquired a distaste for the scholastic method of doing theology. He was beginning to move in the circles of French humanism, and he may have shared the opinion of Erasmus who blasted the Paris masters as "pseudo theologians . . . whose brains are rotten, their language barbarous, their intellects dull, their learning a bed of thorns, their manners rough, their life hypocritical, their talk full of venom, and their heart as black as ink."[12] Calvin never put it quite like that, but he did describe a course of divinity given to young theologues as "mere sophistry, and sophistry so twisted, involved, tortuous and puzzling that scholastic theology might well be described as a kind of esoteric magic. The denser the darkness in which anyone shrouded a subject and the more he puzzled himself and others with preposterous riddles, the greater his fame for acumen and learning."[13]

In 1528 Calvin left all of that behind when, at his father's behest, he moved from Paris to Orléans to take up a new discipline, the study of law. Gérard Cauvin was no longer in the good graces of the cathedral chapter at Noyon and, facing old age, he also realized that his bright son was likelier to earn a better income as a lawyer than as a servant of the church. In any

10. CO 13, cols. 525-526; CNTC, 8, p. 331.

11. *Calvin's Tracts and Treatises,* Henry Beveridge, trans. (Grand Rapids: Eerdmans, 1958), I, p. lx.

12. EE 1, pp. 87-88 (no. 64); CWE 1, p. 138.

13. *Tracts and Treatises,* I, p. 40.

event, Calvin acquiesced to his father's will. The contrast with Luther is striking: Luther, in defiance of his father, forfeited a career in the law in order to become a monk; Calvin, in obedience to his father, gave up the study of theology in order to become a lawyer.

Calvin threw himself enthusiastically into the study of law, first at Orléans, then at Bourges. Soon he was good enough to give lectures and to substitute as a kind of "teaching fellow" when the professors were absent from class. Calvin's legal training had two important influences on his future work: First, it provided a thorough grounding in practical affairs which would be of enormous benefit in his efforts to reshape the institutions of Geneva; secondly, it opened his eyes to the world of classical antiquity and to the study of ancient texts. While at Bourges he also took up the study of Greek, being tutored by an evangelical scholar from Germany, Melchior Wolmar.

When his father died in 1531, Calvin felt free to forsake the study of law for his real love, classical literature. He moved back to Paris and in 1532 published his first book, an edition of Seneca's treatise *On Clemency,* complete with a textual apparatus and lengthy commentary. It was a masterpiece of erudition, and he hoped it would establish him as a scholar of note in humanist circles. In the preface, he felt it necessary to apologize for the fact that, although he was just twenty-three, this was only his first book: "I would much prefer to bring forth no 'children' at all than to bring forth abortions, as usually happens."[14] Commercially speaking, however, this book was a complete flop! It only went through one edition, and Calvin had to pay for that himself. It was nonetheless an impressive effort and paved the way for his extensive literary labors.

Calvin's Conversion

Calvin's transition from humanist to reformer was marked by what he once described as a "sudden conversion" *(conversio subita).* However, it has been notoriously difficult for Calvin scholars to agree on a probable date for this turning point. The guesses range from 1527 to 1534. There are several reasons for this difficulty. In the first place, Calvin was reticent about himself. In part, this was because of his natural bent toward shyness and introversion, and, in part, because he took seriously Paul's admonition, "For we preach not ourselves, but Christ Jesus the Lord" (2 Cor. 4:5). The glory belonged to God and not to John Calvin.

Furthermore, while the conversion may have been "sudden," it was

14. *Battles and Hugo,* p. 4.

surely prepared for by a period of struggle, unease, and doubt. Calvin, no less than Luther and Zwingli, had a traditional Catholic upbringing and must have known the sense of anxiety and burdensomeness which characterized late medieval culture. As a very young boy he once made a pilgrimage with his mother to Ourscamp Abbey, where he was permitted to kiss a holy relic, the finger of Saint Anne. Later he presented a vivid picture of the kind of preaching he must often have heard, designed, it would seem, to produce a spirituality of guilt:

> They informed us we were miserable sinners dependent on thy mercy; reconciliation was to come through the righteousness of works. The method of obtaining thy mercy was by making satisfaction for offenses. Then, because thou wert a stern judge and strict avenger of iniquity, they showed how dreadful thy presence must be. Hence they bade us flee first to the saints, that by this intercession thou mightest be easily entreated and propitious toward us.[15]

How Calvin first came into contact with new evangelical ideas we cannot be certain. Some of Luther's writings were translated into French in the early 1520s, and Calvin may well have read them. He also had close ties with the circle of French evangelical humanists inspired by the great scholar Jacques Lefèvre d'Etaples. Some of these, including his future co-worker Guillaume Farel, had attempted a tentative reform of the church in the diocese of Meaux near Paris until they were suppressed by the stronger forces of orthodoxy. Calvin's earliest biographers Beza and Colladon attributed a significant role in his conversion to his cousin, Robert Olivétan, for whose French New Testament (1535) Calvin wrote a preface entitled, "To all lovers of Jesus Christ and his Gospel." That was his first published work as a Protestant. Of one thing we can be sure: Calvin did not embrace the new gospel in a quick or facile manner.

> Offended by the novelty, I lent an unwilling ear, and at first, I confess, strenuously and passionately resisted; for (such is the firmness or effrontery with which it is natural to men to persist in the course which they have once undertaken) it was with the greatest difficulty I was induced to confess that I had all my life long been in ignorance and error.[16]

In 1555, over twenty years after the event, Calvin looked back on his conversion and wrote about it in the preface to his *Commentary on the*

15. *Tracts and Treatises,* I, p. 62; OS 1, pp. 484-485.
16. *Tracts and Treatises,* I p. 62; OS 1, p. 485.

Psalms. Since this is Calvin's most explicit reference to this crucial event, we quote it here at length:

> My mind which, despite my youth,
> Had been too hardened in such matters,
> Now was readied for serious attention.
> By a sudden conversion
> God turned and brought it
> To docility.
>
> Having therefore received
> Some taste and knowledge
> Of true piety,
> I was suddenly fired
> With such a great desire to advance
> That, even though I had not forsaken
> The other studies entirely,
> I nonetheless worked at them
> More slackly.
>
> But I was utterly amazed
> That before a year had passed
> All those who yearned
> For pure doctrine
> Were coming again and again to me
> To learn it.
> Even though I had scarcely commenced
> To study it myself.
>
> For my part, being of a nature
> Somewhat unpolished and retiring,
> I always longed for repose and quiet.
> Hence I began to seek
> Some hiding place
> And way to withdraw from people.
> But, far from attaining my heart's desire,
> All retreats and places of escape.
> Became for me like public schools.
>
> In short, although I always cherished
> The goal of living in private, incognito,
> God so led me and caused me to turn
> By various changes
> That he never left me at peace in any place
> Until, in spite of my natural disposition
> He brought me into the limelight.

Leaving my native France,
I departed into Germany
With the express purpose
Of being able to live,
At peace in some unknown corner,
As I had always hoped.[17]

Three important strands in Calvin's piety and personality are evident in this revealing recollection. First, he saw his conversion as the result of divine initiative: "God turned my heart." Perhaps this was the real intention behind his description of this even as "sudden"—not so much a lightning-quick occurrence (though it may have been that too) as a sense of being completely overwhelmed by God's grace. Calvin had no illusions that he would have ever drifted into a proper relationship with God apart from the prevenient "turning" on God's part. "So obstinately addicted to the superstitions of the papacy did I remain that it would have been hard indeed to have pulled me out of so deep a quagmire," he observed.[18] "I did nothing, the Word did it all." Calvin's experience echoed that of Luther. Here too are the experiential roots of the much-discussed doctrine of predestination. As we shall see, Calvin's view of election can only be understood in the context of the particular appropriation of salvation through Jesus Christ.

A second motif in Calvin's approach to faith arises from the comment that God subdued his heart to docility. This word, *docilitas,* might also be translated, *teachableness.* There is a sense in which Calvin aspired to be nothing more than a faithful disciple of Jesus Christ, *disciple* in its root meaning (from the Latin *disco,* to learn) of learner, one who is capable of being taught. This theme resounds throughout his writings on the Christian life. For Calvin true piety did not consist in a servile fear of an all-powerful God but rather "in a sincere feeling which loves God as Father as much as it reverences him as Lord." The evidence of such piety was precisely a

17. This is a strophic translation by Ford L. Battles, printed in the introduction to his translation of the 1536 *Institution of the Christian Religion* (Atlanta: John Knox Press, 1975), pp. xxiii-xxiv. Battles' translation has been reprinted by Eerdmans (1986) as *Institutes of the Christian Religion: 1536 Edition.* Subsequent citations will be to this latter printing.

18. CO 31, col. 22: "Ad primo quidem, quum superstitionibus papatus, magis pertinaciter addictus essem, quam ut facile esset e tam profundo luto me extrahi, animum meum, qui pro aetate nimis obduruerat subita conversione and docilitatem subegit." In his commentary on Seneca's *De Clementia* Calvin noted that *"subita* means not only 'sudden' but also 'unpremeditated.' " Cf. Battles and Hugo, *Commentary on De Clementia,* pp. 56 f.

willingness to become docile, teachable before the true God. "Whoever has been endowed with this piety dare not fashion out of their own rashness any God for themselves. Rather, they seek from him the knowledge of the true God, and conceive him just as he shows and declares himself to be."[19] Significantly, this definition derives from Calvin's *Catechism* of 1537, a document intended for the instruction of children in the faith. Later, in his *Commentary on Acts* (18:22) he said that there can be no *pietas* without true instruction, as the name *disciples* indicates. "True religion and worship of God," he said, "arise out of faith, so that no one duly serves God save him who has been educated in his school."[20]

Throughout the description of his conversion, Calvin protested his shy and retiring nature, the desire to live in scholarly seclusion, "at peace in some unknown corner." We will not understand Calvin the person unless we take into account this reticence, this genuine reluctance to enter the fray of battle. In this respect he differed from the two other great reformers we have already examined. Luther was made for the part, a veritable volcano of a personality exploding at Worms, "Here I stand!" Zwingli too was a person of action; after all, he died in battle wielding a double-edged sword! But Calvin was different. Shy to the point of being unsociable, he would not have done well with small talk at a modern party. He had to be pulled, kicking and screaming as it were, into the ranks of the reformers. Yet the God who had subdued his heart to teachability also steadied his nerves for the momentous tasks which lay before him.

Calvin's Vocation

On All Saints' Day 1533, exactly sixteen years to the day after Luther had posted the famous theses against indulgences on the church door in Wittenberg, Nicholas Cop, a friend of Calvin and rector of the University of Paris, delivered a convocation address which shocked his hearers. Though not what we would call a hot gospel sermon, it had enough evan-

19. OS 1, p. 379: "Or la vraye piete . . . consiste plustot en un pur et vray zele qui ayme Dieu tout ainsi comme Pere et le revere tout ainsi comme Seigneur. . . . Et tous ceulx qui ont ce zele ilz nentreprenent point de forger ung tel Dieu quilz veullent selon leur temerite, mais ilz cherchent la cognoissance du vray Dieu de luy mesmes et ne le concoivent point aultre que tel quil se manifeste et declare a eulx." Cf. *Instruction in Faith,* Paul T. Fuhrmann, trans. (Philadelphia: Westminster Press, 1949), p. 19.

20. CO 32, col. 249; CNTC 7, p. 142. See Ford L. Battles, *The Piety of John Calvin* (Grand Rapids: Baker Book House, 1978), pp. 13-26.

gelical content to offend the defenders of Catholic orthodoxy. On All Saints' Day, Cop did not praise the saints but rather proclaimed Christ as the only mediator with God. Cop was forced to flee for his life.

Calvin, too, was implicated in the event. According to an old legend, he escaped from Paris in the nick of time, his friends hoisting him down out of a window on bed sheets while the police were knocking at the door—shades of Paul's hurried flight from Damascus in a basket![21] Calvin's papers were seized; from that time forth he became persona non grata in Paris. About a year after Cop's address, some of the more advanced Protestants in Paris decided to make a startling, radical display of their faith. A fiery attack on the Mass and its accoutrements—"bell-ringing, anointings, chantings, ceremonies, candlelightings, censings, disguises, and such sorts of buffooneries"—was printed on a placard and posted all over the city. One even appeared, mysteriously, on the door to the bedchamber of King Francis I. In Germany Luther had launched the Reformation by attacking indulgences, a linchpin in the late medieval sacrament of penance. The French Reformation began with a frontal assault on "the horrible, great and unbearable abuses of the papal mass," as the title on the placards ran.[22] Now the forces of persecution were unleashed against the French evangelicals. Calvin left the country in haste and found refuge in the Reformed city of Basel, the home city of Cop who was there already.

Erasmus was also living in Basel at the time. The prince of the humanists, aged and sick, had returned to his favorite city to live out his last days on earth. Erasmus died at Basel in June 1536, three months after the publication of the first edition of Calvin's *Institutes* in the same city. With Erasmus died his dreams of universal peace and learning, his hopes that a revival of letters would usher in a "golden age" of reformation. In the very next year, 1537, the Spanish Inquisition prohibited the reading of Erasmus's works. A few years later, in 1542, the books of John Calvin, including his *Institutes,* were also declared off limits for good Christians and were ceremoniously burned before the Cathedral of Notre Dame in Paris. Erasmus and Calvin in Basel signify the intersection of two eras. Calvin had learned much from the great scholar, not the least of which was how to study the Scriptures. Calvin did not cease to be a humanist after he became a reformer. But his conversion and his immersion in the biblical and patristic sources led him

21. This story is given credence by Emanuel Stickelberger, *Calvin: A Life,* David Gelzer, trans. (Richmond: John Knox Press, 1954), p. 22.

22. The text of the placards of 1534 have been translated by Ford L. Battles and appear as appendix I in his edition of the 1536 *Institutes,* pp. 339-342.

down a very different path than that taken by Erasmus. Calvin's path was much closer to, but still distinct from, Erasmus's old adversary in Wittenberg.

Calvin did not make a big splash in Basel: "I dwelt there hidden, as it were, and known only to a few people." But he was not idle. The fruit of his labors rolled off the presses of the printer Thomas Platter in March, 1536. It was called, to give the full title:

> The Basic Teaching of the Christian Religion comprising almost the whole sum of godliness and whatever it is necessary to know on the doctrine of salvation. A newly published work very well worth reading by all who are studious of godliness. A Preface to the most Christian King of France, offering to him this book as a confession of faith by the author, Jean Calvin of Noyon.[23]

"A . . . work very well worth reading" *(lectu dignissimum opus)* was a modest advertisement for a book destined to become the principal document of Protestant theology in the sixteenth century. Unlike Calvin's first book on Seneca, the *Institutes* became a bestseller almost overnight. The first edition, "only a little booklet" as Calvin once described it, was small enough to be hidden beneath one's coat or secretly stashed away with one's wares. Thus evangelical colporteurs and merchants carried it throughout Europe.

What accounts for the remarkable success of the *Institutes?* We can answer this question in part by pointing to two distinct functions it served. First, it was a powerful tract for the times. As Calvin said in the prefatory epistle to Francis I, he had not originally intended to address this work to the king. Calvin at first planned the book to be a kind of basic theology primer for "our French countrymen, very many of whom I saw to be hungering and thirsting for Christ."[24] But the intervening persecution of French Protestants had moved Calvin to present the case of fellow believers to the king in the hope that he might adopt a more moderate course. Calvin lamented that "the poor little church has either been wasted with cruel slaughter or banished into exile." His own homeland had become "like a hell" to him, as he put it a few years later in a letter to a friend. He tried to clear the French evangelicals of the charges of sedition and schism—they were not sectarians bent on the overthrow of order, but honest citizens who

---

23. OS 1, p. 19. The translation is that of T. H. L. Parker, *John Calvin: A Biography* (London: Dent and Sons, 1975), p. 34.

24. 1536 *Institutes,* p. 1; OS 1, p. 21.

desired only to restore the purity of the gospel. What was most at stake was—this was the keynote of Calvin's entire theology—"How God's glory may be kept safe on earth . . . how Christ's Kingdom may be kept in good repair among us."[25] Throughout the letter Calvin was polite and deferential toward the king. But the closing sentence is filled with all the thunder of Elijah: If Francis would not mend his ways, then in due season the Lord would surely appear, "coming forth armed to deliver the poor from their affliction and also to punish their despisers."[26] Without knowing it, Calvin had fired the first volley in the battle of words which would lead finally to the bloody wars of religion in France.

The primary purpose of the *Institutes,* though, was catechetical. From the time of his conversion Calvin had been pressed to serve as a teacher of those who were hungry for the true faith. One can still see a cave near the city of Poitiers where Calvin was said to have ministered to the needs of a (literally!) underground congregation. He knew firsthand the urgent need for a clearly written manual of instruction which would present the rudiments of a biblical theology and lead young Christians into a deeper understanding of the faith. The time was ripe for such a book. Other reformers had attempted to do something on this order, but with limited success. Melanchthon first published *Common Places* in 1521; Zwingli brought out *Commentary on True and False Religion* in 1525. Farel had even written a *Summary* of evangelical theology in French, which was published in 1534. Each of these works had its strengths, but fell short of meeting the need which the *Institutes* supplied.

We shall return to the story of the *Institutes* which grew, through many revisions, from the modest "little booklet" of 1536 into a huge tome and treasury of Protestant dogmatics in the definitive edition of 1559. Six brief chapters constituted the first edition. Chapter 1, "On the Law," was largely an exposition of the Ten Commandments. Chapter 2, dealt with faith and contained a commentary on the Apostles' Creed. In this context the doctrine of predestination was presented, though only in a cursory, nonpolemical manner. Chapter 3, on prayer, contained Calvin's earliest exegesis of the Lord's Prayer. Chapter 4 took up the sacraments, by which he meant baptism and the Lord's Supper. Chapter 5 was a refutation of "the five false sacraments" while Chapter 6 was concerned with three themes: Christian liberty, church polity, and civil government. The sequence of topics is the

25. 1536 *Institutes,* p. 3; OS 1, p. 23.
26. 1536 *Institutes,* p. 19; OS 1, p. 36.

same as the one used by Luther in his catechisms, which Calvin may have deliberately imitated. For the section on prayer, Calvin owed a great deal to Martin Bucer's discussion of the Lord's Prayer in *Commentary on the Gospels* (1530). But, all in all, Calvin presented more clearly and more masterfully than anyone before him the essential elements of Protestant theology.

Perhaps too modestly, Calvin said that, when the *Institutes* were published in Basel, no one knew that he was the author. The first printing, though, was exhausted within a year. The timid, young scholar became known more and more as an up-and-coming proponent of the Reformation. This led in turn to what, next to conversion, was the most privotal event of Calvin's life.

In the summer of 1536 Calvin, with his brother Antoine and his half-sister Marie, was traveling from Paris to Strasbourg where he hoped to settle down to his long-desired life of leisure and study. However, the armies of Francis I and the Emperor Charles V were engaged in military maneuvers which required the little Calvin caravan to take a southern detour. Thus they arrived at the city of Geneva, situated on the borders of France, Savoy, and Switzerland. Calvin did not have a good impression of the city and planned to stay only one night. Earlier Guillaume Farel had led the city to embrace the Reformation; at a citizen assembly on May 25 of the same year the Genevans had voted unanimously to "live henceforth according to the law of the gospel and the Word of God, and to abolish all papal abuses."[27] Still, the actual work of reform had barely begun.

Farel, having been informed that Calvin was in the city, burst into his hotel room and implored him to stay in Geneva and assist in completing the newly won Reformation. Calvin was genuinely shocked at the idea and protested that he was ill-suited for such a task. He could better edify the church by his quiet study and writing. "The summit of my wishes," he later wrote to Cardinal Sadolet, "was the enjoyment of literary ease, with something of a free and honorable station."[28] Just give me a carrel in the library, and let the rest of the world go by! Farel, however, was undaunted by the young man's meager excuse. With his flashing eyes and his formidable red beard, Farel thundered down the curse of God upon Calvin in words which he could never forget:

27. Quoted, William Monter, *Calvin's Geneva* (New York: John Wiley and Sons, 1967), p. 56.

28. *Calvin: Theological Treatises*, p. 225. "nempe ut otio literario cum honesta aliqua ingenuaque conditione fruerer." OS 1, p. 461.

> At this point Farel
> (Burning with a wondrous zeal
> To advance the gospel)
> Suddenly set all his efforts
> At keeping me.
> After having heard
> That I was determined
> To pursue my own private studies—
> When he realized
> He would get nowhere by pleas—
> He came to the point of a curse:
> That it would please God
> To curse my leisure
> And the quiet for my studies
> That I was seeking,
> If in such a grave emergency
> I should withdraw and refuse
> To give aid and help.
> This word so overwhelmed me
> That I desisted from the journey
> I had undertaken.[29]

From that moment, Calvin's fate was linked to that of Geneva. In his earliest letters after his call, he referred to himself as "Reader in Holy Scripture to the Church in Geneva." Though he took on many other duties over the years, his primary vocation remained that of pastor and teacher. It is important to point out that Calvin never felt at home in Geneva. In the first mention of him in the records of the city council, he is referred to as "*ille Gallus*—that Frenchman!" He became a citizen of Geneva in 1559, only five years before his death. To this day the Swiss are famous for their snobbery and provincialism, the Genevans especially so. For example, *L'Eglise protestante nationale* refers not to the national church body of Switzerland, the Swiss Reformed Church, but rather to the church of the canton of Geneva. Calvin's first sojourn in Geneva lasted less than two years. He accomplished some significant things—his first catechism and a confession of faith were adopted—but conflict with the council over the proper discipline of the church led to a crisis. In April 1538 Calvin and Farel were expelled from the city. After another short stay in Basel, Calvin was persuaded to move to Strasbourg, where he had been headed before being waylaid, so to say, by the fiery Farel.

29. Battles, p. 33; CO 31, col. 26.

Calvin spent three years in Strasbourg, and they were undoubtedly the happiest years of his life. They were also perhaps the most decisive years for his development as a reformer and a theologian. Let us look at five dimensions of his life during this crucial period.

First, Calvin was a pastor. At that time Strasbourg did not belong to France but was a free imperial city of the Holy Roman Empire. But it was close enough to France to attract a sizable number of French refugees seeking asylum from persecution in their native land. Calvin was called as pastor of the *ecclesiola Gallicana,* the little French congregation, which met in the church of Saint Nicholas. Here Calvin celebrated the sacrament of the Lord's Supper and carried out the various details of his pastoral ministry. He gave serious thought to the role of worship in the church and translated a number of psalms into French meter. Thus began the congregational singing of psalms which became such an integral part of French Reformed worship. A refugee who visited Calvin's church gave the following description of the service:

> Everyone sings, men and women, and it is a lovely sight. Each has a music book in his hand. . . . As I looked on this little company of exiles, I wept, not for sadness but for joy to hear them all singing so heartily, and as they sang giving thanks to God that he had led them to a place where his name is glorified.[30]

Calvin must have had scenes like this in mind when he later declared that "we know by experience that singing has great force and vigor to move and inflame the hearts of men to invoke and praise God with a more vehement and ardent zeal."[31]

Secondly, Calvin was a teacher. John Sturm, also a native of France and a scholar at the University of Paris, had organized a school in Strasbourg to which Calvin was appointed as "lecturer in Holy Scripture." Here Calvin lectured three days a week, offering exegetical courses on the Gospel of John and the Pauline Epistles. He also preached four sermons each week to his congregation. The curriculum at Sturm's school, with its strong emphasis on classical literature, became a model for Calvin's academy in Geneva. At first Calvin was paid only one florin per week for his lectures. He supplemented his income by giving private lessons, taking in boarders, lawyering on the side, and, what must have pained him most, selling some of his precious library. He complained about the high cost of living in Strasbourg:

30. Parker, p. 69.
31. This is from the preface to Calvin's Psalter of 1542. Cf. McNeill, *History and Character,* p. 148.

"I can't call a single penny my own. It is astonishing how money slips away in extraordinary expenses."[32]

Thirdly, Calvin was a writer. His most important publication was a thoroughly revised edition of the *Institutes* which appeared in August 1539. It was approximately three times larger than the 1536 version. Its stated purpose was "to prepare and train students in theology for the study of the divine Word that they might have an easy access into it and keep on in it without stumbling."[33] In 1541 the first French translation of the *Institutes* was published. It was a landmark in the development of the French language, comparable in its effect to the Luther Bible in German or the Authorized Version in English. Also in 1539 Calvin published his *Commentary on Romans,* a masterful treatment of what for him no less than for Luther was the most important book in the Bible. This was the first of Calvin's biblical commentaries; eventually he published commentaries on most of the Old Testament and on every book in the New Testament except Revelation and 2 and 3 John.[34]

We must mention three briefer but brilliant pieces Calvin penned during these years. One was an answer to Cardinal Jacopo Sadoleto, a reform-minded Catholic prelate who had written to the church at Geneva seeking to woo it back to Rome. Calvin's *Reply to Sadolet* is a literary tour de force, perhaps the best apology for the Reformed faith written in the sixteenth century. He also published a book of liturgy, *The Form of Ecclesiastical Prayers and Hymns* which would have a lasting effect on Reformed worship. *Little Treatise on the Holy Supper* was Calvin's first considered effort to state a median position between the Lutheran and Zwinglian extremes on the Eucharist. Had Calvin died in 1541 at the ripe age of thirty-two, he would still be revered today as one of the greatest theologians and one of the ablest writers among the reformers.

Fourthly, Calvin was a church statesman. The reformers of Strasbourg, Bucer and Wolfgang Capito, tried desperately to mend the schism between the Protestants of Germany and Switzerland. They also participated in a series of conferences aimed at reuniting Protestants and Catholics. Unity

32. Parker, p. 69.

33. Ibid., p. 72; OS 1, pp. 25-256.

34. The most recent critical edition of the Romans commentary has been edited by T. H. L. Parker, *Iohannes Calvini Commentarius in Epistolam Pauli ad Romanos* (Leiden: E. J. Brill, 1981). See also, T. H. L. Parker, *Calvin's New Testament Commentaries* (London: SCM Press, 1971) and *Calvin's Old Testament Commentaries* (Edinburgh: T. and T. Clark, 1986).

still seemed possible in 1540 since the Council of Trent had not yet con-vened nor had the fierce wars of religion taken their toll. Calvin was in-volved in many of these discussions. He traveled to Frankfort, Hagenau, and Worms as a kind of adviser to the Protestant delegations at these interfaith conferences. At one of these he met Philip Melanchthon with whom he struck up a lifelong friendship. The real importance of these meetings for Calvin was the worldwide vision of the church they confirmed for him. He lamented the fragmented character of Christendom: "Amongst the greatest evils of our century must be counted the fact that the churches are so divided one from another and that there is scarcely even a human relationship between us."[35] Calvin was not willing to compromise essentials for the sake of a false peace, but he sought to call the church back to the true basis of its unity in Jesus Christ.

Fifthly, at Strasbourg Calvin became a husband. Calvin was doubtless the most eligible bachelor in the city. Bucer, the matchmaker among the re-formers, tried several times to find a suitable bride for the young pastor. One of the proposed young women could speak no French. Since Calvin knew no German, it was concluded that they might have a communication prob-lem. In a letter to Farel, Calvin described what he really wanted in a wife:

> I am not of the wild race of lovers who, at the first sight of a fine figure, embrace all the faults of their beloved. This is the only beauty which allures me, if she is chaste, if not too nice or fastidious, if economical, if patient, if there is hope that she will be interested about my health.[36]

As one of my women students remarked, with that kind of recipe it is a wonder that he ever found a wife! In fact, he married one of his own parishoners, Idelette de Bure, the widow of a French-speaking Anabaptist converted to the Reformed faith by Calvin himself. She was described by Farel, who performed the wedding, as an "upright and honest" and "even pretty" woman.[37]

We would like to know more about family life in the Calvin household, but again much of this lies hidden behind the veil of reticence. We can

35. Calvin to Archbishop Cranmer: CO 14, col. 313. Cf. Jean Cadier, "Calvin and the Union of the Churches," *John Calvin: A Collection of Essays,* ed. G. E. Duffield (Grand Rapids: Eerdmans, 1966), pp. 118-130.

36. Jules Bonnet, ed., *Letters of John Calvin* (New York: Burt Franklin, 1972; original ed., 1858), I, p. 141.

37. A. L. Herminjard, ed., *Correspondence des Réformateurs dans les pays de langue francaise* (Geneva and Paris: 1866-1897), VI, p. 285.

assume that Calvin and Idelette's relationship was not the fiery love affair of an Abelard and Heloise, nor even perhaps the rollicking domestic content of a Luther and Katie. But neither was it the stoical, sexless arrangement often portrayed by Calvin's detractors. Idelette bore Calvin only one child, a son named Jacques who was born prematurely and died in infancy. We get a glimpse of Calvin's grief in a letter he wrote to his friend Pierre Viret: "Certainly the Lord has afflicted us with a deep and painful wound in the death of our beloved son. But he is our Father: he knows what is best for his children."[38] When Idelette herself died in 1549, Calvin again wrote to Viret: "You know the tenderness or rather the softness of my soul. . . . The reason for my sorrow is not an ordinary one. I am deprived of my excellent life companion, who, if misfortune had come, would have been my willing companion not only in exile and sorrow, but even in death."[39] Calvin survived Idelette by fifteen years, but we should not imagine that even then his life was free from the rush and bother of daily domesticity. Idelete left behind two children by her first husband for whom Calvin continued to provide solicitous care, as he had promised to his wife on her deathbed. In addition, Calvin's brother Antoine and his family—he had eight children by two wives, the first of whom he divorced because of her adultery with a servant—along with various other friends and relations shared the modest dwelling of the reformer at Number Eleven, Rue des Chanoines in Geneva. For most of his life Calvin's house was full of little children. As one biographer has wisely remarked, "no doubt the womenfolk protected both him and the children from one another." Still, it is sobering to realize that Calvin's *Institutes* and commentaries, his many treatises and sermons were "not written in an ivory tower, but against the background of teething troubles."[40]

When the Genevans implored Calvin to return to their church, where things had gone from bad to worse, he demurred. He much preferred the happy situation in Strasbourg to that dangerous "gulf and whirlpool" he had left three years before, "that cross on which I had to perish daily a thousand times over."[41] But had not Jesus promised His followers precisely that—a cross? The consensus of Calvin's friends was that he should return. This time Bucer brought up the theme of divine judgment: If you refuse to resume your ministry, you will be acting just like Jonah who tried to run

38. Ibid., VIII, p. 109.
39. CO 13, col. 230. Partially quoted in Stauffer, p. 45.
40. T. H. L. Parker, *Calvin: A Portrait* (London: SCM, 1954), p. 72.
41. Herminjard, VI, pp. 199, 325-326.

away from God![42] Fully persuaded to return, Calvin reentered Geneva on September 13, 1541. The remainder of his career as reformer was symbolized by the first two official acts he undertook upon his return. One was to present to the city council a detailed plan for the order and governance of the church. These *Ecclesiastical Ordinances* called for the installment of the four offices of pastors, doctors (teachers), elders, and deacons, which corresponded to doctrine, education, discipline, and social welfare.[43] The council approved Calvin's blueprint, but he spent the rest of his career trying, never completely successfully, to secure its enforcement.

Calvin's other act was also of decisive importance. On the first Sunday after his return, he entered the pulpit of Saint Pierre. The great Gothic cathedral was crammed with curious Genevans who expected to hear an exultant Calvin lambast his opponents, who had driven him from the city, and deliver a burning "I-told-you-so" sermon to the whole assembly. In a letter to Farel, Calvin told what he did: "After a preface, I took up the exposition where I had stopped—by which I indicated that I had interrupted my office of preaching for the time rather than that I had given it up entirely."[44] Nothing could have been less dramatic or more effective. Calvin merely picked up where he had left off three years before, at the very chapter and verse of whatever book of the Bible (we don't know which one, nor does it matter) from which he had been preaching. In this way Calvin signaled that he intended his life and his theology to be, not a device of his own making, but a responsible witness to the Word of God.

Calvin as Theologian

Calvin's Writings

Whoever wishes to make a thorough study of Calvin's theology must consult at least six distinct sources within his vast literary corpus.

The *Institutes.* Calvin has often been thought of as a "man of one book." It is possible—and tempting—to confine one's investigation of Calvin's theology to the one volume he hoped would "be a key to open a way for all children of God into a good and right understanding of Holy Scrip-

42. So Beza reported in his "Life of Calvin." *Tracts and Treatises,* I, p. lxxv.
43. Karl Holl, *Johannes Calvin* (Tübingen: J. C. B. Mohr, 1909), p. 12: "Wenn Calvin die vier Aemter der Pastoren, Lehrer, Aeltesten, Diakonen aus dem Neuen Testament übernahm, so fand er in ihnen zugleich die Frunktionen der Kirche ausgedrückt, die er für konstitutiv hielt: Lehre, Zucht, Jugendunterricht und soziale Fürsorge."
44. CO 3, p. xxxiii.

ture."[45] We have already mentioned the origin and early success of this work. We have also outlined the six chapters of the 1536 edition, which contained 520 octavo pages of about six and one-eighth by four inches. The Strasbourg edition of 1539 was already significantly expanded to 346 pages, thirteen by eight inches in size, with wide margins for readers' comments. Calvin continued to enlarge, revise, and reorganize the *Institutes* throughout his life. In all he produced eight editions of the Latin text (1536, 1539, 1543, 1545, 1550, 1553, 1554, 1559) and five translations into French (1541, 1545, 1551, 1553, 1560). Not until the definitive edition of 1559 was Calvin pleased with the structure of his magnum opus: "Although I did not regret the labor spent, I was never satisfied until the work had been arranged in the order now set forth."[46] The *Institutes* of 1559 is a massive work, roughly equal in size to the Old Testament plus the Synoptic Gospels. It is arranged in four books which follow in general the pattern of the Apostles' Creed. We can illustrate the final form of the *Institutes* in this way:

Book 1: The Knowledge of God the Creator
—twofold knowledge of God
—Scripture
—Trinity
—Creation
—providence

Book 2: The Knowledge of God the Redeemer
—the fall, human sinfulness
—the Law
—Old and New Testaments
—Christ the Mediator: His Person (Prophet, Priest, King) and work (atonement)

Book 3: The Way in Which We Receive the Grace of Christ, Its Benefits and Effects
—faith and regeneration
—repentance
—Christian life

45. "Subject Matter of the Present Work" in *Calvin: Institutes of the Christian Religion,* John T. McNeill and Ford Lewis Battles, eds. (Philadelphia: Westminster Press, 1960), p. 3. All further quotations from the *Institutes* will follow the McNeill-Battles translation unless otherwise noted. This quotation is from the preface to the French edition of 1560: Jean Calvin, *L' Institution Chretiene,* Jean Cadier, ed. (Geneva: Labor et Fides, 1955), p. xix.

46. "John Calvin to the Reader," *Institutes,* p. 3; OS 3, p. 5.

—justification
—predestination
—the final resurrection
Book 4:   The External Means by Which God Invites Us into the
Society of Christ
—church
—sacraments
—civil government

Commentaries. We make a mistake if we view the *Institutes* as a systematic theology in the modern sense of that term. It was intended to serve as a guide to the study of the Bible, to show the reader "what he ought especially to seek in Scripture, and to what end he ought to relate its contents." As a complement to the *Institutes,* Calvin referred his readers to his biblical commentaries. On the basis of these commentaries Joseph Scaliger, the great classical scholar, pronounced Calvin "the greatest wit the world had seen since the Apostles." Likewise Jacob Arminius, who modified several principles of Calvin's theology, recommended the commentaries next to the Bible, for Calvin "is incomparable in the interpretation of Scripture."[47] Drawing on his superb knowledge of Greek and Hebrew and his thorough training in humanist philosophy, Calvin produced commentaries on all of the New Testament books except 2 and 3 John and Revelation, on the Pentateuch, Joshua, and Psalms, and Isaiah. Calvin's commentaries and his sermon-lectures on the Old Testament fill forty-five volumes in the nineteenth-century English translation published by the Calvin Translation Society. All of Calvin's exegetical work is marked by brevity on the one hand and modesty on the other. His goal was to penetrate to the mind of the author as concisely and clearly as possible, avoiding lavish displays of erudition and digressions into secondary concerns. Nor did he hesitate to admit that he did not understand some passages in the Bible. For example, concerning the implication of Acts 1 for the second coming of Christ, he declared: "It is better that I should leave untouched what I cannot explain," a frank acknowledgment of his own limitations before the mystery of Scripture.[48]

Sermons. Calvin was a master preacher in an age when the pulpit was the primary medium of communication to the entire culture. "When the gospel

47. Quoted, A. M. Hunter, *The Teaching of Calvin* (London: James Clarke, 1950), p. 20.
48. CNTC 6, p. 36; CO 48, col. 14: "quod tamen explicare nequeo, praestat intactum relinquere."

is preached in the name of God," Calvin said, "it is as if God himself spoke in person."[49] Following the pattern Zwingli had instituted in Zurich, Calvin generally preached continuously through the books of the Bible. His practice was to preach from the New Testament on Sunday and the Old Testament on weekdays. He did not follow a manuscript but, having immersed himself in the text for the day, walked directly from his study to the pulpit of Saint Pierre. Calvin preached twice on Sundays and once daily on alternate weeks. His sermons were taken down in shorthand by a band of faithful French refugees. A few sermons were published in Calvin's lifetime, but some have remained in manuscript form to the present day; they are just now being edited critically and published.[50]

Tracts and Treatises. Calvin once said of himself, using the words of Augustine, "I count myself one of the number of those who write as they learn and learn as they write."[51] Calvin wrote more in one lifetime than most people are able to read. In addition to the *Institutes,* commentaries and sermons, he wrote numerous tracts and treatises which shed considerable light on the development of his thought. Some of these writings were directed against theological opponents such as the radical reformers *(Psychopannychia,* 1534; *Against the Libertines,* 1545), Roman Catholics (*An Inventory of Relics,* 1543; *Antidote to the Council of Trent,* 1547), and Lutherans (Westphal, Heshusius). Others are more general treatments of Reformation themes such as *The Necessity of Reforming the Church* (1544), *Short Treatise on the Lord's Supper* (1541), and the *Treatise upon the Eternal Predestination of God* (1552).

Letters. Calvin was a prolific correspondent. A highly selective edition of

49. Calvin's third sermon on Jacob and Esau. Cf. John H. Leith, "Calvin's Doctrine of the Proclamation of the word and Its Significance for Today in the Light of Recent Research," *Calvin Studies II: Presented at a Colloquium on Calvin Studies at Davidson College* (January 1984), p. 62, 31n.

50. Thus far five volumes of Calvin's sermons have appeared in the series *Supplements Calviniana;* 872 sermons were published in the *Corpus Reformatorum* edition of Calvin's writings (CO). The sermon manuscripts have undergone a curious history themselves. Forty-four folio volumes of sermons were deposited in the *Bibliothèque publique et universitaire* in Geneva. In the year 1805 the librarian sold all but one of these volumes—by weight!—since they were not written in Calvin's own hand and were very difficult to decipher. Fortunately, the library was later able to recover thirteen of the original set. These include sermons on Genesis, Psalms, Isaiah, Jeremiah, Micah, Ezekiel, Matthew, Acts, and 1 Corinthians.

51. "John Calvin to the Reader," *Institutes,* p. 5; OS 3, p. 7; "Ego ex eorum numero me esse profiteor qui scribunt proficiendo, et scribendo proficiunt."

his letters collected by Jules Bonnet fills four hefty volumes. Calvin's letters reveal him as a contextual theologian as much alive to the political and social currents of his time as to specific religious concerns. The range of his correspondence is astounding. He wrote to his fellow reformers (Farel, Viret, Melanchthon, Bullinger), to kings and princes (Edward VI and Lady Jane Grey of England, Sigismund Augustus of Poland, Duchess Renée of Ferrara, Admiral de Coligny of France), to persecuted churches and imprisoned Protestants, to pastors and colporteurs and martyrs in waiting. The international scope of Calvin's theology and the extent of his personal influence can be gauged only by looking at his letters.

Liturgical and Catechetical Writings. Perhaps above all else, Calvin was a pastor. We have already seen him versifying French psalms for his church at Strasbourg, a task he extended to Geneva upon his return. He was keenly aware that the only way to recast the moral and religious life of the people was to instruct them in "the school of faith." He spared no efforts in devising an adequate confession of faith and catechism to complement *The Form of Prayers* (1542).

In our overview of key themes in Calvin's theology, we shall make use of each of these six genres of literature. Most of our attention, however, will be directed to the *Institutes* and the biblical commentaries.

Calvin's Perspective

"Business with God." "Nearly all the wisdom we possess, that is to say, true and sound wisdom, consists of two parts: the knowledge of God and of ourselves." Thus Calvin opened the first chapter of the *Institutes*. The fact that he chose to speak of the "knowledge" of God rather than the "being" or "essence" of God points to the centrality of revelation in his thought. Indeed, it is impossible for human beings to penetrate into the essence of God, to discover "what God is" *(quid Deus sit)* in and of Himself. We can only know "of what sort God is" *(qualis Deus sit),* and this only insofar as God has chosen to reveal Himself first.

But which comes first, the knowledge of God or the knowledge of ourselves? Calvin recognized that we cannot easily discern "which one precedes and brings forth the other." Both are true simultaneously. There is no proper knowledge of God which does not involve self-understanding. Yet no one can know who he really is without first looking upon God's face. We are not dealing with two levels of knowledge. It is not as though one could gain a thorough knowledge of the self, by earning a Ph.D. in psychology perhaps, and then transfer to a divinity school to pursue the knowledge of God. At every step of the way, and in every area of life, we are confronted by a seeming contradiction: The knowledge of ourselves drives us to look at God while it presupposes that we have already contemplated Him.

However, when Calvin spoke of the twofold knowledge of God *(duplex cognitio dei),* he was not talking about the ever-present duality of the divine-human encounter. Rather he referred to the knowledge of God as Creator, manifested in the fashioning of the universe, and the knowledge of God as Redeemer, seen only in the face of Christ.[52]

Every human being is essentially a religious creature. No one is exempt from doing "business with God" *(negotium cum Deo).* Deep within every person God has fixed an awareness of Himself. Calvin called this awareness "the seed of religion," "the sense of divinity," "the worm of conscience." According to Calvin, no matter how far one may drift away from God, even to the point of denying God's very existence, still "that seed remains which can be in no wise be uprooted" *(Inst.* 1.4.4).

Calvin believed that God had not only placed an innate awareness of Himself within all persons but had also revealed Himself in the wonders of the external creation as well. He saw God as a Worker *(Opifex)* who had displayed "innumerable evidences" and "unmistakable marks of his glory" in the whole workmanship of the universe *(Inst.* 1.5.1). Indeed, the universe was "a sort of mirror in which we can contemplate God, who is otherwise invisible." Or, to change metaphors, it was "a dazzling theater" on which the glory of God shone *(Inst.* 1.5.8).

The knowledge of God revealed in nature called forth an inevitable human response. There was no such thing as an objective, disinterested knowledge of God. The knowledge of God was determinative of human existence, hence no neutral response was possible. The "seed of religion" would perforce yield one of two responses: piety or idolatry. Calvin defined piety as "that reverence joined with love of God which the knowledge of his benefits induces" *(Inst.* 1.2.1). Idolatry was the substitution of creaturely deities for the one true God.

All of this is a commentary on Augustine's famous dictum at the beginning of his *Confessions:* "O Lord, thou hast made us for thyself, and our hearts are restless until they find their rest in thee." Still, for Calvin, the ultimate goal of piety was *not* the salvation of the individual. "For the pious

52. *Institutes,* 1.2.1. E. A. Dowey has argued that this construct provides a model for understanding Calvin's entire theology: "The Structure of Calvin's Thought as Influenced by the Two-fold Knowledge of God," *Calvinus Ecclesiae Genevensis Custos,* ed. Wilhelm Neuser (Frankfort: Peter Lang, 1984), pp. 135-48.

mind realizes that the punishment of the impious and wicked and the reward of life eternal for the righteous equally pertain to God's glory (*Inst.* 1.2.2). In a striking line Calvin averred that "even if there were no hell" the truly pious person would shudder at the thought of offending the glory of God.

Lost in the Labyrinth. On the basis of what we have said thus far, one might conclude that Calvin was a proponent of a purely natural theology. At one point he did concede that the order of nature would have led to a correct understanding of God—"if Adam had remained upright" (*Inst.* 1.2.1). Had the Fall never occurred, it would have been possible to move from the vestiges of God's presence in the self and the world into a proper relationship with the Creator. Because of sin, however, this was a never-to-be-realized possibility. "So it happens that no real piety remains in the world" (*Inst.* 1.4.1). The knowledge of God in the natural realm had only a negative function—to render humans inexcusable for their idolatry.

> It is therefore in vain that so many burning lamps shine for us in the work-manship of the universe to show forth the glory of its author. Although they bathe us wholly in their radiance, yet they can of themselves in no way lead us into the right path. They do not go farther than to render us inexcusable (*Inst.* 1.5.14).

One of Calvin's favorite images for human estrangement from God was the labyrinth. As a student of the classics, Calvin would have known the Greek legend of Theseus who entered the labyrinth at Cnossus, slew the Minotaur, and found his way out again by means of the thread given to him by Ariande. Humankind was utterly lost in a maze.

> Hence arises that boundless filthy mire of error wherewith the whole earth was filled and covered. For each man's mind is like a labyrinth, so that it is no wonder that individual nations were drawn aside into various falsehoods; and not only this—but individual men, almost, had their own gods (*Inst.* 1.5.12).

Indeed, the human mind was a veritable "factory of idols" which manufactured one false god after another. "All of the labyrinths of error in the world" came from this common source.[53] "Wretched man, wanting to be somebody in himself, began incontinently to forget and misunderstand the source of his good; and by an act of outrageous ingratitude, he set out to exalt himself in pride against his Maker and the Author of all that is

---

53. *Calvin: Commentaries,* ed. Joseph Haroutunian (London: SCM Press, 1958), p. 131.

excellent in him."[54] Thus while the primal image of God remained in the human, it had been completely spoiled and defaced. In their fallen condition, "natural reason could never guide men to Christ."[55]

Accommodated Revelation. All true knowledge of God derived from one fact: God, in His great mercy, had deigned to reveal Himself. It is important to recognize that, for Calvin, revelation was the result of a free decision of God. No one compelled God to reveal Himself, anymore than God was compelled to create the universe. Even had He left humankind to wander aimlessly in the labyrinth of sin, God would still have remained just. Yet out of His sovereign goodness, he decided to bridge "the great distance between us and his heavenly glory," to come down to us through the Word.[56]

To describe the process of revelation Calvin used the word *accommodation (attemperatio).*[57] "God cannot be comprehended by us," said Calvin, "except as far as he accommodates himself to our standard."[58] Again, God "accommodates himself to our capacity in addressing us."[59] Most likely, Calvin borrowed the principle of accommodation from the tradition of classical rhetoric, which he had studied as a humanist. The precise aim of rhetoric was to accommodate, to adjust, adapt, or fit one's language in a way that would be suitable to the intended audience. This too was what God did in making Himself known.

God's accommodated revelation contained two movements. The first movement in the process of revelation was God's free decision not to keep His Word "shut up in his bosom," but rather to send it forth. In the created order the Word manifested itself in the *opera Dei* which served as "witnesses and messengers of God's glory." In a passage which could have come from Francis of Assisi, Calvin exulted in this "natural revelation": "For the little birds that sing, sing of God; the beasts clamor for him; the elements dread him, the mountains echo him, the fountains and flowing waters cast their

54. Ibid., p. 58.

55. Ibid., p. 132.

56. Ibid., p. 131.

57. The best treatment of this theme in Calvin is Ford L. Battles, "God Was Accommodating Himself to Human Capacity," *Interpretation* 31 (1977), pp. 19-38. See also E. A. Dowey, *The Knowledge of God in Calvin's Theology* (New York: Columbia University Press, 1952), pp. 3-18.

58. *Comm.* Ezek 9:3,4: CO 40, col. 196.

59. *Comm.* 1 Cor. 2:7: CO 49, col. 337; CNTC 9, pp. 53-54.

glances at him, and the grass and flowers laugh before him."[60] Yet, as we have seen, because of human sinfulness the salvific effect of the works of God in nature was nil: They could only leave people without excuse before the bar of judgment. Still, God desired to "render himself near and familiar to us," to communicate His will to us. In order to accomplish this, the Word, accommodating itself to our human sinfulness, was enfleshed in the incarnation, "in-lettered" in Holy Scripture, and visibly and audibly displayed in the ministry of the sacraments and preaching. Only through these *oracula Dei* can we arrive at the proper knowledge of God the Redeemer.

We can learn something about Calvin's theological method when we see how he related the principle of accommodation to his doctrine of Scripture. Calvin used two images to describe the Bible, the first to show how the Bible was given, the second to illustrate its function in the Christian life.

> For who even of slight intelligence does not understand that, as nurses commonly do with infants, God is wont in a measure to "lisp" in speaking to us? Thus such forms of speaking do not so much express clearly what God is like as accommodate the knowledge of him to our slight capacity (*Inst.* 1.13.1).

Here God was likened to a nurse engaged in baby talk with infants! The Bible too was a kind of divine baby talk. When we find "God prattling to us in the Bible in an uncultivated and vulgar style," we should not be offended but grateful since it is only by such condescension that we can know Him at all.[61]

Calvin also compared the Bible to a pair of spectacles:

> Just as old or bleary-eyed men and those with weak vision, if you thrust before them a most beautiful volume, even if they recognize it to be some sort of writing, yet can scarcely construe two words, but with the aid of spectacles will begin to read distinctly; so Scripture, gathering up the otherwise confused knowledge of God in our minds, having dispersed our dullness, clearly shows us the true God (*Inst.* 1.6.1).

The Bible was likened to divine eyeglasses for the spiritually nearsighted. These two different images of the Bible, inspired baby talk and spectacles, point to two important aspects of Calvin's approach to the special task of theology. We can express these in terms of a positive and negative admonition. Positively, true theology is reverent reflection on the revelation of God in the Bible, which is absolutely sufficient (i.e. normative, for belief and conduct). Negatively, theology must not wander into "vain speculations"

60. *Commentaries,* p. 60.
61. Ibid., p. 90; CNTC 4, pp. 70-71.

but stick closely to those things we may legitimately know, namely to the data of revelation in the Scriptures. Let us explore each of these principles further.

The first principle introduces us to Calvin's doctrine of Holy Scripture, the essential elements of which we can summarize in one sentence: The Bible is the inspired Word of God revealed in human language and confirmed to the believer by the inner witness of the Holy Spirit. Each element in this definition requires further elaboration. (1) *The Bible is the inspired Word of God.* Calvin did not spend much time trying to explain precisely how the Scriptures were inspired. However, he clearly asserted the divine origin of the Bible, as in his *Commentary* on 2 Timothy 3:16:

> All those who wish to profit from the Scriptures must first accept this as a settled principle, that the Law and the prophets are not teachings handed on at the pleasure of men or produced by men's minds as their source, but are dictated by the Holy Spirit. . . . We owe to the Scripture the same reverence as we owe to God, since it has its only source in Him and has nothing of human origin mixed with it.[62]

Calvin believed the Bible was the "school of the Holy Spirit." Its writers were instruments, organs, amanuenses of the Holy Spirit.[63] If the Bible was a kind of "prattling," as Calvin had said, then God is the Prattler. It was easy to see that the Scriptures, "which so far surpass all gifts and graces of human endeavor, breathe something divine" (*Inst.* 1.8.1).

(2) *The Bible is the Word of God revealed in human language.* To use Calvin's exact words, it is the Word of God which has "flowed to us from the very mouth of God by the ministry of men" (*Inst.* 1.7.5). As a well-trained humanist Calvin recognized the diverse styles of writing found in the Bible. The Holy Spirit, he concluded, at times uses both "eloquence" and "a rude and unrefined style" in the Bible (*Inst.*, 1.8.2). This is all a part of what G. C. Berkouwer called "the servant-form of Holy Scripture."[64] Calvin explained that "God accommodates Himself to the ordinary way of

62. CNTC 10, p. 330; CO 52, col. 383: "Hoc prius et membrum: eandem scripturae reverentiam deberi quam Deo deferimus, quia ab eo solo manavit, nec quidquam humani habet admistum."

63. *Institutes,* 4.8.9; OS 5, p. 141: "Illi fuerunt certi et authentici Spiritus sancti amanuenses: et ideo eorum scripta pro Dei oraculis habenda sunt."

64. G. C. Berkouwer, *Holy Scripture* (Grand Rapids: Eerdmans, 1975), pp. 195-212.

speaking because of our ignorance, and sometimes even, so to say, stammers."[65] Yet in the "rude and lowly teaching of the gospel" Christians discover the very words of life itself.

Calvin dealt with the text both reverently and critically. He doubted both the Pauline authorship of Hebrews and the Petrine authorship of 2 Peter, the latter on stylistic grounds, although he regarded both as canonical. In Calvin's harmony of the Synoptic Gospels, he usually tried to reconcile apparent discrepancies, such as the number of women at the empty tomb, but he never lost sight of the humanity and distinct personalities of the Gospel writers. He dealt frankly with the different time sequence given for the cleansing of the Temple:

> Matthew and Luke state that as soon as Christ came into the city and temple he turned out those who were buying and selling: Mark is content to say then that he surveyed the scene, and puts the actual expulsion onto the following day. I reconcile these by saying that when he saw that he had not spoken of the cleansing of the temple he put it in later, out of place.[66]

Calvin portrayed Mark as a genuine human author, composing a narrative, sifting through materials, recalling an "omission," then inserting it in his text, "out of place." To be sure, Mark was uniquely inspired by the Holy Spirit throughout this process, but not as a kind of programmed computer or automated typewriter.

Another example from Calvin's exegesis also shows his respect for the human character of Scripture. In his commentary on Acts 7:14 he dealt with the contradiction between Stephen and Moses concerning the precise number of Israelites who accompanied Jacob into Egypt. Stephen said there were seventy-five, but Genesis 46:27 gives only seventy. After surveying several possible solutions, Calvin concluded that the error probably crept in through a copyist's mistaken reading of the Septuagint text. It would have been an easy error to make since, as Calvin pointed out, numbers in Greek are often indicated by letters. "But," Calvin went on to say, "this was not such an important matter that Luke should have confused the Gentiles over it, when they were used to the Greek reading." The purpose of the story is to show the power of God to bring a great people out of such a small

---

65. CNTC 5, p. 226; CO 47, col. 458: "Scimus enim ut se ad communem loquendi modum accommodet Deus ruditatis nostrae causa, imo interdum quodammodo balbutiat."

66. CNTC 3, pp. 2-3.

band. "It suits us better to ponder that miracle which the Spirit commends to us, than to be troubled and anxious about a single letter, by which the number is altered." A bit later, in the same context, Calvin pointed out that "it is obvious that an error has been made" in substituting the name of Abraham for that of Jacob (Acts 7:16). "Hence this verse must be corrected accordingly!"[67] Calvin showed remarkable freedom in dealing with the text of Scripture precisely because he had implicit confidence both in its authority as a God-breathed oracle and in its ability to accomplish its purpose—"to show forth Christ" *(Inst.* 1.9.3).

(3) *The Bible is confirmed to the believer by the inner witness of the Holy Spirit.* How do we know that the Bible is the Word of God? For Calvin there was no independent epistemological platform on which believers could stand and objectively decide for or against the Bible. How could one know that the Bible was the Word of God? Such assurance could could only come if the same Spirit who inspired the prophets and apostles was present to illuminate one's mind and to confirm within one the truth which had been revealed. Calvin said that while some people demand "rational proof" that Moses and the prophets were inspired,

> I reply: the testimony of the Spirit is more excellent than all reason. For as God alone is a fit witness of himself in his Word, so also the Word will not find acceptance in men's hearts before it is sealed by the inward testimony of the Spirit. The same Spirit, therefore, who has spoken through the mouths of the prophets must penetrate into our hearts to persuade us that they faithfully proclaimed what had been divinely commanded *(Inst.* 1.7.4).

67. CNTC 6, pp. 181-82. There is a vast, and generally unedifying, literature on Calvin's doctrine of Scripture. Two recent contributions are Jack Rogers and Donald McKim, *The Authority and Interpretation of the Bible* (San Francisco: Harper and Row, 1979), pp. 89-119; John Woodbridge, *Biblical Authority: A Critique of the Rogers/McKim Proposal* (Grand Rapids: Zondervan, 1982), pp. 56-67. Woodbridge points out a number of weaknesses in the Rogers/McKim book, but he is guilty of the same special pleading he finds so offensive in his opponents. Two older studies worthy of note are Brian A. Gerrish, "Biblical Authority and the Continental Reformation," *Scottish Journal of Theology* 10 (1957), pp. 337-360; John T. McNeill, "The Significance of the Word of God for Calvin," *Church History* 28 (1959), pp. 131-146. On the Acts 7:16 text, see W. Robert Godfrey, "Biblical Authority in the Sixteenth and Seventeenth Centuries: A Question of Transition," *Scripture and Truth,* D. A. Carson and John Woodbridge, eds. (Grand Rapids: Zondervan, 1983). Godfrey points out that the "error" in this text was not attributed by Calvin to the scriptural author, but was accounted for through the process of textual transmission.

The ability "to recognize" the Bible as the Word of God, then, was not a skill acquired through academic study, nor an insight gained by dogmatic presuppositions; it was rather the free gift of God himself. To the believer, enlightened by the Holy Spirit, there was a direct correlation between the moments of inspiration and illumination. Calvin gave short shrift to the various proofs of the Bible's authenticity. He stated frankly that "those who wish to prove to unbelievers that Scripture is the Word of God are acting foolishly, for only by faith can this be known" (*Inst.* 1.8.13). Of course, Calvin was acquainted with many evidences of the Bible's credibility: its great antiquity, miracles, prophecies, the witness of the church and the martyrs. These were not without value to the believer, but they were at best only "secondary aids to our feebleness" compared with "that chief and highest testimony."

Calvin maintained the unity of Word and Spirit against two opposing errors. On the one hand, the Catholics downplayed the role of illumination by subordinating the Scriptures to the church. They took the words of Peter, "no prophecy of Scripture is of private interpretation," to prohibit any individual handling of the Bible and "to arrogate to their councils the final authority to interpret Scripture." Calvin argued that the word "private" in this context did not mean "individual" but "humanly devised":

> Let the whole world be unanimously agreed, and let all the minds of men be of one united opinion, what results would still be private and their own, because the subject is contrasted here with divine revelation, in that the faithful are enlightened by the Holy Spirit and acknowledge only what God wills in his Word.[68]

Calvin, like Luther, affirmed that the Scripture was the womb from which the church was born, and not vice versa.[69] Popes, councils, even the early Church Fathers whom Calvin frequently quoted, could be and often were in error. Through the inner witness of the Holy Spirit, the Scriptures authenticated themselves and disclosed their proper interpretation to the diligent believer.

On the other hand, some of Calvin's contemporaries, "fanatics," he called them, were so enamoured of the Spirit that they saw little need for the written Word. Hence, "these rascals tear apart those things which the prophet joined together with an inviolable bond" (*Inst.* 1.9.1). The Holy Spirit did not bypass the Scriptures, but was recognized in His agreement

68. CNTC 12, p. 343.
69. *Institutes,* 1.7.2. Cf. WA 3, p. 454.

with them. "The Holy Spirit so inheres in his truth, which he expresses in Scripture, that only when its proper reverence and dignity are given to the Word does the Holy Spirit show forth his power" (*Inst.* 1.9.3). All of Calvin's theology was carried out within these bounds: the objectivity of God's revelation in Holy Scripture and the confirming, illuminating witness of the Holy Spirit in the believer.

We can now return to that other favored metaphor of spectacles for the bleary-eyed. This image points to the central function of Scripture: It is for our edification, to enable us to see what would otherwise be indiscernible. Calvin was forever lambasting those theologians who toyed with "idle speculations." Proper theology was theology within the limits of revelation alone. Calvin considered the question of what God was doing before He created the world. No doubt, answered Calvin, with a twinkle in his eye, He was busy creating hell for those theologians with overly-curious minds (*Inst.* 1.14.1)! Those who would "apply ourselves teachably" to God's Word would not be led astray into such frivolous inquiries.

A good example of the spectacles character of Scripture is reflected in Calvin's discussion of an astronomical discovery. In commenting on Genesis 1:16, "the lesser light to rule the night," Calvin was confronted with the fact that the moon was not second in size to the sun among the heavenly bodies since the astronomers had proved, by means of the recently invented telescope, that Saturn was really larger than the moon. Calvin did not deny the findings of astronomy, but neither did he allow these to detract from the main purport of Scripture.

> It must be remembered that Moses does not speak with philosophical acuteness on occult mysteries, but relates those things which are everywhere observed. . . . The dishonesty of those men is sufficiently rebuked, who censure Moses for not speaking with greater exactness. For, as it became a theologian, he had respect to us rather than to the stars. . . . If the astronomer inquires respecting the actual dimensions of the stars, he will find the moon to be less than Saturn. Let the astronomers possess their more exalted knowledge; but, in the meantime, they who perceive by the moon the splendor of night, are convicted by its use of perverse ingratitude unless they acknowledge the beneficence of God. He who would learn astronomy . . . let him go elsewhere.[70]

Calvin understood that the Bible is not a source book of natural science, designed to harmonize with the latest scientific findings. Indeed, how could

70. John Calvin, *The First Book of Moses Called Genesis,* John King, trans (Edinburgh: Calvin Translation Society, 1847), I, pp. 79-80, 86-87.

that be possible, seeing that the "modern" (Latin: *modus,* just now) scientific world view has undergone multiple transformations from Genesis until the present? Rather, the purpose of Scripture was to reveal what was profitable to know about God and ourselves. Calvin said that the Lord in giving us the Scripture "did not intend either to gratify our curiosity or satisfy our desire for ostentation or provide us with a chance for mythical invention and foolish talk; He intended rather to do us good."[71] Thus the Genesis account of the moon's creation does not invite a relative comparison with the size of Saturn; its purpose is to instill gratitude, one of the key ingredients of true piety, in those who bask in the glow of the moon's light. The theologian's task, asserted Calvin, is "not to divert the ears with chatter, but to strengthen consciences by teaching things true, sure, and profitable" (*Inst.* 1.14.4).

To know God was man's chief end and justified his existence. If a man had one hundred lives, said Calvin, this one aim would be sufficient for them all.[72] While we were lost in the labyrinth of sin, God revealed the knowledge of Himself to us in His Word. Approached reverently, obediently, and teachably, the Bible becomes our spectacles into reality, our indispensible aid in the worship and service of God.

The God Who Acts

The Triune God

Neither Luther nor Zwingli devoted much attention to the doctrine of the Trinity. Both accepted the orthodox formulations of the oneness and threeness of God developed by the early councils, but neither felt compelled to elaborate on this teaching. At the beginning of his career Calvin too followed this pattern. The first edition of the *Institutes* contained only a meager statement on the Trinity; the word itself *(sacra trinitas)* is mentioned only twice. On the basis of these sparse statements, Pierre Caroli accused Calvin of Arianism. Calvin had no trouble disproving the false charge, but, from that time on, he became an adamant defender of the doctrine of the Trinity. This stance was reinforced by his close encounters with genuine anti-Trinitarians such as Servetus, Gentile, and Gribaldi. Gribaldi was a Paduan lawyer who freely disseminated his doubts about the Trinity among the Italian-speaking refugees in Geneva. At the instigation of Calvin, Gribaldi

71. CNTC 10, p. 330.
72. *Commentaries,* p. 125.

was banished from the city in 1557 for "sapping and perverting the chief article of our faith."[73] Four years earlier Servetus, for the same offense, had met a fate worse than banishment.

Calvin proved himself impeccably orthodox in his own formulations of the Trinity: "When we profess to believe in one God, under the name of God is understood a single, simple essence, in which we comprehend three persons, or hypostases" (*Inst.* 1.13.20). We must ask whether Calvin in adopting this classical definition of God did not violate his own principle of doing theology within the limits of revelation alone. Calvin was very sensitive to this question and sought to meet it head on. He was well aware that words such as *ousia, hypostases, persona,* and even *Trinitas* were non-scriptural terms. He once said, "I could wish they were buried, if only among all men this faith were agreed on: that Father and Son and Spirit are one God, yet the Son is not the Father, not the Spirit the Son, but that they are differentiated by a peculiar quality" (*Inst.* 1.13.5). Yet precisely because certain heretics, such as Arius, have used scriptural language to affirm nonbiblical concepts of God, it was necessary for Calvin to refute their errors by using words such as *Trinity* and *Persons* in order to render "the truth plain and clear" (*Inst.* 1.13.3).

Even in conceding this point, however, Calvin warned against a speculative incursion into the mystery of God's essence. "Let us then willingly leave to God the knowledge of himself." It was mere presumption for believers to "seek out God anywhere else than in his Sacred Word, or to think anything about him that is not prompted by his Word, or to speak anything that is not taken from his Word" (*Inst.* 1.13.21). Thus Calvin refused to twist the Scriptures in order to bolster the doctrine of the Trinity. Well-worn proof texts for the Trinity, such as the plural form of God *(Elohim)* in Genesis 1 or the thrice-repeated adulation of the seraphim in Isaiah 6:3 or Jesus' statement, "I and my Father are one" (John 10:30) Calvin regarded as weak and spurious proofs for such an important doctrine.

Those who denied the Trinity surely struck a sensitive nerve of Calvin. He referred to them as "slippery snakes," "babblers," "rascals," "certain frenzied persons such as Servetus and his like," who traffic in "chicaneries" and "vile absurdities." Why was the Trinity such an important issue for him? As we have seen, he was not interested in the metaphysical niceties of abstract theology, nor was he slavishly attached to traditional terminology. *The Trinity was crucial because it was a witness to the deity of Jesus Christ*

---

73. Rudolf Schwarz, ed., *Johannes Calvins Lebenswerk in seinen Briefen* (Neukirchen: Neukirchener Verlag, 1962), III, p. 888.

and thus to the certainty of salvation procured by Him. The purpose of
Calvin's Trinitarianism was, like that of Athanasius, soteriological. He
wanted to safeguard the biblical message, "God is manifest in the flesh,"
against false interpretations, such as that of Servetus who "confounded the
Son and the Holy Spirit with the creatures" (*Inst.* 1.13.22). Thus from the
first edition of the *Institutes* onward, he placed the confession of the Trinity
in a liturgical context, namely in the invocation of the Triune God at
baptism. Baptism in the name of the Father, the Son, and the Holy Spirit
witnessed both the unity and the triunity of God. The distinctions within
the Godhead were seen in the particularizing characteristics of each "Person": The free mercy of the Father by the sacrifice of His death, the Holy
Spirit cleansing and regenerating, making us partakers of the benefits of the
Son. Yet, lest anyone think that Christians worship three gods, the very
oneness of baptism pointed to the essential unity of the three divine persons.

> For it is one baptism, which is sanctified by the triune name. What reply will
> the Arians or Sabellians be able to make to this argument? Baptism possesses
> such force as to make us one; and in baptism, the name of the Father, and
> of the Son, and of the Holy Spirit is invoked. Will they deny that it is one
> Godhead who is the foundation of this holy and mystic unity? We must
> necessarily acknowledge that the ordinance of baptism proves the three Per-
> sons in one essence of God.[74]

In sum: The distinctions within the Trinity (Calvin preferred to call these
"subsistencies") were not to be understood as divisions. There was one God
who knows Himself and who has revealed Himself as Father, Son, and Holy
Spirit. The Trinity was the foundation of salvation for only could one who
was truly God redeem those who were utterly lost. In the liturgy of baptism
and in the doxology faith in the Trinity was confessed not in order to fully
define the being of God—for who could ever do that?—but only (as Augustine had said earlier) not to be silent before the mystery of His presence.

Creation

Having derived from Scripture the Triune nature of God, Calvin next
described the activity of God in relation to the world in creation and
providence. These doctrines fall under the general rubric of the "Knowledge of God the Creator" in contrast to the "Knowledge of God the
Redeemer," which Calvin discussed in Books II-IV of the *Institutes.* Calvin
saw the created world as a "dazzling theatre" of God's glory, alive with

74. CNTC 11, p. 173; CO 51, col. 191.

multiple witnesses of His power and majesty. Human beings, too, bore within them an ineradicable "sense of divinity" which left them without excuse for their idolatry and rebellion. Because of the noetic consequences of the Fall, this natural knowledge of God could never lead to salvation. "With nature alone as guide our minds cannot penetrate to him."[75] Once, however, people were illumined by the Holy Spirit, and with the aid of the "spectacles" of Scripture, creation could yield a more lucid and spiritually edifying knowledge of God. Strictly speaking, this biblically informed knowledge of God in creation was not a "natural theology," but rather a "theology of nature."

While Calvin distinguished the knowledge of God the Creator from that of God the Redeemer, he did not doubt that the one Triune God was the Subject of both acts. In commenting on Ephesians 3:9, he stated: "By Christ as God, the Father created all things. It is not surprising, then, if by the same Mediator all the Gentiles are now restored into the whole."[76] Again, the purpose for the enhanced knowledge of God revealed in nature was to strengthen the faith of believers: "Therefore it was his will that the history of creation be made manifest, in order that the faith of the church, resting upon this, might seek no other God but him who was put forth by Moses as the Maker and Founder of the universe" (*Inst.* 1.14.1).

Calvin strongly countered the notion that in creation God was merely reworking an already existent material mass. This idea, as old as Plato and Aristotle and as current as process philosophy, was to Calvin's mind a blatant denial of the aseity (Latin: *a se,* from himself) and lordship of God. God created the world *ex nihilo,* out of nothing. For Calvin, no less than for Zwingli, this affirmation was the benchmark of biblical faith. The Hebrew word *bara,* he pointed out, means "to create," to bring into being what was not, rather than to form or fashion something already made.[77] The Manicheans went so far as to attribute creation to two equally powerful deities, one a benevolent god who created good, the other a sinister spirit who brought forth evil. Such a view not only robbed God of His omnipotence but also (and more damaging in Calvin's view) deprived Him of His glory.

Although God lacks nothing, still the principal aim he had in creating men

75. CNTC 7, p. 119; CO 48, col. 416: "Sequitur sola natura duce non posse illuc penetrare mentes nostras."

76. CNTC 11, p. 162; CO 51, col. 182.

77. *Commentairies de Jean Calvin sur l'Ancien Testament,* André Malet, ed. (Geneva: Labor et Fides, 1961), I, pp. 24-25.

was that his name might be glorified in them. . . . The wicked are created for the day of their perdition: for that does not happen save in so far as God wills to reveal his glory by them; even as he has said in another place, that he raised up Pharaoh in order that his name should be manifest among the peoples. And were this not so, what would become of so many evidences of Scripture which tell us that the sovereign aim of our salvation is the glory of God?[78]

The world was created for the glory of God, but it was not created without consideration for the benefit of humankind. Why, for instance, did God take six days to create the world? He could have done it all in a moment, but He accommodated his power to human capacities, distributing "his work into six days that we might not find it irksome to occupy our whole life in contemplating it" (*Inst.* 1.14.2). For precisely the same reason, God created the angels—not for his own sake, but for ours, "to comfort our weakness, that we may lack nothing at all that can raise up our minds to good hope, or confirm them in security" (*Inst.* 1.14.11). Indeed, all of creation was intended to enhance human life:

> Now when he disposed the movement of the sun and stars to human uses, filled the earth, waters, and air with living things, and brought forth an abundance of fruits to suffice as foods, in thus assuming the responsibility of a foreseeing and diligent father of the family he shows his wonderful goodness toward us (*Inst.* 1.14.2).

Unlike some theologians, such as Thomas Aquinas, Calvin did not seek to prove the existence of God by arguing from the effects of creation back to a First Cause, the Creator. To his mind such a proof, even if it were possible, was redundant since all persons had within them an intuitive awareness of God. But the creation did have tremendous significance for believers. They were not meant to exploit nature for their own selfish ends, nor to study it merely to satisfy their wanton curiosity. Rather believers were to contemplate the goodness of God in His creatures in such a way that their very hearts were moved. Calvin said "to recognize that God has destined all things for our good and salvation and at the same time to feel his power and grace in ourselves and in the great benefits he has conferred upon us, and so bestir ourselves to trust, invoke, praise, and love him" (*Inst.* 1.14.21-22).

The following "Hymn to Creation," adapted from the *Institutes,* is a

---

78. CO 8, cols. 293 *f.* Quoted in François Wendel, *Calvin: The Origin and Development of His Religious Thought* (London: Collins, 1963), p. 171.

beautiful example of the proper response to creation which Calvin enjoined upon the believer:

> God has set all things for our good
> And our salvation; in our very
> Selves we feel His pow'r and grace,
> His great, unnumber'd benefits,
> Freely conferr'd upon us.
>
> What else can we then do but stir
> Ourselves to trust, invoke, to praise and love Him?
> For all God's handiwork is made for man.
> Ev'n in the six days he shows a Father's care
> For His child as yet unborn.
>
> Away, ingratitude, forgetfulness
> Of Him! Away with craven fear He may
> Fail us in our need! For He
> Has seen to it that nothing will be
> Lacking to our own welfare.
>
> Whene'er we call on God, Creator
> Of heav'n and earth, we must be mindful
> That all He gives us is in His hand
> To give; our ev'ry trust and hope
> We hang on Him alone
>
> Whatever we desire, we are
> To ask of Him and thankfully receive
> Each benefit that falls to us.
> Let us then strive to love and serve
> Him with all our hearts.[79]

Providence

More than any other reformer of the sixteenth century, Calvin was keenly aware of the precarious and utterly contingent character of human life. If Luther was preoccupied with the anxiety of guilt, and Zwingli moved to a deeper understanding of the gospel by his close brush with death, then Calvin was haunted by the specter of the apparently haphazard and meaningless course of existence. Just as Luther continued to wrestle with the devil after his evangelical breakthrough, so too Calvin recognized the perpetual conflict and struggle in the believer's search for meaning: "While we teach that faith ought to be certain and assured, we cannot imagine any

79. Battles, *Piety,* pp. 169-170.

certainty that is not tinged with doubt, or any assurance that is not assailed by some anxiety" (*Inst.* 3.2.17).

The sources of anxiety were present in every conceivable human situation. In a striking passage, which anticipates the sense of "thrownness" so evident in modern existentialist literature, Calvin described the fragility of the human condition:

> Innumerable are the evils that beset human life; innumerable, too, the deaths that threaten it. We need not go beyond ourselves: since our body is the receptacle of a thousand diseases—in fact holds within itself and fosters the causes of diseases—a man cannot go about unburdened by many forms of his own destruction, and without drawing out a life enveloped, as it were, with death. For what else would you call it, when he neither freezes nor sweats without danger? Now, wherever you turn, all things around you not only are hardly to be trusted but almost openly menace, and seem to threaten immediate death. Embark upon a ship, you are one step away from death. Mount a horse, if one foot slips, your life is imperiled. Go through the city streets, you are subject to as many dangers as there are tiles on the roofs. If there is a weapon in your hand or a friend's, harm awaits. All the fierce animals you see are armed for your destruction. But if you try to shut yourself up in a walled garden, seemingly delightful, there a serpent sometimes lies hidden. Your house, continually in danger of fire, threatens in the daytime to impoverish you, at night even to collapse upon you. Your field, since it is exposed to hail, frost, drought, and other calamities, threatens you with barrenness, and hence, famine. I pass over poisonings, ambushes, robberies, open violence, which in part besiege us at home, in part dog us abroad. Amid these tribulations must not man be most miserable, since but half alive in life, he weakly draws his anxious and languid breath, as if he had a sword perpetually hanging over his neck? (*Inst.* 1.17.10).

To pretend that we are exempt from such dangers, to imagine that we can neutralize their impact by taking out large insurance policies, for example, or by worshiping at the modern shrine of the health spa is to deny our humanity or, as Calvin put it, to "overlap our finitude."[80] Calvin's doctrine of providence did not reflect the pious optimism of "God's in his heaven, all's right with the world." It arose from an utterly realistic assessment of the vicissitudes of life and of the anxiety they produce.

Calvin distinguished his view of providence from two popular misconceptions, that of fatalism on the one hand and (what would become known later as) deism on the other. The Stoic doctrine of fate presupposed that all events were governed by the necessity of nature which contained within itself an

---

80. *Comm.* on Matt. 6:27: CNTC, 1 p. 221.

intimately related series of cause and effect. Calvin was accused of teaching precisely this doctrine. He denied the charge, pointing out that in the Christian view "the ruler and governor of all things" was not an impersonal force or chain of necessity, but rather the personal Creator of the universe "who in accordance with his wisdom has from the farthest limit of eternity decreed what he was going to do, and now by his might carries out what he has decreed" (*Inst.* 1.16.8).

Calvin expended more energy in refuting the other error, namely the idea that God having constructed the world in the beginning had since left it to run its course more or less on its own. Such a view imagined God idly observing from heaven what takes place on earth, distant and removed from the daily goings-on of everyday life. Some who subscribed to this view held that God foresaw what would happen but did not intervene in the actual unfolding of the events themselves. Against this concept of "bare foreknowledge," Calvin asserted that providence "pertains no less to his hands than to his eyes" (*Inst.* 1.16.4). God so attended to the regulation of all events, which proceed from His set plan, that "nothing takes place by chance." Slightly better, but still deficient, was the belief that certain events were allowed by God's permission, but not sustained by His direct action. But this view too limited God's omnipoitence by conjuring up a deity who reposes idly in a watchtower.[81] "Bare permission" was no better than "bare foreknowledge." Both denied to God what the Scriptures everywhere attributed—a watchful, effective, active, ceaseless engagement with the governance of the world He had created.

Providence, then, was inseparably joined to creation and was itself a kind of continuation of the creative process *(creatio continuata):* "We see the presence of divine power shining as much in the continuing state of the universe as in its inception" (*Inst.* 1.16.1). Not only the great events of history but even the most minute occurrences within nature were subject to God's direction. "It is certain that not one drop of rain falls without God's sure command" (*Inst.* 1.16.5). Thunder and lightning, too, obeyed His voice. The emphasis on God's direct, immediate activity in the world led Calvin to reject the traducianist theory of the origin of the soul. According to this view, which was held by Luther, the soul is transmitted from generation to generation through the process of human procreation. Calvin, on the other hand, believed that each time a child is given life, God creates

81. *Institutes*, 1.16.8; CO 34, col. 302: "Ainsi donc cognoissons que Dieu ne se pourmene point là haut comme en des galleries: mais qu'il remplit tout le monde, et qu'il faut que nous le contemplions tousjours prochain de nous."

a new soul *ex nihilo*. This meant that God must be very busy for each day He created thousands of souls every minute.

God's direct interaction with the world did not mean for Calvin, however, that He could not also use secondary causes to effect His will. Indeed, these played an important role in the unfolding of God's purposes.

> Therefore the Christian heart, since it has been thoroughly persuaded that all things happen by God's plan, and that nothing takes place by chance, will ever look to him as the principal causes of things, yet will give attention to the secondary causes in their proper place (*Inst.* 1.17.6).

God did not hesitate to use even Satan and his hosts to achieve His divine goals. The question arises whether in so doing God did not become an accomplice in their evil deeds. To get around this difficulty Calvin distinguished between the will and the precept of God. "While God accomplishes through the wicked what he has decreed by his secret judgment, they are not excusable, as if they had obeyed his precept which out of their own lust they deliberately break" (*Inst.* 1.18.4). In commenting on Paul's "thorn in the flesh" which was inflicted by "a messenger of Satan" Calvin asked how Satan, who was a murderer from the beginning, could become in this way a sort of physician to the apostle, since through infirmity Paul gained much spiritual strength!

> My answer is that Satan's only intention, in accordance with his character and customs, was to kill and destroy, and the good of which Paul speaks was dipped in deadly poison, so that it was a special act of mercy for the Lord to turn into a means of healing what was by nature the means of death.[82]

In His great and boundless wisdom, God "knows right well how to use evil instruments to do good" (*Inst.* 1.17.5). Of course, God did not simply give free rein to the devil and his demonic cohorts, but bridled them in their fury and mad raging. Calvin found this fact to be of great comfort to believers under duress from the evil one:

> Let them recall that the devil and the whole cohort of the wicked are completely restrained by God's hand as by a bridle, so that they are unable either to hatch any plot against us or, having hatched it, to make preparations or, if they have fully planned it, to stir a finger toward carrying it out, except so far as he has permitted, indeed commanded (*Inst.* 1.17.11).[83]

82. *Comm.* on 2 Cor. 12:7: CNTC, 10 P. 160.

83. Cf. also CO 34, col. 15: "Si nous cognoissons que Dieu tiene la bride à Satan et à tous les siens, ... alors nous pourrons recourir à lui hardiment."

In his book, *My Lady of the Chimney Corner,* Alexander Irvine told a story which illustrates this distinctively Calvinist perspective on providence. A starving Irish family is provided a good meal as the result of a wager made during a gambling game. Anna, the pious mother, thanks God for bringing them relief. Boyle, whose nefarious activity had won them the dinner, replies: "Anna, if aanybody brought us here th' night, it was th' ould devil in hell." "Deed yer mistaken," Anna answers sweetly, "When God sends a maan aanywhere, he always gets there, even if he has to be taken there by th' devil."[84]

A common objection to Calvin's doctrine of providence is the charge that, since God decrees every event, there is no basis for human responsibility. Why should believers not step calmly into the path of a speeding car or leap exuberantly from a tall skyscraper, certain that they will be protected from harm by divine providence? Calvin, however, not one to suffer fools gladly, repulsed this line of reasoning by arguing that believers are not excused from due prudence since human precaution itself is one of the means by which God preserves life. Thus, "if the Lord has committed to us the protection of our life, our duty is to protect it; if he offers helps, to use them; if he forewarns us of dangers, not to plunge headlong; if he makes remedies available, not to neglect them" (*Inst.* 1.17.4). The providence of God does not work in such a way as to negate or make unnecessary human endeavor. Even when God works through an evil person to achieve a divine purpose, he does not do it "as if he were a stone or a piece of wood, but he uses him as a thinking creature, according to the quality of his nature which he has given him."[85]

Yet the question remains whether Calvin's insistence upon the divine governance of all events does not in the end (or in the beginning, seen from the perspective of the eternal decrees) make God the author of sin. This is a serious objection and one which Calvin did not take lightly. The last chapter in Book 1 of the *Institutes* seeks to show how God carries out His judgments while, at the same time, "he remains pure from every stain." Calvin argued first that "God's will" is not a universal term but one which carries a multiple meaning. Luther too had spoken of God's revealed will

84. Quoted, Hunter, p. 144, 100n.

85. John Calvin, *Treatises Against the Anabaptists and Against the Libertines,* Benjamin W. Farley, ed. (Grand Rapids: Baker Book House, 1982), p. 245; CO 7, col. 188: "Car il ne faut pas imaginer que Dieu besongne por un homme inique, comme par une pierre ou par un trone de bois: mais il en use comme d'une creature raisonnable, selon la qualité de sa nature qu'il luy a donnée."

and His concealed will. The former He has manifested in His Word, which includes the law with the Commandment "Thou shalt not kill." The latter is the secret plan by which God carries out His eternal plan and which includes, for example, the delivering up of Christ to be crucified. In sending Christ to the cross, the Bible says that Herod and Pilate were fulfilling what God in His counsel had determined before to be done (Acts 4:27-28). At the same time they were also violating the expressed will of God revealed in His law. This does not mean that there are two contrary wills in God, else His unity would be disrupted. We do not, indeed we cannot, understand *how* God wills to take place what He also forbids to be done. "But even though his will is one and simple in him, it appears manifold to us because, on account of our mental incapacity, we do not grasp how in diverse ways it wills and does not will something to take place" (*Inst.* 1.18.3).

Time and again Calvin appealed to the mystery and incomprehensibility of God's actions: "Let us recall our mental incapacity, and at the same time consider that the light in which God dwells is not without reason called unapproachable because it is overspread with darkness" (*Inst.* 1.18.3). The problem of evil is so acute precisely because we cannot understand *how* the tragedies of life redound to the greater glory of God. In commenting on the man born blind whose malady was the occasion of God's glory (John 9:1-4), Calvin warned against prematurely judging the reasons for such conditions: "God sometimes has another purpose than punishing men's sins when he sends them afflictions. Consequently, when the causes of afflictions are hidden, our curiosity must be restrained so that we may neither injure God nor be malicious to our brethren."[86]

In the face of suffering and tragedy, the temptation is either to deny God's ability to prevent the disaster, and thus posit a God who is impotent in the face of radical evil, or, more commonly, to blame God for not intervening. A well-known pastor tried to comfort a fellow minister whose young daughter had died of cancer by saying to him that "God will have a lot to give account for in heaven." No one who has faced such a crisis can deny the fact of such feelings. Indeed, the Bible itself, especially the Psalms, is filled with them: How long, O Lord? Why is your mercy gone forever? Why do the evil triumph and the righteous suffer? Calvin did not deny the legitimacy of posing such questions out of the throes of pain, but he also knew that such anger against God is like "spitting at the sky" (*Inst.* 1.18.3). It is folly, he said, to "try to make God render account to us" (*Inst* 1.17.1). True piety will realize that behind the suffering we experience, which in itself is not

---

86. *Comm.* on John 9:3: CNTC, 4 p. 239; CO 47, col. 218.

good but evil, God remains in His justice, wisdom, and love the Father who has promised never to leave or forsake us. The root error of those who charge God with complicity in evil is their facile belief that God and humans are subject to the same standards of judgment. Yet an "infinite qualitative difference" exists between the two. To judge God's providential acts by criteria of justice and wisdom applicable to humans only is to compare apples and oranges; it is like asking how many inches are in a pound. "There is a great difference between what is fitting for man to will and what is fitting for God, and to what end the will of each is directed, so that it be either approved or disapproved" (*Inst.* 1.18.3). Finally, then, there is no answer to the problem of evil, at least no answer which is available to the human mind in this life. God's method of governing the universe Calvin called an "abyss"—an abyss we ought reverently to adore rather than try curiously to penetrate (*Inst.* 1.17.2). For all of his reputation as a theologian of rigorous logic, Calvin preferred to live with mystery and logical inconsistency rather than to violate the limits of revelation or impute blame to the God Scripture portrays as infinitely wise, utterly loving, and perfectly just.

In his treatise *Against the Libertines* (1545) Calvin distinguished three aspects of providence. The first is God's general or universal providence which is manifested in the order of nature. By this operation God governs all creatures according to the quality and inclination which He has placed within them. The second level of providence, God's "special" providence, pertains to God's involvement with the human community, the acts of God by which He helps His servants, punishes the wicked, and tests or chastises the faithful. At this level of providence, God's good gifts are distributed without discrimination among all peoples; He sends the rain and sunshine to just and unjust alike. God distributes His "common grace," as later theologians would call it, to the whole human race without exception. Calvin observed with a wry humor that "the most evil people eat and drink . . . sometimes they are even fatter than the faithful."[87] There is yet a third level of providence, however, which pertains particularly to the elect. This is the form of God's operation by which He "governs his faithful, living and

---

87. *Supplementa Calviniana,* I, p. 709. Richard Stauffer has shown how Calvin's treatment of providence in his sermons both reflects and expands his exposition in the *Institutes.* See his *Dieu, la création et la Providence dans la prédication de Calvin* (Bern: Peter Lang, 1978), esp. pp. 261-302. Cf. also the fine discussion on universal and particular providence in Calvin by Charles Partes, *Calvin and Classical Philosophy* (Leiden: E. J. Brill, 1977), pp. 126-45.

reigning in them by his Holy Spirit."[88] Calvin mentioned this third aspect of providence in Book 1 of the *Institutes*—"because God has chosen the church to be his dwelling place, there is no doubt that he shows by singular proofs his fatherly care in ruling it" (1.17.6)—but postponed any extended discussion of it until he had first treated the great themes of redemption (Book 2) and regeneration (Book 3). We note here what we shall have to examine more closely a little later: The doctrine of predestination, which would logically fit better under the discussion of providence, Calvin placed in the context of soteriology, in relation to his treatment of the work of the Holy Spirit in the life of the believer (*Inst.* 3.21-24).

Our discussion of Calvin's doctrine of providence would not be complete without looking at its pastoral implications. As a pastor in Geneva, and in his correspondence with thousands of Christians in widely differing circumstances, Calvin was an experienced "director of souls" or, as we would say, spiritual counselor. He never tried to minimize or deny the reality of the suffering which confronts the believer. To Madame de Budé, recently widowed and about to face the turmoil of being uprooted from her family and sent into exile, Calvin wrote: "True it is, that we shall not cease to be subject to many troubles and annoyances; but let us pray him that having been strengthened by his word, we may have wherewithal to overcome them."[89] With another noblewoman in France, the Comtesse de Seninghen, Calvin commiserated in her illness:

> I hear . . . that you are weak in body and afflicted with many diseases, of which I too have my share to exercise me in the same manner. But however that may be, we have great cause to be satisfied that in our languishing we are supported by the strength of God's Spirit, and moreover, that if this corruptible tabernacle is falling to decay, we know that we shall be very soon restored, once and for ever.[90]

As a pastor Calvin recognized the legitimacy of human emotions and did not counsel a Stoic indifference in the face of suffering. He interpreted the scene of Jesus weeping before Lazarus's tomb as an example of Christ's suffering with us: "When the Son of God put on our flesh he also of his own accord put on human feelings. . . . Herein he proved himself to be our brother, so that we might know that we have a Mediator who willingly excuses and is ready to help those infirmities which he has experienced in

88. *Treatises Against Anabaptists*, p. 247; CO 7, col. 190.
89. Bonnet, ed., II, p. 92.
90. Ibid., IV, p. 333.

himself."[91] Again, we are "companions of the Son of God" who came "down to our condition to encourage us by his example."[92] Thus while nothing happens to the believer which is not in an ultimate and incomprehensible way directed by divine providence, God does not leave His children to suffer alone, but shares with them "the slings and arrows of outrageous fortune."

Calvin was frequently called on to counsel those Protestants who had been imprisoned for their faith and who often faced imminent martyrdom. The practical application of his doctrine of providence is best seen in these letters. In 1553 he addressed the following words to "the prisoners of Lyons" who awaited execution in France.

> Be then assured, that God who manifests himself in time of need, and perfects his strength in our weakness, will not leave you unprovided with that which will powerfully magnify his name. . . . It is strange, indeed, to human reason, that the children of God should be so surfeited with afflictions, while the wicked disport themselves in delights; but even more so, that the slaves of Satan should tread us under foot, as we say, and triumph over us. However, we have wherewith to comfort ourselves in all our miseries, looking for that happy issue which is promised to us, that he will not only deliver us by his angels, but will himself wipe away the tears from our eyes. And thus we have good right to despise the pride of these poor blinded men, who to their own ruin lift up their rage against heaven; and although we are not at present in your condition, yet we do not on that account leave off fighting together with you by prayer, by anxiety and tender compassion, as fellow-members, seeing that it has pleased our heavenly Father, of his infinite, goodness, to unite us into one body, under his Son, our head. Whereupon I shall beseech him, that he would vouchsafe you this grace, that being stayed upon him, you may in no wise waver, but rather grow in strength; that he would keep you under his protection, and give you such assurance of it, that you may be able to despise all that is of the world. My brethren greet you very affectionately, and so do many others.—Your brother, John Calvin.[93]

One of the prisoners wrote back to Calvin, describing how his letter had found its way into the prison and was read by "one of the brethren who was in a vaulted cell above me . . . as I could not read it myself, being unable to see anything in my dungeon." He expressed his gratitude for Calvin's

91. *Comm.* on John 11:33; CNTC 5, p. 12; CO 47, col. 265.
92. *Comm.* on Heb. 12:3; CNTC 12, p. 189.
93. Bonnet, ed., II, pp. 412-413.

consolation, "for it invites us to weep and to pray."[94] In this way the doctrine of providence, far from inspiring passive resignation in the face of evil, sustained countless men and women in moments of crisis, danger, and death.

The Christ Who Saves

Harmatology: The Doctrine of Sin

Having set forth the knowledge of God the Creator in Book 1 of the *Institutes*, Calvin then moved to the knowledge of God the Redeemer in Book 2. However, before unpacking the great theme of redemption, he first discussed the nature and extent of human sinfulness. There was an important reason for this order. In his commentary on Isaiah 53:6, he put it this way:

> For unless we realize our own helpless misery, we shall never know how much we need the remedy which Christ brings, nor come to him with the fervent love we owe him. . . . To know the true flavor of Christ, we must each of us carefully examine ourselves, and each must know himself condemned until he is vindicated by Christ. No one is exempt. The prophet includes *all*. If Christ had not brought help, the whole human race would perish.[95]

Thus only by seeing ourselves as we really are, in our utter perversity and alienation, can we enter fully into the benefits of salvation.

Calvin is commonly thought of as the author of a thoroughly pessimistic view of humanity. Certainly many passages in Calvin can be cited in support of such a position. Take, for example, his description of the human as a "five-foot worm" (*Inst.* 1.5.4) or his even more extreme pronouncement that man is unfit to be ranked with "worms, lice, fleas, and vermin."[96] Read out of context, statements like these portray Calvin as a gloomy misanthrope guilty, in psychological terms, of a morbid self-aversion. Such a caricature, however, does not accord with Calvin's deep appreciation for human achievements in science, medicine, literature, art, and other disciplines. "We see implanted in human nature some sort of desire to search out the truth" and this desire can only be attributed to God's common grace. The Lord had left "many gifts" to human nature even in its spoiled and lost condition (*Inst.* 2.2.15). As we have seen already, the image of God in the

94. Ibid., p. 411, 1n.

95. *Commentaries*, p. 154; CO 37, col. 259.

96. Cf. David Cairns, *The Image of God in Man* (London: SCM Press, 1953), p. 139.

human, while horribly defaced, had not been—indeed could not be—totally erased. Still, despite the many virtues and excellent gifts which grace human nature, "before the throne of God's judgment they will not be worth a straw for obtaining justification."[97] In relation to "things below," human nature, by virtue of its natural endowments, was creative, perceptive, capable of truly remarkable achievements; however, in relation to "things above," it was corrupt, impotent, unable to contribute the smallest step toward its salvation.

We have observed how Calvin's discussion of the knowledge of God in Book 1 was governed by a hypothetical premise—"if Adam had remained upright" (*Inst.* 1.2.1). We find a similar construction at the beginning of Book 2: ". . . how great our natural excellence would be *if only it had remained unblemished*" (*Inst.* 2.1.1). Since, however, this wishful condition was contrary to fact (i.e., Adam did not remain upright, nor did our natural excellence remain unblemished), one could not understand the human condition merely by examining human beings in their present lapsed state. For this reason the philosophers, though their works contained "droplets of truth" were of negligible worth. In a graphic metaphor, Calvin compared them to a traveler passing through a field at night who in a momentary lightning flash sees far and wide, but then is suddenly plunged again into the darkness of the night before he can even take a single step (*Inst.* 2.2.18). To truly understand human nature we must look neither to the philosophers, nor to ourselves, nor even to Adam in his prefallen state for he was not yet at that stage a "finished product." Calvin pointed instead to Jesus Christ, the True Human, in whom we can see the restoration of our corrupted nature fully embodied (*Inst.* 1.15.4). Before describing how, in fact, Christ has restored our nature, Calvin first outlined the form of its corruption.

The problem of original sin, while posed already in the New Testament especially by Paul, became acute in Christian theology only in the struggle between Augustine and Pelagius. Indeed, Calvin admitted that the early Fathers spoke too obscurely on the matter, "at least they explained it less clearly than was fitting" (*Inst.* 2.1.5). Calvin heartily agreed with Augustine who taught that Adam's sin had had disastrous consequences for the whole human race. He defined original sin as "a hereditary depravity and corruption of our nature, diffused into all parts of the soul, which first makes us liable to God's wrath, then also brings forth in us those works which Scripture calls 'works of the flesh' " (*Inst.* 2.1.8).

97. Wendel, p. 1921.

Let us observe three aspects of Calvin's doctrine of sin. First, while Adam's fall plunged the whole human race into depravity—"the beginning of corruption in Adam was such that it was conveyed in a perpetual stream from the ancestors into their descendents" (*Inst.* 2.1.7)—we cannot merely blame our sinful condition on Adam since "a contagion imparted by him resides in us, which justly deserves punishment" (*Inst.* 2.1.8). Adam's sin is our sin as well. Put otherwise, Adam is not only the progenitor of the human race but also, as it were, the root of human nature as well. Unlike Zwingli, Calvin did not shrink from pressing the implications of this doctrine even to infants. They, too, are not guilty of another's fault but of their own since they carry within them the "seed of sin" even if the fruit of their iniquity have not yet blossomed forth. Secondly, as to how this sin is spread from one generation to the next, Calvin rejected the traducianist idea that the corrupted soul of Adam is transmitted biologically from parent to child. In commenting on Jesus' statement, "That which is born of the flesh is flesh" (John 3:6), Calvin noted, "The corruption of all mankind in the person of Adam alone did not proceed from generation but from the ordinance of God. As in one man he adorned us all, so he has also in him deprived us of his gifts."[98] Thirdly, for this reason Calvin refused to limit the scope of original sin to one dimension of the human person (e.g., bodily existence or sexuality), but saw it pervading the total life. "The whole man is of himself nothing but concupiscence." Again, "the whole man is overwhelmed—as by a deluge—from head to foot, so that no part is immune from sin and all that proceeds from him is to be imputed to sin" (*Inst.* 2.1.9).

Sin, then, according to Calvin is not simply the name for evil acts which we commit; it is rather the direction and inclination of human nature itself in its fallen condition. We do sins because we are sinners. Sin consists both in the loss of original righteousness (deprivation) and the powerful propensity to bubble forth into every kind of specific evil and misdeed (depravation). The essence of Adam's first sin, replicated in various degrees in all of his descendants, is pride, disobedience, unbelief, all of which issue in ingratitude. Despite the awful lostness in which we humans now find ourselves entrapped, our lives are marked by a "sighing and groaning for that lost worthiness," an ability somehow not to forget our "original nobility" (*Inst.* 2.1.3). Calvin's writings do not drag us down into the depths of our own perversity in order to leave us there, but rather to prepare us to hear the good word of our liberation from sin through Jesus Christ the Lord:

98. *Comm.* on John 3:6; CNTC 4, p. 66; CO 47, col. 57.

"No one is permitted to receive God's blessings unless he is consumed with the awareness of his poverty" (*Inst.* 2.2.10).

Christology: The Person of Christ

In our discussion of Luther and Zwingli, we pointed out the thoroughly Christocentric character of their theology, despite the different nuances they placed on this important emphasis. Calvin, no less than the two other great exponents of mainline Protestant theology, never lost sight of this Christological foundation. In his *Commentary on Colossians,* he set forth what may well be taken as the orienting focus of his entire theological program:

> Again he returns to thanksgiving, as an opportunity for enumerating the blessings given them through Christ, and thus he enters upon a full description of Christ. For the only remedy for the Colossians against all the snares by which the false apostles endeavoured to trap them was to grasp thoroughly what Christ was. For how comes it that we are carried about with so many doctrines, but because the power of Christ is not perceived by us? For Christ alone makes all other things suddenly disappear. Hence there is nothing that Satan tries so hard to do as to raise up mists to obscure Christ; for he knows that by this means the way is opened up for every kind of falsehood. Therefore, the sole means of retaining as well as restoring pure doctrine is to set Christ before our eyes, just as He is with all His blessings, that His power may be truly perceived.[99]

This passage is significant because here Calvin asserted that the task of true theology is to restore the doctrine of Christ, "just as he is with all his blessings." In other words, the theme which dominates Calvin's Christology is not the knowledge of Christ in His essence, but in His redemptive role as Mediator. Even on a text which could be taken as evidence for a more speculative Christology (e.g., "I am in the Father and the Father in me," John 14:10), Calvin commented: "Christ is here speaking not of what he is in himself, but of what he is toward us, it is a question of power rather than of essence."[100] Although Calvin was careful to stay within the confines of classical Catholic Christology, he would have readily assented to Me-

99. *Comm.* on Col. 1:12; CNTC 11, p. 306; CO 52, cols. 82-83.

100. *Commentaries,* p. 160. Cf. also his comment on Hebrews 13:8, "Jesus Christ the same yesterday, and today, and forever": "The apostle is speaking not of Christ as he is in eternity, but of our knowledge of him. . . . He is not speaking of Christ's being but, so to say, of his quality, or of how he acts towards us." Ibid., p. 142.

lanchthon's statement that to know Christ is not to study His natures or properties, but rather to know His benefits.

The revelation of God in Christ is also the supreme example of God's accommodation of Himself to human capacities. We can detect this idea in the word for Christ which Calvin used more than any other: *Mediator*. Even apart from our sin, we need a mediator with God because of our creaturely finitude. "Even if man had remained free from all stain, his condition would have been too lowly for him to reach God without a Mediator" (*Inst.* 2.12.1). Indeed, even the elect angels, who have never fallen from their pristine purity, look to Christ as their Head and Mediator. The tragic fall of the human race doubled, as it were, the necessity for the Mediator. Plunged by his mortal ruin into death and hell, defiled with so many spots, befouled with his own corruption, and overwhelmed with every curse, Adam and all his lost progency would have had no hope of rescue had God not sent His Son "familiarly among us as one of ourselves." Indeed, "the situation would surely have been hopeless had the very majesty of God not descended to us, since it was not in our power to ascend to him" (*Inst.* 2.12.1).

Calvin affirmed without equivocation that Jesus Christ as Mediator was both true God and true man. The Redeemer in the flesh is one with the Eternal Son of God. Calvin's favorite designation of the Incarnate Christ was the Pauline expression, "[God] was manifested in the flesh" (1 Tim. 3:16, RSV). Calvin rejected every kind of adoptionist or minimalist Christology as totally inadequate. Christ was not "an upstart and temporary God" but "the eternal Word of God begotten of the Father before all ages."[101] Christ must have been truly God, for

> it was his task to swallow up death. Who but Life could do this? It was his task to conquer sin. Who but very Righteousness could do this? It was his task to rout the powers of the world and air. Who but a power higher than the world and air could do this? Therefore our most merciful God, when he willed that we be redeemed, made himself our Redeemer in the person of his only-begotten Son (*Inst.* 2.12.2).

But Calvin's stress on the deity of Christ in no way weakened his insistence on the other pole of the classical Christological dogma: Christ was also true man. In the incarnation Christ did not, of course, renounce His divinity, but rather concealed it under the "veil" of His flesh. Does this imply a kind of docetic Christology? Was Christ a phantom-like figure who

101. Ibid., pp. 158-159.

merely pretended to be a human being without entering fully into the pathos of human existence? Calvin insistently denied this. In a sermon on "The Nativity of Jesus Christ" Calvin described the lowly circumstances of the Savior's birth: "He was, as it were, banished from every house and fellowship. There was nothing except a stable and a manager to receive him. . . . He was in extreme poverty without any honor, without any reputation, as it were, subject to servitude."[102] In Gethsemane the Son of God was "plunged into such an extremity that it seemed he was at the depth of the abyss."[103] Far from acting out a charade, Christ was "oppressed by real sorrows, and prayed the Father in all earnestness to send help."[104] There are no depths to which Jesus did not stoop in order to become our Brother. Calvin had an interesting twist on the motive for the incarnation. Christ did not need to be clothed with humanity to become accustomed to mercy, but because He could not persuade people that He was kind and ready to help unless He had been tested by human misfortunes. "When, therefore, all kinds of evil press upon us, let this be our immediate consolation, that nothing befalls us which the Son of God has not experienced himself, so that he can sympathize with us; and let us not doubt that he is in it with us as if he were distressed along with us."[105]

Jesus Christ was true God and true man, but while the two natures were united in one person they were not by reason of the union fused or amalgamated to one another. Calvin has sometimes been accused of leaning toward a Nestorian view of Christ since he insisted so sharply on distinguishing the divinity and humanity of the Redeemer. Yet Calvin sharply refuted this very heresy—"Away with the error of Nestorius, who in wanting to pull apart rather than distinguish the nature of Christ devised a double Christ!" (*Inst.* 2.14.4)—and devoted an entire chapter in the *Institutes* to showing "how the two natures of the Mediator make one person." In this connection we should also mention another formulation which has prompted some to question the orthodoxy of Calvin's Christology, namely the so-called *extra Calvinisticum*. This term was invented by seventeenth-century Lutheran dogmaticians to designate the Reformed doctrine that the Son of God had an existence "also beyond the flesh" *(etiam extra carnem)*. Calvin's clearest statement on the subject is found in the *Institutes* 2.13.4:

102. John Calvin, *Sermons on the Saving Work of Christ,* tr. Leroy Nixon (Grand Rapids: Baker Book House, 1950), pp. 36-37. Cf. CO 46, cols. 955-956.

103. Calvin, *Saving Work,* p. 54.

104. *Comm.* on Heb. 5:7: CNTC 12, p. 64.

105. *Comm.* on Heb. 2:17: CNTC 12, p. 33.

Even if the Word in his immeasurable essence united with the nature of man into one person, we do not imagine that he was confined therein. Here is something marvelous: the Son of God descended from heaven in such a way that, without leaving heaven, he willed to be borne in the virgin's womb, to go about the earth, and to hang upon the cross; yet he continuously filled the world even as he had done from the beginning!

Calvin did not develop this idea consistently or systematically—to have done so would have violated his own principle of "theology within the limits of revelation alone." Does it signify, as some interpreters claim, a reserve in his Christology, a penchant for taking the disclosure of God in the incarnation with less than full seriousness? Had Calvin been less committed to the full humanity of Christ, this argument would have more force. As it stands, the *extra Calvinisticum* was for Calvin a way of underlining the identity between the Redeeming Word in the flesh and the Eternal Word who, with the Father and the Spirit, was the source of creation and redemption. As David Willis has shown, it thus "functions to support a fully Trinitarian doctrine of man's knowledge of God and of himself."[106] Calvin's real concern was to show that in the Incarnate Christ we are not dealing with human nature raised to the thousandth degree, but with "God manifested in the flesh." At the same time, we must admit that this formulation led Calvin to minimize the importance of Christ's bodily presence during His earthly ministry (without giving way to docetism) and to assign a kind of "division of labor" to the humanity and divinity of Christ (without succumbing to Nestorianism).

Christology: The Work of Christ

While Calvin stayed within the bounds of strict Chalcedonian orthodoxy in his restatement of the person of Christ, he recognized that adherence to correct doctrine was not sufficient to prevent the abuses he saw about him in the dependence on relics, indulgences, the rosary, and the Mass. He alleged that "the papists have nothing but a little shadow of Christ because while they were concerned to grasp the bare essence they neglected his kingdom, which consists in the power of serving." There was little profit, he thought, in knowing who Christ was (i.e., his person), unless "this second thing happened, that Christ be known as he willed to be toward us and for

106. E. David Willis, *Calvin's Catholic Christology: The Function of the So-Called Extra Calvinisticum in Calvin's Theology* (Leiden: E. J. Brill, 1966), p. 153. For a recent critique of the extra-Calvinisticum, see Selinger, pp. 62-64. Cf. also the discussion in Karl Barth, *Church Dogmatics* I/2, pp. 168-169; IV/1, pp. 180-181.

what purpose he was sent by the Father" (i.e., his work).[107]

Calvin explained the work of Christ in relation to Christ's threefold office as Prophet, King, and Priest.[108] In the Old Testament each figure was inducted into office by an anointing with holy oil which foreshadowed a fulfillment in the "anointed one," the Messiah Himself. In his prophetic office, Christ was anointed by the Spirit to be the herald and witness of the Father's grace. He fulfilled this office not only by His teaching ministry on earth but also in the continual preaching of the gospel. To recognize Christ as Prophet also means that outside of him "there is nothing worth knowing, and all who by faith perceive what he is like have grasped the whole immensity of heavenly benefits" (*Inst.* 2.15.2). However, Christ did not merely proclaim God's reign as Prophet, He also brought it with Him as King. In this office Christ serves as the Father's vice-regent in governing the world. Even in the midst of his humiliation and death, the penitent thief "adores Christ as King on the gallows tree, celebrates his reign in the fearful and unspeakable loss, and proclaims him author of life in the hour of dying."[109] Calvin admonished Christians to learn from this contrast that, although they may live their entire life "under the cross" God will emerge as the ultimate Victor:

> Thus it is that we may patiently pass through this life with its misery, hunger, cold, contempt, reproaches, and other troubles—content with this one thing: that our King will never leave us destitute, but will provide for our needs until, our warfare ended, we are called to triumph. Such is the nature of his rule, that he shares with us all that he has recieved from the Father (*Inst.* 2.15.4).

Christ fulfilled the priestly office when, in His capacity as a pure and stainless Mediator, He appeased the wrath of God and made perfect satisfaction for human sins. Through Christ's atoning act God the Father takes away all cause for enmity and reconciles believers utterly to Himself. Thus He "wipes out all evil in us by the expiation set forth in the death of Christ" (*Inst.* 2.16.3). This sounds very much like the theory of penal, substitutionary atonement set forth by Anselm in his famous treatise, *Why God Became Man*. There is no doubt that Calvin was influenced by Anselm, but Calvin's formulation of the doctrine of atonement is not a mere echo of the earlier

107. *Comm.* on John 1:49: CO 47, col. 36.

108. This schema, which Calvin may have adapted from Bucer, was not present in the *1536 Institutes.* Cf. Wendel, *Calvin,* p. 225, 125n. Cf. also John F. Jansen, *Calvin's Doctrine of the Work of Christ* (London: James Clarke, 1956).

109. *Comm.* on Luke 23:42: CNTC 3, pp. 202-03; CO 45, col. 774.

theory. Let us briefly look at five aspects of Calvin's doctrine which bear the marks of his unique theological concerns.

First, Anselm presupposed an almost ontological necessity for the incarnation: God wanted to rescue fallen humanity; He could only do that by becoming man Himself. Calvin denied any simple or absolute necessity for the incarnation. Its *raison d'être* "stemmed from a heavenly decree, on which men's salvation depended" (*Inst.* 2.12.1). In one sermon on the passion of Christ, Calvin stated that "God was well able to rescue us from the unfathomable depths of death in another fashion, but he willed to display the treasures of his infinite goodness when he spared not his only Son."[110] The atonement, then, is the supreme example of God's accommodation of Himself to our weak and sinful condition. It has no necessity outside of God's gracious will toward us.

Second, while Anselm was concerned primarily to show how through the atonement the justice of God was rectified, Calvin's focus is more on the wrath and love of God which are both illustrated in the work of Christ. Following Paul (Rom. 5:10), Calvin asserted that before reconciliation all persons were held to be the enemies of God. At the same time, the work of atonement derived from God's love: God does not love us because Christ died for us; Christ died for us because God loves us. Calvin quoted Augustine to show how both the love and wrath of God are held in juxtaposition:

> Therefore, God loved us even when we practiced enmity toward him and committed wickedness. Thus in a marvelous and divine way he loved us even when he hated us. For he hated us for what we were that he had not made; yet because our wickedness had not entirely consumed his handiwork, he knew how, at the same time, to hate in each one of us what we had made, and to love what he had made (*Inst.* 2.16.4).

Third, in Anselm's theory the life of Christ was of no salvific value since as a human being Christ owed a perfect, sinless life to the Father anyway. Only Christ's death which, because He had not sinned, He did not deserve could accrue merit for human salvation. As George H. Williams has shown, the dominant role of the Mass, understood as the sacramental reenactment of Christ's "passive" sacrifice, reflected Anselm's emphasis on the exclusively salvific character of Christ's death.[111] Now Calvin certainly did not

---

110. CO 46, col. 833: "Et defait il nous pouroit bien retirer des abysmes de mort d'une autre façon: mais il a voulu desployer les thresors de sa bonte infinie, quand il n'a point espargné son Fils unique."

111. George H. Williams, *Anselm: Communion and Atonement* (St. Louis: Concordia, 1962).

minimize the decisiveness of the death of Jesus; he even said, "the substance of life is set in the death of Christ" (*Inst.* 2.16.5). But—here is his unique emphasis—the salvific efficacy of the atonement was not limited to Christ's death. It extended throughout the "whole course of his obedience." Hence, Christ's birth, life, teachings, miracles, alongside His suffering and death, belong to His work of atonement. "In short, from the time when he took on the form of a servant, he began to pay the price of liberation in order to redeem us" (*Inst.* 2.16.5). Indeed there is no disjunction between Christ's death on the cross and His continual ministry of intercession at the right hand of the Father. The fruit of Christ's death is ever fresh and lasting for believers, for "by his intercession he propitiates God to us and sanctifies our prayers by the odor of his sacrifice and helps us by the goodwill of his advocacy."[112]

Fourth, although the legal language of penal satisfaction and substitution predominates in Calvin's discussion of atonement, he did not neglect the theme of *Christus Victor,* the motif of atonement as Christ's triumph over the devil:

> In taking the curse upon himself he crushed, broke, and scattered its whole force. . . . Paul with good reason, therefore, magnificently proclaims the triumph that Christ obtained for himself on the cross, as if the cross, which was full of shame, had been changed into a triumphal chariot! (*Inst.* 2.16.6).

Christ's resurrection, ascension, and the promise of His *Parousia* are all evidences of His victory over the hosts of evil. These great triumphs of Christ are not only a clear mirror of His divinity but also "the firm support of our faith." Jesus does not keep the victor's prize for Himself but shares it with the members of His body. This is clearly expressed in that petition of the Lord's Prayer where believers ask to be freed from the evil one:

> Mark this clearly:
> Not in our power is it for us
> To engage in combat
> That great warrior the devil
> Or bear alone the force of his onslaught.
> Otherwise pointless it would be
> To ask of God what already
> We have in ourselves.

112. *Comm.* on 1 John 2:2; CNTC 5, p. 244. While Calvin is sometimes said to have denied the doctrine of limited atonement, this passage, among others, is proof to the contrary: "Under the word 'all' he does not include the reprobate."

Those who, self-assured,
Ready themselves for combat, know not
Their ferocious, well-equipped adversary.
As from the jaws of a mad and raging lion,
We seek now to be freed from his power.

If the Lord did not snatch us
From the midst of death,
We would by his fangs and claws immediately
Be torn to pieces,
Swallowed down his throat.
Still we know
If the Lord is with us,
If He fights for us while we keep still,
In His might we shall do mightily.
Let others trust in their free choice,
Their own capacities—
For us enough it is
To stand, be strong
In God's power alone.[113]

Fifth, Calvin surely belongs to that family of theologians who stressed the "objective" character of Christ's atoning work. But he did not leave out the subjective aspect, either of Christ's work on our behalf or of our response to His sacrifice. By our participation in Christ's redeeming work we are called to a life of radical obedience. An efficacy inheres in the death of Christ "which ought to be manifest in all Christians, unless they intend to render his death useless and unfruitful" (*Inst.* 2.16.7). This appropriation of Christ's work in the life of the believer is the theme of Book 3 of the *Institutes* which Calvin entitled, "The Way in Which We Receive the Grace of Christ, What Benefits Come to Us from It, and What Effects Follow."

Life in the Spirit

Very few studies have been written on the "spirituality of John Calvin."[114] This is surprising when one considers how much attention Cal-

---

113. Battles, *Piety,* pp. 109-110.
114. Among the better studies devoted to this theme are two books by Wilhelm Kolfhaus: *Die Seelsorge Johannes Calvins* (Neukirchen: Moers, 1941); *Vom Christlichen Leben nach Johannes Calvin* (Neukirchen: Moers, 1949). In English, see Ronald S. Wallace, *Calvin's Doctrine of the Christian Life* (London: Oliver and Boyd, 1959); Lucien Richard, *The Spirituality of John Calvin* (Atlanta: John Knox Press, 1974). Cf. also John H. Leith, "A Study of John Calvin's Doctrine of the

vin himself devoted to this theme. Indeed, Calvin's life's work can be interpreted as an effort to formulate an authentic spirituality, that is to say, a *modus vivendi* of life in the Spirit, based on the revealed Word of God, lived out in the context of the church of God, and directed toward the praise and glory of God: *soli deo gloria!* We have seen already that in Calvin's view every person is implanted with a "seed of religion," a "sense of divinity" which inevitably issues in either piety, which consists of love mingled with reverence for God, or in idolatry, the production and adoration of false gods. According to Calvin, the human is by nature a worshiping being, *homo religiosus.* The problem of human existence is that this immense appetite for the divine has been tragically misdirected, turned in on itself, satiated with transient goods. To redirect and redeem fallen humanity, God became man in the person of His Son, Jesus Christ. Yet so "long as Christ remains outside of us, and we are separated from him, all that he has suffered and done for the salvation of the human race remains useless and of no value for us" (*Inst.* 3.1.1). This is the point in the *Institutes* where Calvin began to unfold how believers "come to enjoy Christ and all his benefits." All of Book 3 is a marvelous treatise on the Christian life in which Calvin elaborated successively on the following topics: the work of the Holy Spirit, faith and regeneration, repentance, self-denial, crossbearing, meditation on the future life, justification, sanctification, Christian freedom, prayer, election, and the final resurrection. Since within a short compass it is impossible to treat all of these important doctrines, we will focus on three of them, faith, prayer, and predestination. Admittedly, these three themes are not often viewed synoptically. Yet each is very close to the heart of Calvin's spirituality.

Faith

Calvin devoted a brief chapter to faith in the 1536 *Institutes;* by 1559 it had grown into a long chapter with forty-three sections. This reflects Calvin's lifelong struggle with this great theme of the gospel. Before setting forth his positive definition of faith, let us clear away several popular misunderstandings which he rejected. First, some people's faith is no deeper than "a common assent to the gospel history" (*Inst.* 3.2.1). Calvin, like Luther, denied that such a bare historical faith, a shaking of one's head *yes* to what the Bible declares to be true, was sufficient for salvation. Evidently, even the demons are capable of this kind of faith (cf. Jas. 2:19). Calvin also disallowed the term *implicit faith* as it was propounded by the Roman

Christian Life," (Yale University, Ph.D., 1949).

theologians to refer to a kind of pious submission to the collective judgment of the church. True faith rests not on ignorance but on knowledge. It is not enough to embrace what someone else has declared to be true; we must penetrate further to the personal knowledge of God the Father through Jesus Christ His Son. Finally, Calvin had no use for the scholastic distinction between "formed" and "unformed" faith, the latter being a kind of preliminary first stage of faith which must be completed by the infusion of the habit of love in order for it to be effective in the process of justification.[115] Calvin was one with Luther in this totalistic concept of faith: "For the beginning of believing already contains within itself the reconciliation whereby man approaches God" (*Inst.* 3.2.8).

What, then, is faith? Calvin defined it as "a firm and certain knowledge of God's benevolence toward us, founded upon the truth of the freely given promise in Christ, both revealed to our minds and sealed upon our hearts through the Holy Spirit" (*Inst.* 3.2.7). We can see from this definition that faith for Calvin was far from being an innate capacity within corrupted human nature. To believe or not to believe is not within the range of possibilities open to those outside the orbit of God's redeeming activity. Again and again, Calvin reiterated that faith is the unique gift of the Holy Spirit. Indeed, faith is "the principal work of the Holy Spirit," a supernatural gift that those who would otherwise remain in unbelief receive by grace (*Inst.* 3.1.4). "Whomsoever God wills to snatch from death, he quickens with the Spirit of regeneration" (*Inst.* 3.3.21). In referring to faith as knowledge, did not Calvin reduce salvation to an intellectual exercise? Not at all, for while the mind is involved in the act of faith, it is "more of the heart than of the brain, more of the disposition than of the understanding" (*Inst.* 3.2.8). By calling it "knowledge" Calvin was thinking of faith as "a lively awareness" by which we grasp the grace of our adoption as well as the newness of life and the other gifts of the Holy Spirit. There is then a dual aspect to faith. On the one hand, it is the work of the Holy Spirit; and on the other, it is the genuine human response by which those whom God has elected enter into their new life in Christ.

This being placed into Christ *(insitio in Christo)* occurs in regeneration which, Calvin was careful to point out, follows from faith as its result: Since

115. *Institutes,* 3.2.8. Cf. also Calvin's discussion of this distinction in his *Commentary* on James 2:14-17: CNTC 3, pp. 282-285. For a comparative study of Luther, Zwingli, and Calvin on this passage, see Timothy George, " 'A Right Strawy Epistle': Reformation Perspectives on James," *Review and Expositor* 83 (1986), pp. 369-82.

faith receives Christ, it leads us to the possession of all His benefits. Repentance too, which is a part of regeneration, is the consequence of faith. "Now, both repentance and forgiveness of sins—that is, newness of life and free reconciliation—are conferred on us by Christ, and both are attained by us through faith" (*Inst.* 3.3.1). What is repentance? "It is the true turning of our life to God, a turning that arises from a pure and earnest fear of him; and it consists in the mortification of our flesh and of the old man, and in the vivification of the Spirit" (*Inst.* 3.3.5). For Calvin repentance was nearly synonymous with conversion; he explained that both the Hebrew and Greek words for *repentance* imply a radical change in the repenter, a turning away from, and a turning toward: "Departing from ourselves, we turn to God, and having taken off our former mind, we put on a new." Calvin would not be pleased with the kind of evangelism which preaches an easy believism, which calls for a decision for Christ without radical, life-changing consequences. The two aspects of repentance, mortification and vivification, are not limited to the initial moment of conversion, but persist as the pattern of the whole Christian life. In referring to the spirituality of the Anabaptists and Jesuits, whom Calvin lumped together, he lambasted "that giddy spirit which brings forth such fruits that it limits to a paltry few days a repentance that for the Christian man ought to extend throughout his life" (*Inst.* 3.3.2). This sounds very much like the first of Luther's *Ninety-five Theses.* Indeed, Calvin even more than the German reformer, stressed the lifelong necessity for continual repentance and, consequently, the lifelong process of gradual growth in grace, or sanctification. Though we can and should make progress in the Christian life, being conformed more and more into the image of Christ, we never attain such perfection as to render repentance unnecessary. Even the regenerate, as long as they dwell in mortal bodies, carry within them "a smouldering cinder of evil, from which desires continually leap forth to allure and spur them to commit sin" (*Inst.* 3.3.10). Thus we never outgrow the need for the disciplines of self-denial and the bearing of the cross.

Among the many other dimensions of faith which Calvin treated, there are two we want to mention here: the relation of faith to testing and doubt and its indefectibility. Calvin declared faith to be the gift of the Holy Spirit whereby we are regenerated and led into a life of repentance and renewal. Faith is not mere conjecture which "flits around in the top of the brain," but a knowledge, certain and sure which "takes root in the depth of the heart" (*Inst.* 3.2.36). But what about the existential fact that even believers, perhaps *especially* believers, are frequently tempted by doubts and shaken from their steadfast confidence? In a passage which we have quoted partially already, Calvin offered a realistic assessment of this experience:

> Surely, while we teach that faith ought to be certain and assured, we cannot imagine any certainty that is not tinged with doubt, or any assurance that is not assailed by some anxiety. . . . We say that believers are in perpetual conflict with their own unbelief. Far, indeed, are we from putting their consciences in any peaceful repose, undisturbed by any tumult at all (*Inst.* 3.2.17).

Sometimes doubts arise from the incessant conflict between flesh and spirit within the believer, sometimes from the direct assaults of Satan, at other times from the seemingly fortuitous events which engulf us. Faith which has never passed through the fires of doubt and temptation will remain weak and flaccid. But—here is the second point Calvin wanted to make—in the end true faith will ultimately triumph over the difficulties which beseige and seem to imperil it. Thus Calvin affirmed the final perseverance of the saints. In his commentary on John 10:28, Calvin declared:

> It is the incomparable fruit of faith that Christ bids us be sure and untroubled when we are brought by faith into his fold. . . . This is a remarkable passage, teaching us that the salvation of all the elect is as certain as God's power is invincible. . . . We are surrounded by powerful enemies, and so great is our weakness that we are not far from death every moment. But he who keeps what we have committed unto him is *greater* and more powerful *than all;* and so we have nothing to be afraid of, as if our life were in danger.[116]

This is a rich and nuanced doctrine and cannot be reduced to the shorthand formula, "once saved, always saved." Calvin did not minimize the sin of apostasy, that is a complete falling away and utter renunciation of the gospel. However, this sin could be committed only by one who had not received the "incorruptible seed" of the Spirit in the new birth. Such unbelievers might show evidence of the Christian life, and even possess what Calvin called "temporary faith," but in the end they would prove to be false saints since "God certainly bestows his Spirit of regeneration only on the elect." On the other hand, true believers might fall into sin, even gross sin, but, sustained by the Spirit, they would not totally or finally be lost. Those who took this teaching as an occasion for laxity were presuming on the grace of God and stood in jeopardy of divine judgment. In his commentary on Hebrews 6, often cited as a proof text to *disprove* the doctrine of perseverance, Calvin gave his clearest and most eloquent description of the indefectibility of faith amid the storms of life:

116. *Comm.* on John 10:28: CNTC 4, p. 273; CO 47, cols. 249-250.

"Which hope we have as an anchor of the soul, both sure and steadfast"
(Heb. 6:19).

This is an eloquent comparison between an anchor and faith resting upon
the Word of God. It is obvious that while we wander in this world, we do
not stand on firm ground; on the contrary, we are as in the middle of the sea,
tossed about by turbulent waves. The devil does not cease stirring up innumerable storms, which almost overturn and sink our ship, unless we throw
our anchor deep in the sea. Our eyes see no harbor anywhere. In whatever
direction we look, we see only water, and the waves keep rising with deadly
threat. Just as the anchor is thrown into the midst of the waters to some dark
and secret place, and while it remains there, it keeps the ship from being
broken up by the waves surrounding it—so our hope needs to hold fast to the
invisible God. But there is a difference between the anchor and our hope; the
former is thrown down into the sea because the earth is at the bottom of it;
the latter, on the other hand, is lifted up and soars on high because it finds
nothing to hold on to on this earth. For our hope must not cling to the
creature, but must find its quietness in God. As the cable tied to the anchor
connects the vessel with the earth at a long distance through the dark waters,
so God's truth is a bond which connects us with himself; and no distance, or
foggy darkness, can keep us from clinging to him. When we are thus tied to
God, even when we struggle constantly with storms, we remain beyond the
danger of shipwreck. This is why he says that the anchor is sure and firm.
It can, of course, be that the rush of the waters will pull the anchor off, or
break the cable, and tear the beaten ship to pieces. Such a thing can happen
in the sea. But the power of God which sustains us is different; different is
the fortitude of hope, and different the firmness of his Word.[117]

Prayer

The longest chapter in the 1559 *Institutes* is devoted to prayer which
Calvin called "the chief exercise of faith, and the means by which we daily
receive God's benefits." At the outset Calvin was confronted with a question
posed by his own theological presuppositions: If the entire Christian life
from the first step through final perseverance is a gift of God, then why
pray? Can we not just go about our business in the certain knowledge that
God will take care of everything quite apart from our prayers? Those who
reason this way, Calvin said, do not understand the purpose for which God
has ordained prayer—it is "not so much for his sake as for ours." Calvin
condemned the hypocrisy of those who "believe in breaking God's ear-

117. *Comm.* on Heb. 6:19: CNTC 12, p. 86; CO 55, cols. 80-81.

drums . . . to persuade him of what they want."[118]

> The faithful do not pray to tell God what he does not know, or urge him to
> his duties, or hurry him on when he delays, but rather to alert themselves to
> seek him, to exercise their faith by meditating upon his promises, unburden-
> ing their cares by lifting themselves into his bosom. . . . Keep hold of both
> of these points: our prayers are anticipated by him in his freedom, yet, what
> we ask we gain by prayer.[119]

Calvin set forth four rules of prayer to guide the Christian in his "conver-
sation with God." The first rule is that we approach God reverently, that
we frame our prayers "duly and properly." This means that we should avoid
the kind of levity and frivolity which appeals to God as a sort of heavenly
chum, the "man upstairs." To come truly into the divine presence is to be
"moved by God's majesty" (*Inst.* 3.20.5). Neither should we use vain and
ostentatious words. "When we come to pray with serious intention, the
tongue does not outrun the heart, nor is God's favor secured by an empty
flow of words, but rather, the longings which the devout heart sends out
like arrowshots are those that reach to heaven."[120] This rule also means that
we will not arrogantly demand of God any more than He allows, but will,
as Scripture teaches, ask everything in accordance with His will.

The second rule of prayer is that we pray from a sincere sense of want
and with penitence. Prayer is more than pious mutterings. It must come
from the heart, "out of the depths," as the psalmist said. The verbs Calvin
used to describe true prayer underline this principle: in prayer we yearn,
desire, hunger, thirst, seek, request, beseech, cry out. Nor is the element of
repentance to be absent from our prayers.

> God did not set forth prayer
> Haughtily to puff us up before him
> Or greatly to value our own things.
> Prayer is for us to confess, weep for
> Our tragic state,
> As children unburden their troubles
> To their parents,
> So it is with us before God.

118. Calvin, *Saving Work,* p. 68.

119. *Comm.* on Matt. 6:8: CNTC 1, p. 203; CO 45, cols. 193-94.

120. *Comm.* on Matt. 6:7: CNTC 1, p. 203; CO 45, p. 193: "Nam ubi serio affectu
concipitur precatio, lingua non anteit pectus: deinde non captatur Dei gratia inani
verborum fluxu, sed potius suos affectus, non secus ac sagittas, pium cor emittit, qui
in coelum penetrent."

> This sense of sin spurs, goads,
> Arouses us to pray.[121]

The third rule of prayer follows on the second: We must yield all confidence in ourselves and humbly plead for pardon. The entire purpose of prayer, and indeed of the whole Christian life, is the glory of God. This means that anyone who stands before God to pray must in true humility "abandon all thought of his own glory, cast off all notion of his own worth, in fine, put away all self-assurance" (*Inst.* 3.20.8). It is appropriate, then, that we begin our prayer by confessing our sins and claiming the promise of forgiveness.

The fourth rule is that we pray with confident hope: "Cast down and overcome by true humility, we should be nonetheless encouraged to pray by a sure hope that our prayer will be answered" (*Inst.* 3.20.11). Calvin went as far as to say that the only prayer that is acceptable to God is born out of the "presumption of faith." The real basis of our hope, of course, is the object toward which our prayers are directed: We pray to our Heavenly Father, the Father of all mercies, the God of all comfort; we pray through Jesus Christ, His Son our Lord, in whom all the promises of God are confirmed and fulfilled; we pray through the Holy Spirit, who is our teacher in prayer and who "arouses in us assurance, desires and sighs, to conceive which our natural powers would scarcely suffice" (*Inst.* 3.20.5).

These four rules are to guide the individual believer in his private prayer, but they also apply to the common prayers of the church. Indeed, Calvin held that the "chief part of worship lies in the office of prayer" (*Inst.* 3.20.29). He had no patience with those who claimed they could worship just as well at home as they could in church. Public prayer should be simple, direct, not the "windy prayers" of the hypocrites. Singing, too, belongs to the ministry of prayer, although he warned that we should not be more attentive to the melody than to the spiritual meaning of the words. And, of course, prayer should be offered in the vernacular, not in Greek among Latins, nor in Latin among French or English, but in the daily language understood by the whole assembly. By 1536 Calvin had described the role of prayer in the worship of God:

> Shifty, slippery, inattentive
> Is the mind toward thinking of God
> Unless exercised by prayerful
> Speech and song.

121. Battles, *Piety,* p. 93.

The glory of God ought to shine
In the various parts of our bodies,
And especially in the tongue,
Created to sing, speak forth,
Tell, proclaim
The praise of God.
And the tongue's chief task is,
In the public prayers offered
In the assembly of believers,
With one common voice,
With a single mouth,
To glorify God together,
To worship him together
In one spirit, one faith.[122]

Predestination

Pietro Nelli, a sixteenth-century Italian satirist, described the popular attitude toward the doctrine of election in these lines:

The porter, the maidservant, and the bondsman
dissect free will
and make hash of predestination.[123]

Contempt for this doctrine is a recurrent theme in the history of the church. In the eighteenth century John Wesley, who owed more to John Calvin than he was willing to admit, wrote the following verses of a hymn in which the Calvinist teaching is held up to ridicule:

'Thou has compell'd the Lost to die;
'Hast reprobated from thy Face;
'Hast Others sav'd, but them past by;
Or mock'd with only Damning Grace.'

How long, thou jealous God, how long
Shall impious Worms thy Word disprove,
Thy Justice stain, thy Mercy wrong,
Deny thy Faithfulness and Love.

Still shall the Hellish Doctrine stand?
And Thee for its dire Author claim?

122. Ibid., p. 99.
123. Quoted, Carlo Ginzburg, *The Cheese and the Worms: The Cosmos of a Sixteenth-Century Miller* (London: Routledge and Kegan Paul, 1980), p. 20.

> No—let it sink at thy Command
> Down to the Pit from whence it came.

Our purpose in this section is to describe briefly what Calvin taught about predestination and how it functioned in his theology. In 1844 Alexander Schweizer wrote a book in which he called predestination the *Zentraldogmen* in the theology of Calvin. This opinion has been repeated by numerous scholars and has become a part of the common caricature of the Genevan reformer. Others, however, have questioned this assumption. The word *predestination,* in its nominal form, was first used by Calvin only in the 1539 *Institutes.* He certainly did not set out to organize his entire theological program around this idea. On closer examination, one is impressed with the unoriginality of Calvin's doctrine of election. His teaching on this subject is in all essentials identical to that we have already observed in Luther and Zwingli, and the same could be said for Bucer as well. Like all of these he appealed frequently to his favorite Father, Augustine, and had affinity with the radical Augustinian tradition of the Middle Ages, including such theologians as Thomas Aquinas (in his later writings), Gregory of Rimini, and Thomas Bradwardine. Where Calvin did make an original move was in his placement of the doctrine within his theological schema. Predestination is usually, and most logically, treated in the context of the doctrine of God as a special application of the doctrine of providence. For example, this is where Thomas, Zwingli, and later Reformed theologians, such as Beza and William Perkins, placed it. Calvin, too, in early editions of the *Institutes* held providence and predestination in tandem. But in the definitive edition of 1559 he separated the two, keeping providence under the doctrine of God the Father in Book 1, while placing predestination under the general rubric of the work of the Holy Spirit near the end of Book 3. Just as providence in a sense completes the doctrine of God the Creator, so predestination is the capstone to the doctrine of God the Redeemer.

Calvin did not begin with predestination and then proceed to atonement, regeneration, justification, and other doctrines. Predestination became an issue in the context of the history of salvation. Calvin introduced it in fact as a problem occasioned by the preaching of the gospel. Why, he asked, when the gospel is proclaimed, do some respond and others not? In this diversity, he said, the wonderful depth of God's judgment is made known. For Calvin predestination was from first to last a pastoral concern. For the believer the fact of election is an *ex post facto* reflection on how, amid the darkness and death of sin, God's grace has broken through. It is not an occasion to glory in one's chosenness, nor to play the game of "I'm in, you're out." True enough, this attitude has too often been associated with adherents of Calvin's doctrine of election. This has led to smugness and ugly exclusivism, as in the old Particular Baptist hymn:

> We are the Lord's elected few,
> Let all the rest be damned;
> There's room enough in hell for you,
> We won't have heaven crammed!

More in keeping with Calvin's perspective is the sentiment of John Newton, himself a great Calvinist:

> Amazing grace! how sweet the sound,
> That saved a wretch like me!;
> I once was lost, but now am found,
> Was blind, but now I see.

We can summarize Calvin's doctrine of predestination in three words: *absolute, particular,* and *double.* Predestination is absolute in the sense that it is not conditioned upon any finite contingencies, but rests solely on God's immutable will. Calvin rejected the scholastic notion that election depends on God's foreknowledge of human achievement *(ante praevisa merita).* "God's foreknowledge cannot be the reason of our election, because when God [looks into the future and] surveys all mankind, he will find them all, from first to last, under the same curse. So we see how foolishly triflers prattle when they ascribe to mere naked foreknowledge what must be founded on God's good pleasure."[124] Secondly, predestination is particular in that it pertains to individuals and not to groups of people. Of course, Calvin was aware that God elected Israel as His special covenant people. Yet not every single member of the nation was elected to salvation, as Paul pointed out (Rom. 9:1-16). The covenant of grace applies to each person individually. With respect to the atonement, this means that Christ died not for everyone indiscriminately, but only for the elect. This doctrine, which became one of the hallmarks of Calvinist orthodoxy, was adopted by many Baptists in seventeenth-century England, in consequence of which they were called Particular Baptists as opposed to the General Baptists who believed in the unlimited scope of Christ's atoning work. Finally, predestination is double; that is, God to the praise of His mercy has ordained some individuals to eternal life, and to the praise of His justice has ordained others to eternal damnation. Calvin put it plainly: "election itself could not

124. *Commentaries,* p. 294.

stand except as set over against reprobation" (*Inst.* 3.23.31). Since all are justly condemned by virtue of their desertion from God, God remains both free and perfectly just in His decision. He is not "liable to render an account," nor are we mere earthlings "competent judges to pronounce judgment in this cause according to our understanding" (*Inst.* 3.23.2). Both are true: The reprobate are chosen for damnation by God's eternal decree and, nonetheless, the wicked bring upon themselves the just destruction to which they are destined. If asked why God has chosen this one and rejected that one, Calvin replied that the questioner was seeking something greater and higher than God's will, which could not be found.

Calvin did not teach this doctrine because he was a "dour despot" or a mean man, but because, rightly or wrongly, he believed it was clearly found in the Scriptures. He warned against parading the message of the "horrible decree" before novices in the faith and desired to say no more about predestination than could be derived from the Bible: "We should not investigate what the Lord has left hidden in secret . . . nor neglect what he has brought out into the open, so that we may not be convicted of excessive curiosity on the one hand, or of excessive ingratitude on the other" (*Inst.* 3.21.4). Later Calvinists, often forgetting these words, tended to become embroiled in endless debates over the precise ordering of God's decrees, evidences of election in one's activity in the world, and so forth. Calvin's doctrine remained Christocentric in its focus: "We have in the very head of the church the clearest mirror of free election" (*Inst.* 3.22.1). Nor did he permit the doctrine of predestination to be used as an excuse for not proclaiming the gospel to everyone: Since God alone knows whom He has elected to salvation and whom not, we preach the gospel promiscuously, trusting the Holy Spirit to use it as an external means for the effectual calling of the very ones who have been chosen in Christ before the foundation of the world. Throughout the history of the church some of the most effective evangelists and missionaries have been staunch defenders of a high doctrine of predestination. For example, during the Great Awakening of the eighteenth century, George Whitefield, a Calvinist, won far more people to Christ than his Arminian friend, John Wesley. Predestination, as Calvin understood it, is neither a church steeple from which to view the human landscape, nor a pillow to sleep on. It is rather a stronghold in times of temptation and trials and a confession of praise to God's grace and to His glory.

External Means of Grace

The Presuppositions of Calvin's Doctrine of the Church

Luther's predominant concern was with the evangelical center of the church; later reformers took up the difficult task of determining with some precision its circumference. Zwingli, Bucer, and Oecolampadius struggled with this problem; yet it remained for Calvin, the "poor, timid scholar" as he described himself, to exploit fully the theory and practice of the Protestant congregation.

Beset by a resurgent Catholicism on the one hand and a proliferating sectarianism on the other, Calvin developed a more formal theory of the relation of the invisible church and the church as an external institution recognizable as true by certain distinguishing marks. At the beginning of Book 4 of the *Institutes,* Calvin clarified the function of the "marks": "For, in order that the title church may not deceive us, every congregation that claims the name 'church' must be tested by this standard as by a touchstone" (*Inst.* 4.1.11). By so directly associating the marks with the act of testing and verification, Calvin surpassed Luther's concept of the marks as mere indicators of the visible church. They became in some sense causative, constitutive of the visible church. Thus, in the Reformed confessions, the notes are distinguished from the traditional Nicene attributes (one, holy, catholic, apostolic) precisely because they are not merely descriptive, but dynamic: They call into question the unity, holiness, catholicity and apostolicity of every congregation which claims to be a church, and so subject it to an outward, empirical investigation. "In this way," said Calvin, "the face of the church emerges into visibility before our eyes" (*Inst.* 4.1.9).

Significantly, Calvin did not follow Bucer, as did the Reformed tradition generally, in elevating ecclesiastical discipline to the technical status of a *nota.*[125] For Calvin, as for Luther, the more certain *(certeoribus)* marks remained the Word purely preached and the sacraments duly administered. However, he did not for that reason disparage the importance of discipline for the well-being of the church. If the saving doctrine of Christ was the soul of the church, then discipline served as its sinews *(pro nervis),* through which the members of the body were held together, each in its own place. Discipline, then, pertained to the constitution and organization, if not to the

125. However, in the first edition of the *Institutes* Calvin did include "example of life" among the "certain sure marks." Cf. CO 1, col. 89. On Bucer, see P. D. L. Avis, *The Church in the Theology of the Reformers* (Atlanta: John Knox Press, 1981), pp. 48-50.

definition, of the true congregation. It belonged to the arena of visibility insofar as it too was a criterion of testing, both individually in self-examination and corporately in the public procedures of admonition, censure, and excommunication.

Calvin's concern for the order and form of the congregation derived from his emphasis upon sanctification as both the process and goal of the Christian life. In contrast to the unilateral accentuation of justification in the Lutheran confessions, Calvin gave precedence to sanctification in his systematic arrangement of the "benefits of Christ." The two are connected as distinct but interrelated "moments" in the grace of double cleansing, so that "actual holiness of life, so to speak is not separated from free imputation of righteousness" (*Inst.* 3.11.1). In this life the locus of sanctification is the congregation, the visible church, in which the elect participate in the benefits of Christ not as isolated individuals, but as members of a body in which "all the blessings which God bestows upon them are mutually communicated to each other" (*Inst.* 4.1.3). In this way the visible church becomes a "holy community," an agent of sanctification in the large society where every aspect of life is to be brought within the orbit of Christian purposes and Christian regulations.

Having examined the presuppositions of Calvin's doctrine of the local church, we now turn to a more specific elucidation of them as set forth in his commentaries on three of the Pastoral Epistles, namely those of 1 and 2 Timothy and Titus. The choice of these commentaries is suggested by the content of the epistles which deals explicitly with the order and organization of the congregation. Moreover, the commentaries were written in the late 1540s, seven to eight years after Calvin's return from Strasbourg, but six to seven years before the consolidation of his power in what has been called the second Genevan revolution of 1555. Calvin admitted that he had not made as much progress in reforming the church at Geneva as he had wished: "We know by experience that it is not the work of one or two years to restore a fallen church to a tolerable state."[126] These documents, then,

---

126. *Comm.* on Titus 1:5: CNTC 10, p. 356. The commentaries on Timothy were published in 1548, prefaced by a dedicatory epistle to the Duke of Somerset, Protector of England and tutor of the boy king, Edward VI. To this well-placed partisan of reform Calvin commended the Epistles to Timothy as providing "a living picture of the true government of the church." He urged him to follow the pattern laid down by Paul as "there is hardly anything needful for the building up of the church that cannot be drawn from them." Here we see Calvin as the *episcopus* of Geneva looking beyond national boundaries and the particularities of his local situation in the

written in the thrust of battle as it were, reflect Calvin's intense efforts to establish a godly congregation amid disturbances without and struggles within.

Calvin's Bipolar Ecclesiology

In his book, *The Christian Polity of John Calvin,* Harro Höpfl argued that while Calvin's theology "began almost as apolitically as Luther's," with the visible church receiving only scant attention in the 1536 edition of the *Institutes,* in fact his thought came to be more and more centered on the visible church until his early emphasis on the church as the communion of saints was almost entirely eclipsed.[127] It is true that in successive editions of the *Institutes* Calvin's discussion of the visible church was greatly expanded, eventually achieving the status of an entire book. However, this was *not* done at the expense of emphasis on the invisible church. The two poles of Calvin's ecclesiology, divine election and the local congregation, are held together in the closest possible connection, frequently in the same sentence. The church is called God's house, explained Calvin, because "not only has He received us as His sons by the grace of adoption (election), but He Himself dwells in the midst of us" (the congregation). Again, the upbuilding of the church is for the sake of the elect.[128]

Only when we realize that Calvin never relaxed the visible/invisible tension can we understand his diverse characterizations of the church. On the one hand, the church appears in mortal danger. If false doctrines are allowed to spread, they will "completely destroy the church." Indeed, Calvin said that there was good reason to fear that the recently kindled light

interests of an ecumenical congregational reform. The commentary on Titus, published the following year in 1549, was dedicated to Guillaume Farel and Pierre Viret, Calvin's predecessors in the reform of the Genevan church—Calvin says he came to Geneva as their "assistant." Calvin claimed to stand precisely in the same relationship to these colleagues, who were then laboring at Neuchâtel and Lausanne, as Titus had stood to Paul: he was their successor, charged with putting the "finishing touches" to the building which they had begun but left uncompleted (Ibid., p. 347).

127. Harro Höpfl, *The Christian Polity of John Calvin* (Cambridge: University of Cambridge Press, 1982), pp. 34, 84-85. Cf. the following claim: "The universal church, the communion of saints, continued to recede inexorably from view, becoming at last no more than a device for dealing with the Creed's assertion of the one-ness of the church in such a way as to wrest this weapon from the Romanists," *ibid.,* p. 84.

128. *Comm.* on 1 Tim. 3:15: CNTC 10, p. 231.

of reformation would soon be put out.[129] At the same time, *sub specie aeternitatis,* human fickleness and unfaithfulness "cannot prevent God from preserving His Church to the end."[130]

For Calvin the visible church was not a progressive approximation of the invisible. The former was a *corpus permixtum,* wheat and tares growing in the same field, whereas the latter included elect angels, Old Testament worthies, and assorted predestined souls who find themselves outside the "Lord's walled orchard." Indeed, the inscrutability of election and the objectivity of Word and sacrament (but *not* discipline!) underlay Calvin's reluctant extension of the title "church" to select congregations still in Roman obedience—"to the extent that some marks of the church remain, we do not impugn the existence of churches among them" (*Inst.* 4.2.12). This provided, we might add, a convenient rationale for not rebaptizing papist converts to Protestantism.

Ecclesia Externa as Mater et Schola

Calvin began his discussion of the visible church in Book 4 of the *Institutes* by applying to it the well-worn metaphors of *Mater* and *Schola.* We are conceived in the womb of Mother Church, nourished at her breast, and enrolled as pupils in her school all the days of our lives (*Inst.* 4.1.4). The interlacing images of the church as mother and school also recur throughout the commentaries on the Pastoral Epistles. The church is the mother of all believers "because she brings them to new birth by the Word of God, educates and nourishes them all their life, strengthens them and finally leads them to complete perfection."[131] The church is also "God's school"—the "pillar and ground of the truth" as the text reads—which instructs its students in "the study of a holy and perfect life."[132]

The maternal character of the church is seen especially in its dispensing of the sacraments of baptism and the Lord's Supper. Calvin called baptism "our entrance into the Church and the symbol of our engrafting into Christ." He interpreted the phrase "the washing of regeneration" in Titus 3:5 as baptism by water, noting that "God does not play games with us with empty figures [perhaps a swipe at Zwingli?] but inwardly accomplishes by

129. *Comm.* on 2 Tim. 2:17: CNTC 10, pp. 314-315.
130. *Comm.* on 2 Tim. 2:19: CNTC 10, p. 316.
131. *Comm.* on 1 Tim. 3:15: CNTC 10, p. 231; CO 52, col. 288.
132. *Comm.* on 1 Tim. 5:7: CNTC 10, p. 254; CO 52, col. 308.

His own power the thing He shows us by the outward sign."[133] For Calvin baptism was designed to confirm faith in the elect, a view characterized by Karl Barth as "cognitive sacramentalism."[134] Nonetheless, Calvin required that baptism be applied indiscriminately to everyone in the visible church.

There is precious little about the Lord's Supper in the Pastoral Epistles, and Calvin the exegete was properly silent about it. There is, however, one reference to the supper which distinguishes the blessing of ordinary food at table from the blessing of the sacramental meal. "We bless the food that we eat to nourish the body in order to receive it legitimately and without uncleanness, but we consecrate the bread and wine in the sacrament supper in a more solemn manner that they may be to us pledges of Christ's body and blood."[135]

Along with predestination, the doctrine of the Lord's Supper elicited more controversial writings from Calvin than any other subject. On the presence of Christ in the bread and wine, he tried to steer a middle course between Zwingli, whom he felt had too little regard for the outward signs, and Luther, who extolled them immoderately thus obscuring the mystery itself. Calvin agreed with Zwingli that Christ was locally present at the right hand of the Father in heaven and should not be thought of as "attached to the element of the bread," to be touched by the hands, chewed by the teeth, and swallowed by the mouth (*Inst.* 4.17.12). But he agreed with Luther that the supper is not an empty symbol—"the truth of the thing signified is surely present there"—but a means of "true participation" in Christ (*Inst.* 4.17.10-11). How can Christ be at once at the Father's right hand and present at the "spiritual banquet" of communion? "What our mind does not comprehend, let faith conceive: that the Spirit truly unites things separated in space" (*Inst.* 4.17.10). So important was the supper as spiritual nourishment for the church that Calvin advocated its weekly celebration.

For Calvin the church was not only mother but also school. Indeed, he frequently combined the two metaphors. Speaking of Timothy's education he said: "Having been rightly instructed in the faith from your infancy, and having, so to speak, sucked in sound doctrine with your mother's milk, and having made till now continual progress in it, take pains by a faithful ministry to prove that you are still the same."[136] The church, of course, is a school from which one never graduates (this side of heaven, if then!),

133. *Comm.* on Titus 3:5: CNTC 10, p. 382.
134. Barth, *Church Dogmatics,* IV/4, p. 130.
135. *Comm.* on 1 Tim. 4:5: CNTC 10, pp. 241-242; CO 52, col. 296.
136. *Comm.* on 1 Tim. 4:6: CNTC 10, pp. 242-243; CO 52, col. 298.

hence the need for continual instruction. The church is also, in the best sense of the term, a "reform school," complete with specified dress code, censored reading matter, compulsory attendance at chapel, and truant officers to deal with recalcitrant students! Calvin, in fact, insisted that special care be given to the instruction of rebels: "Since the conversion of a man is in God's hands, who knows whether those who today seem unteachable may be suddenly changed by God's power into different men?"[137]—a statement markedly similar to his description of his own "sudden conversion" by which God subdued his heart to *docilitas,* teachableness.

Order and Office

The installment of a fourfold office of pastor, teacher, elder, and deacon was an essential component of the Genevan settlement of religion which took Calvin back to his adopted city in 1541. Alexandre Ganoczy, among others, argued that Calvin borrowed this fourfold schema from Martin Bucer whose 1536 *Commentary on Matthew* had presented just such an arrangement.[138] In any event, by 1541 Calvin had come to believe that such a pattern was mandated by Scripture; it was in fact the cornerstone of the new polity embedded in the *Ecclesiastical Ordinances.*

One would think that a structure so essential to a "well proportioned" congregation would be amply set forth in the New Testament, especially in epistles expressly designed as manuals of church order. (Calvin, of course, nowhere questioned the Pauline authorship of the Pastorals; in agreement with modern biblical scholarship, however, he did see them as public letters on church order rather than private correspondence.) This proves *not* to be the case. Of the four offices, the lion's share of attention is devoted to the pastorate. Nothing at all is said of the teaching office, and Calvin tended to conflate it with the pastorate. On the other hand, Calvin seemed almost embarrassed by Paul's lengthy comments of the diaconate as opposed to the eldership, given the inverted importance of these two lay offices in his own polity.

Calvin did in fact hold the office of deacon in high esteem. Deacons were public officers in the church entrusted with the care of the poor. He urged that they be skilled in the Christian faith since, in the course of their ministry, "they will often have to give advice and comfort." Indeed, the deacons in Calvin's Geneva should have been experts in what we call today

---

137. *Comm.* on 2 Tim. 2:25: CNTC 10, p. 321; CO 52, col. 374.

138. Alexandre Ganoczy, *Calvin: Théologien de l'Eglise et du Ministère* (Paris: Editions due Cerf, 1964), pp. 298-299.

social work as well as pastoral care. Calvin admitted that the diaconate could sometimes serve as a "nursery [again the maternal motif] from which presbyters are chosen," yet he opposed the Roman custom of making the deacon the first step toward the priesthood. This practice was an invidious undermining of "a highly honorable office."[139]

As to the eldership, Calvin noted that the word *presbyteros* describes not an age but an office. Timothy, to whom Paul was writing, was quite young; Calvin was only twenty-seven when he was called to Geneva. As applied both to himself and to Timothy, however, the word *presbyteros* was synonymous with *episcopus* or pastor. Calvin discovered that there are in fact two kinds of presbyters in the New Testament. The textual basis for this "discovery" is the verse: "Let the elders that rule well be counted worthy of double honor, especially those who labor in the word and in teaching" (1 Tim. 5:17, RSV). He explained:

> The plain meaning of the words is that there were some who ruled well and honourably, but who did not hold a teaching office. The people elected earnest and well-tried men, who, along with the pastors in a common council and with the authority of the Church, would administer discipline and act as censors for the correction of morals.[140]

If this sounds surprisingly similar to the institution of the consistory in Geneva, we must allow that not even Calvin was beyond reading the exigencies of his own situation back into the New Testament.

The Reformed Pastor

Calvin believed that the offices of prophet, apostle, and evangelist, so prominent in the New Testament, were temporary in nature and had ceased at the end of the apostolic age. Of the offices which are extant in this dispensation, that of the pastor is clearly the most honorable and the least dispensable for the proper order and well being of the church.[141]

In the spiritual upbuilding of the congregation, the appointment of pastors was second in priority only to the acceptance of pure doctrine. Indeed in Calvin's mind these two goals were so closely intertwined, they could

139. *Comm.* on 1 Tim. 3:9; 3:13: CNTC 10, pp. 229-230.

140. *Comm.* on 1 Tim. 5:17: CNTC 10, p. 262; CO 52, col. 315. Calvin's other "proof text" for the lay eldership is Romans 12:8. Cf. *Inst.* 4.3.8. Cf. also Höpfl, pp. 94-95, 137-139.

141. Cf. Ganoczy's comment: "Le Pasteur est *le* ministres par excellence. Il peut assumer la fonction des autres ministres, mais les autres ministers ne peuvent pas assumer la fonction pastorale," p. 300.

hardly be separated. The New Testament terms *bishop, elder (presbyter), minister, pastor,* and sometimes *teacher (doctor)* all refer to the same office. What is the role of the pastor?—to represent God's Son (Calvin elsewhere used the term *lieutenant* in the etymological sense of *tenant lieu de),* to erect and extend God's kingdom, to care for the salvation of souls, to rule the church which is God's inheritance.[142] Calvin held that there should be at least one pastor in every town, though of course some towns, such as Geneva, might have need of several pastors—in due course Geneva could boast an entire "company" of pastors.

How was a pastor to be chosen? Calvin considered whether in fact one should deliberately seek the office. While it was certainly wrong for an individual to "thrust himself forward" out of self-seeking ambition, it was proper for one moved by a godly desire to prepare for the office. "What are theological schools if not nurseries for pastors?"[143] Yet one had to be publicly called according to the order the church prescribed. In Geneva this required a prior examination and selection by the company of pastors (an intimidating prospect!), presentation to the city council, and approval by the common consent of the congregation.

This process was followed by ordination, which Calvin described as a "solemn rite of institution" into the pastoral office. Calvin elsewhere referred to ordination as a sacrament and admitted that grace was conferred through this outward sign. Indeed, he used language strikingly similar to his description of baptism. Ordination was not a vain or useless sign, but a faithful token of the grace received from God's own hand. Again, it was a "legitimate act of consecration before God, something that could be done only by the power of the Holy Spirit."[144] We must be careful, however, not to impugn to Calvin an absolutist view of church polity. He rebuked the refugee congregation at Frankfort for seeking to depose their pastor, Valérand Poullain, on the grounds that he had not been properly ordained. Concerning Poullain he wrote: "Those who first worked to plant the Gospel ought to be accepted as pastors without further formalities."[145] Calvin, then, was willing to allow a certain leeway in the method of choosing ministers. The pastoral office itself is never adiaphorous, but the details of appoint-

142. *Institutes,* 4.3.1. Cf. Jacques Courvoisier, *De La Réforme au Protestantisme: Essai d'Ecclesiologie Réformée* (Paris: Beauchesne, 1977), pp. 66-71.

143. *Comm.* on 1 Tim. 3:1: CNTC 10, p. 222; CO 52, col. 280.

144. *Comm.* on 2 Tim. 1:6: CNTC 10, p. 293; CO 52, col. 350: "consecratio coram Deo legitima, quia non perficitur nisi spiritus sancti virtute."

145. Hunter, p. 203.

ment may be. It was precisely this kind of flexibility which enabled Calvin to influence, if not direct, an international reform movement in such diverse political settings as France, Poland, Scotland, England, and the Palatinate.

But *why* are pastors so important to the church? "Does not everyone have a chance to read the Scriptures for himself?" asked Calvin.

Yes, but pastors had to carve or divide the Word, "like a father dividing the bread into small pieces to feed his children."[146] Pastors must be thoroughly taught in the Scriptures, so that they can *rightly* instruct the congregation in heavenly doctrine.

The importance of preaching in Calvin's thought can hardly be exaggerated. Calvin had no truck with those who arrogated to themselves the title of bishop, who went about dressed up in theatrical clothes, but who in fact were "dummies who never preach"—an epithet which would resound in the Puritan excoriation of Anglican divines as "dumb dogs" who have a "bare reading" ministry. In a pastor profound learning had to be accompanied by a talent for teaching.

> There are many who, either because of defective utterance or insufficient mental ability, or because they are not sufficiently in touch with ordinary people, keep their knowledge shut up within themselves. Such people ought, as the saying goes, to sing to themselves and the muses—and go and do something else. . . . What is required is not merely a voluble tongue, for we see many whose easy fluency contains nothing that can edify. Paul is rather commending wisdom in knowing how to apply God's Word to the profit of His people.[147]

The purpose of preaching is edification. The pastor must not "fly about among the subtleties of frivolous curiosity"; he must not, to use Calvin's delightful word, be a "questionarian." Preaching must not only be sound doctrinally but must also seek the "solid advantage" of the church, that is, it must be practical, applicable, discriminating.

The pastor is charged with preaching and governing. "A pastor needs two voices," said Calvin, "one for gathering the sheep and the other for driving away wolves and thieves."[148] The disciplinary role of the pastor requires that his own conduct be above reproach. Calvin did not hesitate to advocate a double standard for clergy/laity. In discussing Paul's prohibition of polygamy for pastors (his interpretation of "the husband of one wife" requirement), Calvin observed: "He might have to some extent tolerated in others

146. *Comm.* on 2 Tim. 2:15: CNTC 10, p. 313; CO 52, col. 367.
147. *Comm.* on 1 Tim. 3:2: CNTC 10, p. 225; CO 52, col. 282.
148. *Comm.* on Titus 1:9: CNTC 10, p. 361; CO 52, col. 412.

something that in bishops was quite intolerably disgraceful."[149] Calvin had not here relapsed into the two-tiered morality of medieval Christendom. Rather, he was concerned with the visibility of the church, with the "face" of the church. As unworthy minister can do irreparable harm to the congregation. For this reason he must hold to a stricter accountability.

The Church and the World

By rejecting the Anabaptist concept of the congregation as a conventicle sequestered from the environing culture, Calvin rooted his reformation in the "placed Christianity" of the medieval *corpus christianum.* In a perceptive article on "The 'Extra' Dimension in the Theology of Calvin," Heiko Oberman argued that the relatively more progressive element in the Reformed concept of the state could be traced to Calvin's view of God as Legislator and King and that the rule of God was not limited to the congregation only but also extended *etiam extra ecclesiam:* even beyond the church.[150] Calvin's commentaries on the Pastorals reveal a pattern of both interaction and tension between the church and the world.

At times Calvin spoke in a manifestly sectarian tone about the exclusivity of the visible church. A right relationship with God is prerequisite for even the enjoyment of natural blessings. Every gift we touch is defiled by our sins and unclean "till God graciously helps us and, by incorporating us into the Body of his Son, makes us anew lords of the earth, so that we may legitimately enjoy as our own all the wealth He supplies."[151] Unbelievers are, in fact, usurpers and thieves! Everything which they enjoy may be regarded as "the property of another which they rob and steal."[152] Rhetoric we might have expected from a communitarian sectary, not from a proprietary theologian like Calvin! His intention, however, was not to disendow all non-Christians, but rather to emphasize the unity of redemption and creation and to assert the sovereignty of Christ over the entire created realm.

Far from advocating withdrawal from the world, Calvin urged Christians to be engaged in it. Their prayers are to be universal in scope; they are "to include all men in their prayers and not to restrict them to the body of the

149. *Comm.* on 1 Tim.3:2: CNTC 10, p. 224; CO 52, col. 282.

150. Heiko A. Oberman, "The 'Extra' Dimension in the Theology of Calvin," *Journal of Ecclesiastical History,* 21 (1970), pp. 43-64.

151. *Comm.* on 1 Tim. 4:5: CNTC 10, p. 241; CO 52, col. 297.

152. *Comm.* on 1 Tim. 4:3: CNTC 10, p. 240; CO 52, col. 294.

Church."[153] Christians are not to exalt themselves proudly over others, but to deal with *sympathea,* fellow-feeling, toward those who are *extra ecclesiam,* in hopes that tomorrow they may be added to it.[154]

The rule of Christ was to be manifested, ideally, in the institution of a godly magistracy. Calvin listed three advantages of a well-ordered government: transquility, gravity or modesty, and piety. In the words of Isaiah, Calvin urged the magistrates to be "nursing fathers" to the Reformation. They were to maintain not only civic order but also religious uniformity. Yet the *ius reformandi* was not an authority the magistrates should exert independently of the congregation. The proper relationship of the two is illustrated by the example of a pertinacious heretic. After thorough examination—Calvin warned Christians not to be hasty in labeling as heretics everyone who disagreed with them—and patient admonition, the obstinate heretic may be, must be, expelled from the congregation by excommunication. Beyond this the church cannot go. However, the magistrate was well within his bounden duty in bringing to bear what Calvin called, somewhat euphemistically, "further measures of greater rigor." There was, Calvin noted, a difference between the duty of a bishop and that of a magistrate.

At the time Calvin wrote these words, most of the magistrates of Europe were, of course, inveterately opposed to the very reformation Calvin felt they should be supporting. Calvin nonetheless counseled obedience to such rulers, just as Paul had done with respect to the magistrates of his day, all of whom were "sworn enemies of Christ." In the face of opposition and persecution, Calvin called for perseverance and prayer. The institution of the magistracy was ordained by God no matter how abused it may be by a particular occupant. "That is why believers, in whatever country they live, should not only obey the laws and the behests of the magistrates, but should also in the prayers commend their welfare to God."[155]

Nowhere in the commentaries on the Pastorals is there a hint of the concept of resistance by the lesser magistrates, much less the right of tyrannicide advanced by later Calvinists. The decade following the writing of these commentaries, however, witnessed a heightened persecution of the Protestant congregations in France. Calvin's doctrine of passive obedience was pushed to the limit. Yet as late as 1561 he counseled Admiral de Coligny against armed revolt: "It would be better should we all perish a

153. *Comm.* on 1 Tim. 2:1: CNTC 10, p. 205; CO 52, col. 265.
154. *Comm.* on Titus 3:3: CNTC 10, pp. 278-379; CO 52, col. 427.
155. *Comm.* on Tim. 2:2: CNTC 10, p. 207; CO 52, col. 266.

hundred times than expose the gospel to such a disgrace."[156] However, the Genevan Company of Pastors was drawn more and more into open support of the French Protestant party. Calvin's own reticence gave way to full endorsement of the war efforts of the Huguenots on the grounds that legitimate magistracy was represented by a prince of the blood, Louis de Condé.

Despite the advances of the Reformation in Geneva, Calvin wrote for a congregation beseiged by physical and spiritual enemies alike. The overriding impression which emerges from these commentaries is one of a church at war, in combat, its very survival a matter of intense struggle.

> Satan . . . a thousand times a day draws us away from the right course. I say nothing of fire and sword and exiles and all the furious attacks on our enemies. I say nothing of slanders and other such vexations. How many things there are within that are far worse! Ambitious men openly attack us, Epicureans and Lucianists mock at us, impudent men insult us, hypocrites rage against us, those who are wise after the flesh do us harm, and we are harassed in many different ways on every side. The only remedy for all these difficulties is to look forward to Christ's appearing and always to put our trust in it.[157]

The consummation of the congregation, the final establishment of law and order and reformation, must be awaited in patience by the faithful as the eschatological act of God.

Post Tenebras Lux!

From his student days in Paris, Calvin had been frail and frequently sick. His last years were marked by unremitting pain. Early in 1564, in a letter to French physicians who had sent him some medicine, he enumerated the physical ailments which afflicted him: arthritis, kidney stones, hemorrhoids, fever, nephritis, severe indigestion ("whatever nourishment I take sticks like paste to my stomach"), cholic, ulcers, the discharge of blood instead of urine. "All these ailments as it were in troops assail me."[158] Two days before he wrote these words, he had preached what proved to be his last sermon, carried to the pulpit of Saint Pierre on his bed. When the end was very near, the ministers of Geneva crowded into his home to hear his farewell address. He reminisced over the turbulent course of his career and tried to put his own life in perspective.

156. Jules Bonnet, ed., *Les Lettres de Jean Calvin* (Paris, 1884), II, p. 382.
157. *Comm.* on 1 Tim. 6:14: CNTC 10, p. 279; CO 52, col. 330.
158. Bonnet, ed., IV, pp. 358-360.

When I first came here there was almost no organisation. The Gospel was preached and that was all. Everything was in upheaval. I have lived through many marvellous conflicts. I have been greeted in mockery in the evening before my own door with fifty or sixty shots. You may imagine how this affected a poor, timid scholar such as I am and, I confess, always have been. Then I was hunted out of the town, and on my return from Strassburg, I had as great difficulty as before in performing my office. People set their dogs on me, which caught at my robe and my legs. . . . When I went to the Council of Two Hundred to appease a tumult, I was greeted with cries to withdraw. "I shall do nothing of the sort," I replied. "Kill me, you rascals, if you will. My blood will witness against you, and these benches will require it of you." So it will be with you, my brethren, for you are in the midst of a perverse and unhappy people. However many persons of goodwill there be, it is a wicked and perverse folk, and you will have experience of its perversity when I am gone. But take courage and fortify yourselves; for God will make use of this Church and maintain and preserve it. I have had many failings with which you have had to put up, and all I have done is worth nothing. The wicked will lay hold of this saying. But I repeat that all I have done is of no worth, and that I am a miserable creature. This, however, I can say, I have wished to do good and my failings have always displeased me, and the fear of God has been rooted in my heart. So that you can say that my intention has been good, and I pray that the evil may be pardoned me, and if there has been anything good, that you will conform to it and follow it.

Concerning my doctrine, I have taught faithfully and God has given me the grace to write. I have done this as faithfully as possible and have not corrupted a single passage of Scripture, nor knowingly twisted it. When I have been tempted to subtlety, I have withstood the temptation and always studied simplicity. I have never written anything from hatred of anyone, but have always faithfully set before me what I deemed to be the glory of God.[159]

On May 2 he wrote his last letter, a final farewell to his old friend Farel: "Since it is the will of God that you should survive me in the world, live mindful of our intimacy, which, as it was useful to the church of God, so the fruits of it await us in heaven. . . . It is enough that I live and die for Christ, who is to all his followers a gain both in life and death."[160] On May 27 his sufferings came to a close. Beza, who was with him to the end, wrote: "On that day, with the setting sun, the brightest light that was in the world for the guidance of God's church, was taken back to heaven."[161]

Beza's poignant eulogy seems to reverse the motto of the Genevan Refor-

159. CO 9, cols. 891-892. Cf. Monter, pp. 94-97.
160. Bonnet, ed., IV, p. 364.
161. McNeill, *History and Character,* p. 227.

mation, *post tenebras lux*—after the darkness, light—into *post lucem tenebrae*—after the light, darkness. When one visits Geneva today one is shown the imposing Monument of the Reformation where Calvin stands in stone, larger than life, flanked on either side by statues of famous reformers and statesmen. (Luther and Zwingli merit an honorable mention but no statue!) Somehow this monument, impressive as it is, seems out of character for the man it was built to commemorate. Calvin did not seek his own glory, but died confessing that "all I have done is of no worth . . . I am a miserable creature." Calvin was buried in the common cemetery. At his own request, no stone was erected over the site of his interment. On the occasion of his eightieth birthday Karl Barth compared his own work as a theologian to the donkey who carried Jesus into Jerusalem.

> If I have done anything in this life of mine, I have done it as a relative of the donkey that went its way carrying an important burden. The disciples had said to its owner: "The Lord has need of it." And so it seems to have pleased God to have used me at this time, just as I was, in spite of all the things, the disagreeable things, that quite rightly are and will be said about me. Thus I was used. . . . I just happened to be on the right spot. A theology somewhat different from the current theology was apparently needed in our time, and I was permitted to be the donkey that carried this better theology for part of the way, or tried to carry it as best I could.[162]

Calvin too was such a donkey who happened to be "on the right spot" at the right time. His life's goal was to be a faithful servant of the Word of God. The light which emanates from his witness still shines—*post tenebras lux!*—not, to be sure, as a reflection of his own brilliance, but as a means of illumination to point men and women toward the adoration of the true God, whose glory is revealed in the face of Jesus Christ.

Today we are removed by five hundred years and an ocean from sixteenth-century Geneva. We cannot simply deracinate Calvin from his context and venerate him as the perfect theologian and churchman. Many of his emphases are still relevant today. His stress on the sovereign initiative of God in salvation would be a healthy corrective to the prevailing neo-Pelagianism of contemporary American Christianity. We also need to be reminded that the church is not a social agency with only a slightly more spiritualized mandate than the Rotary Club. In the midst of our secular culture, we need to appropriate Calvin's vision of the church as the special creation of the Holy Spirit, a community which can point men and women

162. Karl Barth, *Fragments Grave and Gay,* ed. Martin Rumscheidt (London: Collins, 1971), pp. 116-117.

beyond itself to the transcendent source of their lives and of life itself. On the other hand, we can only deplore Calvin's coercive view of society, his intolerance of dissenters, his acquiesence in the death of Servetus, notwithstanding his plea for leniency in the mode of execution. Yet, even here, we cannot condemn him self-righteously when we ourselves belong to a society which, in the name of national survival, a motive no better than Calvin's, destroyed the civilian population of two Japanese cities in 1945. Perhaps we can all agree with the words of John Robinson, pastor of the Pilgrim Fathers, a devoted Calvinist and defender of the Synod of Dort, who remarked to the departing Pilgrims that he was determined to follow Calvin no further than he had followed Christ, since he was very confident that the Lord had more truth and light yet to break forth out of his Holy Word.[163]

Select Bibliography

The standard critical edition of Calvin's works remains the fifty-nine-volume series edited by G. Baum, E. Cunitz, E. Reuss, et al. in the *Corpus Reformatorum: Ioannis Calvini Opera quae supersunt omnia*. The Barth-Niesel anthology, *Opera Selecta*, contains a critical edition of the *Institutes* and several other major writings. The series *Supplementa Calviniana* is bringing out many of Calvin's hitherto unpublished sermons. The McNeill-Battles edition of the *Institutes* (vol. 20-21 in Westminister Press' Library of Christian Classics) is far superior to earlier English versions. Two additional volumes in this series are devoted to Calvin: *Calvin: Commentaries*, ed. Joseph Haroutunian and *Calvin: Theological Treatises*, ed. J. K. S. Reid. David and Thomas F. Torrance have edited an excellent translation of *Calvin's New Testament Commentaries*, 12 vols. (Grand Rapids: Eerdmans, 1957-70). Baker Book House has reprinted the entire collection of Calvin's works (commentaries, tracts, and letters) first published in the nineteenth century by the Calvin Translation Society. A brief anthology of Calvin texts is G. R. Potter and M. Greengrass, eds., *John Calvin* (New York: St. Martin's Press, 1983). The 1536 edition of the *Institutes,* tr. Ford Lewis Battles, has been jointly published by the Meeter Center for Calvin Studies and Eerdmans Publishing Company as the first volume in *Bibliotheca Calviniana,* a new series devoted to making available in English the yet untranslated works of Calvin as well as major European studies of Calvin. Benjamin W. Farley has translated Calvin's *Sermons on the Ten Commandments* (Grand Rapids: Baker Book House, 1980) and his *Treatises Against the Anabaptists and*

163. For an assessment of Robinson's theology and its indebtedness to Calvin, see Timothy George, *John Robinson and the English Separatist Tradition* (Macon, Ga.: Mercer University Press, 1982).

Against the Libertines (Grand Rapids: Baker Book House, 1982). Peter De Klerk publishes an annual comprehensive bibliography of Calvin literature in the *Calvin Theological Journal.*

Balke, Willem. *Calvin and the Anabaptist Radicals.* Grand Rapids: Eerdmans, 1981. A thorough study of Calvin's relationship with the Anabaptists containing both a chronological review and a systematic analysis of this topic.

Bouwsma, William J. *John Calvin: A Sixteenth-Century Portrait.* New York: Oxford University Press, 1987. A sympathetic and nuanced treatment of Calvin by one of the leading historians of the Renaissance and Reformation.

Douglass, Jane Dempsey. *Women, Freedom, and Calvin.* Philadelphia: Westminster Press, 1985. A stimulating essay on the implication of Calvin's theology for women and their struggle for equality.

Hall, Charles A. M. *With the Spirit's Sword.* Richmond: John Knox Press, 1968. Examines the motif of spiritual warfare in the theology of Calvin.

Leith, John H. *An Introduction to the Reformed Tradition.* Atlanta: John Knox Press, 1977. An excellent survey of a major Protestant tradition.

McDonnell, Kilian. *John Calvin, the Church, and the Eucharist.* Princeton: Princeton University Press, 1967. An insightful, ecumenically oriented study of Calvin's eucharistic theology written by a Benedictine monk.

McKee, Elsie A. *John Calvin on the Diaconate and Liturgical Almsgiving.* Geneva: Droz, 1984. A well-researched study of an oft neglected aspect of Calvin's ecclesiology.

McKim, Donald K., ed. *Readings in Calvin's Theology.* Grand Rapids: Baker Book House, 1984. A helpful collection of essays by prominent Calvin scholars.

McNeill, John T. *The History and Character of Calvinism.* London: Oxford University Press, 1954. Somewhat dated, but generally reliable survey by the doyen of Calvin scholarship in America.

Parker, T. H. L. *Calvin's New Testament Commentaries.* Grand Rapids: Eerdmans, 1971. An indispensable introduction to the study of Calvin's New Testament commentaries.

Parker, T. H. L. *Calvin's Old Testament Commentaries.* Edinburgh: T. and T. Clark, 1986. A companion volume to the above mentioned study.

Parker, T. H. L. *John Calvin: A Biography.* Philadelphia: Westminster Press, 1975. The most recent full-length life of Calvin in English. A respectable work, though not without its flaws. Should be compared with the earlier biographies by Walker (1906), Reyburn (1914), Hunt (1933), and MacKinnon (1936).

Richard, Lucien J. *The Spirituality of John Calvin.* Atlanta: John Knox Press, 1974. A study of Calvin's distinctive approach to the spiritual life by a noted Catholic theologian.

Selinger, Suzanne. *Calvin Against Himself.* Hamdon, Conn.: Archon Books, 1984). A study of Calvin's religion, its relation to Luther, and its impact on the history of ideas. A creative study even if at points the conclusions outrun the evidence.

Shepherd, Victor A. *The Nature and Function of Faith in the Theology of John*

Calvin. Macon, Ga.: Mercer University Press, 1983. Originally a doctoral dissertation at the University of Toronto, this able study draws on the commentaries as well as the *Institutes* in setting forth Calvin's doctrine of faith.

Van Buren, Paul. *Christ in Our Place: The Substitutionary Character of Calvin's Doctrine of Reconciliation.* Grand Rapids: Eerdmans, 1957. An excellent exposition of Calvin's doctrine of atonement. Originally a dissertation directed by Karl Barth.

Wendel, François. *Calvin: The Origins and Development of His Religious Thought.* Durham: Ladyrinth Press, 1987. Originally published in French in 1950, this is perhaps the best single volume on Calvin.

Willis, E. David. *Calvin's Catholic Christology.* Leiden: E. J. Brill, 1966; A careful examination of the so-called "extra Calvinisticum" theme in Calvin's thought.

6

No Other Foundation
Menno Simons

Let it now be said that the worth of [the Anabaptists'] endeavor is not to be judged in the light of their contribution to history. They took their stand in the light of eternity regardless of what might or might not happen in history.

Roland H. Bainton[1]

The Radical Reformation

The Radical Reformation was a tremendous movement of spiritual and ecclesial renewal which stood on the margins of the major territorial churches, Catholic and Protestant, during the great religious upheaval of the sixteenth century. However, this movement was neither marginal nor peripheral in its basic drives and spiritual vitalities. Embracing both ecumenicity and sectarianism, violent revolution and pacifistic communalism, sublimating ascetical, mystical, and rationalist impulses from the Late Middle Ages, the Radical Reformation considered as an entity posed a thoroughgoing critique of the *corpus christianum* in both its mainline Protestant and Tridentine Catholic mutations.

Only in recent years have the radical reformers begun to emerge from the shadow of opprobrium cast over them by their sixteenth-century opponents. Heinrich Bullinger, for instance, called them "devilish enemies and destroyers of the church of God."[2] Luther's preferred term was *Schwärmer,* which recalls the uncontrollable buzzing of bees around a hive, and which the German reformer applied indiscriminately to a wide host of adversaries. Calvin's epithets were no less pejorative: "fanatics," "deluded," "scatterbrains," "asses," "scoundrels," "mad dogs."[3] Interpreting the radicals in

1. Roland H. Bainton, *Studies on the Reformation* (Boston: Beacon Press, 1963), p. 206.
2. Heinrich Bullinger, *Von dem unverschampten fräfel* (Zurich, 1531), fol. 75r.
3. John Calvin, *Treatises Against the Anabaptists and Against the Libertines,* Benjamin W. Farley, ed. (Grand Rapids: Baker Book House, 1982), p. 30. Cf. also the study of Willem Balke, *Calvin and the Anabaptist Radicals* (Grand Rapids:

252

terms of the negatives of dissent and nonconformity has skewed efforts to understand their own spiritual motivation. A contemporary British historian of note reflects this failure in his depiction of the "true nature" of Anabaptism as "a violent phenomenon born out of irrational and psychologically unbalanced dreams, resting on a denial of reason and the elevation of that belief in direct inspiration which enables men to do as they please."[4]

Sometimes the radical reformers are lumped together as "the left wing of the Reformation." In this designation we can hear a faint echo of Luther's own accusation that both the papists and the *Schwärmer* erred on "the left and the right side," neither remaining on the path of true freedom. Luther, however, reversed the modern positioning, placing the Catholics on the left and the radicals on the right!

Recognizing the anachronistic use of "left-wing" when applied to sixteenth-century dissent, George H. Williams proposed "the Radical Reformation" as a collective term for all those groups of religious innovators who remained in neither the Roman Catholic nor mainline Protestant churches. Williams's typology of the radicals is the most comprehensive and most durable to date, despite the fact that it was first put forth thirty years ago.[5] Williams divided the radicals into three major groupings: Anabaptists, Spiritualists, and Evangelical Rationalists. These are not hard and fast categories but general rubrics for describing common affinities among a wide range of heterogeneous Christians. Despite their many differences they all wanted to cut back through the accretions of ecclesiastical tradition, through what Balthasar Hubmaier called "the mud holes and cesspools of human dogma," to the authentic root (*radix*) of faith and order. Each branch of the Radical Reformation attached itself to a distinctive "root." For the Anabaptists it was the Bible, especially the New Testament. They

4. G. R. Elton, *Reformation Europe, 1517-1559* (New York: Harper and Row, 1963), p. 103.

5. George H. Williams and Angel Mergal, eds., *Spiritual and Anabaptist Writers* (Philadelphia: Westminster Press, 1957), pp. 19-38. In *The Radical Reformation,* Williams fleshed out his typology in a volume of nearly 1000 pages. This classic study has been amplified and brought up to date in Spanish translation: *La Reforma Radical* (Mexico City, 1982). Cf. also Williams' response to the scholarly discussion of his book in "The Radical Reformation Revisited," *Union Seminary Quarterly Review* 39 (1984), pp. 1-28. On the viability of the term "radical reformation," see Roland Crahay, "Le non-conformisme religieux du XVIe siècle entre l'humanisme et les Eglises," in *Les Dissidents du XVIe siècle entre l'Humanisme et le Catholicisme,* ed. Marc Lienhard (Baden-Baden: Valentin Koerner, 1983), pp. 15-34.

desired not merely to reform the church, but to restore it to its pristine, apostolic purity. The Spiritualists, on the other hand, were less concerned with the external, visible church than with the experience of the Spirit within. Some of them, such as Caspar Schwenckfeld, came to believe that all *externalia,* even water baptism and the Lord's Supper, could be eliminated in favor of the witness of the Spirit within, the "inner word." The Evangelical Rationalists appealed to reason. To be sure, it was not autonomous reason in the later sense of the Enlightenment, but reason illuminated by the Spirit and informed by Holy Scripture. This emphasis led many of them to question the traditional Trinitarian and Christological dogmas of the ancient church.

The Radical Reformation, then, was not merely a "wing," a side effect that merely revealed a more extreme form of the Reformation; it was instead a movement which gave birth to a new form of Christian faith and life. As one scholar put it, it was a "reformation of the Reformation" or "a correction of the correction of Catholicism."[6] Precisely this, together with the fact that for the most part the radicals were forced to develop their model of the Christian life outside the confines of the official churches, gave their spirituality and church life a distinctive cast. Radical reformers lived outside the established order. Many of them accepted exile, torture, and capital punishment rather than deny the Lord Who had called them to take up their cross and follow him.

Menno and Anabaptism

Menno Simons was the most outstanding leader of the Anabaptist branch of the Radical Reformation, but he was neither the first nor the most original exponent of this tradition. We have seen already how Swiss Anabaptism emerged out of the cradle of the Zwinglian reformation. Its earliest leaders, Conrad Grebel and Felix Mantz, were radical disciples of Zwingli who felt that they were merely carrying to logical consequences ideas they had learned from Master Huldrych. Through their study of the Bible, they became convinced that the baptism they had received as infants was invalid and that, in defiance of Zwingli since he could not be persuaded, they had to restore true baptism of believers only. We have seen how on January 21, 1525, the little group met in the home of Felix Mantz on Neustadtgasse in Zurich, within the very shadow of the Great Minster itself. A letter, written

6. J. A. Oosterbaan, "The Reformation of the Reformation: Fundamentals of Anabaptist Theology," *MQR* 51 (1977), p. 176. Cf. also Walter Klaasen, *Anabaptism: Neither Catholic nor Protestant* (Waterloo, Ont.: Conrad Press, 1973).

a few years after the event, describes what happened at this meeting: "And it happened that they were together. After fear lay greatly upon them, they called upon God in heaven, that he should show mercy to them. Then George arose and asked Conrad for God's sake to baptize him; and this he did. After that, he baptized the others also."[7] The "George" referred to here was George Blaurock, so called because he wore a blue coat (*blaurer Rock*). Blaurock, a Roman priest turned fiery evangelist, was the central figure in the Anabaptist revival at Zollikon, a village just five miles out of Zurich on the lake. On one occasion, he blocked the duly appointed minister from entering the pulpit, declaring, "Not thou, but I, have been called to preach."[8] The Zurich magistrates were not slow in acting against such commotions. Blaurock was imprisoned, Grebel was sent into exile where he died of the plague, Mantz was drowned in the Limmat River. Despite persecution the movement spread throughout other Swiss cantons, as well as into Southern Germany and Austria.

The Anabaptists were characterized neither by doctrinal homogeneity nor organizational efficiency. Various leaders imparted their own distinctive stamp to the movement. Hans Hut, a sometime disciple of Thomas Müntzer, predicted that Christ would return to earth on Pentecost Sunday, 1528. He set about to gather the 144,000 elect saints (Rev. 7:4) whom he "sealed" by baptizing them on the forehead with the sign of the cross. He was dead by 1528. Hut's charred body (he had set fire to his prison cell in a futile effort to escape) was condemned posthumously. His movement soon splintered, although his apocalyptic message was taken up by other prophets, such as Melchior Hofmann who set a different date (1534) and place (Strasbourg) for the second coming—with similar results. Although both Hut and Hofmann counseled their followers to wield only the "sheathed sword," that is to absorb violence but not to inflict it, their drastic predictions and scathing invective against emperor, pope, and "bloodsucking anti-Christian Lutheran and Zwinglian preachers" created an atmosphere in which the

7. *Bibliotheca Reformatoria Neerlandica* ('s-Gravenhage: Martinus Nijhoff, 1910), VII, p. 516; translated in C. J. Dyck, ed., *An Introduction to Mennonite History* (Scottdale, Penn.: Herald Press, 1981). The more familiar account of the January 21 baptisms derives from the *Hutterite Chronicle,* written many years after the event. The letter quoted here was written around 1530 by Swiss Brethren in Klettgau, Switzerland in response to an inquiry from a group in Cologne.

8. Williams, *The Radical Reformation,* p. 124.

overtly revolutionary kingdom of Münster could flourish.[9]

Through Hofmann's evangelizing efforts, Anabaptism came to the Netherlands. In 1530 he baptized around three hundred converts in the city of Emden and also commissioned lay preachers to carry his message into nearly every corner of the Low Countries. Convinced that he was the Elijah whom Jesus had said would prepare the way for His coming again, Hofmann returned to Strasbourg, had himself committed to prison where he awaited the *Parousia*. He remained in prison until his death some ten years later, pathetically hoping to the end for the descent of the New Jerusalem.

When Hofmann was imprisoned at Strasbourg in 1533, one of his disciples, a baker from Haarlem named Jan Mathijs, declared himself to be a prophet sent by the Holy Spirit: as Hofmann was Elijah, he was Enoch, the second of the two witnesses prophesied in Revelation 11. He proceeded to ordain twelve apostles, among them Jan Beuckels of Leyden. Possessed of Hofmann's eschatological urgency, they moved the site of New Jerusalem from Strasbourg to Münster, which they took over in a storm of violence. All of the "godless" (i.e. those who refused to be baptized) were to be killed. When Mathijs himself was killed on Easter Sunday, 1534, Jan of Leyden assumed the leadership. He had himself crowned the "king of righteousness over all" and introduced polygamy in literal imitation of the Old Testament practice. Three times each week King Jan appeared in the market place in his royal robes to receive obeisance from his subjects. This experiment in theocracy ended in a bloody holocaust when the city of Münster was beseiged by Protestant and Catholic troops fighting side by side against the violent Anabaptists within. When the blood bath was over, Jan of Leyden and two of his associates were captured and tortured to death with red-hot tongs on January 22, 1536. The bodies were put on display in iron cages in the tower of Saint Lambert's Church on the main street in Münster. These cages can still be seen today, grim reminders of the tragedy of 1534-1535.

At this point the stories of Menno Simons and Dutch Anabaptism come together. Menno was born in 1496, four years after Colombus had discovered America, exactly thirteen years after Luther's birth and thirteen before Calvin's. He was the son of a dairy farmer in the village of Witmarsum, less

---

9. Hans-Jürgen Goertz, ed., *Radikale Reformatoren* (Münich: C. H. Beck, 1978), p. 163. Hofmann referred to the emperor, pope, and false teachers as the "höllische Dreieinigkeit." on Hofmann's relation to Menno, see Klaus Deppermann, *Melchior Hofmann: Soziale Unruhen and apokalyptische Visionen im Zeitalter der Reformation* (Göttingen: Vandenhoeck and Ruprecht, 1979).

than ten miles from the North Sea. We know little about Menno's early education. He probably studied at the monastery school at Bolsward near his home. He developed good proficiency in Latin and could read some Greek but no Hebrew. He was also acquainted with certain Church Fathers, such as Tertullian, Cyprian, and Eusebius. He claimed never to have read the Bible until two years after his ordination as a priest although, of course, he would have had some acquaintance with it through the Roman liturgy.

Menno was ordained to the Catholic priesthood in March, 1524, when he was twenty-eight years old. He was first appointed parish priest in the village of Pingjum, his father's ancestral home. There he served seven years before being called to his home village of Witmarsum in 1531. During this time Menno performed the perfunctory duties of a country priest and did them rather well; the move to Witmarsum was a promotion. At the same time, he spent much time in frivolous activities, such as drinking and playing cards. He later confessed that even after he had begun to read the Bible, "I wanted that knowledge through the lusts of my youth in an impure, sensual, unprofitable life, and sought nothing but gain, ease, favor of men, splendor, name and fame, as all generally do who sail that ship."[10] Apparently he was something of a born leader even though he was, as he put it, "a lord and a prince in Babylon." "Everyone sought me and desired me. The world loved me and I it . . . I was pre-eminent among men, even aged men. Everyone revered me. When I spoke they were silent. When I beckoned they came. When I waved them away they went. What I desired they did." Later Menno came to realize, with the writer of Ecclesiastes, that all such allurements are really "vanity." When the bon vivant became a Christian, he lost his erstwhile friends. "Heretofore I was honored; now debased. . . . Once I was a friend, now I pass for an enemy."[11]

Like Luther, Zwingli, and Calvin, Menno had to struggle through to the gospel. Menno's biographers have been puzzled as to why he took so long before breaking with the Roman Church and fully embracing the Anabaptist cause. We can better understand Menno's later career if we look some-

---

10. CWMS, p. 669. This volume contains a brief biography of Menno by Harold S. Bender. Other biographical accounts include the article on "Menno Simons" by Cornelius Krahn in *Mennonite Encyclopedia*, III, pp. 577-584; Christoph Bornhauser, *Leben und Lehre Menno Simons'* (Neukirchen: Neukirchener Verlag, 1973); Jan A. Brandsma, "The Transition of Menno Simons from Roman Catholicism to Anabaptism as Reflected in His Writings" (Baptist Theological Seminary, Rüschlikon-Zurich: B.D., 1955).

11. CWMS, p. 71.

what closely at the process which led to this decision. There are three important clusters of events and ideas in Menno's developing consciousness of the true church and his role in it.

We have seen what an important role the Eucharist played in the process of Calvin's break with Rome, as well as in the dispute between Luther and Zwingli. The same issue surfaced in Menno's early career as a Catholic priest. In 1525, the very year that Grebel and Mantz were organizing the first Anabaptist congregations in Switzerland, Menno began to entertain doubts about the dogma of transubstantiation.

> It occurred to me, as often as I handled the bread and wine in the mass, that they were not the flesh and blood of the Lord. I thought that the devil was suggesting this, that he might separate me from my faith. I confessed it often, sighed and prayed; yet I could not come clear of the idea.[12]

That Menno should have had "heretical" ideas like these was not so unusual, for the real presence of Christ in the supper was being questioned among various circles in the Netherlands. As early as 1521 Cornelius Hoen, a leader of the Dutch Sacramentists, had taught that the bread and wine in the Eucharist were merely symbols of Christ's suffering and death. We do not know whether Menno had access to Hoen's teachings, but we are certain that he had read some of Luther's tracts. In *The Babylonian Captivity of the Church* (1520) Luther declared transubstantiation to be a figment of human opinion, since it was based neither on the Scriptures nor sound reason. Menno later declared that Luther's writings had helped him to realize that "human injunctions cannot bind unto eternal death."[13] He did not follow Luther's own explanation of the Sacrament of the Altar, but adopted one much closer to that of Zwingli. Still, Menno's initial doubting of the doctrine of transubstantiation was an important break from his earlier devotion to the Mass, which he later described in the following way:

> Yes, I have said to a weak, perishing creature that came forth from the earth, that was broken in a mill, that was baked by the fire, that was chewed by my teeth and digested by my stomach, namely, to a mouthful of bread, Thou hast saved me. . . . O God, thus have I, a miserable sinner, toyed with the harlot of Babylon for many years.[14]

This last sentence about "toying with . . . Babylon for many years" may

12. Ibid., p. 668.
13. Cornelius Krahn, *Dutch Anabaptism: Origin, Spread, Life and Thought*, p. 171.
14. CWMS, p. 76.

refer to the fact that Menno continued to celebrate Mass long after his radical questioning had begun.

Menno might have quietly remained within the Roman fold had he not come to question another pillar of the established tradition, infant baptism. As early as 1529 Menno read a book by a South German preacher, Theobald Billicanus, which cited Cyprian as an advocate of adult baptism. However, an event closer to home was really the catalyst for Menno's thinking on this subject. On March 20, 1531, in the city of Leeuwarden, capital of the Dutch province of Friesland, an itinerant tailor named Sicke Freerks was beheaded because he had been baptized a second time. Menno later commented, "It sounded very strange in my ears that one spoke of a second baptism."[15] Freerks had been re-baptized by one of Hofmann's disciples at Emden. Menno referred to him as "a devout, pious hero." Freerks's brutal execution must have made a lasting impression on Menno. In any event, he began to investigate the basis for infant baptism. He examined the arguments of Luther, Bucer, Zwingli, and Bullinger but found them all lacking. He consulted with his fellow priest at Pingjum; he read the Church Fathers. Finally, he "searched the Scriptures diligently and considered the question seriously but could find nothing about infant baptism." He came to the conclusion that "all were deceived about infant baptism."[16] Menno's recourse to the Scriptures was a momentous step in his pilgrimage. He began to preach from the Bible, so much so that he gained a reputation as an "evangelical preacher," though, he later said, he was unworthy of that designation for his preaching at that time was "without spirit and love" and bore no positive fruit.

Possessed of new convictions on the Lord's Supper and baptism, Menno nonetheless did not break with the Roman Church until he was deeply stirred by events surrounding the tragedy of Münster. As early as 1532 some people in the area around Witmarsum had been rebaptized. Some of these had also been drawn into the vortex of the violent, revolutionary kingdom of the two Jans at Münster, including Menno's own brother, Peter Simons. On March 30, 1535, a group of some three hundred violent Anabaptists captured the Old Cloister near Bolsward. For eight days they withstood the assaults of the authorities, but on April 7 the cloister was retaken and the radicals savagely slain. Among them was Menno's brother. This event precipitated a crisis in Menno's life.

15. Ibid., p. 7.
16. Ibid., p. 8.

After this had transpired the blood of these people, although misled, fell so hot on my heart that I could not stand it, nor find rest in my soul. I reflected upon my unclean, carnal life, also the hypocritical doctrine and idolatry which I still practiced daily in appearance of godliness, but without relish. I saw that these zealous children, although in error, willingly gave their lives and their estates for their doctrine and faith. And I was one of those who disclosed to some of them the abominations of the papal system. But I myself continued in my comfortable life and acknowledged abominations simply in order that I might enjoy physical comfort and escape the cross of Christ.

Pondering these things my conscience tormented me so that I could no longer endure it. I thought to myself—I, miserable man, what am I doing? If I continue in this way, and do not live agreeably to the Word of the Lord, according to the knowledge of the truth which I have obtained; if I do not censure to the best of my little talent the hypocrisy, the impenitent, carnal life, the erroneous baptism, the Lord's Supper in the false service of God which the learned ones teach; if I through bodily fear do not lay bare the foundations of the truth, nor use all my powers to direct the wandering flock who would gladly do their duty if they knew it, to the true pastures of Christ—oh, how shall their shed blood, shed in the midst of transgression rise against me at the judgment of the Almighty and pronounce sentence against my poor, miserable soul!

Menno realized that he had not lived up to the light which he had received. He implored God for forgiveness and a new life in Christ:

My heart trembled within me. I prayed to God with sighs and tears that He would give to me, a sorrowing sinner, the gift of His grace, create within me a clean heart, and graciously through the merits of the crimson blood of Christ forgive my unclean walk and frivolous easy life and bestow upon me wisdom, Spirit, courage, and a manly spirit so that I might preach His exalted and adorable name and holy Word in purity, and make known His truth to His glory.[17]

From April 1535 until January 1536 Menno tried, as the priest of Witmarsum, to carry out an evangelical reform. Before he had dissimulated and compromised; now he spoke out clearly and without hesitation. Menno's first writing, *The Blasphemy of Jan van Leyden,* comes from this period. This is a stirring tract in which Menno opposed the kingship of Christ to the false pretensions of "King John." Menno showed the un-Christlike character of the "proponents of the sword philosophy" and called for a life of nonresistance:

17. Ibid., pp. 670-671.

It is forbidden to us to fight with physical weapons. . . . This only would I learn of you whether you are baptized on the sword or on the cross? Let every one of you guard against all strange doctrine of swords and resistance and other like things which is nothing short of a fair flower under which lies hidden an evil serpent which has shot his venom into many.[18]

In the same month that Jan of Leyden was tortured to death, Menno made his decisive break with the Church of Rome. He felt a special compassion for the "poor misguided sheep" who wandered about without a shepherd. About a year after he had left the comfortable parish at Witmarsum to become an itinerant underground evangelist, seven or eight Anabaptist brethren near Groningen entreated him to accept the office of elder or chief shepherd of the brotherhood. After a time of struggling with this decision, he consented and so began "to teach and to baptize, to labor with my limited talents in the harvest field of the Lord, to assist in building up his holy city and temple and to repair the dilapidated walls." Having been baptized earlier, Menno was now duly ordained, probably by Obbe Phillips who with his brother Dirk had emerged as early leaders of the non-Münsterite Dutch Anabaptists. As George Williams pointed out, Menno, like many other former Roman priests, became not only an *ana*baptist but also a *re*ordinationist.[19] A few years after he had ordained Menno, Obbe Phillips became disillusioned with the divisiveness of the Anabaptist movement and forsook the brotherhood altogether. Had he remained steadfast in his leadership, the Dutch Anabaptists may well have been called "Obbenites" rather than Mennists or later Mennonites. Dirk Phillips did not defect from the faith but became Menno's great colaborer. He was also a great theologian, perhaps more creative if less influential than Menno.

From his ordination in 1537 until he died in 1561, Menno exerted a remarkable influence on the Anabaptists of the Netherlands and Northern Germany. During most of these years he lived the life of a hunted heretic, preaching by night to secret conventicles of brothers and sisters, baptizing new believers in country streams and out of the way lakes, establishing churches and ordaining pastors from Amsterdam to Cologne to Danzig. When we consider the dangers Menno faced, we are amazed that he was able to die a natural death at the age of sixty-six. A letter, addressed to Mary, regent of the Netherlands, and dated May 19, 1541, shows clearly the hazards which confronted Menno:

18. Ibid., pp. 45, 49.
19. Williams, *The Radical Reformation,* pp. 392-393.

Most gracious Lady, the error of the cursed sect of the Anabaptists which in the last five or six years has very strongly prevailed in this land of Friesland . . . would doubtless be and remain extirpated, were it not that a former priest Menno Symonsz who is one of the principal leaders of the aforesaid sect and about three or four years ago became fugitive, has roved about since that time once or twice a year in these parts and has misled many simple and innocent people. To seize and apprehend this man we have offered a large sum of money, but until now with no success. Therefore we have entertained the thought of offering and promising pardon and mercy to a few who have been misled . . . if they would bring about the imprisonment of the said Menno Symons.[20]

Such intrigues and harassment pursued Menno wherever he went. In 1542 Emperor Charles V published an edict against him and offered one hundred gold guilders for Menno's arrest. Menno referred to himself as a "homeless man." But he did not have only himself to think about. His wife Gertrude and their three children suffered the same fate. In 1544 he lamented that he "could not find in all the countries a cabin or hut in which my poor wife and our little children could be put up in safety for a year or even half a year."[21] His wife and two of the children preceded Menno in death. The earliest portraits of Menno show him with crutches, and it is certain that he lived his last years as a cripple. From the beginning of his career Menno knew that there was no way for the true Christian to avoid the cross. "If the Head had to suffer such torture, anguish, misery, and pain, how shall his servants, children, and members expect peace and freedom as to their flesh?"[22] On the twenty-fifth anniversary of his renunciation of the Roman Church, Menno died and was buried in his own garden at Wüstenfeld.

Like the other reformers we have studied, Menno's theology was situational; it emerged in the context of his active involvement in the life of the church. His writings reflect the course of his chequered career. Menno never had the leisure to produce learned tomes or to develop a systematic theology. Yet he wrote with vigor and insight, drawing both on the earlier Anabaptist heritage and the wider Christian tradition but primarily on his own intensive engagement with the Scriptures. He wrote approximately twenty-five books and tracts in addition to numerous letters, meditations, and hymns. On the title page of all of his works he quoted the Pauline text 1 Corinthians 3:11, "For other foundation can no man lay, than that is laid,

20. CWMS, p. 17.
21. Ibid., p. 424.
22. Ibid., pp. 109-110.

which is Jesus Christ." This verse became the motto of his life and of his theology.

In 1540 Menno published what was to become his most influential writing, *Dat Fundament des Christelycken Leers,* or *The Foundation of Christian Doctrine.* In some ways this treatise is comparable to the first edition of Calvin's *Institutes,* published just four years earlier. It was at once a tract for the times and a sort of catechetical instruction for new believers. Calvin had written a prefatory epistle to King Francis I, pleading for toleration for the persecuted Protestants in France. Menno too addressed himself to the princes and magistrates whose agents were hunting and persecuting the Anabaptists. He pleaded for them to be not exterminators but defenders of righteousness. "Do not be Jeroboam, Ahab, and Manasseh any longer, but be David, Hezekiah, and Josiah so that you need not because of your office be ashamed in the great and dreadful day of the Lord."[23] He appealed for tolerance on the basis of a common humanity: Anabaptists too were clothed with the same nature; they too yearned for rest and peace, for wives and children; they too were by nature as fearful of death as any other people. Yet they had to endure daily the tyrannical sword of lords and princes. Menno made it clear that he spoke for pacifistic, nonresistant Anabaptists; he explicitly condemned the characteristics of the Münsterites: "the sword, polygamy, an external kingdom and king, and other like errors on account of which the innocent have to suffer much."[24] The *Foundation* was an apology for those Anabaptists who chose the way of the cross over that of the sword. Menno recognized the legitimacy of the civil authorities and pledged obedience to them in all areas which did not violate the requirements of faith. Menno's book had little if any impact on the rulers, who continued their unabated assault against all Anabaptists. Its real influence was on the believers, who found in it a succinct summary of Anabaptist theology and churchmanship. The *Foundation* was translated and reprinted several times in the sixteenth century.

The *Foundation* was Menno's masterpiece, but earlier he had published several treatises to clarify the doctrinal position of the Anabaptists. These include: *The Spiritual Resurrection* (1536), a booklet in which Menno contrasted the bodily resurrection at the end of time with the spiritual resurrection from sin to "a new life and change of heart"; *Meditation on the Twenty-Fifth Psalm* (1537), a personal exegesis of Psalm 25 modeled on the style of Augustine's *Confessions; The New Birth* (1537), a scathing denun-

23. Ibid., p. 106.
24. Ibid., p. 107.

ciation of the "ugly, leavenous dung of human commands, statutes and glosses" coupled with an urgent call for repentance and regeneration. Menno's later writings became more polemical as he was forced to define his views over against various opponents. Some of his writings were directed against fellow Anabaptists such as David Joris, who saw himself as the eschatological "David" and who attracted many of the disillusioned Münsterites. Adam Pastor, a former priest whom Menno had ordained to the ministry, came to doubt the divinity of Jesus Christ. Against him Menno directed his *Confession of the Triune God* (1550). Menno also engaged in extensive dialogue with three Reformed ministers, John à Lasco, Martin Micron, and Gellius Faber. These discussions were rehearsed in several long treatises. Menno's other writings were largely pastoral admonitions related to church discipline (he wrote three treatises on this subject), spirituality (e.g. *The Nurture of Children,* 1557; *Meditations and Prayers for Mealtime,* 1557), and sufferings (e.g. *Confession of the Distressed Christians,* 1552; *The Cross of the Saints,* 1554). We shall draw on all of these writings in our survey of the principal themes in Menno's theology.

The New Life

Coursing through all branches of the Radical Reformation was a decided emphasis on the interiorized process of salvation. For all of the radicals, true Christianity was ipso facto personal, experiential, and individual. Indeed, the Anabaptist branch of the Radical Reformation has been characterized recently as a "charismatic movement."[25] Their practice of adult baptism earned them the name *Anabaptist,* but they clearly insisted that an *experience* of the new birth was a prerequisite for water baptism. Baptism sometimes came as the climax of conversion, a process which often involved an intense emotional struggle. This seems to have been the case with the baptisms administered in the early Anabaptist congregation at Zollikon.

> Hans Bruggbach of Zumingen arose crying and shouting that he was a great sinner and that they should pray God for him. Thereupon Blaurock asked whether he desired to receive the grace of God, and he said yes. Then Mantz arose and asked 'Who will prevent me that I should not baptize him?' And Blaurock answered, 'No one.' So he took a dipper of water and baptized him in the name of God the Father, God the Son, and God the Holy Spirit.[26]

25. Kenneth R. Davis, "Anabaptism as a Charismatic Movement," *MQR* 53 (1979), pp. 219-234.

26. Leonard von Muralt and Walter Schmid, eds., *Quellen zur Geschichte der Täufer in der Schweiz* (Zurich: S. Hirzel Verlag, 1952), pp. 42-43. Fritz Blanke

As we have seen, Menno's own baptism was preceded by a similar period of wrenching struggle, of sighing and crying and praying, until the "God of mercy . . . touched my heart, gave me a new mind, humbled me in his fear, taught me in part to know myself, turned me from the way of death and graciously called me into the narrow path of life."[27] As long ago as 1848 the historian Max Göbel recognized that "the essential and distinguishing characteristic of this [Anabaptist] church is its great emphasis upon the actual personal conversion and regeneration of every Christian through the Holy Spirit."[28]

Although Luther described himself as "born again," and both Zwingli and Calvin commented on Jesus' words to Nicodemus, Menno placed the greatest emphasis on the necessity for the new birth. "If now you desire to have your wicked nature cleared up, and desire to be free from eternal death and damnation . . . then you must be born again."[29] The process of conversion involved the two interrelated moments of faith and repentance. Faith was the inward appropriation of the gospel, which Menno defined as "the blessed announcement of the favor and grace of God to us, and of forgiveness of sins through Christ Jesus." When the sinner cast himself wholeheartedly upon the grace and promises of God, "the heart is renewed, converted, justified, becomes pious, peaceable and joyous, is born a child of God, approaches with full confidence the throne of grace, and so becomes a joint heir of Christ and a possessor of eternal life."[30] Menno did not prescribe a precise pattern of conversion through which every believer must go. But he did describe the new birth as an experience by which "the heart is pierced and moved through the Holy Ghost with an unusual regenerating, renewing, vivifying power, which produces first of all the fear of God."[31] Faith did not stop with fear but led on to love. Having received the great riches of God's grace in Christ, the believer, moved by an unfeigned faith, was able to love God, returning love for love. Here Menno came close to Calvin's definition of true piety as reverence joined with love of God which the knowledge of His benefits induced (*Inst.* 1.2.1).

Faith was the positive response to God's grace, but it was incomplete

interprets this early phase of Anabaptism as a "revival movement." See his *Bruder in Christo* (Zurich: Zwingli-Verlag, 1955).

27. CWMS, p. 671.
28. Max Göbel, *Geschichte des Christlichen Leben* (Coblenz, 1848), p. 37.
29. CWMS, p. 92.
30. Ibid., p. 115.
31. Ibid., p. 329.

without the prior act of repentance or, as Menno called it, true penitence *(ware penitencie)*. He lambasted those who held to a "mere historical faith" which gave no evidence of a changed life. It will not "help a fig," he averred, to be called Christians or boast of the Lord's blood, death, merits, grace, and gospel, as long as believers were not genuinely converted from their wicked, sinful lives. Repentance, then, involved a change of life; it had nothing to do with external religious practices such as "hypocritical fastings, pilgrimages, praying and reading lots of Pater Nosters and Ave Marias, hearing frequent masses, going to confessionals." These were vain and empty commandments of men. True penitence is "possessed of power and works."[32]

In the treatise *The True Christian Faith* (1541), Menno presented ten "case studies" of true faith drawn from the Bible, five from the Old Testament and five from the New. Menno's examples were Noah, Abraham, Moses, Joshua and Caleb, Josiah, the centurion of Capernaum, Zacchaeus, the thief on the cross, the sinful woman of Luke 7, and the Syrophenician woman of Matthew 15. All of these people shared in common a lively faith which led to decisive action and service for God: Abraham left the country of his fathers and obediently offered up his son Isaac; Moses forsook the luxuries of Egypt in order to lead his people out of slavery; the thief on the cross confessed Christ before all the people and reproved the blasphemy of his fellow criminal. Zacchaeus was one of Menno's favorite illustrations. Zacchaeus, the wealthy tax collector, reminded Menno of many people with whom he had dealings—unethical merchants and financiers, money-mad judges and lawyers, drunken innkeepers and corrupt clergy. But once Zacchaeus had received Christ into his house with joy, his life was radically altered. "He believed and was renewed; he reformed his life; he walked no more in his former evil ways." If believers had the faith of penitent Zacchaeus, Menno claimed, then few lords would continue in their violent and luxurious lives, few judges and lawyers in their courthouses, few merchants in their unfair business practices, and few preachers, priests, and monks in their salaries, incomes, and cloisters. "There would soon be a different and better situation because, it cannot fail, the righteous must live his faith."[33]

In order to understand more fully Menno's doctrine of salvation, we must review briefly his concept of sin. Menno distinguished four kinds or levels of sin. The first kind was the corrupt, sinful nature inherited at birth by all descendants of corrupt, sinful Adam. Menno accepted the traditional theo-

32. Ibid., p. 111.
33. Ibid., p. 369.

logical term *original sin* as an apt designation for this corruption. He also quoted in support of it the traditional proof text, Psalm 51:5, "Behold, I was brought forth in iniquity, and in sin did my mother conceive me." Menno believed that in the Garden of Eden Adam and Eve had been bitten by the satanic serpent and thus became, as it were, carriers of a sinful nature which was subject to eternal death, "so we, their descendants, are also born of sinful nature, poisoned by the serpent, inclined to evil, and by nature children of hell, of the devil, and everlasting death."[34] Indeed, little children "often show, as they grow, the evil seed of Adam"; the older they become, the more obvious it is! For this reason Menno admonished Christian parents not to spare the rod in correcting their children, since "a child unrestrained becomes headstrong as an untamed horse."[35] By nature children were rebellious against the Word of God, inclined to be loud, stubborn and self-willed. All of this sounds very traditional, yet at one decisive point Menno departed from the orthodox doctrine of original sin. While all persons inherited a corrupt nature which inevitably leads to actual sins, the death of Christ on the cross removed the *guilt* of original sin for everyone! This is one of Menno's major arguments for not submitting infants to baptism. Although they were capable of neither faith nor baptism, infants were universally in "a state of grace" until they reached the age of "shame" or of the "discrimination of good and evil."

> For Jesus Christ's sake original sin (as men call it) is not imputed by God against [children] unto damnation, but they are in one respect like Adam and Eve were before the fall, namely that they are innocent and blameless, understanding neither good and evil. But just as soon as they come to the knowledge of good and evil, they step out of innocent ignorance into known wickedness, and by their own disobedience sin against the Lord.[36]

No one was condemned because of original sin, devastating and long-lasting though its effects may be. Only those who were capable of responsible moral and ethical decisions could incur guilt.

Original sin was the "mother" of actual sins, according to Menno's second category. Actual sins were the fruit of the flesh (Gal. 5). They included adultery, fornication, avarice, hatred, envy, theft, murder, and idolatry. These were sins of willful commission and incurred God's just condemnation unless repented of. Only by being born again by faith and

34. Ibid., p. 504.
35. Ibid., p. 951.
36. Quoted, William Keeney, *The Development of Dutch Anabaptist Thought and Practice from 1539-1564,* pp. 68-69.

true repentance could believers "resist" original sin and die to actual sins. One who experienced the new birth was "transferred from Adam to Christ." The regenerate "live no longer after the old corrupted nature of the earthly Adam, but after the new upright nature of the new and heavenly Adam, Christ Jesus."[37] Does this mean that true believers are capable of sinless perfection? Menno denied that it does, since even after conversion inherited sinful nature remains, although it should no longer dominate. This prompted Menno to introduce his third category of sins: human frailties, errors, and stumblings which are still found daily among saints and regenerate ones. Believers sin but they do not do it in the same way as unbelievers, (i.e. "with relish and boldness" perhaps a slap at Luther's advice to "sin boldly.")[38] The Christian life was a continual struggle after holiness and sanctification: "Their poor weak life they daily renew more and more, and that after the image of him who created them. . . . They put on Christ and manifest his nature, spirit, and power in all their conduct."[39] The saints were not rejected by God for their sinful lapses as long as they sighed and lamented about their errors and daily implored God for forgiveness. There was, however, a fourth category of sin through which a believer might "fall from grace by willfulness and wickedness." This was the sin of apostasy, the sin against the Holy Spirit. One who committed this sin, which involved open wickedness and trampling on of Christ, would receive his proper reward, eternal damnation.

Time and again Menno reiterated the basic theme of his soteriology: Genuine, evangelical faith produces genuine, evangelical fruit; true faith cannot be idle—it changes, renews, purifies, sanctifies, justifies more and more; all those who through the new birth have been grafted into Christ are "fruit bearing twigs of the true vine."[40] Menno stated this not only as a positive principle but also spelled out its negative implication: If you do not do as Christ commands, this is proof that you do not really believe in Christ, despite your profession to the contrary. Faith and its fruit are inseparable. Menno, and Anabaptists generally, did not accept Luther's forensic doctrine of justification by faith alone because they saw it as an impediment to the true doctrine of a "lively" faith which issues in holy living. Melchior Hofmann lambasted those who cried "Believe, believe;

37. CWMS, pp. 93, 507.
38. Ibid., p. 564.
39. Ibid., p. 93.
40. Ibid., p. 99.

grace, grace," but whose faith was fruitless and dead. Menno explicitly refuted Luther's famous denigration of James as a "strawy epistle."

> The Lutherans teach and believe that faith alone saves, without any assistance by works. They emphasize this doctrine so as to make it appear as though works were not even necessary; yes, that faith is of such a nature that it cannot tolerate any work alongside of it. And therefore the important and earnest epistle of James is esteemed and treated as a 'strawy epistle.' What bold folly! If the doctrine is straw, then the chosen apostle, the faithful servant and witness of Christ who wrote and taught it, must also have been a strawy man; this is as clear as the noonday sun. For the doctrine shows the character of the man.

Menno was disturbed by the antinomian tendencies which he felt were latent in Luther's doctrine of justification, at least as that doctrine had been appropriated by many Lutherans with whom he had contact.

> They strike up a psalm, *Der Strick ist entzwei und wir sind frei,* etc. ("Snapped is the cord, now we are free, praise the Lord") while beer and wine verily run from their drunken mouths and noses. Anyone who can but recite this on his thumb, no matter how carnally he lives, is a good evangelical man and a precious brother.[41]

The Anabaptist concept of discipleship *(Nachfolge)* as a deliberate repudiation of the old life and a radical commitment to Jesus as Lord could not tolerate such a lackadaisical abuse of the grace of God.

At the same time Menno insisted that salvation was by grace and not by works. "Far be it from us that we should comfort ourselves with anything but the grace of God through Christ Jesus."[42] Menno attributed the entire *ordo salutis,* from creation through eternal life, to the work of grace. By grace the human race was created when as yet it was not, by grace it was again accepted through Christ when it was still lost, by grace Christ was sent to earth, by grace we are taught repentance, by grace it is given us to believe, by grace we receive the Holy Spirit, and by grace we attain eternal life.

Such language could well have come from any one of the mainline reformers we have studied in this volume. Upon closer examination, however, we find that there is an important difference between Menno and the

41. Ibid., pp. 333-334. Menno's attitude toward James is reviewed alongside those of Luther, Zwingli, and Calvin in Timothy George, "'A Right Strawy Epistle': Reformation Perspectives on James," *Review and Expositor* 83 (1986), pp. 369-383.

42. CWMS, p. 506.

magisterial Protestants as to the ultimate source and modus operandi of grace. It is significant that Menno began his listing of the "moments" in salvation history with creation and not with the eternal decrees or secret design of God. Menno shared with all adherents of the Radical Reformation a stiff aversion to the twin doctrines of predestination and bondage of the will which, as we have seen, bound the mainline reformers together along with the strict Augustinians in the Roman Catholic tradition (cf. the seventeenth-century Jansenist movement). Menno frequently addressed his followers as "the elect" and "the chosen of God"; he also spoke very strongly of Jesus Christ as the object of predestination, as the eternal Word of God who became incarnate "in time and in the town of Nazareth, according to the predestination of God, according to the decree of God."[43] But he was clearly not pleased with the presumed fatalism he thought was implied in the predestinarian theology of Luther and Zwingli. The German (i.e. Lutheran) churches proclaimed "this matter of [God] working in us both good and bad," while Zwingli taught that "when a thief stole, or a murderer killed, God's will compelled them to it." Menno referred to Zwingli's doctrine as "an abomination of abominations."[44] Had he been familiar with Calvin's doctrine, he would doubtless have accorded it no more respect. The idea of double predestination he repelled vigorously:

> Shall I say that thou hast ordained the wicked to wickedness, as some have said? God forbid. . . . Water, fire, life, and death hast thou left to our choice. . . . O dear Lord, how sadly have they blasphemed thine unspeakably great goodness, eternal mercy, and almighty majesty in this matter!

Menno was moved by two concerns in his rejection of rigid predestinarianism: first, he felt that it did damage to God's goodness in making him the author of evil; secondly, like the Lutheran version of justification, it provided a handy excuse for carnal minds to "continue upon the broad way and have a cover for their sins."[45]

In summary we can say that Menno tried to strike a balance between the "works righteousness" of medieval Catholic soteriology and the theological determinism of the mainline Protestants. Salvation is by grace not by works,

43. Ibid., p. 832.
44. Ibid., pp. 301, 760.
45. Ibid., p. 75. The most detailed study of Anabaptist soteriology to date is Alvin J. Beachy, *The Concept of Grace in the Radical Reformation* (Nieuwkoop: B. de Graaf, 1977). Cf. also Robert Friedmann, *The Theology of Anabaptism* and J. A. Oosterbaan, "Grace in Dutch Mennonite Theology," *A Legacy of Faith: A Sixtieth Anniversary Tribute to Cornelius Krahn,* C. J. Dyck, ed., pp. 69-85.

and yet it is "of my own choice" that I accept the proffered means of divine grace. If Menno's position is less satisfactory than we could hope for, it must be said that he approached the subject with neither the subtle sophistication of a Calvin or a Luther nor the scholastic refinement of a Balthasar Hubmaier, who wrote an elaborate treatise *On Free Will*. It is also well to remember that he was struggling with issues which neither originated nor terminated with the controversies of the sixteenth century. A major segment of English Baptists in the seventeenth century embraced an understanding of salvation not far distant from Menno's, while the Arminian wing of Dutch Calvinism —not to say the Methodists still later—developed concepts of "resistible grace" and "unlimited atonement," which also recall the theology of the Anabaptists.

The Infallible Word

In his book *The Theology of Anabaptism,* Robert Friedmann did not include a separate section on the doctrine of Scripture. At least superficially, one could justify this procedure with references to Menno since he nowhere explicitly developed his views on the authority, nature, and meaning of the Bible. Yet no one can read very far in Menno's writings without realizing that he was thoroughly saturated with the language and themes of Holy Scripture. Menno may have been the most biblical of the radical reformers if only from the sheer quantity of quotations, references, and allusions to Holy Writ.

We may begin by recalling the decisive role which the Bible played in Menno's own conversion and break with Rome. His questioning of transubstantiation and infant baptism was resolved ultimately by a searching engagement with the Scriptures. This had the effect of relativizing all other human authorities and traditions:

> Behold, my worthy brethren, against the doctrines, sacraments, and life just considered, imperial decrees, papal bulls, councils of the learned, long standing practices, human philosophy, Origen, Augustine, Luther, Bucer, imprisonment, banishment, or murder mean nothing; for it is the eternal, imperishable Word of God; I repeat, it is the eternal Word of God, and shall so remain forever.[46]

The *primary* importance of the Bible in Menno's theology is its crucial role in the process of conversion. Drawing on the analogy of the Word to the

46. Henry Poettcker, "Menno Simons' View of the Bible as Authority," Dyck, p. 32.

seed in Jesus' parable of the sower (Luke 8:11), Menno likened the Scriptures to a spiritual seed from which the new life springs forth. The Holy Spirit germinates the seed and brings forth its fruit in faith and repentance. Menno sometimes used the distinction between law and gospel to show the various ways the seed of the Word brings about regeneration. The function of the law is to produce the knowledge and conviction of sin, while that of the gospel is to present the remedy of salvation through Jesus Christ. In the early days of the Anabaptist movement, the *preaching* more often than the reading of the Word yielded this result. "So also where the gospel is preached in true zeal, so that it penetrates the hearts of the listeners, there one finds a converted, changed and new mind."[47] Many of those who heard and responded to the Anabaptist message were poor farmers, unskilled workers, and displaced persons. Often they were completely or almost illiterate. Yet, once converted, they began to "hide the Word in their hearts." When hailed before the civil authorities, these unlearned believers would frequently confound their judges by their ability to quote and reason from the Scriptures.

Menno based his entire program of reform on an urgent appeal to the authority of the Bible. He urged his readers not to trust in ancient traditions, papal decretals, imperial mandates, or "the wisdom and glosses of the learned ones," but only in "God's infallible Word."[48] Menno's severe prun-

47. Ibid., p. 45.

48. CWMS, pp. 100, 102. The following dialogue between the Franciscan inquisitor, Friar Cornelis, and the Belgian Anabaptist, Jacob de Roore, shows how the Bible had become a powerful weapon in the hands of common people. When Jacob quoted from the Apocalypse, equating the Church of Rome with the whore of the Babylon, Friar Cornelis interrupted:

"Ah, bah! What do you understand about St. John's Apocalypse? At what university did you study? At the loom, I suppose; for I understand that you were nothing but a poor weaver and chandler before you went around preaching and rebaptizing out here in the Gruthuysbosch. I have attended the university of Louvain and studied divinity so long, and yet I do not understand anything at all about St. John's Apocalypse; that is a fact."

To which Jacob replied: "That's why Christ thanked his heavenly Father, that he had revealed and made it known to babes and hidden it from the wise of this world, as it is written, Matthew 11:25." Friar Cornelis' sarcastic response betrays his exasperation in dealing with such theological upstarts:

"Exactly; God had revealed it to the weavers at the loom, to the cobblers on their bench, and to the bellows-menders, lantern-tinkers, scissors-grinders, broom-makers, thatchers, and all sorts of riff-raff, and poor, filthy, and lousy beggars. And

ing of the liturgical tradition of the church was based on a strict application of the principle that what the Bible does not expressly enjoin should not be permitted. "There is not a word to be found in Scripture," Menno asserted, "concerning their anointing, crosses, caps, togas, unclean purifications, cloisters, chapels, bells, organs, choral music, masses, offerings, ancient usages, etc."[49] Hence all of these had to be eliminated from true Christian worship.

Many of the Anabaptists resorted to a simplistic literalism in their interpretation of the Bible. This led to extreme practices, such as polygamy in Münster and the incident of running naked through the streets of Amsterdam (based on Isa. 20:2-3). Guy de Brès, Reformed leader of Belgium, told of certain Anabaptists who preached from the roof because Jesus had said "and what you hear whispered, proclaim upon the housetops" (Matt. 10: 27), while others masqueraded as little children because Jesus had said that one must become as a little child to enter the kingdom of heaven (Matt. 10:2-4).[50] Menno did not agree with these extremists, yet he did insist that Jesus' prohibition of oaths and his admonition to nonresistance be followed literally. His basic hermeneutical principle was (shades of Luther) Christocentric. "All doctrines both of the Old and New Testament rightly explained and understood according to the intent of Christ and his apostles are profitable for doctrine and reproof."[51]

Menno's understanding of the Bible was developed in dialogue with the major reformers on the one hand and the radical spiritualists on the other. Against the background of a common adherence to the principle of *sola scriptura*, Menno's use and appeal to the Bible differed from the mainline Protestants in at least three aspects. First, *he chided the reformers for tempering their appeal to Scripture with human traditions and vain learning*. We recall that Menno had been "helped" by Luther's writings in his early struggles to wrest himself free from his Roman background. Menno quoted favorably Luther and Melanchthon's remarks concerning the nonbinding character of extra-biblical traditions, but then he added: "Here Luther and

to us ecclesiastics who have studied from our youth night and day, he has concealed it. Just see how we are tormented. You Anabaptists are certainly fine fellows to understand the holy Scriptures; for before you are rebaptized, you can't tell A from B, but as soon as you are baptized, you can read and write. If the devil and his mother have not a hand in this, I do not understand anything about you people."

49. CWMS, p. 172.
50. Quoted, Keeney, p. 33.
51. CWMS, p. 312.

Melanchthon have correctly expressed themselves according to the Scripture, although alas, they did not follow their own advice!"[52] In his debates with Reformed pastors, Menno frequently charged them with having insufficient Scriptural bases for their positions. In writing to Gellius Faber, for example, Menno enjoined him to "read through the entire Scriptures— Moses and the prophets, Christ and the apostles." He claimed that Faber could prove his point "by a single letter of Scripture."[53]

We have earlier observed how a dispute over the deity of Christ arose among the Dutch Mennonites, fueled by a former follower of Menno, Adam Pastor. In his *Confession of the Triune God* (1550), Menno attempted to set forth the traditional, orthodox doctrine of the Trinity by appealing only to the Bible. He made no reference to the Councils of Nicea or Constantinople or to any of the patristic controversies which consumed the early church for the first four centuries. "These plain Scriptures, testimonies, and references" are quite sufficient! He declared that for fifteen years he had been averse to "human sophistry and glosses." To go beyond the simple language of the Bible in matters like this was "like trying to pour the river Rhine or Meuse into a quart bottle." At the same time we must admit that Menno was not able to stick by his own rule. When he moved from merely quoting traditional proof texts to a description of the deity of Christ and the Holy Spirit, he fell back on terminology which was developed in the history of theology. Christ was called a "person" by the Church Fathers; the Holy Spirit "proceeds from the Father through the Son, although he ever remains with God and in God," and so forth. Nor is this the only instance of Menno's appeal to the wider church tradition. He found, for example, that "the worthy martyr Cyprian" advocated, like the Anabaptists, baptism upon confession of faith. Still, these are clearly *exceptions* to Menno's usual practice of speaking where the Bible speaks and being silent where the Bible is silent.

Luther, we remember, validated his teaching office by appealing to his vocation as a *Doctor in Biblia;* Zwingli and Calvin brought to their study of the Scriptures a thorough immersion in the humanist disciplines. Menno was different on both accounts. As a former priest he would have been literate in Latin, and in fact he did provide Latin summaries of some of his works. Nonetheless, he admitted that he had never attained proficiency in languages despite his having "coveted" them from his youth. In fact, Menno preferred to write in the vernacular since his intended audience were

52. Ibid., p. 514.
53. Poettcker, p. 33.

common people who could not follow learned discourses in Latin. Menno set himself against scholasticism, both Roman and Protestant; in the *Foundation* he had declared that the wisdom which we teach is "not to be brought from afar nor taught in colleges. It must be given from above and be learned through the Holy Ghost."[54]

Second, *for Menno the New Testament took precedence over the Old in his interpretation of Scripture.* We have encountered this issue before in our discussion of Zwingli's defense of infant baptism against the Swiss Brethren. It is significant that Menno quoted more from the New Testament than the Old at a ratio of 3:1. Even his *Meditation on the Twenty-Fifth Psalm* has many more references from the New Testament than from the Old. Surely, the Bible as a whole was authoritative for Menno. The thrust of the whole Scripture is to direct us to Christ. The Old Covenant was a period of preparation and promise which was fulfilled with the coming of the Messiah. According to Menno, Jesus Christ really did bring something new. The Old Covenant was displaced by the radical newness of Christ's kingdom. The mainline reformers stressed the continuity of the two testaments; for them there was really only *one covenant in two dispensations.* This principle enabled them to justify infant baptism by analogy to its Old Testament counterpart, circumcision. They also found in the Old Testament a pattern for church-state relationships. The Anabaptists denied the legitimacy of this appeal to the Old Testament by pointing to the *normative* status of the New Covenant. For Menno this was not only an issue in his debates with the major reformers but also in his struggles with apocalyptic militants such as Jan of Leyden. Jan justified his use of the sword by claiming that he was the third David appointed by God to usher in his kingdom by force; Menno insisted that the Christian leave the armour of David to the physical Israelites.

> Now we should not imagine that the figure of the Old Testament is so applied to the truth of the New Testament that flesh is understood as referring to flesh; for the figure must reflect the reality; the image, the being; and the letter, the Spirit. If we take this view of it we shall easily understand with what kind of arms Christians should fight, namely with the Word of God which is a two-edged sword.[55]

In this way Menno depicted the reality of the New Testament over against the Old. Seen in the perspective of his entire theology, this principle is the

54. CWMS, p. 107.
55. Ibid., p. 42.

hermeneutical corollary to fundamental Christocentrism, his oft-repeated reminder that "no other foundation can anyone lay than that which is laid, which is Christ Jesus."

Third, *Menno accepted the apocryphal writings as canonical.* The Reformation principle of *sola scriptura* raised a new the question of the canonicity of the Bible. We have observed Menno's strong reaction to Luther's disparaging evaluation of James as a "strawy epistle." Another point of difference between the mainline reformers and the radicals concerned use of the apocryphal books. Most of the major Protestant theologians rejected the Apochrypha as spurious, or at best of inferior and negligible value. Since a number of Roman Catholic teachings, such as purgatory, were justified by appealing to the Apocrypha, Protestants were eager to devalue their authority. The Church of England, true to its pattern of *via media,* regarded the apocryphal books as edifying literature which could be read appropriately in worship, but not on the same level with the undisputed canonical writings. At the Council of Trent the Roman Church recognized the full canonical status of the Apocrypha. The Radical Reformation, in all of its expressions, was much closer to the Catholic position on this issue. Menno quoted freely from all of the apocryphal books and made no distinction between their authority and that of the undisputed writings. At one point he appealed to the apostle Peter and the apocryphal character Susanna in the same sentence: "We think with the holy Peter that we should obey God rather than man, and with dear chaste Susanna that it is better to fall into the hands of man than into the hands of God."[56] In the Middle Ages the apocryphal books had circulated in separate editions and were very popular in medieval preaching and iconography. The Radical Reformation, as a popular movement which drew on several streams of medieval piety, continued to regard the Apocrypha as fully inspired, as a part of God's uttered Word which "can neither be bent nor broken."[57] The lingering influence of this tradition is illustrated by the fact that to this day the Amish Mennonites base their marriage service on the Book of Tobit.

Menno was forced to stress the figurative meaning and spiritual character of the Old Testament over against the mainline Protestants and apocalyptic militants such as Jan of Leyden. He also found himself defending the objectivity and binding authority of the entire Bible against the radical spiritualists. Following the debacle of the Münsterite kingdom, disillusioned followers of the late King Jan of Leyden found themselves pulled in

56. Ibid., p. 177.
57. Ibid., p. 341.

several directions. Some of them, led by John of Batenburg, continued to believe that the second advent of Christ could be brought about only through violent attacks against the "godless" (i.e. the non-Batenburgers). Known as the *Zwaardgeesten* (sword-minded), these terrorists of the Radical Reformation plundered churches and slaughtered innocent people over a wide expanse of the Low Countries. Although Batenburg was executed in 1538, his followers continued to wreak vengeance on others. As late as 1552 the city of Leyden was concerned about a Batenburger attack.

Against the violent extremists Menno hurled the same arguments he had used against Jan of Leyden even before he had joined the brotherhood. However, another more subtle opposition arose among other dissidents who shared Menno's aversion to violence but could accept neither his positive biblicism nor his program of organizing peaceful Anabaptists into visible congregations.

It must have been a great personal blow to Menno when Obbe Phillips, who had baptized and ordained him to the ministry, forsook the Anabaptist fellowship in 1540. In his *Confession,* written near the end of his life, Obbe recounted his disillusionment with the emerging Anabaptist movement which was led by Menno and his own brother Dirk. He wrote that when the prophecies had deceived them on all sides—a reference to the failed predictions of Hofmann, Mathijs, and Jan of Leyden—then "the letter of the Scriptures took us prisoner"—an allusion to Menno's insistence on following literally the model of the church in the New Testament.[58] We gain a vivid impression of Obbe's deep psychic revulsion through his description of the execution of "fifteen or sixteen teachers and brethren" which he witnessed at Haarlem in 1534.

> Some were smothered and put on the pike; then the others were beheaded and set on the wheel. This I myself thereafter saw and stood among the executed with some brethren who had travelled with me because I was curious to know which in the heap those three were who had baptized us and had proclaimed such calling and promise to us. But we could not identify them, so frightfully were they changed by the fire and smoke, and those on the wheels we could not recognize either, nor tell one from the other.[59]

This event must have indelibly seared Obbe's conscience. He came to regret his part in the origins of Dutch Anabaptism and eventually ended his life as a kind of solitary spiritualist.

58. SAW, p. 223.
59. Ibid., p. 219.

Menno faced a more serious challenge from the spiritualist wing of Anabaptism in the person of David Joris who, like himself, had been ordained to the ministry by Obbe Phillips. In 1538 Joris received a letter from an admiring follower, a wealthy woman named Anneken Jans which proclaimed him a prophet of God, the "fan" in the hand of the Lord to winnow and "prepare for him an acceptable people that he may speedily come to his temple."[60] Joris soon came to regard himself as the "true" Third David, in contrast to the discredited Jan of Leyden. From 1539 to 1544 Joris lived in Antwerp where he developed a thoroughly spiritualistic approach to the Christian faith. Whereas Menno stressed the written Word, Joris placed emphasis on the inward Word. Eventually he came to reject all "externals," including adult baptism. The guidance of the Spirit was to take precedence over the objective, historical aspects of the faith:

> Faith is revealed in the power of the Spirit and in the power of truth, not in the telling of the Biblical story, nor in the story of the miracles of the apostles and prophets, nor in the corporeal proof of the outer cross of Christ, nor in his incarnation, his death or his resurrection, nor in his second coming.[61]

Faced with persecution in the Low Countries, Joris moved to Basel with his wife and eleven children in 1544. He took an assumed name, "Johann van Brugge," outwardly conformed to the Reformed Church and lived out his days in relative ease and leisure. He continued to direct his followers, known as Davidjorists, through his prolific literary output. From his example many of them sought to disguise their true beliefs through dissimulation and external compliance with the demands of the established churches.

As early as the first edition of the *Foundation,* Menno perceived the danger posed by "the corrupt sects." He lamented that so many have been "so sadly misled from one unclean sect to another: first to that of Münster, next to Batenburg, now Davidian." He also attacked the claims of the false teachers:

> Do you mean to say that the doctrine of Christ and his apostles was incomplete and that your teachers bring forth the perfect instruction? I answer that to teach and believe this is the most horrible blasphemy. . . . Deceived children, where is there a letter in the whole doctrine of Christ and the

60. Williams, *The Radical Reformation,* p. 383.

61. Quoted, Roland Bainton, *David Joris: Wiedertäufer and Kämpfer für Toleranz im 16. Jahrhundert* (Leipzig, 1937), p. 80. Cf. also the recent article by James M. Stayer, "David Joris: A Prolegomenon to Further Research," *MQR* 59 (1985), pp. 350-361.

apostles . . . by which you can prove and establish a single one of your erring articles?[62]

Challenged by Menno's strong attack, Joris wrote a letter to Menno warning him to prepare for a great battle. Menno answered in a "Sharp Reply to David Joris" (1542). To sense just how "sharp" Menno's reply was, we need only to hear his characterization of Joris as "a dunghill of a man, ashes, and a vapor." He criticized the Davidjorist policy of duplicity and conformity to the environing religious culture as mere cowardice. The root of Joris's heresy, Menno alleged, lay in his displacement of Christ's Word with that of his own: "You treat as obsolete the doctrine of Christ and your own as perfect and abiding."[63] With these words Menno bade Joris not to write to him any more until he had repented and was willing to submit his own ideas to the revealed Word of the Lord in Holy Scripture. Shortly after Joris died in 1556, the authorities in Basel discovered that the respectable merchant they had known as Johann van Brugge was really the notorious heretic. They ordered his body exhumed and burned posthumously. His ideas continued to live on, however, and Menno was forced to deal with a recurrent spiritualistic tendency in Dutch Anabaptism throughout his career. In an early work, *Why I Do Not Cease Teaching and Writing* (1539), Menno set forth the principle which would be the touchstone for the rest of his ministry.

> Brethren, I tell you the truth and lie not. I am no Enoch, I am no Elijah, I am not one who sees visions, I am no prophet who can teach and prophesy otherwise than what is written in the Word of God and understood in the Spirit. . . . Once more, I have no visions nor angelic inspirations. Neither do I desire such lest I be deceived. The Word of Christ alone is sufficient for me.[64]

The Incarnate Lord

We have observed how Menno Simons tried to restate the classical doctrine of the Trinity in purely biblical terms, avoiding the speculative, philosophically weighted language of the patristic debates. A similar issue arose with respect to the person of Christ, or more precisely, with the mode of the incarnation. The Council of Chalcedon (451) had declared the incarnate Christ to be "one person in two natures." This was a compromise formula intended to refute the error of the Monophysites (who held Christ possessed

62. CWMS, pp. 215-217.
63. Ibid., pp. 1019-1020.
64. Ibid., p. 310.

only one nature) on the one hand and the Nestorians (who too radically separated the humanity and divinity of Christ) on the other. Christological schisms continued to divide the church after Chalcedon, especially in the East. We should not be surprised that the Radical Reformation, with its desire to cut back through ecclesiastical accretions to the roots of Christianity, occasioned further controversy over this perennial theological dilemma.

Among certain Spiritualists, Anabaptists, and Evangelical Rationalists there appeared in a variety of forms the teaching that when Christ became incarnate He brought with Him His own body from heaven. Caspar Schwenckfeld, the Spiritualist, claimed to have introduced this doctrine in the Reformation, having learned it from his reading of the Bible and the Church Fathers. Schwenckfeld defended his version of the "celestial flesh" Christology against other reformers such as Sebastian Franck and Melchior Hofmann who, alleged, took "their errors from our truth, like spiders who suck poison out of a beautiful flower."[65] Hofmann, rather than Schwenckfeld, transmitted this doctrine to the Netherlandish Anabaptists and hence to Menno Simons. Drawing on the imagery of medieval mysticism, Hofmann likened the descent of Christ into the womb of the virgin Mary to a drop of dew descending from heaven into an oyster where it crystallizes into a pearl. Hofmann also echoed the early Gnostic leader Valentinus when he claimed that Christ took nothing of His substance from Mary, but merely passed through her "as water through a pipe." Using a different metaphor, Menno explained the incarnation in terms of the divine Christ passing through Mary's womb as a ray of sunshine passes through a glass, without assuming sinful flesh.

Menno seems to have only reluctantly entered into controversy with his Reformed opponents on the doctrine of the incarnation. In his *Brief and Clear Confession* (1544), written at the request of John à Lasco, he referred to a conference at Emden at which they had discussed the incarnation, "a subject to which you know I had been invited and constrained against my will." In the same document he further described how he had at first doubted this teaching, when it "was first mentioned by the [Hofmannite?] brethren, fearing that I might be in error about it." He spent many days fasting, praying, seeking the advice of other Christians.

> At last, after much fasting, weeping, praying, tribulation, and anxiety, I became by the grace of God comforted and refreshed at heart, firmly acknowledging and believing, assured by the infallibly sure testimony of the Scripture, understood in the Spirit, that Christ Jesus forever blessed is the Lord from

65. Williams, *The Radical Reformation*, p. 332.

heaven; the promised spiritual seed of the new and spiritual Eve.[66]

Though he never wavered again in his adherence to the doctrine, Menno refrained from teaching it publicly, holding that "there are few who can understand this intricate matter, even after it has been explained to them!"[67] Yet Menno obviously felt that his doctrine of the incarnation was worth defending in large treatises as he devoted more attention to it than to any other doctrinal concern.

Since Menno's formulation of the incarnation differed slightly from Hofmann's, it will be well to listen to his own explanation of it:

> The heavenly Seed, namely, the Word of God, was sown in Mary, and by her faith, being conceived in her by the Holy Ghost, became flesh, and was nurtured in her body; and thus it is called the fruit of her womb, the same as a natural fruit or offspring is called the fruit of its natural mother. For Christ Jesus, as to his origin, is no earthly man, that is, a fruit of the flesh and blood of Adam. He is a heavenly fruit or man. For his beginning or origin is of the Father, like unto the first Adam, sin excepted.[68]

Time and again, Menno cited as his basic proof text, "The Word became flesh," (John 1:14). He rejected the preferred expression of his opponents, "The Word took unto itself human flesh," in favor of a literal interpretation of the Johannine declaration. Menno could not allow that Christ received his human nature from Mary, else he would have been tainted with the Adamic sin which is common to all his descendants. The Roman Catholics solved this problem by appealing to the doctrine of the Immaculate Conception of the Virgin Mary: Mary was preserved by a supernatural conception in her mother Anna from original sin and so was able to bear a sinless Christ. The Reformed tradition generally held that the Holy Spirit miraculously cleansed the corrupt seed of Adam so that Jesus was free from original sin despite the fact that he inherited a fully human nature. Menno set aside both of these explanations: The former elevated Mary to the status of a divine goddess, the latter split Christ into two parts, destroying the unity of His person. Menno sought to resolve the problem by pointing to the celestial origin of Christ's entire being: "The entire Christ Jesus, both

66. CWMS, pp. 422, 427.
67. Ibid., p. 430.
68. Ibid., p. 437.

God and man, man and God, has his origin in heaven and not on earth."[69]

Menno attempted to define the process of the incarnation as carefully as possible so as to allow both for Jesus' natural birth and for His supernatural origin. He consciously chose certain prepositional phrases to clarify this point: Jesus Christ was conceived *in* Mary *through* or *from* the Holy Spirit, but He was born *out of* Mary and not *from* Mary. A somewhat shorthand version of this formula declared that Jesus was born *from* God *out of* Mary.[70] Unlike Hofmann, Menno explicitly stated that Jesus drew nourishment as he experienced the normal fetal development in His mother's womb. The Eternal Word "conceived and came forth of the Holy Ghost; nourished and fed in Mary, as a natural child is by its mother." At the same time, Menno insisted that Mary contributed nothing to the origin of Jesus' human nature. Menno's theory was confirmed by the then current physiological theory (stemming from Aristotle) that the female was a wholly passive member in the generation of progeny. Modern biology has, of course, discredited this view; we now know that male and female are equal partners in the process of procreation. In Menno's day, however, his view was the dominant scientific theory, shared by doctors and philosophers alike. The male seed was believed to be the source of the newborn nature, which was only nourished and given birth by the mother. Menno also believed that this pattern was confirmed by the scriptural example of Abraham and Sarah, which proved "beyond challenge, that a child takes its origin in its father and not in its mother."[71]

Menno believed his formulation had preserved both the sinlessness of Christ and the reality of his humanity. His opponents, however, accused him of teaching a docetic Christology, the ancient heresy that Christ only appeared or seemed to be human. Calvin, who never met Menno but knew of his views through his opponent Martin Micron, said of the Dutch Anabaptist that he could imagine nothing "prouder than this ass or more impudent than this dog."[72] He also criticized the biological theory on which Menno, at least in part, based his understanding of the incarnation: "In order to disguise their error—to prove that Christ took his body out of nothing—the new Marcionites too haughtily contend that women are 'without seed.' Thus they overturn the principles of nature" (*Inst.* 2.13.3). In retrospect, Calvin clearly had the better argument with respect to the role

69. Ibid., pp. 797-798.
70. Cf. the excellent discussion in Keeney, pp. 91-92, 207-209.
71. CWMS, p. 793.
72. CO 10, p. 167; Williams, *The Radical Reformation,* p. 487, 31n.

of the female in procreation. However, as we have seen, Menno had no intention of denying the true humanity of Christ. Against the Gnostics (including Marcion), he asserted that Christ "was truly human and not a mere phantasm. . . . He was afflicted, hungry, thirsty, subject to suffering and death, according to the flesh."[73] Menno's concern was to show how Christ remained unsullied from original sin, able to offer a perfect sacrifice on the cross for the sins of the world. He thus tended to emphasize the unity of the person of the God-Man rather the distinctiveness of Jesus' natures. Thus Menno did not hesitate to say that God the Son suffered and died in His divinity as well as in his humanity, a formulation which the Reformed theologians were reluctant to embrace. Menno construed the Reformed emphasis on the distinctive properties of the two natures as producing "two sons, one the Son of God without any mother and not subject to suffering, and the other the son of Mary without any father and subject to suffering." Against such a schizoid Christ, Menno declared that "the Lord Jesus Christ is not an impure and divided Christ of two persons or sons, but an undivided and pure Christ, a single person, God's own first-born Son and only begotten Son."[74] Like all theologians Menno was driven to explain his point by means of analogy—as the Emperor Charles V was a son of Austria on his father's side and a son of Spain on his mother's side, yet was not two sons but a single, undivided son; so likewise Christ Jesus was on the side of His Father the Son of God and on the side of His mother a son of man. Still, Christ remained "not one son out of two sons—but an only and undivided Son, the Son of God and of Mary."[75]

The Swiss Brethren and Hutterites did not follow the Dutch Anabaptists in adopting Menno's distinctive doctrine of the incarnation and later Mennonites have abandoned it as well. The editor of the English translation of Menno's writings admitted that "modern Mennonites are therefore a bit embarrassed by the peculiar views of Menno on this subject."[76] However, during the sixteenth and seventeenth centuries Menno's doctrine had important soteriological and ecclesiological implications for Dutch Anabaptism. The crucial importance of the new birth depends on the incarnation through which believers are made partakers of the divine nature. Menno's concept of the church as a community without spot or wrinkle, feasting at communion on the heavenly "manna" which Jesus identified with his body

73. CWMS, pp. 428, 794.
74. Ibid., pp. 792-793.
75. Ibid., p. 808.
76. Ibid., p. 784.

(John 6:51 *ff.*), is also related to the miracle of the incarnation. Dirk Phillips expressed the close connection between Christology and eucharistic piety in this way: "Christ Jesus is the living bread which came like dew or manna from heaven, and what was the food of angels has also become the food of men (Ps. 78:25). But the bread, which he is himself, and gives men—that is, believers—to eat, is his flesh, which he has given for the life of the world."[77]

The True Church

The Congregation

Menno Simons is reported to have said, while on his sickbed—which was to become his deathbed—that nothing on earth was as precious to him as the church. For twenty-five years he labored throughout the Netherlands and Northern Germany to establish fellowships of believers into organized congregations committed to one another and to their mission in the world. Through the ministry of Menno and his fellow workers, Dutch Anabaptism recovered from its disillusionment at Münster to become the most enduring expression of the Radical Reformation.

Much of Menno's writings were devoted to showing the character of the true church over against the false Antichristian churches which were legally recognized and supported by the state.

> They verily are not the true congregation of Christ who merely boast of his name. But they are the true congregation of Christ who are truly converted, who are born from above of God, who are of a regenerate mind by the operation of the Holy Spirit through the hearing of the divine Word, and have become the children of God, have entered into obedience to him, and live unblamably in his holy commandments, and according to his holy will with all their days, or from the moment of their call.[78]

The true church, then, was an intentional community consisting of regenerate members who willingly embraced a life of discipleship and who pledged themselves one to the other in conventional love and mutuality. Menno referred to the Roman Catholics, Lutherans, and Zwinglians as "the great and comfortable sects." He grouped them with the Arians, the Circumcellions, and the Münsterites. They shared one feature in common: "It is the custom of all the sects who are outside of Christ and his Word to make valid

77. SAW, p. 243, 16n.
78. CWMS, p. 300.

their positions, faith, and conduct with the sword."[79] Menno and the Anabaptists denied the legitimacy of the *corpus christianum,* whereby church and society formed an organic unity and religion was undergirded by the coercive power of the state. This attitude was truly revolutionary in the sixteenth century and led to violent reprisals against the nonconforming Anabaptists. Often enough, it was the leaders of the official churches who egged on the authorities to persecute the radical reformers. It is not surprising that Menno reserved some of his choicest epithets for the religious leaders: "hypocritical liars . . . good-for-nothing slander mouths . . . this Herodian tribe . . . devil's preachers."[80]

The Anabaptists did not deny that the magistrates were ordained of God to maintain law and order. They pledged obedience to civil authority in every area which did not violate the requirements of their faith. In 1550 a Dutch Anabaptist named Hans van Overdam explained the position of his fellow Christians to the secular magistrates:

> Be it known to you, noble lords, councilors, burgomasters, and judges, that we recognize your offices as right and good; yes, as ordained and instituted of God, that is, the secular sword for the punishment of evil-doers and the protection of the good, and we desire to obey you in all taxes, tributes, and ordinances, as far as it is not contrary to God. And if you find us disobedient in these things, we will willingly receive our punishment as malefactors. God, who is acquainted with every heart, knows that this is our intention.
>
> But understand, ye noble lords, that the abuse of your stations, or offices we do not recognize to be from God but from the devil, and that antichrist through the subtlety of the devil has bewitched and blinded your eyes . . . Be sober, therefore, and awake, and open the eyes of your understanding, and see against whom you fight, that it is . . . against God.
>
> Therefore we will not obey you; for it is the will of God that we shall be tried thereby. Hence we would rather, through the grace of God, suffer our temporal bodies to be burned, drowned, beheaded, racked, or tortured, as it may seem good to you, or be scourged, banished, or driven away, and robbed of our goods, than show you any obedience contrary to the Word of God and we will be patient herein, committing vengeance to God.[81]

Unlike Luther, Zwingli, and Calvin who wanted to *reform* the church on the basis of the Word of God, the radical reformers were more concerned

79. Ibid., p. 175.
80. Ibid., p. 180.
81. Quoted, John C. Wenger, *Even Unto Death* (Richmond: John Knox Press, 1961), p. 71.

to *restore* the primitive church which they believed had "fallen" or apostasized. The *Volkskirche* (lit., "people's church") which the mainline reformers retained was itself a mark of the church's fallenness. New wine could not be stored in old wineskins. Rather the New Testament church had to be restored "according to the true apostolic rule and criterion." In his *Confession of the Distressed Christians* (1552), Menno described the restitution of the true church which he had witnessed in his own day:

> The brightness of the sun has not shone for many years; heaven and earth have been as copper and iron; the brooks and springs have not run, nor the dew descended from heaven; the beautiful trees and verdant fields have been dry and wilted—spiritually, I mean. However, in these latter days the gracious, great God by the rich treasures of His love has again opened the windows of heaven and let drop the dew of His divine Word, so that the earth once more as of yore produces its green branches and plants of righteousness which bear fruit unto the Lord and glorify His great and adorable name. The holy Word and sacraments of the Lord rise up again from the ashes by means of which the blasphemous deceit and abominations of the learned ones are made manifest. Therefore all the infernal gates rouse themselves, they rave and rant and with such subtle deceit, blasphemous falsehood, and blood tyranny that if the strong God did not show forth His gracious power, no man could be saved. But they will never wrest from Him those that are His own.[82]

Menno's favorite word for the church was *Gemeente* (cf. *Gemeinde*), by which he designated the living fellowship or community of believers, the true communion of saints. In his *Reply to Gellius Faber* Menno listed the following six characteristics by which the church is known: (1) an unadulterated, pure doctrine; (2) scriptural use of the sacramental signs; (3) obedience to the Word; (4) unfeigned, brotherly love; (5) a bold confession of God and Christ; (6) oppression and tribulation for the sake of the Lord's Word. It is significant that four of these six marks of the church are concerned with the ethical and moral dimensions of the Christian life.

Baptism

The importance of baptism for the followers of Menno Simons is indicated by the term *Anabaptist* (*Wiedertäufer*), which was the label given to them by their opponents. Menno declared that "for the sake of baptism we are so miserably abused, slandered, and persecuted by all men."[83] In 1529

---

82. CWMS, pp. 502-03.
83. Ibid., p. 236.

Emperor Charles V issued an imperial mandate which required the death penalty for all rebaptizers:

> Whereas it is ordered and provided in *common* [i.e., canon] *law* that no man, having once been baptized according to Christian order, shall let himself be baptized again or for the second time, nor shall he baptize any such, and especially is it forbidden in the *imperial law* to do such on pain of death.[84]

While this law was based on the ancient codes against the Donatists and other schismatics of the early church, it was clearly aimed at "the recently arisen, new error and sect of anabaptism." The Anabaptists, of course, denied that they were rebaptizers at all, since they did not recognize the baptism they had received as infants as valid in any sense.

We can summarize Menno's doctrine of baptism in three affirmations: (1) *Faith does not follow from baptism, but baptism follows from faith.* Menno opposed the sacramental understanding of baptism, which both Catholic and most Protestant theologians taught. He held that water baptism was an outward sign consequent to the inward experience of faith. The new birth consisted not in being plunged into the water, not in having the baptismal formulation pronounced by a priest.

> The new birth consists, verily, not in water nor in words; but it is the heavenly, living, and quickening power of God in our hearts which flows forth from God, and which by the preaching of the divine Word, if we accept it by faith, quickens, renews, pierces, and converts our hearts, so that we are changed and converted from unbelief to faith. . . . And these regenerate ones are those to whom alone he has taught and commanded the holy, Christian baptism as a seal of faith."[85]

Menno declared that even if the emperor or king came to him desiring baptism, he would refuse to administer it unless there was evidence of a changed life. "For where there is no renewing, regenerating faith leading to obedience, there is no baptism."

(2) *Infants are not capable of faith and repentance and should not be baptized.* Menno insisted on following the strict order of the Great Commission where Jesus instructed his disciples first to teach then to baptize. Yet "little irrational infants" were not able to receive such teaching, hence they should not be submitted to baptism. "Since infants do not have the ability to hear, they cannot believe, and because they do not believe they cannot

84. Quoted, Williams, *The Radical Reformation,* p. 238.
85. CWMS, p. 265.

be born again."[86] As we have noted earlier, Luther and Zwingli solved the problem of faith and infant baptism in different ways. For Zwingli the faith of the infant being baptized was not in question, but rather that of his parents or of the church itself. Luther recognized the intrinsic relation of faith and the one being baptized, and thus he posited a sleeping, dormant faith within the infant. Against the former view Menno insisted on the personal faith of the recipient of baptism. Against Luther's view he stated: "We do not read in Scripture that the apostles baptized a single believer while he was asleep. They baptized those who were awake, and not sleeping ones."[87] Anabaptist soteriology, with its emphasis on the universal salvific efficacy of Christ's death for all children who had not reached the age of accountability, dissolved the traditional argument for infant baptism as the sacrament for the remission of original sin. Instead, Menno insisted that

> little ones must wait according to God's Word until they can understand the holy gospel of grace and sincerely confess it; and then, and then only is it time, no matter how young or old, for them to receive Christian baptism. . . . If they die before coming to years of discretion, that is, in childhood, before they have come to years of understanding and before they have faith, then they die under the promise of God, and that by no other means than the generous promise of grace given through Christ Jesus. Luke 18:16.[88]

Another familiar argument in favor of infant baptism was the analogy to circumcision in the Old Testament. Menno refuted this argument by pointing out that if it were followed literally then only male infants should be baptized! His main argument, of course, was the lack of any positive command either from Jesus or the apostles regarding the baptism of infants. Hence he could only regard the practice as a ceremony of human invention, "a horrid stench and abomination before God."[89]

(3) *Baptism is the public initiation of the believer into a life of radical discipleship.* Menno spent more time refuting the errors of his opponents than setting forth his own positive theology of believers' baptism. Like Zwingli he wanted to separate clearly the sign and the thing signified. "If we ascribe the remission of sins to baptism and not to the blood of Christ, then we mold a golden calf and place it in the stead of Christ."[90] At the same time, water baptism was an ordinance of great significance for Menno in

86. Ibid., p. 134.
87. Ibid., p. 126.
88. Ibid.
89. Ibid., p. 272.
90. Ibid., p. 243.

contrast to the Spiritualists, such as David Joris who eliminated it altogether or Melchior Hofmann who called for a temporary suspension (*Stillstand*) of the outward rite. For Menno baptism signaled a response of obedience to the gospel, a literal imitation and initiation taken by a novice upon his entrance to the monastic order. In the monastic tradition, such a vow implied a radical break with one's past life and the assumption of a new identity within the community, symbolized by the receiving of a new name and investiture in new garments. Baptism among the Anabaptists was symbolic of a similar radical change in identity and lifestyle. It involved the "putting off " of the old man and the "rising to walk in the newness of life." In contemporary American culture, baptism seldom involves personal sacrifice or hardship. To the Anabaptists of the sixteenth century, it often meant the loss of livelihood, the forfeiture of home, land, and family, and the assumption of a strange country. Acceptance of baptism meant a sharing with Christ not only in the power of his resurrection but also in the fellowship of his sufferings. In 1554 Menno described in graphic language the consequences of such a baptism for so many of his followers:

> For how many pious children of God have we not seen during the space of a few years deprived of their homes and possessions for the testimony of God and their conscience; their poverty and sustenance written off to the emperor's insatiable coffers. How many have they betrayed, driven out of city and country, put to the stocks and torture? How many poor orphans and children have they turned out without a farthing? Some they have hanged, some have they punished with inhuman tyranny and afterward garroted them with cords, tied to a post. Some they have roasted and burned alive. Some, holding their own entrails in their hands, have powerfully confessed the Word of God still. Some they beheaded and gave as food to the fowls of the air. Some have they consigned to the fish. They have torn down the houses of some. Some have they thrust into muddy bogs. They have cut off the feet of some, one of whom I have seen and spoken to. Others wander aimlessly hither and yon in want, misery, and discomfort, in the mountains, in deserts, holes, and clefts of the earth, as Paul says. They must take to their heels and flee away with their wives and little children, from one country to another, from one city to another—hated by all men, abused, slandered, mocked, defamed, trampled upon, styled 'heretics.' Their names are read from pulpits and town halls; they are kept from their livelihood, driven out into the cold winter, bereft of bread [and] pointed at with fingers. . . .[91]

91. Ibid., pp. 599-600. It is difficult for one living in a modern, secularized culture to appreciate the deep-rooted revulsion directed against those who challenged the rite of infant baptism. Karl Barth once characterized infant baptism as

The Lord's Supper

In 1549 a young woman named Elizabeth Dirks was arrested in the city of Leeuwarden and interrogated in the town hall by the members of the city council. The following is a part of the dialogue between this Anabaptist sister and her examiners:

Lords:	'What are your views with regard to the most adorable, holy sacrament?'
Elizabeth:	'I have never in my life read in the holy Scriptures of a holy sacrament, but of the Lord's Supper. . . .
Lords:	'Be silent, for the devil speaks through your mouth.'
Elizabeth:	'Yea, my lords, this [charge] is a small matter, for the servant is not better than his lord.'
Lords:	'You speak from a spirit of pride.'
Elizabeth:	'No, my lords, I speak with frankness.'
Lords:	'What did the Lord say, when He gave His disciples the Supper?'
Elizabeth:	'What did He give them, flesh or bread?'
Lords:	'He gave them bread.'
Elizabeth:	'Did not the Lord remain sitting there? Who then would eat the flesh of the Lord?'[92]

Even more than baptism, the Lord's Supper was a neuralgic concern for those who saw in Anabaptism a threat to the state-church system. Like Elizabeth, who was later executed by drowning, the Anabaptist martyrs were frequently questioned about their eucharistic theology. An Anabaptist from West Friesland was asked: "What do you hold concerning the sacrament?" He replied: "I know nothing of your baked God." A widow named Weynken, from The Hague, was sentenced to death by strangling because she stubbornly denied the sacramental efficacy of the supper. On the morning of her execution, a Dominican friar offered to administer the sacrament to her. She said: "What God would you give me? one that is perishable and sold for a farthing?" And to the priest who had celebrated Mass that day, she said that he had "crucified God anew."[93]

Before turning to Menno's eucharistic theology, we might well look in

"a part of the landscape . . . mightier than the wall of Berlin and the cathedral of Cologne or whatever you please." "Gespräch mit Karl Barth," *Stimme,* Dec. 15, 1963, p. 753.

92. Wenger, p. 76.

93. Thielman J. van Braght, *The Bloody Theater or Martyrs' Mirror,* pp. 484, 423.

on the celebration of the supper as it was observed among the Anabaptists of the Lower Rhine in the late sixteenth century.

> When the Lord's Supper was distributed the minister took the bread and broke a piece of it for each, and as soon as it was given out and each had a piece in his hand, the minister also took a piece for himself, put it into his mouth and ate it; and immediately, seeing this, the congregation did the same. The minister, however, used no words, no ceremonies, no blessing. As soon as the bread was eaten, the minister took a bottle of wine or a cup, drank, and gave each of the members of it. On this wise they observe the breaking of bread.[94]

The simplicity of this liturgy recalls the observance of the supper among the early Swiss Brethren who did not allow for priestly vestments, singing, or anything which could create "a false reverence." The simultaneous eating of the bread and the drinking from a common cup are practices which have endured in some fellowships. There is no hint that the early Anabaptists used anything other than real wine in communion, although certain Gnostic sects (and today the Mormons) preferred water. Grape juice became the norm among many American Protestants in the nineteenth century in connection with the modern temperance movement.

Although the Anabaptists repudiated the elaborate ritual and liturgical accoutrements of the Mass, the Lord's Supper as celebrated among them was not a shallow casual observance, but rather a vivid reenactment of Jesus' last meal and an anticipation of the eschatological Messianic banquet. In his *Foundation* Menno set forth a fourfold rationale for the supper which he designated as "this holy sacrament." First, Menno disowned the sacramental literalism which regarded the perishable elements of bread and wine as the actual flesh and blood of Christ. In agreement with Zwingli and Calvin, he insisted on the bodily presence of the ascended Lord at the right hand of the Father in heaven. The supper was rather "an admonishing sign and memorial" to Christ's salvific sacrifice of himself on the cross together with his deliverance of us into the kingdom of his grace. Secondly, the supper was a great proof or pledge of Christ's love for us. At the Lord's Table believers not only remember His death as a past event but also call to mind "all the glorious fruits of divine love manifested toward us in Christ." This love is active in the participants of communion, "progressively renewing" their faith. Menno described the deep spiritual fervor which grips believers gathered around the Lord's Table:

94. Cornelius Krahn, "Communion," *Mennonite Encyclopedia* I, p. 652.

Their hearts are flooded with joy and peace; they break forth with joyful hearts in all manner of thanksgiving; they praise and glorify God with all their hearts because they have with a certainty of mind grasped it in the spirit, have believed and known that the Father loved us so that he gave us poor, wretched sinners his own and eternal Son with all his merits as a gift, and eternal salvation.[95]

Thirdly, the supper was a bond of Christian unity, love, and peace. Drawing on an ancient Christian metaphor which goes back to the *Didache,* Menno likened the community of believers gathered around the table to a loaf of bread:

Just as natural bread is made of many grains, pulverized by the mill, kneaded with water, and baked by the heat of the fire, so is the church of Christ made up of true believers, broken in their hearts by the mill of the divine Word, baptized with the water of the Holy Ghost, and with the fire of pure, un-feigned love made into one body.[96]

Thus Christians who partook of the supper together had to put aside all quarrelling and contentions. They had to forgive one another, serve one another, reprove and exhort one another and also, as the phrasing about being baked in the fire suggests, they had to be ready to suffer and die for one another and together, if necessary, for their Lord.

In the fourth place, the supper was the communion of the body and blood of Christ. Menno derived this idea directly from Paul's expression in 1 Corinthians 10:16 which identifies the cup and bread as a *koinonia* (sharing, fellowship, participation) in the body and blood of Christ. We have alluded already to the inner renewal which the supper is intended to effect in believers. With connotations of the heavenly flesh of Christ, Menno declared that in communion Christians were made "flesh of his flesh, bone of his bone." Wherever the Holy Supper was celebrated with love, peace, and unity, "there Jesus Christ is present with his grace, Spirit, and promise, and with the merits of his sufferings, misery, flesh, blood, cross, and death." Menno was exalted in describing the blessings of such a meal: "Oh, the delightful assembly and Christian marriage feast . . . where hungry consciences are fed with the heavenly bread of the divine Word, with the wine

95. CWMS, p. 144.
96. Ibid., p. 145.

of the Holy Ghost, and where the peaceful, joyous souls sing and play before the Lord."[97]

In connection with the Lord's Supper, many Anabaptists also observed the ordinance of footwashing. Menno said little about this rite. He simply instructed the church to wash the feet of brothers and sisters who had come to them from a long distance. Dirk Phillips, however, listed "the foot washing of the saints" as one of seven ordinances which Jesus intended the church to practice. He gave three reasons for the importance of footwashing. First, it was commanded by Christ and, thus, should not be neglected. Here we see the motif of the restitution of the apostolic church, understood as a model to be as literally restored as possible. Secondly, the outward washing of the feet signified the inward cleansing of Christ. Whereas baptism (again like the monastic vow) was a once-for-all sacrament of initiation, footwashing, like the supper, needed to be repeated as the symbol of continual renewal and purgation. Thirdly, footwashing was an occasion for the believers to enact liturgically the true humility which the supper called forth and also embodied. Dirk derided those religious leaders who disdained to have their feet washed, preferring instead to be called "Doctors, Masters, and Sirs." Such puffed up pride and arrogance was the opposite of the Christian virtues of humility and love.

The Ban

Despite the differences among themselves, Luther, Zwingli, and Calvin agreed on two essential marks or characteristics (*notae*) of the true church: the correct preaching of the Word and the proper administration of the sacraments. Calvin, it is true, stressed the importance of church discipline for the well ordering of the Christian life, but he too refused to elevate discipline to the level of the Word and sacraments. The Anabaptists, on the other hand, insisted that discipline, carried out in accordance with the instruction of Jesus in Matthew 18:15-18, was an indispensable mark of the

97. Ibid., p. 148. One of the Dutch Anabaptist hymns reflects the spiritual joy and Christocentric devotion which must have characterized the early Mennonite celebration of the Supper:
"Dit Auontmael van Broot en wijne
Is een ghenieten geestelijck
Des Lichaems en Bloets Christi devijne
Als ghemeynschap keestelijck,
Voreent in een Lijf te zijne
Dits Christi mitten feestelijck."
Rudolk Wolkan, *Die Lieder der Wierdertäufer* (Nieuwkoop: B. de Graaf, 1965; originally published, 1903), p. 85.

true church. Significantly, in the very context of declaring the use of the sword off-limits for Christians, the *Schleitheim Confession* contrasted its purpose in the world to that of church discipline within the congregation: "In the perfection of Christ, only the ban is used for a warning and for the excommunication of the one who has sinned, without putting the flesh to death." In Anabaptist thinking, the authority of internal governance was in some sense parallel to the power of the magistrate. Like the pre-Constantinian church which existed in polemical parallelism with the Roman Empire, the radical sectarians of the sixteenth century refused to conform to their environing culture and conceived of the church as an "alternative society" with its own gospel-sanctioned instruments of order and discipline.

The ban, or evangelical separation as Menno often termed it, was the means by which unworthy and corrupt church members were excluded from the congregation. So prominent did the role of excommunication become in the Dutch Anabaptist tradition that one historian has dubbed the entire movement as "Anabanism."[98] It must be remembered that the evangelical or pacifist Anabaptist movement in the Netherlands emerged in the context of revolutionary disturbances. In his later years Menno regarded the strict practice of discipline as one of the features which distinguished the peaceful Anabaptists from their violence-proned rivals: "It is more than evident that if we had not been zealous in this matter these days, we would be considered and called by every man the companions of the sect of Münster and all perverted sects."[99]

Menno's emphasis on the purity of the church was related directly to his "celestial flesh" Christology and to his view of the supper as a marriage feast or fellowship meal with the sinless Christ. As Adam had but one Eve, and Isaac but one Rebecca, and even as Christ had but one body

> which was heavenly and from heaven, and was righteous and holy in all its members, so also he has but one Eve in the Spirit, but one new Rebecca, who is his spiritual body, spouse, church, bride, namely, those who are believers, the regenerate, the meek, merciful, mortified, righteous, peaceable, lovely, and obedient children in the kingdom and house of his peace; pure, chaste virgins in the spirit, holy souls, who are of his divine family and holy flesh of his flesh, and bone of his bone.[100]

Those who erred in either doctrine or life, and who remained obstinate in

98. Williams, *The Radical Reformation,* p. 485.
99. CWMS, p. 962.
100. Ibid., pp. 967-968.

their errors, "shall not be allowed a place in the holy house, camp, city, temple, church, and body of Christ." Such erring members were like a contagion which had to be eliminated like extraneous matter from a living organism. The inability of the established churches to maintain proper discipline, along with their false doctrines and "idolatrous" sacraments, was cited as a major reason for separation.

Along with preserving the purity of the church, the exercise of the ban was aimed at the recovery of the wayward brother or sister. The remedial intent of discipline is seen in Menno's desire that those who had been excluded "may be frightened by this ban and so brought to repentance, to seek union and peace and so to be set free before the Lord and his church from the satanic snares of their strife, or from their wicked life."[101] The three stages of fraternal admonition enjoined by Matthew 18 were followed patiently before the severe act of exclusion was taken. Moreover the formal ban was, at least in theory, only a social confirmation of a severance from Christ which had already occurred in the heart of the unrepentant member:

> No one is excommunicated or expelled by us from the communion of the brethren but those who have already separated and expelled themselves from Christ's communion either by false doctrine or improper conduct. For we do not want to expel any, but rather to receive; not to amputate, but rather to heal; not to discard, but rather to win back; not to grieve, but rather to comfort; not to condemn, but rather to save.[102]

The pastoral tone of this statement, which comes from Menno's *Admonition on Church Discipline* (1541), was in fact often betrayed by the vindictive and harsh recriminations often involved in the shunning of expelled members. This policy required the avoidance of all social contact with the impenitent. This did not mean, according to Menno, that one should not exchange a common greeting of "good morning" or "good day" with the fallen member, nor did it require the withholding of works of mercy and kindness in times of distress. It did mean, however, that no social intercourse or business dealings were to be entered into with the lapsed ones. "It is manifest that a pious, God-fearing Christian could have no apostate as a regular buyer or seller. For as I have daily to get my cloth, bread, corn, salt, etc. and exchange for it my grain, butter, etc., it cannot fail but that intercourse will arise therefrom."[103] The ban was to be applied without

101. Ibid., p. 969.
102. Ibid., p. 413.
103. SAW, p. 269.

discrimination to family members, including husbands and wives and parents and children, though Menno did counsel leniency especially in the case of an excommunicated spouse. In 1550 a dispute arose in the Emden congregation of a sister, Swaen Rutgers, who refused to abstain from sexual intercourse with her backslidden husband. While some in the church argued in favor of banning her as well, Menno would not consent to such an action. Stricter Anabaptists, however, continued to insist on shunning among lapsed spouses. Some of these went so far as to require bride and groom on their wedding day to promise to obey the law of avoidance in case the ban were applied against one or the other.

Among the offenses punished by banning were heavy drinking, adultery, oath-swearing, marriage to an unbeliever, teaching false doctrines, unrelieved quarreling with spouses, and embezzling the congregation's money. Most of these were matters of personal holiness or congregational concern. However, the wider concern to present a pure witness to the world was not taken lightly. For example, a certain tailor was excommunicated from his church for charging seven shillings for making "a doublet and hose" when the going rate was five! The strenuous use of discipline could, and doubtless often did, degenerate into petty legalism. Yet it also contained elements of social protest which reached beyond the confines of a single congregation.

Faced with persecution and hostility from without, the Anabaptist churches were especially on guard against corruption or laxity from within. Membership in an Anabaptist church was neither casual nor assumed; participation was perforce hearty and vigorous. A true, visible church was at once a rebaptized company of gathered saints, *separated from* the world in its autonomous polity and eschewal of all violent connections, and a squad of spiritual shock troops *separating back to* the world through congregational discipline those members whose lives betrayed their profession.

The Bloody Theater

The theme of suffering found concrete expression in the example of the martyrs of the Radical Reformation whose stories, printed and sung, became a major genre of Anabaptist spirituality. The first ceremony of rebaptism in Zurich (January 21, 1525) was carried out in defiance of the mandate of the town council. From the beginning Anabaptists were regarded as seditious and heretical. In 1527 Zwingli summed up in one phrase his great fear of the Anabaptist movement: "They overturn everything."[104] As we have noted, the imperial diet at Speyer (April, 1529) revived the ancient

104. Z 6, p. 46: "Omnia turbant inque pessimum statum commutant."

Code of Justinian which specified the death penalty for the practice of rebaptism. The radical reformers were ruthlessly suppressed by Protestant and Catholic magistrates alike. Servetus, for example, who was both an ana-baptist and an anti-Trinitarian, held the dubious distinction of being burned in effigy by the Catholics in France and in actuality by the Protestants in Geneva.

Leonhard Schiemer lamented the effects of persecution before he was beheaded in 1528. "And now that we remain as a little flock, they have driven us with reproach and disgrace into every country. . . . They make the world too small for us."[105] Jakob Hutter, leader of the Moravian Anabaptists, wrote the following letter to the governor of Moravia on behalf of the distressed brothers and sisters who had been driven off their lands:

> So now we find ourselves out in the wilderness, under the open sky on a desolate heath. This we accept patiently, praising God that he has made us worthy to suffer for his name. . . . Yet we have among us many widows and orphans, many sick people and helpless little children who are unable to walk or travel. Their fathers and mothers were murdered by that tyrant Ferdinand, an enemy of divine justice![106]

Hutter himself was executed with the sword in 1536, following prolonged torture on the rack.

A vast literature of martyrdom developed in the wake of persecution. Many treatises and sermons were in effect exhortations to martyrdom. An excellent example of this was Menno's booklet to his oppressed followers, *The Cross of the Saints* (1554). Taking as his theme the beatitude, "Blessed are they which are persecuted for righteousness' sake," Menno reminded his readers that they were not the first to undergo "the angry, wolfish tearing and rending, the wicked animal-like torturing and bloodshedding of this godless world against the righteous."[107] He rehearsed the biblical examples of martyrdom, beginning with Abel, and appealed to Eusebius of Caesarea's *Ecclesiastical History* in order to establish the continuity between the martyrs of the early church and those of his own fellowship. He then refuted the charge of sedition and the spurious efforts to link all Anabaptists with the violent Münsterites. In conclusion he called upon his followers as

105. A. Orley Swartzentruber, "The Piety and Theology of the Anabaptist Martyrs," *MQR* 28 (1954), p. 25.

106. Jacob Hutter, *Brotherly Faithfulness: Epistles from a Time of Persecution* (Rifton, N.Y.: Plough Publishing House, 1979), pp. 67-68.

107. CWMS, p. 595.

"soldiers and conquerors in Christ" to face with steadfastness and courage the supreme sacrifice:

> Therefore, O ye people of God, gird yourselves and make ready for battle; not with external weapon and armor as the bloody, mad world is wont to do, but only with firm confidence, a quiet patience, and a fervent prayer. . . . The thorny crown must pierce your head and the nails your hands and feet. Your body must be scourged and your face spit upon. On Golgotha you must pause and bring your own sacrifice. . . . Be not dismayed, for God is your captain.[108]

A kind of "cult of martyrs" emerged among the radicals of the sixteenth century, as it had in the early church. Hans Hut's ashes were gathered and preserved as relics by his disciples. There is no evidence that the Anabaptists deliberately provoked their own deaths or rushed with glee to the pyre as some of the early Christian martyrs seem to have done. Yet, if not possessed of a martyrdom-lust, they were nonetheless heroic in their final anguished moments. When Balthasar Hubmaier was being prepared for the flame by having sulphur and gunpowder rubbed into his hair and long beard, he cried out: "Oh, salt me well, salt me well!" When the fagots were lit, he repeated in Latin the words Jesus had uttered from the cross: *"In manus tuas, Domine, commendo spiritum meum."*[109] Hubmaier and his wife, who was drowned in the Danube with a stone tied around her neck, were both remembered and revered as martyrs. Stories like this lent themselves to dramatic retelling. A number of martyr ballads found their way into the famous *Ausbund,* the hymnal of the Swiss Brethren which is still used today by the Amish in North America. One of these hymns, "Wer Christo jetzt will folgen nach," commemorates the martyrdom of George Wagner who, though apparently not an Anabaptist, was accused of denying priestly mediation of forgiveness and the salvific efficacy of water baptism. We give here four of the eighteen stanzas:

> Who Christ will follow now, new born,
> Dare not be moved by this world's scorn,
> The cross must bear sincerely;
> No other way to heaven leads,
> From childhood we're taught clearly.

> This did George Wagner, too, aspire,
> He went to heav'n 'mid smoke and fire,

108. Ibid., p. 621.
109. Williams, *The Radical Reformation,* p. 229.

The cross his test and proving,
As gold is in the furnace tried,
His hearts' desire approving.

Two barefoot monks in grey array,
George Wagner's sorrows would allay,
They would him be converting;
He waved them to their cloister home,
Their speech he'd be averting.

Men fastened him to ladder firm
The wood and straw was made to burn,
Now was the laughter dire;
Jesus! Jesus! did he four times
Call loudly from the fire.[110]

Second only to the Bible, the single most important document of Anabaptist piety was *The Bloody Theater or Martyrs' Mirror of the Defenseless Christians Who Baptized Only Upon Confession of Faith, and Who Suffered and Died for the Testimony of Jesus their Saviour.* This remarkable book, first published in Dutch in 1660 as a folio volume of 1290 pages, was based on earlier Dutch martyr books and included a wide assortment of memorials, testimonies, court transcripts, and excerpts from Anabaptist confessions and chronicles. In its shaping influence on Anabaptist spirituality, the *Martyrs' Mirror* is comparable to John Foxe's *Acts and Monuments of the Christian Martyrs* in the Puritan tradition.

The first part of the *Martyrs' Mirror* recounts the stories of heroic Christian martyrs up to the sixteenth century. The first "Anabaptist" martyr according to this reckoning was John the Baptist beheaded by King Herod presumably for administering the "true baptism of repentance" as well as for condemning the loose morality of the royal court. The trail of blood leads on through the early Church Fathers, the Donatists—"not strange, unknown, erring spirits, but such people as are also in our day styled Anabaptist"—the various medieval sectarian groups and concludes with the death of Savonarola in 1498.[111]

Having covered fifteen bloody centuries through the first half of the book, the *Martyrs' Mirror* next turns to those "who gave their lives for the truth since the great Reformation." The purpose was clearly "to unite the first

110. This appears as hymn no. 11 in the *Ausbund*. The complete hymn with German text is found in *The Christian Hymnary* (Uniontown, Ohio: The Christian Hymnary Publishers, 1972), p. 418.
111. Van Braght, p. 198.

martyrs with the last," thus proving the continuance of the suffering church through all the ages.[112]

In 1552 Cornelius Aertsz de Man, a young man of seventeen, was interrogated before his execution. The judge alleged that the Mennonite church had only been in existence about thirty years. Cornelius replied that since Christ had promised to be with his church to the end of the world, "I do not doubt that he has been the preserver of his body. . . . Although the church has been wiped out in some countries through bloodshed and persecution, it has not been annihilated throughout the world."[113]

The circumstances of the martyrs' deaths are described in gripping detail: Felix Mantz drowned in the Limmat at Zurich while his mother and brother stood on the river's bank encouraging him to remain steadfast; Ottilia Goldschmidt at the site of her execution was offered a proposal of marriage three times by a young man who thought to save her life in that way; Augustine, a Dutch baker, being taken to the fire said to the burgomaster who had sentenced him, "I cite you to appear within three days before the judgment seat of God." As soon as the execution was over, the burgomaster was smitten with a severe illness and died within three days. Stories like these circulated among the faithful and served to encourage those who might likely be faced with similar tests.

Many of the letters printed in the *Martyrs' Mirror* were written from prison to friends and family members. They show the humanity of the martyrs who, even in their hour of distress, did not despise the ties of intimacy which bound them to their dear ones. They commended those they had to leave behind to the loving care of the fellowship. Often they mentioned how difficult it was to leave them behind. One of the most moving examples of this genre is the letter of Janneken Munstdorp to her infant daughter, also named Janneken. The baby had been born in prison while her mother awaited execution. It is addressed as a testament "to Janneken my own dearest daughter, while I was (unworthily) confined for the Lord's sake, in prison, at Antwerp, A.D. 1573."

> My dear little child, I commend you to the almighty, great and terrible God, who only is wise, that He will keep you, and let you grow up in His fear, or that He will take you home in your youth, this is my heart's request of the Lord: you who are yet so young, and whom I must leave here in this wicked, evil, perverse world.
>
> Since, then, the Lord has so ordered and foreordained it, that I must leave

112. Ibid., p. 411.

113. Myron S. Augsburger, *Faithful Unto Death* (Waco: Word Books, 1978), pp. 13-14.

you here, and you are here deprived of father and mother, I will commend you to the Lord; let Him do with you according to His holy will. He will govern you, and be a Father to you, so that you shall have no lack here, if you only fear God; for He will be the Father of the orphans and the Protector of the widows.

Hence, my dear lamb, I who am imprisoned and bound here for the Lord's sake, can help you in no other way; I had to leave your father for the Lord's sake, and could keep him only a short time. We were permitted to live together only half a year, after which we were apprehended, because we sought salvation of our souls. They took him from me, not knowing my condition, and I had to remain in imprisonment, and see him go before me; and it was a great grief to him, that I had to remain here in prison. And now that I have abided the time, and borne you under my heart with great sorrow for nine months, and given birth to you here in prison, in great pain, they have taken you from me. Here I lie, expecting death every morning, and shall now soon follow your dear father. And I, your dear mother, write you, my dearest child, something for a remembrance, that you will thereby remember your dear father and your dear mother.

And now, Janneken, my dear lamb, who are yet very little and young, I leave you this letter, together with a gold ring, which I had with me in prison, and this I leave you for a perpetual adieu, and for a testament; that you may remember me by it, as also by this letter. Read it, when you have understanding, and keep it as long as you live in remembrance of me and your father. And I herewith bid you adieu, my dear Janneken Munstdorp, and kiss you heartily, my dear lamb, with a perpetual kiss of peace. Follow me and your father, and be not ashamed to confess us before the world, for we were not ashamed to confess our faith before the world, and this adulterous generation.

Let it be your glory, that we did not die for any evil doing, and strive to do likewise, though they should also seek to kill you. And on no account cease to love God above all, for no one can prevent you from fearing God. If you follow that which is good, and seek peace, and ensue it, you shall receive the crown of eternal life; this crown I wish you and the crucified, bleeding, naked, despised, rejected and slain Jesus Christ for your bridegroom.[114]

We do not know what became of little Janneken, but in her mother's beautiful will and testament we have a poignant witness to the theology of martyrdom which sustained ordinary men and women of the Radical Reformation in their efforts to follow the "bitter Christ."

114. Van Braght, pp. 984-987. The letter is reprinted in Hans Hillerbrand, *The Protestant Reformation* (New York: Harper and Row, 1968), pp. 146-152.

The Anabaptist Vision

In his *Foundation Book* Menno set forth the purpose and goal of his life's work in the following words:

> This is my only joy and heart's desire: to extend the kingdom of God, reveal the truth, reprove sin, teach righteousness, feed hungry souls with the Word of the Lord, lead the straying sheep into the right path, and gain many souls to the Lord through his Spirit, power, and grace. So would I carry on in my weakness as he has taught me who has purchased me, a miserable sinner, with his crimson blood, and has given me this mind by the gospel of his grace, namely, Jesus Christ.[115]

During long, hard years of struggle and persecution, amid the personal distress of caring for displaced family and bearing with a crippling physical ailment, Menno never wavered from this ideal. Today a modest memorial stands near the site of what is believed to be Menno's grave at Wüstenfeld in Holstein. His name as well as his ideals survive in the worldwide fellowship of the Mennonites and in a host of other spiritual descendants who still revere his memory and who are still moved by his piety, courage, and hope.

There is a sense in which Menno is the "odd fellow out" in our profile of reformers. He did not possess the theological genius of Luther, the political acumen of Zwingli, or the intellectual breadth of Calvin. He also lacked the advantage of Luther's professorial lectern and of Zwingli's and Calvin's prestigious pulpits. From 1535 to 1561 he also lacked the leisure and amenities of a well-settled ministry, being hounded from pillar to post by the authorities of both church and state. He was not exaggerating when he declared that he had

> renounced name and fame, honor and ease, and all, and have willingly assumed the heavy cross of my Lord Jesus Christ which at times assails my poor weak flesh quite grievously. I seek neither gold nor silver (the Lord knows) but am ready with faithful Moses to suffer affliction with the people of God rather than to enjoy the pleasures of sin for a season.[116]

Other Anabaptist leaders, such as Balthasar Hubmaier, Pilgram Marpeck, or even Dirk Phillips, may have surpassed Menno in theological depth and originality. Yet no other reformer embodied so faithfully what Harold Bender called "the Anabaptist vision." Nor was any other Anabaptist as successful as Menno in transforming that vision into an enduring tradition.

115. CWMS, p. 189.
116. Ibid.

What was the Anabaptist vision? Bender identified it with three major emphases: (1) a new conception of the essence of Christianity as discipleship; (2) a new conception of the church as a brotherhood; (3) a new ethic of love and nonresistance.

For Menno *following* rather than *faith* was the great word of the Christian life. Or, perhaps more accurately, faith which did not issue in following was ipso facto barren and false. Menno, with other radical reformers, rejected Luther's doctrine of forensic justification *sola fide* along with Calvin's concept of absolute double predestination. Both of these formulations struck him as abstractions divorced from the reality of "living" faith. Menno would have agreed with Ludwig Haetzer's depiction of the classical Protestant position:

> Yes, says the world, there is no need
> That I with Christ should suffer,
> Since Christ did suffer death for me
> I may just sin on his account,
> He pays for me, this I believe,
> And thus the point is settled.
> O brethren mine, it's but a sham,
> The devil has contrived it.[117]

The literal imitation of Christ was reflected in the practice of adult, believer's baptism, the ordinance of footwashing, the refusal to swear an oath or to bear arms, and the willingness to embrace suffering and martyrdom. In 1553 Menno received a letter from the wife of Leonard Bouwen who had recently been ordained an elder in the church. She begged Menno to use his influence to dissuade her husband from undertaking this work as she feared for his life because of the severe persecution of the Anabaptists. In his reply Menno refused her request though he admitted that "the sorrow and sadness of your flesh pierces my heart as often as I think of it." He reminded her that her husband—and she too—had committed themselves to the cross by their baptism. Since both life and death were in the hands of the Lord, she should strengthen and not weaken her husband. "In short," he advised, "prove yourself to do to your neighbor what Christ has proved

117. "Ei, spricht die Welt, es ist ohn Not/Daso ich mit Christo leide . . ." *Lieder der Hutterischen Bruder* (Scottdale, Penn.: Herald Press, 1914), p. 29. The translation is that of Friedmann, p. 69.

to be to you, for by this only sure and immutable rule must all Christian action be measured and judged."[118]

The new conception of the church was, of course, intended not as an innovation but as a restoration of "the old glorious face of primitive Christianity." In order to carry out this program in its full rigor including the ban the Anabaptists were willing to separate themselves from empire, nation, territory, city-state, and all of the official churches which were allied with these structures of civil authority. Thus the phenomenon of Anabaptism was not merely the most radicalized form of Protestant protest against the Church of Rome—Protestants in a hurry, so to speak—but also a distinctive quest for a new sense of Christian community at odds on crucial points with both Protestant and Catholic models. Perhaps more so than with most other Christian groups, it is difficult to separate the ecclesiology of the Anabaptists from their ethics. Menno felt that genuine compassion for the poor was one of the marks which distinguished his movement from that of the mainline reformers. He criticized the "easygoing gospel and barren bread-breaking" of the established clergy who lived in luxury while their poor members begged for food, and the old, lame, blind, and suffering ones were shunted. By contrast true Christians

> do not suffer a beggar among them. They have pity on the wants of the saints. They receive the wretched. They take strangers into their houses. They comfort the sad. They lend to the needy. They clothe the naked. They share their bread with the hungry. They do not turn their face from the poor nor do they regard their decrepit limbs and flesh. This is the kind of brotherhood we teach. . . .[119]

The Hutterites went even further than this, insisting, after the model of the New Testament church, that all property be held in common and used as needed for the welfare of the whole group.

The new ethic of love and nonresistance was perhaps the single most distinguishing mark of the evangelical Anabaptists. Even Erasmus who abhorred war and worked for peace was willing to allow for a crusade against the Turks. Menno repudiated all resort to physical coercion on the part of true Christians: "Christ is our fortress; patience our weapon of defense; the Word of God our sword; and our victory a courageous, firm, unfeigned faith in Jesus Christ. And iron and metal spears and swords we

118. CWMS, p. 1040.
119. Robert Friedmann, "Community of Goods," *Mennonite Encyclopedia* I, p. 659.

leave to those who, alas, regard human blood and swine's blood about alike."[120]

Echoing throughout Menno's writings are numerous, eloquent pleas for religious toleration. He believed that the true church of Christ was characterized by the fact that it suffers and endures persecution but does not inflict persecution upon anyone. The gospel was to be preached to everyone, but no one was to be compelled by force to accept it. These principles are accepted as axiomatic by large segments of modern society. Yet we should not forget that they were first enunciated at great risk by the early Anabaptists. Nor should we now take them for granted for the price of religious liberty is nothing less than eternal vigilance. The philosopher Ernst Bloch has written a fitting epitaph for Menno and all of the radical reformers who struggled against the stream for the sake of conscience, and whose legacy is a vital part of our common Christian heritage:

> Despite their suffering,
> their fear and trembling,
> in all these souls
> there glows the spark from beyond,
> and it ignites the tarrying kingdom.[121]

Select Bibliography

The most complete collection of the writings of Menno Simons is the English translation of Leonard Verduin: *The Complete Writings of Menno Simons,* ed. John C. Wenger (Scottdale: Herald Press, 1956). H. W. Meihuizen edited a critical text of the first edition of Menno's *magnum opus: Menno Simons, Dat Fundament des Christelycken Leers 1539-1540* (The Hague: Martinus Nijhoff, 1967). Four volumes have appeared in the series *Documenta Anabaptistica Neerlandica.* Most of these consist of archival sources related to Dutch Anabaptism. A new critical edition of Menno's writings is projected in this series. Irvin B. Horst has provided a very helpful *Bibliography of Menno Simons, ca. 1496-1561, Dutch Reformer* (Nieuwkoop, B. de Graaf, 1962). Menno's treatise on the ban and several other documents related to the Dutch Anabaptists are translated in *Spiritual and Anabaptist Writers,* eds.

120. CWMS, p. 198.
121. "Soviel Leid, soviel Furcht und Zittern auch gesetz sein mag, so glüht in allen Seelen doch neu der Funke von drüben, und er entzündet das zögernde Reich." I follow the translation in Hans Jürgen Goertz, ed., *Profiles of Radical Reformers,* trans. Walter Klaassen (Kitchener, Ontario: Herald Press, 1982), p. 9.

George H. Williams and Angel M. Mergal (Philadelphia: Westminster Press, 1957).

Braght, Thieleman J. van. *The Bloody Theater or Martyrs' Mirror.* Scottdale: Mennonite Publishing House, 1951. Originally published in Dutch in 1660, this classic recounts the dramatic stories of the Anabaptist martyrs of the sixteenth century.

Dyck, C. J., ed. *A Legacy of Faith: A Sixtieth Anniversary Tribute to Cornelius Krahn.* Newton, Kansas: Faith and Life Press, 1962. Contains several helpful essays on Menno.

Estep, William R. *The Anabaptist Story.* Grand Rapids: Eerdmans, 1963. One of the most popular surveys of Anabaptism.

Friedmann, Robert. *The Theology of Anabaptism.* Scottdale, Penn.: Herald Press, 1973. One of the better assessments of the theological significance of Anabaptism.

George, Timothy. "The Spirituality of the Radical Reformation," *Christian Spirituality, II: Late Middle Ages and Reformation,* ed. Jill Raitt et al. New York: Crossroad, 1987. A survey of spiritual currents in the Radical Reformation based on primary sources.

Horst, Irvin B., ed. *The Dutch Dissenters: A Critical Companion to Their History and Ideas.* Leiden: E. J. Brill, 1986. Contains twelve articles on the early Dutch Anabaptists as well as a bibliographical survey of recent research in the field.

Keeney, William E. *The Development of Dutch Anabaptist Thought and Practice from 1539-1564.* Nieuwkoop: B. de Graaf, 1968. A systematic presentation of the major themes in Dutch Anabaptist theology.

Krahn, Cornelius. *Dutch Anabaptism: Origin, Spread, Life and Thought (1450-1600).* The Hague: Martinus Nijhoff, 1968. A standard historical study on the context and growth of Anabaptism in the Low Countries.

Loeschen, J. R. *The Divine Community: Trinity, Church, and Ethics in Reformation Theologies.* Kirksville, Mo.: Sixteenth Century Journal Publishers, 1981. Contains a major section on Menno.

Stayer, James M. *Anabaptists and the Sword.* Lawrence, Kan.: Coronado Press, 1976. A major revisionist study of Anabaptist positions on violence and peace. Has a section devoted to the Netherlands.

Williams, George H. *The Radical Reformation.* Philadelphia: Westminster Press, 1962. A comprehensive survey of religious dissent in the sixteenth century. Surpassed in some details, but still the standard study in the field.

7

The Abiding Validity of Reformation Theology

The light is not to be put under a bushel.
Even if the whole world goes to smash, God can make another world.

Martin Luther[1]

In the introductory chapter of this volume we referred to the debate among historians as to whether the Reformation was primarily medieval or modern in its basic impulse and perspective. Frequently, those who argue the latter—that the Reformation signaled the dawn of a new age—do so with a sense of rejoicing at having been liberated from the shackles of superstition and dogmatism which are thought to have characterized the so-called "Dark Ages." The great church historian Adolf von Harnack believed that the entire history of Christian dogma had been culminated and transcended in the theology of Luther: Luther was the end of dogma in the same way as Christ was the end of the law! However, any attempt to evaluate the importance of Reformation theology for the church today must recognize the utter impossibility of such a view. Against Erasmus's boast that he took no delight in assertions, Luther replied that assertions, which he defined as a constant adhering, affirming, confessing, maintaining and persevering, belonged to the very essence of Christianity. "One must delight in assertions, or else be no Christian." For all of their critique of the received doctrines of medieval Catholicism, the reformers saw themselves in basic continuity with the foundational dogmas of the early church.

Still, the reformers did not merely repeat the classical dogmas of the patristic period. They found it necessary to extend and apply them into the realm of soteriology and ecclesiology. For example, at the Council of Nicea (325) the theologians of the early church confessed Jesus Christ to be *homoousios,* "of the same essence," with the Father. They were concerned— as opposed to Arianism with its mythological view of Jesus Christ as neither

1. Quoted, Bainton, *Erasmus,* p. 195.

fully human nor fully divine—with the being and nature of the incarnate Son. The reformers agreed fully with this insight, but they applied it to the issue of salvation in Christ. Put otherwise, they were more concerned with the work of Christ than with the person of Christ. To know Christ, said Melanchthon, is not to investigate the modes of His incarnation; to know Christ is to know His benefits. The early church had emphasized that when God revealed Himself in Jesus Christ, none other than God Himself in His own divine being was revealed. The reformers declared that when God rescued fallen human beings from their sin and estrangement, God Himself was at work in His acts of saving grace. These are not contradictory but complementary emphases. Indeed, the Reformation doctrines of justification and election are not only inconceivable apart from the basis of the Trinitarian and Christological consensus of the early church but also are the necessary outcome and application of the latter.

As a movement in history, the Reformation of the sixteenth century is now behind us. Of course, we can still learn much about its causes and effects as we study the social, political, economic, and cultural factors which rendered it such a pivotal epoch in the history of Western civilization. However, as a movement of the Spirit of God the Reformation has an enduring significance for the church of Jesus Christ. This has been our primary concern throughout this book, and we must focus on it now in these closing pages. We must ask not only *what it meant* but also *what it means*. How can the theology of the reformers challenge and correct and inform our own efforts to theologize faithfully on the basis of the Word of God?

Just as the reformers found it necessary to return to the Bible and the early church in order to address the spiritual crises of their time, so too we cannot neglect the great themes of the Reformation as we seek to proclaim the good news of Jesus Christ in our time. This does not mean that we can merely parrot the theological formulae of the reformers as if we ourselves were living in the sixteenth or seventeenth century instead of in the twentieth. To be sure, Jesus Christ is "the same yesterday, today, and forever" (Heb. 13:8). Likewise, the anxieties of guilt, death, and meaninglessness plague modern men and women as severely as they did princes and peasants in the late Middle Ages. But the way we process those anxieties has changed. Furthermore, we face new and even more dreadful realities such as the possibility of sui-genocide by nuclear self-annihilation. The spectre of multiple holocausts has jarred the sensitivity of the most optimistic humanists. In a world of death camps and terrorism, of mass starvation and AIDS, the Christian faces the same question which was posed to the children of Israel during their captivity in Babylon: "Where now is your God?"

Today we are tempted to answer this question in terms of the possibilities inherent within our own human condition, to extrapolate our theology out of our reason or experience, our philosophy or worldview. The vanity and final bankruptcy of this perspective is evident in the kind of theological faddism which has resulted in what Thomas J. J. Altizer, not known for his traditionalism, has called "a moment of profound theological breakdown . . . the ultimate moment of breakdown of theological tradition in the West."[2] The reformers remind us that God is to be found by us only where it pleases Him to seek us. All of our efforts to find God from within ourselves issue only in baseless speculation and projection which, ultimately, becomes idolatry. The abiding validity of Reformation theology is that, despite the many varied emphases it contains within itself, it challenges the church to listen reverently and obediently to what God has once and for all said *(Deus dixit)* and once and for all done in Jesus Christ. How the church will respond to this challenge is not a matter of academic speculation or ecclesiastical gamesmanship. It is a question of life or death. It is the decision of whether the church will serve the true and living God of Jesus Christ, the God of the Old and the New Testaments, or else succumb to the worship of Baal.

Sovereignty and Christology

The theme of the sovereignty of God resounds unmistakably throughout the writings of all four reformers we have examined. At first glance it might seem that this emphasis was peculiar to the mainline reformers with their stress on God's freedom and eternal decision in election. However, Menno and the Anabaptists were in their own way no less insistent on God's ultimate rulership over the world and history. If anything, their opposition to the cultural norms of the day and their willingness to follow Jesus even to the point of living defenseless in a violent society reflected an even stauncher confidence in the priority and ultimate victory of God's rule.

Nonetheless, the mainline Reformation doctrine of election or predestination stood out as a clear witness to the sovereignty of God in human salvation. It was and has remained a major stumbling block for those who see in it a pernicious undercutting of human freedom and human morality. The reformers, however, found in this teaching a tremendous liberation from the intolerable burden of self-justification. They understood human beings to be so deeply enthralled by sin that only God's sovereign grace

2. Mark C. Taylor, *Deconstructing Theology* (New York: Crossroad, 1982), p. xi.

could make them truly free. Luther's famous treatises *The Freedom of the Christian* (1520) and *The Bondage of the Will* (1525) are two sides of the same coin. God's unmerited and incomprehensible election is the only real basis for human freedom!

None of the reformers had the slightest intention of denigrating human participation in the process of salvation. Augustine had said that while God does not save us by ourselves, neither does he save us apart from ourselves. The doctrine of justification by faith presupposes the subjective appropriation of the divine gift of salvation, but it also recognizes that even that faith by which we are justified is itself also a gift. As Luther put it in his preface to the Epistle to the Romans: "Faith is a divine work in us which changes us and makes us to be born anew of God . . . O, it is a living, busy, active, mighty thing, this faith."[3]

God is the sovereign Lord not only in redemption but also in creation. All of the reformers, including Menno, repudiated the pantheistic tendencies in certain strands of late medieval mysticism. They affirmed the patristic doctrine of *creatio ex nihilo*. The radical distinction between Creator and creature was fundamental to Zwingli's entire theology. Of all the reformers he developed the most elaborate and philosophically informed doctrine of providence (cf. his treatise *De Providentia Dei,* 1529). But all of the reformers eschewed the concept of what Calvin called the "lazy god" *(deus otiosus),* a distant and aloof deity who created the world but who seldom, if ever, interfered with the goings-on in it. Such a god smacked of the deities of Greek mythology or even of the Stoic notion of impersonal fate rather than the biblical God who acts in judgment and deliverance. The reformers were quite willing to concede that we do not always (perhaps not even very often) understand *how* the providence of God is at work in the tragic sufferings and vicissitudes of our earthly existence. Calvin talked about God's "naked providence," and Luther referred to God's "left hand" and even to the "hidden God." The Anabaptists were convinced that somehow (though they did not claim to know how) God would use their sufferings and persecutions in His redemptive purpose for humankind. Indeed, who could have guessed that in that great miscarriage of justice at Calvary God was at work reconciling the world unto Himself?

Our modern disquiet with the Reformation doctrine of providence stems in part from our inordinate craving for clarity. We cannot understand how a sovereign God could permit innocent suffering. "Don't just stand there. Do something!" is at once a prayer and a protest. We would prefer a God

3. LW 35, p. 370; WA DB 7, p. 10.

we can understand or at least like, a God we can hold accountable, or a limited God who struggles with us against the chaos but who finally is too impotent to prevent it or even possibly to overcome it. The reformers felt the force of similar theodocies in their own day.

They were not ignorant—what reader of the Psalms is?—of passionate protests against an inscrutable providence. Calvin admitted that there is no true faith which is not tinged with doubt. In the throes of his *Anfechtungen* Luther himself had cried out, "My God, my God . . . why?" In the end, however, angry outbursts against heaven are, as Calvin put it, like spitting into the sky. The God with whom we have to do is not a God we can explain or manipulate or domesticate. "Our God is a consuming fire" (Heb. 12:29). The reformers provide no more adequate "answer" to the problem of evil than did the prophets or the apostles. Instead, they point us to the God who sustains in the midst of trials, the God who does not just "do something" but who indeed "stands there" in his sovereign compassion, the God who stands beside us and goes before us, who promises never to abandon us even—especially—when all of the evidence is to the contrary.

For all of their emphasis on the priority and absolute authority of the living God, the reformers did not understand sovereignty in an abstract or metaphysical sense. They were not interested in penetrating into the essence of God, nor in talking about God's "absolute power" or sheer omnipotence. The sovereignty of God was qualified and concretized in the historical existence of Jesus Christ, the incarnate Son of God.

Each of the reformers had his own distinctive way of expressing the centrality of Jesus Christ. Luther declared that "the only glory of Christians was in Christ alone."[4] This "glory," however, was manifested in the extent to which the "dear Lord Christ" identified Himself with the depths of the human condition. Luther refused to separate the human lowliness of Christ from His divine power. Luther's Christmas hymns graphically portray the self-humbling of the Almighty God who in the person of His Son took unto Himself our sinful human flesh:

> Th' eternal Father's only Son
> Now is to the manger come:
> In our poor human flesh and blood
> Hath clothed Himself th' eternal good.
>   Kyrioleis.
>
> Whom all the world could not confine
> See on Mary's bosom lying;

4. WA 13, p. 570: "Unica Christianorum gloria est in solo Christo."

He Who doth the world sustain
A tiny infant child became.
Kyrioleis.[5]

Zwingli distinguished more sharply than Luther the humanity and divinity of Christ, placing stronger emphasis on the latter which he saw as the crucial element in the procurement of salvation. As we have seen, this Christological difference was a major factor in the disagreement of these two reformers about the Eucharist. Luther's view of the omnipresence of Christ's body was unthinkable to Zwingli, who insisted on the localized presence of Christ's risen body at the right hand of the Father. Zwingli's theology, however, was no less Christocentric than that of Luther. In the third of the *Sixty-seven Articles* Zwingli insisted that "Christ is the only way to salvation of all who were, are now, or shall be."[6] Even the so-called pious heathen, whom Zwingli surmised we might meet among our neighbors in heaven, are not allowed to climb up "some other way," but are, like all sinners, elected through God's grace and redeemed through Christ's atoning death.

With Calvin the connection between the sovereignty of God and Christology becomes explicit when he designated Jesus Christ as the *speculum electionis,* the "mirror of election." In His role as the Mediator between God and human beings, Christ is in fact a two-way mirror. First of all as the elected One, the specially chosen and predestinated One, He is the mirror through which God looks upon those who are reconciled through His Son. But Jesus Christ is also the mirror through which believers look to find assurance of their own election. In our own century, Karl Barth (*Church Dogmatics* II/2) has drawn on Calvin's insight and extended it even further in his analysis of Jesus Christ as the paradigm of the election of humanity.

Just as Zwingli believed that Luther's doctrine of the ubiquity of Christ's body denigrated the reality of His risen humanity, so Calvin opposed Menno's doctrine of the "heavenly flesh" of Christ as dangerously docetic. Calvin's understanding of atonement presupposed the full participation of the incarnate Christ in the human condition. This required Him to have been born not only "from" the virgin Mary but also "of" her. While we must agree with Calvin's emphasis here, we should note that Menno's concern to safeguard the sinless character of Christ stemmed not from any Gnostic disparagement of the created realm, but rather from his desire to

5. WA 35, p. 434.
6. Z 1, p. 458: "Dannenher der einig weeg zur säligkeit Christus ist aller, die ie warend, sind und werdend."

protect the salvific efficacy of Christ's sacrifice of Himself on the cross. Alongside this stress on the objectivity of the atonement, which he shared with the other reformers, Menno pointed to Christ's life and death as a model of suffering and self-expenditure to which all Christians are intended to conform.

The different Christological nuances among the reformers were substantial and significant, but Menno's favorite text (1 Cor. 3:11) could serve as the basic theme for each of them: The revelation of God in Jesus Christ is the only foundation, the only compelling and exclusive criterion, for Christian life and Christian theology. From this perspective Jesus Christ is not merely a religious idea, not even the best religious idea among many from which we are free to choose; Jesus Christ is the actual realization within space and time of God's sovereign decision to be our God, to be for us and not against us, to save us from ourselves and from the powers which aim at our destruction, and finally to receive us into partnership and friendship with himself. All the reformers agree that theology, insofar as it is true to itself, finds both its point of departure and its final goal in the one authentic *fundamentum,* Jesus Christ its Lord. This perspective is beautifully expressed in the first question and answer of the Heidelberg Catechism (1563):

Q: What is your only comfort in life and in death?

A: That I, with body and soul, both in life and in death, am not my own,
      but belong to my faithful Saviour Jesus Christ, who with his precious
      blood has fully satisfied for all my sins, and redeemed me from all the
      power of the devil; and so preserves me that without the will of my
      Father in heaven not a hair can fall from my head; yea, that all things
      must work together for my salvation. Wherefore, by his Holy Spirit, he
      also assures me of eternal life, and makes me heartily willing and ready
      henceforth to live unto him.[7]

Scripture and Ecclesiology

The principle of *sola scriptura* has traditionally been referred to as the "formal principle" of the Reformation as opposed to the "material principle" of justification by faith alone. This distinction, however, is misleading insofar as it suggests that the reformers approached the Bible as a theological axiom or philosophical prolegomenon rather than as the living and powerful oracle of God. Luther's evangelical breakthrough was won only through a persistent and strenuous study of Holy Scripture. The reformers

7. Philip Schaff, ed., *Creeds of Christendom* (New York: Harper and Bros., 1877), III, pp. 307-308.

were all convinced of what Zwingli called "the clarity and certainty of the Word of God." Although they enthusiastically welcomed the efforts of humanist scholars, such as Erasmus, to recover the earliest biblical text and to subject it to rigorous philological analysis, they did not regard the Bible as merely one book among many others. They were unquestioning in their acceptance of the Bible as the unique, divinely inspired Word from the Lord. Moreover, they were not concerned with an abstract or formal theory of inspiration, but rather with the power of the Bible to convey a sense of encounter with the divine and to elicit a religious response from the hearer. In the seventeenth century John Bunyan, one of the most spiritually percep-tive heirs of the reformers, reflected this experiential appropriation of the Bible when he asked, "Have you never a hill Mizar to remember? Have you forgot the close, the milk house, the stable, the barn, and the like, where God did visit your soul? Remember also the Word—the Word, I say, upon which the Lord hath caused you to hope."[8]

In the sixteenth century the inspiration and authority of Holy Scripture was not a matter of dispute between Catholics and Protestants. All of the reformers, including the radicals, accepted the divine origin and infallible character of the Bible. The issue which emerged at the Reformation was how the divinely attested authority of Holy Scripture was related to the authority of the church and ecclesiastical tradition (Roman Catholics) on the one hand and the power of personal experience (spiritualists) on the other. The *sola* in *sola scriptura* was not intended to discount completely the value of church tradition, but rather to subordinate it to the primacy of Holy Scripture. Whereas the Roman Church appealed to the witness of the church to validate the authority of the canonical Scriptures, the Protes-tant reformers insisted that the Bible was self-authenticating, that is, deemed trustworthy on the basis of its own perspicuity (cf. Zwingli's *Klar-heit*) evidenced by the internal testimony of the Holy Spirit. Article V of the Belgic Confession (1561) poses the question of how one comes to accept the dignity and authority of the canonical books. The answer given is: "not so much because the church receives and approves them as such, but more especially because the Holy Ghost witnesseth in our hearts that they are from God, whereof they carry the evidence in themselves."[9]

By insisting on the correlation of Word and Spirit, the mainline reformers also distanced themselves from those spiritualists who placed their own

8. John Bunyan, *Grace Abounding to the Chief of Sinners* (London: Oxford University Press, 1928), p. 5.

9. Schaff, III, pp. 386-87.

private religious experience above the objectively given revelation of God. Even Menno, for whom the experience of regeneration was fundamental to his entire theology, opposed David Joris and other spiritualizing radicals because their privatized visions and revelations ran counter to the expressed will of God in his written Word. The second of the "Ten Conclusions of Berne" (1528) expresses this positive biblicism which governed, albeit with different results, both Reformed and Anabaptist ecclesiology: "The Church of Christ makes no laws or commandments apart from the Word of God; hence all human traditions are not binding upon us except so far as they are grounded upon or prescribed in the Word of God."[10]

In the perspective of the Reformation, then, the church of Jesus Christ is that communion of saints and congregation of the faithful who has heard the Word of God in Holy Scripture and which, through obedient service to its Lord, bears witness to that Word in the world. We should remember that the church did not begin with the Reformation. The reformers intended to return to the New Testament conception of the church, to purge and purify the church of their day in accordance with the norm of Holy Scripture. Even the Anabaptists, who felt that an absolutely new beginning was called for, retained—even as they transmuted—more of the tradition and theology of the church of the Fathers and the creeds than they imagined. While we must not forfeit the hard won victories of the reformers in the interest of a facile ecumenism, we celebrate and participate in the quest for Christian unity precisely because we take seriously the Reformation concept of the church—*ecclesia semper reformanda,* not merely a church once and for all reformed, but rather a church always to be reformed, a church ever in need of further reformation on the basis of the Word of God.

The reformers were master exegetes of Holy Scripture. Their most incisive theological work is found in their sermons and biblical commentaries. They were convinced that the proclamation of the Christian church could not be derived from philosophy or any self-wrought worldview. It could be nothing less than an interpretation of the Scriptures. No other proclamation has either right or promise in the church. A theology which is informed by the Reformation doctrine of Holy Scripture has nothing to fear from the accurate findings of modern biblical studies. Calvin saw no contradiction in affirming at once both the divine origin of the Bible ("dictated by the Holy Spirit") and its accommodated character (God "lisps" as a nurse to an infant). With such a perspective we will see the Bible not as the mere

10. John H. Leith, ed., *Creeds of the Churches* (Atlanta: John Knox Press, 1982), pp. 129-130.

record of human thoughts about God, but rather as the repository of God's thoughts about—and demands and promises to—human beings. As Karl Barth put it, "[The Scriptures] declare that after God sought us in the wonder of his condescension in Jesus Christ, whose witnesses the Prophets and Apostles are, all our efforts to find him from within ourselves have not only become baseless but are demonstrated to be in themselves impossible."[11]

Worship and Spirituality

Throughout the history of the church there has been a strong correlation between the development of Christian doctrine and the practice of Christian worship. According to a popular saying in the early church, "The rule of prayer ought to lay down the rule of faith." The Reformation reminds us that this process is a two-way street: Not only does worship have a shaping effect on theology but also theological renewal can lead to liturgical revision. In the sixteenth century the renewed emphasis on the sovereign grace of God elicited the response of gratitude which the reformers sought to incorporate in their revisions of the medieval liturgy.

As part of their protest against clerical domination of the church, the reformers aimed at full participation in worship. Their reintroduction of the vernacular was itself revolutionary since it required that divine worship be offered to Almighty God in the language used by businessmen in the marketplace and by husbands and wives in the privacy of their bedchambers. The intent of the reformers was not so much to secularize worship as to sanctify common life. Thus Calvin warned that whoever neglected to pray privately would contrive only "windy prayers" in the public assembly (*Inst.* 3.20.29). Prayer was "the principal exercise of faith," thus the entire Christian life was to be suffused with praise and thanksgiving to God.

We have seen how the reformers pared down the medieval sacraments from seven to two. We have also noted how that with regard to these two, baptism and the Lord's Supper, differences among the reformers became a major obstacle to unity among themselves. The Anabaptists insisted that baptism be consequent to faith and further denied that infants could be the proper recipients of faith whether presumed (Luther), parental (Zwingli), or partial (Calvin). Thus they returned to the early church practice of baptism as an adult rite of initiation signifying a committed participation in the life, death and resurrection of Jesus Christ. The ecumenical signifi-

11. Karl Barth, "Reformation as Decision," *The Reformation: Basic Interpretations,* ed. Lewis W. Spitz (Lexington, Mass: D. C. Heath, 1962), p. 161.

cance of the Anabaptist doctrine of baptism is recognized in the *Baptism, Eucharist and Ministry* statement of the Faith and Order Commission of the World Council of Churches. While admitting the validity of both infant and believer's baptism, it is stated that "baptism upon personal profession of faith is the most clearly attested pattern in the New Testament documents."[12]

On the other hand, in some traditions which staunchly affirm believer's baptism as a denominational distinctive, the rite itself has become attenuated and divorced from the context of a decisive life commitment. This is reflected both in the liturgical placement of baptism in the worship service —often tacked on at the end as a kind of afterthought—and also in the proper age and preparation of baptismal candidates. For example, several years ago the average age for baptism in the Southern Baptist Convention was eight, with numerous baptisms of children aged five and under. The practice of such "toddler baptism" can be justified neither on the basis of the mainline Reformation doctrine of infant baptism nor by the Anabaptist rationale for baptism as the public vow of discipleship within the covenanted congregation. As a corrective to the casual role assigned to baptism in much of contemporary church life, we can appropriate two central concerns from the Reformation doctrines of baptism: From the Anabaptists we can learn the intrinsic connection between baptism and repentance and faith; from the mainline reformers (though more from Luther and Calvin than Zwingli) we can learn that in baptism not only do we say something to God and to the Christian community but God also says and does something for us, for baptism is both God's gift and our human response to that gift.

Even for many churches who are able mutually to recognize their various practices of baptism, full participation in the Eucharist can only be hoped for as a goal not yet achieved. There is no easy side-stepping of this serious ecumenical problem, nor is it possible to ignore the scars which remain from the sixteenth-century disputes over the meaning of *"hoc est corpus meum."* In the Enlightenment Voltaire heaped ridicule on the Christians because the one meal which was supposed to symbolize their unity and love for one another had become the occasion for internecine wrangling. The Catholics said they eat God and not bread, the Lutherans said they eat bread and not God, while the Calvinists said they eat both bread and God! "Why," sniped Voltaire, "if someone told us of such a dispute among the Hottentots, we would not believe him!"

What can we learn from the Reformation debates on the Lord's Supper?

12. Leith, p. 610.

First, *we need to reclaim a theology of presence.* For many Protestants the celebration of holy communion has distinct overtones of a mournful funeral service—a solemn observance dutifully performed in memory of an absent Lord. Luther was right to insist on the real presence even if his language about chewing the body of Christ is inappropriate. Calvin's emphasis on the role of the Holy Spirit in eucharistic worship, on the lifting up of our hearts *(sursum corda)* in adoration, thanksgiving, and praise, points beyond the— also valid—memorialist dimension stressed by Zwingli. The Lord's Supper is not "merely" a symbol. To be sure, it is a symbol, but it is a symbol which conveys that which it signifies. In receiving the Eucharist, we "spiritually receive and feed upon Christ crucified and all the benefits of his death: the Body and Blood of Christ being not corporally or carnally but spiritually present to the faith of believers." This formula, which echoes the language of the 1549 *Book of Common Prayer* about "feeding on Christ in thy heart by faith," is actually from the 1677 *Second London Confession* of the English Baptists.[13]

Secondly, *we need to return to the practice of more frequent communion.* The earliest Christians may have celebrated the Lord's Supper daily (Acts 2:42,46) and certainly weekly. Over the centuries regular partaking of the supper became the sole prerogative of monks and priests so that by the late Middle Ages only the one annual communion at Easter was expected of the people. The reformers tried to encourage fuller participation and more frequent celebration of the Lord's Supper. At first Luther advocated its daily celebration, although he later settled for a weekly observance. The city councils of Zurich and Geneva legislated a quarterly communion: Zwingli was happy with this modest improvement over medieval practice while Calvin pushed unsuccessfully for a weekly celebration. The *Schleitheim Confession* refers to the "breaking of bread" as one of the distinguishing marks of the true church, although how frequently the Anabaptists celebrated the supper probably depended on the ad hoc and clandestine character of their worship services prompted by the threat of impending persecution. If the Lord's Supper is given to us for "daily food and sustenance to refresh and strengthen us" (Luther), if it "supports and augments faith" (Zwingli), if it is a "spiritual banquet" (Calvin) and the "Christian marriage feast at which Jesus Christ is present with his grace, Spirit and promise" (Menno), then to neglect its frequent sharing in the context of

13. W. L. Lumpkin, ed., *Baptist Confessions of Faith* (Valley Forge: Judson Press, 1959), p. 293

worship is to spurn the external sign of God's grace to our spiritual impoverishment.

Thirdly, *we need to restore the balance between Word and sacrament in Christian worship.* The reformers did not invent the sermon, but they elevated preaching to a central role in the divine service. The solemn and articulate reading of Holy Scripture was also given a prominent place. At the same time, they believed that the audible Word of God in the Bible should be met with the corresponding "visible words" of God in the sacraments. The Augsburg Confession (1530) put it succinctly: "Where the gospel is preached in its purity and the holy sacraments are administered in accordance with the divine Word, there is the true church."[14] In recent years a propitious reversal in worship patterns has occurred. "The Constitution on the Sacred Liturgy" of Vatican Council Two (1963) recognized that "it is especially necessary that there be close links between liturgy, catechesis, religious instruction and preaching."[15] Since that time many Roman Catholic congregations have emphasized the decisive importance of the Liturgy of the Word in Christian worship. At the same time many Protestant congregations have regained a new appreciation for the central role of the Eucharist in Christian worship. Each of these trends is an encouraging sign. As Christ gathers His people in remembrance around pulpit and table, we will be able truly to worship him in spirit and in truth.

Each of the reformers we have studied embodied a distinct, if not unique, motif of spirituality which both shaped and was shaped by the particular theological expression it assumed. For Luther it was the sense of joy and freedom in the forgiveness of sins; for Zwingli, it was pure religion and obedient service to the one true God. Calvin's spirituality centered on that sense of awe and wonder before the glory of God which is essential to proper piety; Menno's focused on faithful discipleship which meant following Jesus in the fellowship of suffering. For each of them, life itself was liturgical. Preaching, prayer, praise, and sacraments were communal expressions of faith and devotion which issued from the changed lives of men and women who had been grasped by the grace of God. Contemporary Christian worship is motivated and judged by various standards: its entertainment value, its presumed evangelistic appeal, its aesthetic allure, even perhaps its economic return. The liturgical heritage of the Reformation calls us back to

14. Leith, p. 70.

15. Austin Flannery, ed., *Vatican Council II: The Conciliar and Post-conciliar Documents* (Collegeville, Minn.: The Liturgical Press, 1975), p. 46.

the conviction that above all else worship must serve the praise of the living God.

Ethics and Eschatology

There is a kind of adulation of the reformers of the sixteenth century which divorces their theology from their ethics. This perspective rightly recognizes the reformers as great heroes of the faith, but fails to discern their prophetic role and their revolutionary impact on society. However, Reformation faith was concerned with the whole of life, not merely with the religious or spiritual sphere. This was true because the sovereign God of the Reformation was concerned with the whole human being, body, soul, mind, instincts, social relations, and political affiliations. Recalling the four figures we have studied, we can sum up their major contributions to ethics in terms of three overlapping themes.

First, there is Luther's notion of *faith active in love.* By insisting so single-mindedly on justification by faith alone, Luther was able to free ethics from the burdensome system of works righteousness in which it had been entwined in medieval Catholic theology. In that schema, the doing of good works was essentially a means of accruing merits and thus of securing one's standing before God. One's love for the neighbor inevitably involved an invidious, self-serving manipulation of the neighbor in the interest of personal gain (i.e. one's own salvation). Luther's doctrine undercut this system and released the justified sinner/saint to love the neighbor disinterestedly and unreservedly—for the sake of the neighbor. True faith, Luther held, was not dormant but alive and active in love. Though Luther's doctrine of the two kingdoms prevented him from being very optimistic about the possibility of significantly improving this present fallen world, he never forgot the Christians' responsibility to reach out in love, to be "little Christs," as he put it, to their neighbors. This applied especially to family life, for one's spouse, he said, was one's closest neighbor. Luther reminds us that ethics must flow from a proper theological grounding and not vice versa: Good works are a response to, not the cause or condition of, God's gracious initiative in Jesus Christ.

When we turn from Luther to the Reformed tradition, as represented by Zwingli and Calvin, we find ethical concerns expressed in what might be called *the sanctity of the secular.* Today the word *secular* has come to mean irreligious, even anti-God as in "secular humanism." However, the Latin word *saeculum* means simply the world, the world which despite its fallenness is nonetheless, as Calvin called it, "the theater of God's glory." We have seen how that for Zwingli this emphasis meant a restructuring of

political, social and economic life according to the norms of the gospel. For
Calvin it involved a concept of a godly magistracy where the human ruler,
be it absolute monarch or city council, was regarded as the vice-regent of
God. The Reformed concept of the sanctity of the secular has had an
important influence on the development of Christian social ethics since the
Reformation. John Wesley was an heir to this tradition when he exclaimed,
"The world is my parish." Walter Rauschenbusch articulated this concern
in his passion for the "social gospel" which (as Rauschenbusch used the
term) did not mean another gospel separate from the one and only gospel
of Jesus Christ, but simply that *that* gospel must not be sequestered into
some religious ghetto but has to be taken into the real ghettos and slums
of our world. With only slight exaggeration, we can say that while Luther
accepted the world as a necessary evil, Zwingli and Calvin sought to overcome the world, to transform and reform the world on the basis of the Word
of God because it was the theater of God's glory.

Menno Simons and the Anabaptist tradition present us with yet another
ethical imperative: *confrontation with culture.* To the mainline reformers the
Anabaptists said, "You have given us only a half-way reformation because
you still prop up the church with the state. You still render to Caesar the
things that are God's. But Jesus calls us to a different agenda." Thus they
refused to take the oath because Jesus said, "You shall not swear." They
refused to serve in the military, to bear the sword because Jesus said, "Love
your enemies, follow the way of the cross not the way of the sword." They
refused to baptize their infants which was not only heretical but also trea-
sonable in the sixteenth century. Consequently thousands of Anabaptists
were burned at the stake or drowned in the rivers and lakes and streams
of Europe. The Anabaptist vision is a corrective to the ethics of the mainline
reformers. It reminds us that to sanctify the secular must *never* mean simply
to sprinkle holy water on the status quo but always to confront the culture
with the radical demands of Jesus Christ.

Which of these ethical directions is right for the church today? No one
of them is sufficient alone, for each is susceptible to its own distortion. The
Lutheran emphasis on the priority of faith to works can degenerate into
mere formalism because pure doctrine without holy living always results in
dead orthodoxy. The Reformed emphasis on involvement in the world can
turn the church into little more than a political action committee or a social
service organization, while the Anabaptist critique of culture can lapse into
a sterile separatism which has forgotten its sense of mission. We have much
to learn from each of these traditions, but we are bound to none of them.
We are bound only to Jesus Christ. The church is *communio sanctorum,* a

communion of saved sinners, founded on the gospel of the free grace of God in Jesus Christ, sent into the world for which Christ died, ever to confront that world in witness and service with the absolute demands of Christ.

For all of its stress on returning the pristine church of the New Testament and patristic age, the Reformation was essentially a forward-looking movement. It was a movement of the "last days" which lived out of an intense eschatological tension between the "no longer" of the old dispensation and the "not yet" of the consummated kingdom of God. None of the reformers we have studied was much taken with the radical apocalyptic eschatologies which flourished in the sixteenth century. None of them wrote a commentary on the Book of Revelation. But each of them was convinced that the kingdom of God was breaking into history in the events in which he was led to play a part. Imbued with this sense of eschatological urgency, Calvin wrote in 1543 to the Holy Roman Emperor Charles V: "The Reformation of the Church is God's work, and is as much independent of human life and thought as the resurrection of the dead, or any such work is." Today we recognize the truth of Calvin's statement and give thanks to God for the way in which the glory of God and the power of his Word shone forth in the theology of the reformers even while we also confess with John Robinson, the pastor of the Pilgrims, that "the Lord hath yet more truth and light to break forth out of his holy Word."

A well-known document of our time expressed the heart of the Reformation faith and the hope to which the church of Jesus Christ bears witness:

> To those who ask, "What will happen to the world?" we answer, "His kingdom is coming." To those who ask, "What is before us?" we answer, "He, the King, stands before us." To those who ask, "What may we expect?" we answer, "We are not standing before a pathless wilderness of unfulfilled time, with a goal which no one would dare to predict; we are gazing upon our living Lord, our Judge and Savior, who was dead and lives forevermore; upon the one who has come and is coming, and who will reign for ever. It may be that we shall encounter affliction; yes, that must be if we want to participate in him. But we know his word, his royal word: "Be comforted, I have overcome the world."[16]

16. *"Christus, Die Hoffnung für die Welt,"* quoted in Jan M. Lochman, *Living Roots of Reformation* (Minneapolis: Augsburg Publishing House, 1979), p. 65.

Glossary of Reformation Theology

This glossary presents a selection of central concepts, terms and expressions which are germane to the theology of the reformers. This is in no sense a comprehensive listing, but rather a select grouping of more or less technical terms used throughout this book. For some of the terms which derive from late medieval scholastic theology, I am indebted to "A Nominalistic Glossary" in Heiko A. Oberman's *The Harvest of Medieval Theology,* pp. 459-76. Each of the following entries may be cross-referenced in the subject index of this volume. For citations in the writings of Luther, Zwingli, Calvin and Menno Simons, the reader should consult the appropriate indexes of the English translations of each reformer's works. Especially helpful is the index volume of *Luther's Works* (LW 55) and the subject index to the McNeill-Battles edition of Calvin's *Institutes.*

accommodation   A rhetorical metaphor frequently used by Calvin to refer to God's condescension to the limits and needs of the human condition. For example, with reference to Scripture, Calvin asserted that God was wont to "lisp" *(balbutit)* as a nursemaid conversing with an infant *(Inst.* 1.13.1).

ad fontes   To the sources. A popular phrase which epitomized the zealous program of humanist reformers to return to the original sources of classical, biblical, and patristic antiquity.

Anfechtungen   Variously translated as trials, temptations, assault, perplexity, doubt, dread. This word is much stronger than its synonymn, *Versuchung.* Luther's quest for a gracious God was marked with frequent bouts of fear and *angst* which he called *Anfechtungen.* Luther continued to experience these spiritual conflicts, often characterized as combat with the devil, until his death. He once remarked, "If I were to live long enough I would write a book about *Anfechtungen* without which nobody can understand the Scriptures or know the fear and love of God" (WA TR 4, pp. 490-91).

Babylonian Captivity   A term used by Petrarch and other late medieval writers to describe the "exile" of the popes at Avignon from 1309 to 1377, on the analogy of the deportation of the Jews to Babylon under Nebuchadnezzar. In 1520 Luther published his *Babylonian Captivity of the Church* in which he attacked the sacramental system of medieval Catholicism.

ban   The practice of excluding from the congregation a recalcitrant offend-

324

er, based on the disciplinary procedure in Matthew 18:15-18. The use of the ban was a prominent feature of Anabaptist ecclesiology.

celestial flesh Christology   The teaching of Menno Simons and other radical reformers that Jesus received nothing of His human nature from the Virgin Mary: He was born *out of* not *from* Mary. This doctrine was attacked by Calvin as veiled docetism. It was intended by Menno to preserve the sinlessness of Christ.

Christus pro me   Christ for me. A term Luther repeatedly used to express the personal, existential dimension of the gospel.

communicatio idiomatum   The exchange of properties. The doctrine that the attributes of the divine and human natures in Christ may be predicated of each other by virtue of the unity of His person. Luther's belief in the omnipresence of Christ's body derived from his understanding of this patristic motif.

conciliarism   A movement to reform the church "in head and members" by means of a general council. One of the significant achievements of conciliarism was the healing of the Great Schism at the Council of Constance (1414-1417). Two leading apologists of the conciliar movement were the French theologians Jean Gerson (d. 1429) and Pierre d'Ailly (d. 1420). Later fifteenth-century popes effectively opposed conciliar claims. In 1460 Pope Pius II promulgated the bull *Execrabilis* in which he condemned the practice of appealing from the pope to a general council.

coram deo   In the presence of God, before God. The term is often contrasted with *coram hominibus,* in the presence of humans, vis à vis humans. According to Luther all of life is spent *coram deo,* under the scrutiny of the living God or, as Calvin put it, there is no area of life in which we do not have *negotium cum deo,* "business with God."

Ecclesiastical Ordinances   The basic document of Genevan church order. Its acceptance by the city council was made a condition of Calvin's return to Geneva in 1541. It contains Calvin's program of discipline and church polity based on the fourfold office of pastor, teacher, elder and deacon.

extra Calvinisticum   Originally a polemical term devised by seventeenth-century Lutheran theologians to designate the Reformed doctrine that the Son of God had an existence "also beyond the flesh" *(etiam extra carnem).* Whereas Luther began with the unity of the person of Christ, Calvin stressed the distinction between the two natures of Christ.

facere quod in se est   Literally, to do that which is within one's self, hence, to do one's very best. According to the nominalistic theology of the late Middle Ages, by doing the best that is within one's natural power it was possible to love God above all else and thus to earn the infusion of divine grace.

fides ex auditu   Faith by means of hearing. The Vulgate translation of Romans 10:17, "So faith comes from what is heard, and what is heard comes by the preaching of Christ." Used by the reformers to underscore the importance of the preaching office and the salvific significance of hearing the Word.

Hence Luther's comment that "ears are the only organs of the Christian" (LW 29, p. 224).

fiducia   Confidence, trust, reliance. Steadfast hope in the faithfulness of God. In late medieval theology, *fiducia* was related to the acquisition of merits apart from which it was regarded as vain presumption.

Gelassenheit   Letting loose of one's self. A term from the German mystical tradition signifying a posture of utter dependence, humility and passivity before God. Used both by Luther and the Anabaptists.

Gemeinde   Community, congregation. Luther's preferred word (over *Kirche*) for the church. A word which recalls the New Testament concept of *koinonia* and Luther's doctrine of the priesthood of all believers.

humanism   A loose-knit movement for reform and education based on the rediscovery of the literature of classical antituity. The scholarly work of biblical humanists, such as Erasmus, greatly influenced the Protestant reformers, although they broke with him over the doctrines of the unfree will and unconditional election.

imputed righteousness   The "alien" righteousness of Christ which is counted to the believer quite apart from merits or good works but "by faith alone." Imputation is a forensic term which emphasizes that aspect of God's gracious judgment which is *extra nos,* "outside of ourselves."

indulgence   The remission of the temporal penalty owed to God due to sin after the guilt has been forgiven. In his *Ninety-five Theses* Luther attacked many abuses of the indulgence traffic, including the granting of indulgences in return for financial support.

Magisterial Reformation   A term coined by George H. Williams to designate that pattern of church reform which was officially established and supported by civil authority. Often contrasted with the Radical Reformation with its tendency toward disengagement of church and state.

meritum de condigno   A merit based on the standard of God's justice, hence a genuine or "full" merit. As opposed to a *meritum de congruo,* a *meritum de condigno* was an act performed in a state of grace and therefore worthy of divine acceptation.

meritum de congruo   A merit based on God's generosity. According to nominalistic theology, one could merit the infusion of grace by doing one's very best. A "congruent" merit could be earned even in a state of sin. It was based only on the generosity of God.

mysticism   A popular movement of spiritual renewal which stressed inward illumination and immediate union of the soul with God. The "German" mystical theology developed by Meister Eckhart and his disciples taught the absorption of the soul into the being of God *(Wesenmystik);* the "Latin" mystical theology of Bonaventura and others emphasized union of the will and conformity to Christ.

notae ecclesiae   Marks of the church. For Luther and Calvin, the Word and the Sacraments are the two essential characteristics or "notes" of the visible church. Martin Bucer, many Reformed confessions, and the Anabaptists added discipline as a third distinguishing mark.

opera Dei   The works of God. The evidences of God's handiwork in his general revelation. Among these Calvin identified not only the wonders of the created world without but also the image of God within each individual which, despite its effacement by the fall, remains nevertheless intact.

oracula Dei   The oracles of God. In Calvin's theology, the unique *loci* of God's special revelation in Scripture, salvation history, the incarnation, the sacraments, and preaching.

perseverance of the saints   The doctrine that the truly elect, despite their temptations and lapses into sin, are faithfully preserved by the grace of God unto the end. This was one of the five heads of doctrine affirmed at the Synod of Dort in 1619.

philosophia Christi   The philosophy of Christ. A phrase used by Eramus to sum up his moderate approach to the reform of the church based on moral improvement, educational advance, and a pious imitation of Christ combined with a qualified disdain for externals in religion.

potentia Dei absoluta   The absolute power of God by which God could do anything which did not violate the law of non-contradiction. For example, some theologians speculated that by His absolute power God could have become incarnate in an ass or have decreed adultery to be a virtue rather than a vice.

potentia dei ordinata   The ordained power of God. The order by which God has chosen to act in relation to the created world. The power which is regulated by the revealed and natural laws established by God.

"Prophecy"   The name given to those almost daily sessions of rigorous biblical study established by Zwingli and the Zurich reformers in 1525. From these intensive exegetical exercises emerged many of Zwingli's Scripture commentaries and the famous Zurich Bible of 1531.

reprobation   The "shadow side" of the doctrine of double predestination: the hardening of certain sinners by the foreordained counsel of God to their just condemnation. In medieval theology, the reprobate were called *praesciti*, those who are foreknown not to accept the offer of grace and, thus, to die in a state of sin.

sacramentarian   An opponent of the doctrine of the objective presence of the eucharistic Christ in the sacrament of the altar. In the Middle Ages a *sacramentarius* was one who held theologically that any of the sacraments was merely a sign involving no change either in the sacramental *res* or in the recipient. By the time of the Reformation, however, the term was usually restricted to one who questioned the received eucharistic dogma.

Schwärmer   Fanatic. A word which recalls the uncontrollable swarming of bees around a hive. Used somewhat indiscriminately by Luther to describe those reformers, including Zwingli and the Anabaptists, who spiritualized the gospel or who relied greatly on personal experience at the expense of the objectively given Word and Sacraments.

Seelenabgrund   The ground of the soul. Also called the *scintilla animae*, "the spark of the soul," and the *synteresis*, "the conscience." A concept in mystical theology referring to the innate spark of the divine within every individual, the point of contact for union with God.

sola fide   By faith alone. Based on Luther's 1521 translation of Romans 3:28 as, "That a person be justified . . . by faith *alone.*" Luther used this expression to indicate that the justification of the sinner is the work of God, whereby the "alien righteousness" of Christ is imputed to the believer and received by faith alone apart from the performance of good works.

sola gratia   By grace alone. A watchword of Protestant soteriology which recalls the radical Augustinian emphasis on the divine initiative in election and justification.

sola scriptura   By Scripture alone. The so-called formal principle of the Reformation. The reformers appealed to the sole authority of Holy Scripture as the infallible Word of God over against human opinion and ecclesiastical tradition.

solo Christo   By Christ alone. A phrase used by the reformers to show that salvation was accomplished by God solely through the meadiatorship of his Son.

transubstantiation   The doctrine that by the consecration of the bread and wine in the eucharist the substance of the elements is converted into the substance of the body and blood of Christ. Belief in transubstantiation was defined as *de fide* at the Fourth Lateran Council in 1215. It was reaffirmed as the official teaching of the Catholic Church at the Council of Trent and opposed by all of the Protestant and radical reformers.

twofold knowledge of God   A motif which provides the basic structure for the 1559 definitive edition of Calvin's *Institutes:* knowledge of God as Creator and Redeemer.

via antiqua, via moderna   The old way, the modern way. Terms used to designate competing schools of thought in late medieval scholastic theology. Advocates of the old way were loyal to the old doctors of the high Middle Ages such as Thomas Aquinas and Duns Scotus, while the "modernists" followed William of Ockham and disciples of his such as Gabriel Biel. Luther was trained in the *via moderna* whereas Zwingli resonated more with the *via antiqua.*

viator   Wayfarer, pilgrim, one who is "on the road" *(in via).* One who has not yet completed the journey either to the New Jerusalem or to eternal damnation and who consequently lives suspended between God's judgment and His mercy.

Subject Index

Persons

Modern Authors